INTERIORITY POWERED

Rev. Tom Eggebeen

Good to know you & enjoy worthwhile discussions.

Hugh Leonard

June 11, 2013

INTERIORITY POWERED

How to Use Your Inner Energies at Work

HUGH LEONARD

DEIORSE BOOKS

Los Angeles, California

Copyright © 2013 by Hugh Leonard, Leonard Coaching, Training and Consulting

All rights reserved. No part of this book may be reproduced or transmitted in any form or by any means, electronic or mechanical, including photocopying, recording or by any information storage and retrieval system, without written permission from the author, except for the inclusion of brief quotations in a review.

Deiorse Books
5918 South Croft Avenue
Los Angeles, CA 90056

Disclaimer: Let it be known that permissions which were granted for the quotations used in this book were originally sought under the publishing name of InteriorityPublishing.com. Nothing else has changed regarding those permissions except that the name has been changed to Deiorse Books.

This book is designed to provide information on the theories, processes and practices of the development of one's self or organization, particularly through engagement with one's work. It is sold with the understanding that the publisher and author are not engaged in rendering legal, psychological, or other professional services through the medium of this book, related workshops or media. The purpose of this book is to educate the readers and provide information on human development at work. If a reader discovers that legal, psychological or other expert assistance is required, the services of a competent professional, in the relevant field, should be sought. The reason is that the advice and strategies contained herein may not be suitable for an individual's situation.

The author, Deiorse Books, and Leonard Coaching, Training and Consulting shall have neither liability for, nor responsibility to, any person or entity with respect to any loss or damage caused or alleged to be caused directly or indirectly by the information contained in this book. If you do not wish to be bound by the above, you may return this book along with the receipt to the publisher for a full refund.

First Edition, 2013

Published in the United States of America.

Library of Congress Cataloging-in-Publication Data

    Leonard, Hugh

        Interiority powered : How to use your inner energies at work / Hugh Leonard. — 1st ed. — Los Angeles, Calif. : Deiorse Books, c2013.

        p. ; cm.

        ISBN: 978-0-9853415-0-3

    Includes bibliographical references and index.

        Summary: Aimed at helping people at work to gain access to all of their inner energies and use them for innovative creativity and high productivity.

        1. Labor productivity. 2. Human development. 3. Performance improvement. 4. Leadership development. 5. Self-realization. 6. Spiritual life. I. Title.

HC79.L3 L46 2012   2012942894

158.1—dc23   1209

Includes Notes, Bibliography, Glossary, Index

What others are saying about this book:

"This book provides a holistic guide to coaches, organizational development specialists and other professionals in the area of worker development and productivity. At the same time, readers will find practical methods for getting in touch with their own stories and integrating the wisdom embedded there into their personal contribution at work."

—**Sharon Eakes**, Executive Coach,
Publisher of Fresh Views, Director of Hope Unlimited, LLC
Co-Author of *Liberating Greatness—The Whole Brain Guide to An Extraordinary Life*

"Spirituality is sometimes difficult to grasp. However, when our ordinary lives and work become the source of deep reflection and wisdom, we are privileged to be on our journey toward the person we are called to become. In writing this book, Hugh traces his own development through all kinds of difficult experiences on three continents. In reviewing his own story, he provides a model and an opportunity for us to do the same. He also provides a variety of helpful theories and practices. These are indeed much-appreciated gifts."

—**Peter K. Dennis**, SS.CC. Catholic Priest, Pastor, Teacher, Retreat Director

"To survive and prosper in our times, we need a blueprint for how we must live and work. The context in which we work is changing at an extraordinary pace and the thinking and practices advocated in these pages provide the inner anchors and foundations to enable us to ride these waves of change. Each of us needs to read and practice the ways of growing in a holistic manner while doing our very best work and achieving the highest productivity possible."

—**Wilkie Au**, Ph.D. Professor, Loyola Marymount University.
Author of *The Enduring Heart—Spirituality for the Long Haul*

For Ann

Author's Notes (Hugh Leonard)

History of the Word Interiority

Interiority is an ancient word. As understood by St. Augustine (353-430 AD), Interiority is the exercise of coming to know oneself and God. One aspect of Interiority was referred to by St. Thomas Aquinas, (1224-1274) as the dynamic structure of human intelligence, reflected in the desire to know all there is to know.[1]

The Meaning of Interiority has Expanded

Our understanding of Interiority expanded exponentially with Einstein's discovery that energy is the basis of everything. Consequently, our traditionally earth-bound views were radically transformed to encompass the universe and beyond. We moved from thinking of things in a dualistic manner. Dualism means two-sided. Examples are: matter and spirit, body and soul. We came to appreciate that everything is interconnected and changing, driven by developmental energies at the core. So, the wider meaning of Interiority came to express what is at the center of anything and everything.

My Usage of Interiority

In these pages, I use Interiority to refer to the condition and totality of the inner world of a person who is growing toward wholeness. Such wholeness refers to the highest accomplishment to which humans can aspire and that is to become the person that they are called to be. The context of that growth is work. Simply put, people can grow into extraordinary sources of power and influence if they engage with their work from within their Interiority.

Reasons for My Focus on Interiority

The opposite of Interiority is Exteriority, which refers to the outside or to the world that is external to a person. Presently, most people measure themselves by what they own, consume, how they look and what they say and do. The conscious life of moderns is absorbed by externals and, as time moves on, that preoccupation is increasing exponentially. The resultant lack of an inner life generates feelings of anxiety, emptiness and meaninglessness, regardless of the amount of external goods one possesses. Tragically, most are not aware that Exteriority is the cause of such anxiety and consequent loneliness. Interiority is a balancing discipline for people at work to mature and become whole.

Interiority at Work

There are two meanings to this paragraph title. One is that the energies of Interiority are already powering us from within. They do so naturally. The second is that the energies of Interiority power our interactions with our work and make us productive. That is if we allow those energies to guide us. In general, people do not allow for Interiority but desperately try to control outcomes using external means. Conversely, people whose lives and work are based on a robust Interiority tend to be engaged, creative and productive. In addition, they feel fulfilled because they are growing, relating well with co-workers and contributing to the company and society while building the future by virtue of who they are as whole persons.

My Hope for Interiority Powered

Our society is in deep trouble. People are disillusioned and lack direction. Institutions have lost credibility. Trumpeted solutions sound like more empty drivel. We need people who are strong with strengths fueled from within. People working on the energies of Interiority can change themselves. Personal change, energized by Interiority, is the basis of all influence for change in the workplace, society and in everything.

Interiority Powered Communities Require Accountability

My hope is that this book and the programs based on it will be a source of inspiration for change in the becoming of one's self, especially through one's work. Further hopes are that Interiority Powered people will form communities based on respect for what is within each one and for the inner nature of things. The desired result is that they will pursue integrity in the members of the community and accountability for excellent results at work. For this, I have journeyed a long way. I invite you along on the journey to influence how excellent work is done and emergent wholeness grows in the world and in us.

Table of Contents

Preface 1

    Interiority, Work, Productivity and the Worker

    Philosophy, Stories, Practice

Introduction 15

    The Audiences of this Book

    Overview of Chapters

Chapter 1: Questions 25

    Questioning

    Historical Legacies

    Methods (for implementing change)

        Method 1. Interiority more than Spirituality at Work

        Method 2. Conflict and Growth

        Method 3. The Good Worker

        Method 4. Connecting with Meaning through Work

        Method 5. Meaning through Creating the Future at Work

        Method 6. Lessons from Emerging Terminology

        Method 7. The Great Work of Becoming the Self

Chapter 2: Context 73

    Key Principles

        There is Only the Dance Itself

        Evolution of the Cosmos Depends on Us

        Complexity vs. Coordination

    Key Tasks

        The Question of Meaning – The Most Sought-after Pearl

        Revolutions in the Sciences

        Reinterpretations of the Sacred

        Called to Contribute

        Subjective Perspective

        Resisting Repressive Systems

        Responsible Use of Earth's Resources

xii INTERIORITY POWERED

    Accountability of Global Economic Systems
    Implementing Accountability

Chapter 3: Foundations 107

    Foundation #1: Life Integration Quest
        The Resources of Interiority

    Foundation #2: We are Makers of Meaning
        Involvement
        Alignment
        Appreciation

    Foundation #3: Learning from the Energies of Shadow, Paradox and Chaos
        The Energies of Interiority
        Shadow
        Awareness is the First Step
        Embrace our Own Humanity
        Inner Dialogue – Based on Requesting Guidance from Our Soul
        Activate Our Best Qualities
        The Enlargement of the Soul
        Paradox
        Chaos

    Foundation #4: Trust by Way of Fulfilling Our Call
        Cycles of Integration
        Commitment to Personal Development
        The Road Less Traveled Has Made All The Difference

Chapter 4: A Troubled Organization 155

    The Intervention
        A Profile of Dysfunction
        Diagnosis

Chapter 5: Patterns and Issues Influencing Productivity 169

    A Framework of Recognizable Patterns
        Responsible Engagement
        Passivity
        Escapism
        Exploitation

Fear

Conflict

Chapter 6: Intervention 189

    Awareness

    The Intervention

    Below the Surface

        Disengagement from Self

        Unhealthy Co-dependence

        Manifestations of Co-dependency

        Missing Pieces as Indicative of the Need for Interiority

        Incivility in Behaviors

        Lack of Ethics

        Lack of Accountability

        Escape from Freedom

        Paralysis Due to Counteracting Force-Fields

    A Culture of Interiority

        Flummoxed by the Dynamic Tensions of Polarities

Chapter 7: Challenges 219

    Changing Ourselves

        Sacredness

        Called to Serve

        Pain and Compassion

        The Need to Belong

        Personhood through Work

        Relationality as Truth

        Embracing Interiority

        Growing Up with War

Chapter 8: A Culture of Interiority 241

    Realism in Embracing Interiority

    Becoming an IP Worker Requires Awareness of One's Power

        Shoes Too Small

        IP Worker Awareness

        Institution to Individual

Characteristics of an IP Worker
- An Open System
- Life Viewed as a Whole
- From the Center Outward
- Awareness of an IP Worker Regarding Action and No-Action
- Co-creators and Contributors

Competencies of the IP Worker
- Centering Competencies
- Self-Aware Competencies
- Right-Relationships Competencies
- Communications Competencies
- Organizational Competencies
- Client-Centered Competencies
- Good Work Competencies
- Teamwork Competencies
- Productivity Competencies
- Social Benefits Competencies
- Becoming an IP Organization

Characteristics of the IP Organization
- It is the Network
- Open Systems
- Flexible Leaders and Workers Collaborate
- Worker Innovation a Necessity
- Shared Values, Assumptions and Norms
- Recapping the Past for "Jumping" Forward

Competencies of the IP (Interiority-Powered) Organization
- Empowerment Competencies
- Work-that-Matters Competencies
- Work for the "Greater Good" Competencies
- Management Competencies
- Interiority Culture Competencies
- Worker Self-Management
- Stakeholder-Centered Competencies
- Good-Work Competencies

Productivity Competencies

Organizational Competencies

Business Cycle Competencies

The Integrated IP Worker and IP Organization

Chapter 9: Practices 283

Five Approaches to Practicing Interiority

Dimension 1: Personal Story

Dimension 2: The Body/Physical

Dimension 3: Psyche/Psychological

Dimension 4: Others/Relational

Dimension 5: Spirit/Spiritual

Chapter 10: Programs 339

1. Three Workshops for Implementing Interiority
2. The Way of Interiority
3. Additional Principles to Consider
4. A Devil's Brew
5. Personal Issues - Unworkable in the context of such a group
6. Science, Art and Spirit

Conclusion 347

Introducing Interiority into Organizational Life

Nine-Step Interiority Implementation Model

Taking Heart

About the Author 353

Endnotes 355

Glossary 361

Bibliography 379

Index 385

Acknowledgments

Many people helped in the preparation of this manuscript and book. However, special thanks go to my brother, Peter Leonard, who reviewed the manuscript many times and made many helpful comments. I want to acknowledge the assistance of Tom Lenert, Ph.D., Bob Blough and John Williams in providing guidance for the early editions of the manuscript.

I want to thank Julie Orlov who provided helpful guidance in preparation for publishing. My thanks for their encouragement and support throughout the process go to Peter Dennis, SSCC, Bill Murphy, Ph.D., Mary Butler, Sharon Eakes, George Theotocatos, Karim Jaude, Taketoshi Miyamoto, Ava Stanton, Mary Alberici, Ph.D. Ed.S., C.M. Coach, Eileen Spillane, Gerry Brennan, Josef Klus and Shigeharu Higashi.

Gary Hernandez was my great support in providing excellent developmental editing. He went the extra mile in seeing the process through to a workable manuscript. Loreen Murphy also provided editing of the text. Jack Barnard, in his inimitable style, provided very valuable editing services for the sake of the reader.

Many thanks go to Wendy Jane Carrel, Book Shepherd extraordinaire, upon whose insightful and practical advice I depended greatly to bring this book project to a successful conclusion.

Special thanks goes to Patricia Bacall for cover and interior design and illustrations and for generously guiding the whole design process to excellence. I am grateful to Lewis Agrell for his fine work on the illustrations.

I have not attempted to cite in the text all the authorities and sources consulted in the preparation of this book. To do so would require more space than is available.

Lastly, it is no exaggeration to say that this book could not have been completed without the help of my wife, Ann. She provided practical hints, wise reflections and excellent proofreading. This is all the more remarkable because she was and is employed full time even though officially retired.

Preface

"God is good and the devil's not so bad, either." Irish saying

This book is for and about you, the reader. You includes your work, your story, your emergent self, your work relationships and your contributing self—as it pertains to your connection with the human community. I begin with these dimensions because learning from the self revealed in your evolving stories—especially those that emanate from work—becomes your best opportunity for growth, both personal and professional. I especially address how to cultivate your capacity for Interiority which, in turn, can greatly improve work productivity and enhance personal satisfaction.

Interiority, Work, Productivity and the Worker

I assert that Interiority can introduce a revolution in work-related productivity. This is the kind of revolution that not only benefits the individual, but the community and all of humanity as well. A bold assertion, I know. Let's begin at the beginning.

Exactly what is Interiority? One dimension of Interiority discussed throughout this book refers to the **capacities of our inner lives** to **promote personal and professional maturity, which** encompasses **physical**, **intellectual**, **emotional** and **spiritual** functions. Among others, some intellectual functions include **memory**, **consciousness** and **reasoning** processes. **Emotional** functions, such as sensitivity to the nuances of growth in relationships, reactive patterns that hint at difficult past experiences and recurring prompts from within toward the integration of "**shadow**" energies are also encompassed by Interiority. And, finally, matters of a **spiritual** nature, including explorations of meaning, the clarification of one's unique purpose and the vital task of becoming our true selves, are also matters of Interiority.

A second dimension of Interiority is evident in the apparently purposeful transformation of cosmic dust into consciousness in humans over the 13.7 billion years since the Big Bang. This purposefully transformative journey reveals the characteristic Interiority of **energies** that appear to be **continuously seeking consciousness** and **greater complexity** in all forms of life.

In other words, the universe is at work by virtue of the fecundity of its Interiority. Our planet earth, in the fertility of its life-giving energies, is at the center of this journey and the preservation of its resources forms a foundation of our emerging sacred story. These two dimensions of Interiority are embedded in the variety of emergent symbols on the book cover. In giving them expression, I am highlighting Interiority-at-work in the worker, in the work that we do and is accomplished in us.

I believe that Interiority, well implemented, will produce a heightening of productivity comparable to what happened when Frederick Taylor, author of *The Principles of Scientific Management* (1911), applied "knowledge to work." In this context, I quote the words of Peter Drucker, "The application of knowledge to work after 1880 explosively increased productivity."[1] In these pages, we explore how a similar increase in productivity might be achieved with Interiority. The simple matter is that as we actualize the power of Interiority and as we align ourselves with *who we are becoming*, we will release constricted energies that will allow us to creatively ac*complish our work* and realize lives of *profound fulfillment*.

Here, because of the self-absorption and narcissistic tendencies in society today, I want to make a clear distinction between Interiority and introversion, self-analysis and other preoccupations with self. The ultimate goal of Interiority is to make a contribution to the world's needs. This is accomplished primarily through liberating all of one's energies in service to one's work and in being other-centered *(for the benefit of others)*.

The term **work** itself requires an initial definition. Work encompasses the *tasks* of our profession, of individual *sustenance*, community *fulfillment* environmental *stewardship* and *self-development*—perhaps the most significant work of any life. I would also say none of these outcomes can be accomplished without cultivating *relationships*, especially with our co-workers.

Another term for which we need an expanded appreciation is **productivity**. Productivity in its more scientific meaning is the measurement of units of output by the units of input. **Productivity = Output/Input**. A more descriptive explanation of productivity is the identification of *tasks that need doing, research* into how best to complete these tasks, and the *fulfillment* of these tasks in the most efficient manner.

In this book, I wish to emphasize **non-traditional ways** of increasing productivity—namely, by workers tapping into their **inner personal and organizational resources**. Because of this choice for increased productivity, workers will enjoy *expanded creativity* and *satisfaction*. From a lead article (*LA Times* 12/20/09) quoting Nelson Lichtenstein, an economist and director of the Center for the Study of Work, Labor and Democracy at UC Santa Barbara, "Productivity is Up, Workers Worn Down."[2] The article suggests that the reason workers are **increasing** their **productivity** is because of **external pressures,** such as **fear** of losing their jobs.

This fear factor is characteristic not only in the U.S., but worldwide, as is detectable in the comments of the international students in my university classrooms. Students from around the world profess anxiety over *slim job prospects* and *job loss* is a greater fear than almost everything else.

It is precisely the energies of Interiority that are vitally important when one faces job loss. Interiority, as I present it, allows one to engage with one's fears and use them productively.

To further expand on this point, I once again reference Nelson Lichtenstein who, in the article quoted above, explains that because of external pressures, workers often *choose not to be more productive* but are forced into "working more efficiently harder, and more hours." Rather than being driven by fear from external pressures, **Interiority-based productivity** flows **from deep wellsprings of energy** that pull you along in doing your tasks more efficiently and creatively, even to **surpassing** the highest **expectations** of the boss, the customer—or yourself. In the face of the most threatening work circumstances, healthy and creative sources of productivity are available from within.

In coping with these kinds of fears at work, many of us opt only for the acquisition of more material things. This usually proves to be a one-dimensional dead-end. The truth is we live in a rich and multi-dimensional world of *interdependent relationships*. We come to life continuously through our relationships. To truly live life, we must bridge those connections and interdependencies, even those that are seemingly contradictory, paradoxical and chaotic. Interiority grants us access to all dimensions of the human experience, not merely the socially acceptable. Through Interiority, we learn—and grow—from both the good and evil in all the complexities of life, and work, including the wrongs that we commit and the wrongs that are visited upon us.

In the work of growing, we should allow ourselves to be guided by the emergence of our **unique stories**. These stories include our *goal-centered efforts* as well as *life events* which may have forced us to take unanticipated paths. Becoming aware of our unique story is part of healthy self-growth, and is accomplished by listening to the messages that continually stream forth from our inner world. Ideas, dreams and intuitions sometimes arrive unbidden from within but they are always reflective of the fertile realities of our core. Out of this core flows rich seeds of *potentiality*, whether we are aware of them as such or not. In order to realize the potential of these seeds—these treasures of *insight* and *wisdom*—we must link current and past experiences of our lives, both internal and external, through open reflection and disciplined contemplation.

Ultimately, we are the authors of our own stories as they will not become fulfilled without responsible choices of *direction* and *development*. Our **stories** are **not accidental** happenings but life's aspiration for completion through us and a pledge of boundless meaning entrusted to our care. This is the function of reflection on one's story for the flowering of Interiority in us at work.

In the last several decades, access to Interiority has appreciatively diminished, not only in our homes and personal relationships but also in our workplaces and work relationships. This is due to the **weakening of community belonging** and **distance from** the humanizing influences of **nature**. The usual sad surmise is, "I have **no time for the timeless**." Unfortunately, this is all too indicative of the modern preoccupation with self-promotion, a cultural desperation for recognition— which is ultimately self-defeating. What further exacerbates this condition is the shallow nature of our relationships and the externalization of our life's purpose, if even we have one defined.

Other circumstances militate against Interiority: the increasing numbers of **permanently temporary jobs**, **preoccupation with technologies** and **depersonalization**. Let us briefly examine these three job-canceling trends.

First, the cover story of the January 7, 2010 *Business Week* ominously reads, "The Disposable Worker." The subtitle explains the phenomenon of job insecurity: "Pay is falling, benefits are vanishing and no one's job is secure. How companies are making the era of the temp more than temporary."[3] Basically, jobs providing lifelong security are disappearing, never to return, leaving us the incredibly difficult task of redefining ourselves and our work during our lifetimes, perhaps many times.

Regarding the second job-canceling trend of proliferating technologies, I confess to being overwhelmed by the onslaught of ever-newer technological product iterations vying for my attention. If I pursued even the quintessential technologies of our time, I would hardly be able to do anything else. Yet, large populations are being replaced by technological innovations. Consider the digitization of medical records and how many jobs will be replaced by that technology alone. In its evolutionary march, humanity has traversed out of prehistory through the Stone Age, the Bronze, the Iron, the Dark and the Middle Ages, the Age of Enlightenment when reason was king—the Age of Revolution; but rarely have we faced a more fearsome adaptation than in our own Age. This Age, marked by complexity and limitation, requires more than reason; to adapt successfully, you need access to the integrated energies of your whole person, your groups and communities.

George Soros the investor/philosopher says it cogently, "We need to move from the Age of Reason to the Age of Fallibility."[4] It is in the age of limitations that we must come to terms with, and adapt to the recognition of our frailty. My interpretation is that we humans can no longer afford to be at war with each other, or with ourselves. We face limited resources on a limited planet and to survive we must *unite and integrate the resources we have within*. I believe we are entering the Age of Interiority about which this book dialogs with the reader.

Thirdly, regarding depersonalization, the image of workers toiling in cramped rows of cubicles trying to provide personalized customer service to a stream of impatient callers from around the world is claustrophobic. The voice of the service provider echoes obscurely behind walls of protective security and the personal touch is muted by design. Counter-intuitively, these debilitating circumstances that might drain away any thought of Interiority can also encourage us to become more independently responsible for ourselves at work and more aware of our need for building real communities. Unfortunately, these downswing trends toward depersonalization will only increase for the foreseeable future.

Historically, **work was seen** as an **integral** and **sacred** part of life, especially in certain occupations. *Farming* work was considered sacred, as collaboration with nature was an essential part of the almost-magical production of food. In farming communities fertility rituals abounded to entreat the gods to bless the harvests. *Crafts* developed as people sought to beautify their dwellings and places of worship. Think for a moment of the decorative ornaments for hearths and doorway lintels—as well as stained-glass mosaics—flowing with streams of light and sculptured images for the tombs of the dead. *On-the-job relationships* were crucial in the labor-intensive village life as people needed to work together for planting and harvesting the crops. Semi-sacred bonds developed that became further cemented by clan, hamlet or village affiliation.

Today, work has lost much of the sacred character that kept people sensitive to the numinous (mystical) dimensions of life. Due to the transitory nature of work assignments, work relationships tend to be superficially objective, creating only a temporary sense of fulfillment and a superficial commitment to excellence. Excellence and innovation derives from engagement with our work. This seems to be a diminishing characteristic, as can be interpreted from the following statistics cited in a Gallup Survey.[5]

> **"Engaged Employees Inspire Company Innovation."** The Gallup Management Journal (GMJ) Survey discovered that there are "three types of employees." Of the surveyed employees, the following numbers emerged: "engaged employees (29% of respondents) and those who were not engaged (56%) or actively disengaged (15%)." "The cost range, from lost productivity, to the U.S. economy by the actively disengaged is between $287 and $350 billion."

In response to this debilitating trend, Interiority offers a unique combination of holistic approaches to greatly increase *engagement* as well as *productivity* and *satisfaction*.

Lastly, let us explore the idea of "**worker**" more carefully. The term "worker" refers to all employees, in any organization, regardless of the position they occupy, or the work that they perform. The term "workers," more so than "employees" or "associates," emphasizes the *centrality of work and the worker* over any other dimension of organizational life. After all, work is what characterizes the vast majority of us over the greater part of our lives. While the centrality of the worker inverts the traditional importance placed on the institution and management—going against a culture of top-down power and authority—the *increase in productivity* that can be achieved through cultivating individual Interiority is *exponential* to what we have achieved to date.

Using the familiar metaphor of "machine" and "cog," today's worker is more of a one-dimensional cog in a machine; as opposed to a complex living individual, a system unto him/herself, at work within a larger living system.

One of the main differences in these perceptions is the source of authority that guides the life of the worker. In the case of the worker as a cog, authority is vested in management, which exercises control over what the worker does and often who the worker is. In the case of the worker as a living system, the power derives from the inner lives of the individuals who take responsibility for their identities, their work, their co-workers and all aspects of the organization as a living system.

To be clear, Interiority is less about replacing the typical management and supervisory structures than *increasing the productivity of workers*, whose self-image derives from seeing themselves as the central focus of their work, their work relationships and organizational life.

There are multiple **benefits** that flow from Interiority. The most immediate: workers taking responsibility for every aspect of the assigned work so that the job gets done properly. This includes doing the tasks that others may not have completed, fixing flaws in incoming work and reporting possible improvements.

Another advantage from Interiority accrues to the organization because of the commitment to the goals of the company. The clearer his or her identity, the more committed the worker. Commitment means that workers think of themselves as owners and develop solutions from the owners' vantage point.

A further potential benefit: Interiority provides workers with the **strength to be entrepreneurs**, either inside or outside formal organizations. With the rapid **demise** of the traditional **bureaucratically-structured hierarchies**, both in the public and private spheres, only those workers will thrive who are motivated from within to begin again and again in successive workplaces. The future of work will center on self-starters who can do professional work for a time in an organization that needs their skills and are then able to move on and do the same throughout the cloud of global organizations. No longer will workers be able to count on getting lost in the bureaucratic maze long enough to amass wages over a lifetime, and benefits after retirement.

Yet another benefit is the *reduction of stress* and *increase of personal satisfaction* from greater care of oneself. This enhanced self-care includes maintaining a balance in the physical, mental and emotional aspects of one's health in the midst of workplace stresses. This is all the more important because research has shown that the lower one is in an organization, the higher the stress and the more frequent the incidents of ill-health.[6] Through engagement in the practices of Interiority, each worker can better preserve his or her own health while working.

Now for some comments on how the narrative style differs according to the topics presented.

Philosophy, Stories, Practice

Throughout this book, I interweave three different narrative styles covering three different topics:

- **Philosophy**: A **contemporary philosophical approach** to our work/life experiences; without a philosophical basis, no clear thinking about change is possible. The narrative style used is *logical prose*.

- **Stories**: **Personal stories** from my life to prompt the readers to become more aware of their own stories and their significance. Without the personal element, no responsible progress can be made toward wholeness. The narrative style used is more *descriptive and fanciful*.

- **Practice**: Practical **methodologies** for cultivating Interiority and achieving wholeness through work, as individuals and as organizations. Without practice, the desired behaviors for promoting Interiority are not cultivated. The narrative style used is more suited to *human resource development themes*.

One might ask why we need such *complex approaches* to our work. The simple answer: because life comes to us in exactly that manner. Life comes in experiences of varying intensities.

Thankfully, life comes at a pace that allows us to reflect on our experiences, become wise and grow. In appreciation of the panoramas constantly unfolding before us, I quote the great psychologist Carl Jung as he reflected on his arrival at a stunning awareness on an African plain in 1927.

Philosophy

Jung recorded these thoughts:

> To the very brink of the horizon, we saw gigantic herds of animals, gazelle, antelope, gnu, zebra, warthog and so on. Grazing, heads nodding, the herds moved forward like slow rivers. There was scarcely any sound save the melancholy cry of a bird of prey. This was the stillness of the eternal beginning, the world as it had always been, in the state of non-being; for until then no one had been present to know that it was this world…….There the cosmic meaning of consciousness became overwhelmingly clear to me…….Man, in an invisible act of creation put the stamp of perfection on the world by giving it objective existence.[7]

How prescient of **Jung** and how eloquent his positioning of the human within the cosmic. Jung was paying all of us a compliment when he said that we are **capable of "invisible acts of creation" by the simple act of becoming aware of things around us**. Extraordinary as it may seem, all of us, through our lives and especially through our work, participate in that great task of building the consciousness of the universe. In my own story, even while sitting at this computer, the gift of consciousness allows me to link the disappearing rooftops of my hometown (from a later story), my work as missionary-trainer-coach in Japan, Jung in Africa, this sunlit garden, energy absorbing camellia leaves and the clacking of my keyboard. They are all one by virtue of my Interiority-based consciousness. They are one just as the sunlight, painting shadows on the grass, whose blades reflect grainy patterns on the redwood fence and the granite rocks, indomitably tell their stories of life and constant, if non-obvious, transformation.

What a gift is human consciousness! What a continuously unfolding gift is emergent consciousness in all things!

Stories

The reason for getting in touch with one's unique story is hinted at in the words of anthropologist Loren Eiseley when he wrote:

> Man's mind, like the expanding universe itself, is engaged in pouring over limitless horizons. At its heights of genius it betrays all the miraculous unexpectedness which we try vainly to eliminate from the universe. The great artist, whether he be musician, painter, or poet, is known for this absolute unexpectedness. One does not see, one does not hear, until he speaks to us out of that limitless creativity which is his gift.[8]

Eiseley's words emphasize the work of cultivating gifts in response to your calling. In doing so, you avoid taking those gifts for granted and you enter into the core creativity of nature. We are all artists, each in our own way.

I include in my stories certain experiences that were clearly transformative for me. My intent is to provide an opportunity for reflection and learning to you, the reader. To maintain continuity across the topics, as I relate my experiences, I will dialog with you about your meaningful experiences. I want you to become even more aware of your story of growing to maturity and how you might connect with the deeper flow of your energies for work, for life and for contribution to the community.

Overall, I see the book as a help to you, the reader, in your work-life to improve *productivity*, uncover *meaning* and gain personal *satisfaction*. Explanations of many of the terms that I use are provided in the glossary at the end of the book.

Practice

How many times have we heard, "Practice makes perfect" or "Without practice, nothing happens"? During my five years of junior seminary and seven years of major seminary in preparation for the priesthood, I had many opportunities for practices such as prayer, meditation, chanting, housework and the innumerable duties of community life. Some of the practices, such as Custody of the Eyes (keeping one's eyes averted from possible occasions of temptation), consisted of advisable external behaviors. Other practices such as "in medio stat virtus" (which literally means, "virtue stands in the middle") focused on inner habits. In this case, the practice advocated avoiding extremes and choosing the more moderate behavior.

The priests in charge of these seminaries obviously thought that with an abundance of practices, we seminarians would be shaped and habituated for living a virtuous life. One of the weaknesses of this approach was that the seminarians did not always confirm by individual choice that they wanted to engage in such practices and, therefore, many of the proposed habits did not take root. That being said, I believe in the effectiveness of practice, especially if the choice is confirmed by the practitioner. I believe in the efficacy of practices for the development of habits.

In Chapter 9, I include an extensive series of practices for the development of Interiority. When a practice is chosen, it is necessary to practice, practice and then practice some more. This is because the Interiority focus is on our inner worlds at work, yet we likely have well established outer-behavioral habits which divert most of our energies. We tend to resist inner practices that strengthen our core habits of mind and behavior, but in the long run, these are the ones that matter.

Next I touch on the personal style of my writing.

Everything is Personal

I write about work in a personal way because I have the impression we have lost access to what is most personal at work, due to the over-emphasis on objectivity in communication and decision-making. Work-related discussions are expected to be unemotional and devoid of personal opinion. Nevertheless, while we may decry the limits of ordinary memories, it is an extraordinary fact that we never forget anything that we have experienced; and all our lessons contribute to our unique stories and approaches to work. In this sense, everything is personal.

Hopefully, the personal dimension finds its resonance in us when we are at work. Otherwise, we tend to be dispirited, uninvolved and blandly objective about our work. What a loss! If work is not personal, all of the sights, sounds and sensations remain somewhere in our beings, but are unused. If work is personal, *we bring all of that storied resource of energy to the workplace* where it becomes the grist for creative productivity. Today, more often than not, such energy lies fallow.

In addition to that magnificent treasure trove of unique personal data, your soul remembers, and calls you to wholeness and maturity. Your soul requires recognition of its role as the *binding force of everything* and the *source of inspiration at work*. In this sense of soulful guiding energies, everything is personal.

The dynamic exchanges that make up your soulful experiences amount to interdependence between us and all other things. Such experiences are the building blocks of your stories, from which emerges this edifice of consciousness. In the sense of humans as edifices of consciousness, everything is personal.

We are more complex than simple, more constituted from mystery than from vitalized carbon molecules; even though this is also true. Amazingly, everything that happens is a unique, never-to-be-repeated event. In this sense of the unique phenomena that we are, everything is personal.

Three Worlds in One

Spiritual, psychological, personal and professional growth, all coax forth consciousness in us. Throughout the book, I follow three sub-themes related to such growth:

- **Inner** world: **Spiritual** and **psychological** growth (**soul** work)
- **Outer** world: Framework of **cosmic** energies and **consciousness** (**community** work)
- **Work** world: Context of **personal growth** and increased **productivity** (**vocational** work)

The inner world, the first sub-theme, is about the energies of the universe coursing through each of us. These powerful energies, as wide as the universe, are as close to us as our DNA strands. These energies manifest themselves in us, individually and collectively, but mostly through our work in the world. Who would have imagined that our work—that daily toil usually deemed so lowly—could coax forth consciousness in us. The very stuff of the emerging universe. Engaging these energies is what Interiority allows us to do.

But there is a small problem: The only effective way of engagement runs counter to the needs and expectations of our egos, which vainly look for some semblance of comfort in everything, while preferring no dreary darkness at all.

The seemingly titanic struggle between ego and soul that fragments us is characteristic of our human bondage and is known as soul work; worthy to be aligned with the best work the divine ever conceived. In one's inner world, the soul (daimon/daemon as understood in the original Greek meaning of "a tutelary spirit that guides a person on his/her quest for wholeness") pursues reconciliation within the fragmented self by the integration of repressed and "lost" parts.

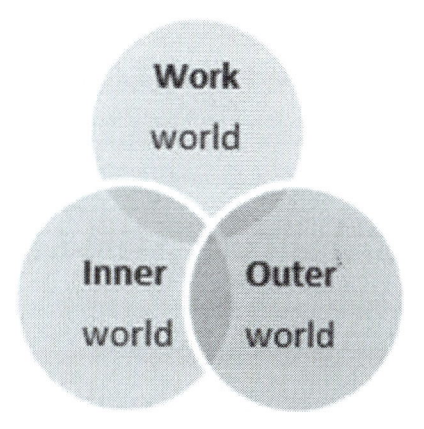

FIGURE 1: **THREE WORLDS IN ONE**

Paradoxically, the greatest of these parts is energy within that is potentially evil and, therefore, culturally merits rejection. Our egos try their best to exercise self-control by denying or repressing the energies of potential evil, but one's soul is the real master— and the soul will have its way.

Because of our soul-guided efforts in the becoming of "self," the energies of potential evil play a part just as important as the energies for potential good. The Irish really were onto something about the complementary nature of all things when they sighed, *"God is good and the devil's not so bad, either."*

The second sub-theme, the **outer world,** is about the **universe and us.** The universe provides the framework for replenishing our energies for transformation and for expanding consciousness; especially regarding the roles that we play in this cosmic drama of increasing complexity and generativity (the power to produce something that influences the emerging period of history). Access to these energies of the universe is through the earth, our home in the cosmos that sustains and protects us.

Optimal response to the universe is the realization that *this whole thing is alive.* Not only is it alive, but every part of it is speaking to us and urging us to wake up. Messages are bombarding our senses with their essential truth: we are *connected* and *interdependent*. If we want to live consciously in the realm of our Interiority, we must allow those messages to flood our beings. If we want to learn how to work productively with the energies available to us, we *must tune in to the patterns of nature* for we are, incontrovertibly, part of the main, part of the same.

"No man is an island entire of itself; every man is a piece of the continent, a part of the main . . . ."[9] John Donne's words remind us to become aware of our relatedness to everything; every living, growing, dying thing and the extraordinary power potentially available to us at work. We dismiss these messages at our peril, for they shape our evolving common story.

In addition, if as a species we wish to survive, we must learn the limits of resource usage and the opportunities for adaptation to changing environmental conditions; imitating every life form that adjusts and progresses according to the formula written in its DNA. We can learn from every physical thing that registers on our senses and every intuition that registers on our souls. The messages are clear: the Earth is a single organism and all parts of its systems are interdependent. Even the violence and chaos that accompany life happen as a precondition of new life—especially in the world of our work.

The **third sub-theme** is the **work** itself, through which we become the people we are called to be. Our work—not just jobs we do—help us discover *who we are*, *why we are here* and *how we contribute* to the building of the whole. The work we often dismiss as meaningless helps define us. The mistakes and the drudgery invite us to deepen and fulfill our unique missions in life.

We want to be productive, cooperative and creative. The good news is we can be. The not-so-good news: good work is hard won and the price tag is a *committed life*. Good work requires action but also the *passion* (in terms of availability to respond to the emerging need) of allowing ourselves to be changed in the process. While we are engaged in our work, in turn, we are being worked on to achieve abiding consciousness and wholeness.

By our work, we are being remade.

The great goal of life is the *becoming of self* through engagement in our own lives; legitimately suffering and embracing the work of our souls. I suggest that we allow this transformation to happen through all of our work experiences. Part of the job is to find out why the work that we do is meaningful for ourselves and every living thing, past, present and future. It is incumbent on us to be aware that how we do our work is unique to us, cannot be done by anyone else or bring the results that we bring.

The Soul

The soul is central to all the worlds of our experience. The three worlds—*inner, outer and work*—are symbolized by three interlocking circles. The obvious meaning: these three worlds influence each other continuously. Additionally, together the circles form a unique and a singular entity that constellates itself around one's being. The center of that entity is your soul, which is on a unique quest that draws you forward throughout your life journey by the evolving inspirations, experiences, intuitions and wisdom you embody and which remains forever. The form and function of your unique soul is distinct from soul in the cosmic context.

FIGURE 2: **SOUL OF THE WORLD**

A certain dimension of the soul governs the world outside of us (or is made manifest in the outer world). In the illustration, I symbolize that soul dimension as the outer ring. Even though we can say we are not the universe, we are united through the soul's energies to everything that exists. The outer circle also symbolizes one's soul which, being without limit, encompasses all things in itself.

It may be surprising, but the very center of these four circles is our work, in its specific and general contexts. The *specific context* of that work is the *tasks* we do or are assigned in the organization. This is represented in the first circle designated as work. The *general context* is the great work of *becoming ourselves*. We are on our paths toward that whole self throughout our lives.

The second circle symbolizes the inner world through which we grow in diverse ways and what I call Interiority. The third circle symbolizes the outer world—the physical context of our lives. The combination of these three circles together tells us we are entering the Age of Interiority.

The Age of Interiority intimates that we must move along the evolutionary path to include the *inner world* and the *outer world* with the *world of work*. While we have learned to live in the world of work according to traditional models where workers are guided by managers in hierarchical systems, it is mostly the outer world that draws our attention and absorbs our energies. If we live only in those two external worlds of work, we are missing the vital world of inner energies, practices and disciplines for resourceful self-management. More details are included in the symbolic figure: The Age of Interiority.

Symbols notwithstanding, there remains the aspect of the mystery of it all. Just now, a small winged insect flew erratically into my view of the garden and just as quickly disappeared. Yet, for that instant there was a conscious connection between me and that gossamer wonder. Why did that insect fly, from whence and whereto, I have not the faintest idea. Events are constantly occurring all around us and the incident of my winged friend engaging my sight joins the innumerable mysteries that make up the whole mystery of our existence; before which we stand muted, and in quiet admiration.

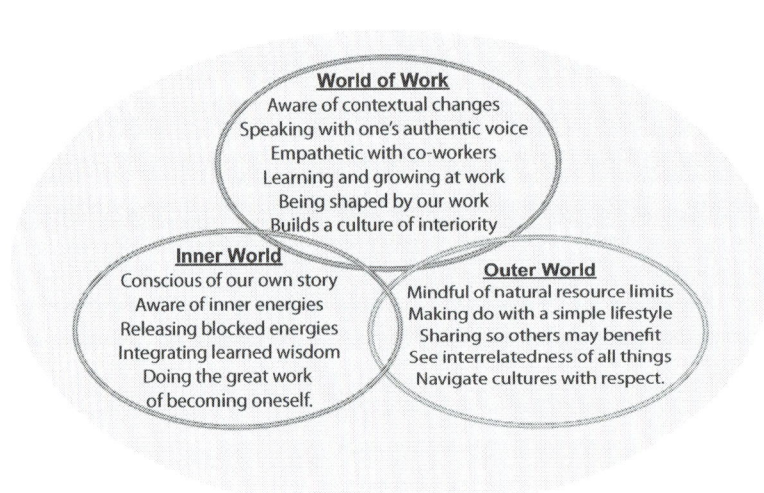

World of Work
Aware of contextual changes
Speaking with one's authentic voice
Empathetic with co-workers
Learning and growing at work
Being shaped by our work
Builds a culture of interiority

Inner World
Conscious of our own story
Aware of inner energies
Releasing blocked energies
Integrating learned wisdom
Doing the great work
of becoming oneself.

Outer World
Mindful of natural resource limits
Making do with a simple lifestyle
Sharing so others may benefit
See interrelatedness of all things
Navigate cultures with respect.

FIGURE 3: **THE AGE OF INTERIORITY**

In this book, it is my intention to include not only our inner worlds, our outer worlds, and the world of our work but also the aspect of *mystery* that can only be comprehended through *silence* and *contemplation*.

In the expression, "the devil's not so bad, either," the whole of the world is taken into account, not merely the manifestly good, but also the manifestly evil...and all degrees of good and evil in between. The reconciliation of the figures popularly represented as God and the devil will hopefully help us realize that they are two sides of the same coin and the human community has for too long been orphaned from the darker side. If we can

FIGURE 4: **THE WINGED WONDER**

reconcile these figures in the context of the mysterious complexity of the human, we can begin to heal in the core of our Interiority a world that is divided against itself. Only then can we move toward a healing embrace of all the dimensions of the unified reality that is our origin, our home and progressively creative, wonderful—yet unpredictable—destiny.

Introduction

The Audiences of this Book

This book is for all who consider themselves to be *workers* and who are interested in reflecting on the formative influence of work on their own development—as human beings and members of their communities. *Leaders, managers, supervisors* and all *stakeholders* belong to this primary audience. They have the responsibility of enabling the organization and its workers to achieve the highest productivity and satisfaction. A secondary audience includes all those who have a professional interest in worker development, performance, productivity, human wholeness and fulfillment. This includes *trainers, coaches* and *mentors*, as well as *consultants, counselors, therapists* and *spiritual directors*.

Professors, teachers, instructors and writers on all aspects of interpersonal dynamics in the workplace can also benefit. In fact, anyone who interfaces with people at work for the purpose of furthering human development will find value in pursuing Interiority. I acknowledge that the secondary audience members are workers in their own rights, who therefore potentially engage in the practice of Interiority for their own benefit. I am making the distinction between the two audiences merely for the purpose of clarifying the ways in which the book may be used.

The general readership will benefit from this book by improving access to their energies for creative work and business success. In these times of extraordinary challenges to worker ingenuity, we should appreciate that each of our inner worlds is an indispensable resource. *Workers need an unshakeable inner foundation* when everything else is constantly shifting in a turbulent business environment. Readers will also benefit by expanding their appreciation of what it means to be human, while deepening their awareness of the centering function of the soul at work.

Readers will gain satisfaction from becoming familiar with *their own stories* and moving toward wholeness. They will more easily adapt to vastly *different work environments* as they realize that the old order of hierarchical authority is passing on and the new order, located within themselves, has begun.

In addition, readers are more likely to consistently integrate their *ethos* and *behaviors* throughout cycles of growth and decline, so their strengths will be sustained. Readers will cement more deeply their *relationships* based on a shared culture of Interiority.

And finally, readers will shape the future of society by contributing to the awareness of shared *communities of concern* and by taking responsibility for outcomes affecting disadvantaged groups in the communities to which they belong.

Poetry of Life at Work

Walt Whitman once wrote, "…and your very flesh shall be a great poem."[10] In this simple yet exquisite phrase, he pointed toward the destiny so many seek: becoming living poems, works of art coaxed forth by mysterious encounters, in task after demanding task. As noted previously, *we are all artists* by virtue of our unique humanity. We make that singular artwork come alive by the disciplined integration of everything we are, even while we work. Becoming a great poet requires virtue, practiced in the unrelenting drudgery of work piled high, yet transformed moment-by-moment.

What we were is now no more. What we are is more alive for having lived with grace. Interiority is our inner world at work, leading us bit by bit toward Whitman's poetic vision.

A Guide, a Right, a Transformation

Clearly we need a roadmap to orient our interior lives so we can leave the fashionable—yet constraining—expressions of ourselves, and speak forthrightly from our hearts. Each of us is called to name the things of our world in a unique way, to carry forward our heritage of work for the purpose of improving and handing it on, and to live from the inside-out our experiences of both fact and mystery. In addition, we get to do this in the most unexpected place in modern society—the workplace.

On this journey into Interiority, we walk not only the predictable path laid out by technocrats, but travel into the fertile areas of mystery that encompass the human at work. At times, our journeys will lead us through the thorny brambles, but it is among the untamed wild of our freedom-seeking spirit we may cultivate the most productive seeds of growth.

As citizens of this world, Interiority is the right of all who consider themselves workers. Interiority is a right in that all workers should not be so overburdened with work and pressure that they cannot develop and grow as the people they are called to become. *Interiority is a gift* to workers, organizations and stakeholders.

Workers will benefit from access to their *creative inner resources, stronger identities,* a clear set of *values,* more effective *working relationships* and by making valuable *contributions to society.*

Organizations will benefit from the stability of a *workforce guided from within* to be as *productive* as possible and from making decisions based on *hard-wrought wisdom.*

Stakeholders will benefit from the reassurance that their *interests* are *considered and acted upon* with due regard for their importance.

Systemic ills in society (and the modern day workplace) require a transformative use of the inner resources of workers everywhere. Such a transformation will derive from energies released when inner barriers are overcome, when reactive patterns obstructing collaboration are dissolved through inner healing and when the inspiration from a clarified purpose drives worker and organizational productivity. I contend our inner worlds of energies are of equal if not greater importance to the outer world of things—and Interiority can enable the worker to gain access to those inner energies.

Einstein said, "Intuition is more important than IQ." Walt Disney said, "If you can dream it, you can do it." Executive Coach Sharon Eakes said, "Organizations are about liberating workers to do their best work." These notables point to the inner life of *intuition* and *dreams* and the *liberation of energies* as having a profound impact on work productivity.

Intuition is knowing something without having to consciously discover or perceive it. Imagination, as expressed in dreams, allows us to create, dismantle, change and create again without ever having to lift a hand. Liberation frees the worker from inner bondage so he/she can channel inner energies into the job at hand.

Imagination is one thing, but turning the dream into an opportunity is another. The worker who is anchored in his/her inner self is also attuned to the needs of the community and can spontaneously turn the dream into an opportunity. The entrepreneur within springs into action as soon as the dream is perceived as an opportunity to contribute and inspired productivity is the result.

Interiority includes faculties of intuition, imagination, liberation and much more. Interiority releases the whole inner world of worker resources for creative innovation and productivity. If workers are possessed of a deep and vital Interiority, they can use imagination to find the innovative means to discover fulfillment at work.

Key Assumptions

Here, I provide some of the key assumptions upon which this book is based. This is so the reader will not have to search for them (assumptions) throughout the text and will have a point of reference for understanding the recurring themes.

1. **External Case for Interiority:** I maintain that our economic future is under threat, specifically in the following three areas:

   - Chronically high unemployment for the foreseeable future is generating a socially-dissatisfied citizenry;
   - The massive national debt is symptomatic of a culture out of control of its finances; and
   - Our democratic systems of government are compromised by wealthy corporations (using lobbyists), politicians (used by lobbyists to make laws for the purposes of corporations), and collusive media which control how people think and behave by providing a minimum of useful information and a maximum of infotainment.

   "Step by step and debate by debate, America's public officials have rewritten the rules of American politics and the American economy in ways that have benefited the few at the expense of the many." So say Jacob S. Hacker and Paul Pierson in their book *Winner-Take-All Politics. How Washington Made the Rich Richer – And Turned Its Back on the Middle Class*.[11] The result: citizens so disillusioned by institutions that they are reacting with distrust and sometimes violence. They have not yet progressed to understanding that the only way to ensure accountability in the institutions and representatives is for the citizens (workers) themselves to become fully informed and strengthened from within. Only then, can they hold those in positions of responsibility fully accountable for their actions—and do so continuously.

   This is one key basis for Interiority. In a word, an informed, accountable worker makes for an informed and accountable citizen, who makes for an informed and accountable politician, who makes for informed and accountable institutions.

2. **The Internal Case for Interiority:** *Stress* and *diminished output* make up the internal case for Interiority. Workers are operating under outdated concepts in the organization and the possibilities for growth through work are diminished by overwork. The release of repressed energies through enhanced creativity and productivity is non-existent because opportunities for reflection are scarce. Supportive collaboration with co-workers is usually anemic and accountability-based connections with leaders, managers and shareholders are almost unimaginable.

   The antidote to the above conditions becomes available to individuals and organizations through the practice of Interiority at work.

3. **Subliminal Levels of Work, Workplaces, Organizations and Managers:** Work can be categorized as personal engagement with the tasks inherent in making a living. The deeper meaning of work, however, is accessible only through creative and transformative challenges—through personal building blocks, our relationships and our communities. Workplaces are special areas where workers apply themselves to making products and delivering services. On a deeper level, workplaces are where workers *collaborate* and *motivate each other* to produce the best possible goods and services in response to community needs; and, in so doing, grow and mature together in *supportive relationships*.

   At present, workplaces have become empty of any reference to the great mysteries that surround the human community and that might allow for transcendent values to be operative. In their place are slogans touting the absolute importance of the organization, the unquestioned authority of the leaders and the assumption that workers are satisfied with financial gain to the exclusion of everything else. This impoverishment of the workplace has to a great degree led to an impersonal, objectified, mechanistic, virtualized work environment bereft of feeling. Workers have almost no access to the deeper meaning of the great mysteries, the eternal, the metaphorical, the transcendent, the numinous; the deep-level connectedness with all things and the wisdom gained.

   When it comes to understanding how we grow into mature people, the following apparent opposites are but two sides of the same coin, namely: work and rest, good and evil, body and soul, light and dark, physical and spiritual, life and death, self and other, joy and suffering, rational and contemplative. Since we live in the tensions between these opposites, our Interiority develops through acceptance of all of these acting in unison within us and is connected to our productivity at work.

We need to become aware of the impact of these opposites in our lives at work so we can learn from everything that happens to us as we grow toward mature selfhood.

4. **This Book is a Means of Reflection:** Whatever one uncovers within, whether it be myths, reactive patterns, emotional conflicts, illusions, fantasies or concepts, all becomes grist for self-understanding and self-management. Making our inner patterns conscious through reflection is a key work of life. In pursuit of this reflection, after I tell my story at various intervals in the book, I offer you, the reader, the opportunity to do your own practical reflection and learning. An important part of that reflection process is to hold an inner dialogue—clarifying what is happening within, asking questions why and making beneficial behavioral choices.

5. **Authentic Power Augmented through the Practice of Centering:** Because modern man is inundated by sensory stimuli, it is almost impossible not to be mentally preoccupied and personally distracted by endless activities. Only by choosing to periodically remove ourselves from being caught up in this busyness and by disciplining ourselves in the practice of inner *silence* and *stillness* can we recapture the core of our living selves. Nothing we can do is more important than engagement with physical quiet and centering within.

6. **Everything is About Relationships:** When we relate to people as *others* worthy of respect, the world around us resolves itself into the field of our personal lives. We become *centers of truth* by the integrity of our relationships with everything. We become enlightened through a non-cerebral way of knowing, which emanates from the inner light of things, correlating wordlessly with our own inner lights.

    Relationships with co-workers are key opportunities for achieving maturity and wholeness. Even the relationships we experience as toxic in our work situations are potentially occasions for the deepest encounters with self and can provide the surest reflections of who we are, and how we behave.

    Relationships are more definitive of the natural order of things than is individuality. Nevertheless, it is up to workers themselves to make work relationships vital and productive. "Only connect," E. M. Forster admonishes in *Howard's End*.[12]

7. **History Means Continuity of Efforts at Improvement:** At the beginning of the 21st Century, we are living through a most profound paradigm shift in the

self-perception of workers. Workers are coming to appreciate they are each on a unique journey and are opting for the freedom to fulfill that call through their work. This is a shift of profound implications because throughout the more recent history of communities everywhere, philosophical theories and social structures have led to patterns of economic and political dominance in the world, the subjugation of people and the destructive misuse of natural resources.

Those oppressive systems will only change when they are subjected to the energies of Interiority, calling them to account in the uplifted voices of people at work.

Overview of Chapters

In writing about Interiority in the life of contemporary workers, I draw from my own experience in the world, and in the workplace. My life has led me across many spectrums. My early life experiences were of physically demanding work in the family forge that focused on farm machinery repair. Then, I spent 27 years engaged in the spiritual development, manual labor and community-building activities of a religious order.

As a priest for 20 years, I ministered to the needs of believers. I assisted in their spiritual development and attended to their needs at significant moments such as birth, marriage and death, as well as in their experiences of triumph and tragedy, sinfulness, celebration and human struggle. In the places where I have worked, I have been an ornamental iron-worker, a welder, carpenter, electrician, plumber, laundryman, musician and general handyman.

As a missionary, I was a teacher, community organizer, human development resource-person, writer and industrial counselor. Much of what I draw from in this book is based on my observations as an organization development consultant and executive coach. I have focused the major portion of my work in these areas over the past 23 years. Additional reflections are derived from real-time struggles in my work and life, as well as from my research and professional experiences in coaching, training and consulting.

I have structured the book in 10 chapters that generally flow from an examination, in Chapter 1, of key historical influences on the evolution of work as we find it today. I do so in order to expose the impoverished environment for human development in the workplace and the dearth of opportunities for human wholeness. Such an examination provides for an exploration of *meaning, purpose* and *contribution,* as well as *fulfillment* in the workers and in the organizations and communities to which they belong. It is my contention that out of this fundamentally humanized workplace will flow Interiority-Powered workers, organizations and communities consonant with the requirements for productive and resourceful business. In this overview, I approach the topic from three angles—philosophy, stories and practice.

In Chapter 1, I lay out the **Questions** and legacies central to work, Interiority and productivity, as well as rhetorical questions that probe the mysterious complexities operating in the world of work.

In Chapter 2, through presenting the prevailing **Context** of work, I explain the basic reasons Interiority is needed in workers and organizations. To this, I add key principles and tasks that enable Interiority to take hold.

In Chapter 3, I explore the four **Foundations** of Interiority, including (1) life integration quest, (2) ourselves as makers of meaning, (3) learning from shadow, paradox and chaos, and (4) developing trust by way of meaning at work.

In Chapter 4, I outline the scenario of **"A Troubled Organization"** experiencing great difficulties because of the dysfunctional relationships of the workers. I provide this scenario from my experience as an organization development consultant. I present an illustration of how the larger system is negatively affected by the lack of Interiority in the workers and the organization as a whole.

In Chapter 5, I examine various **Issues**, which increase or decrease productivity. I begin with the positive element of *engagement*, which increases productivity. This is followed by an examination of five issues that lessen productivity. I also explain why the disengagement from our inner lives at work presently is perceived as "normal." Such disengagement leads to disillusionment and loneliness in the workers and acrimonious battles for advantage over one's co-workers.

In Chapter 6, I describe the methods I used in conducting an **Intervention** in an organization. I was successful to the extent that the organization reached the first stages of Interiority. This meant a heightened awareness of the issues and what needed improvement. Nevertheless, I describe the organization as aware but still weak and I elaborate on the reasons why.

In Chapter 7, I explain the **Challenges** that face all workers in developing Interiority in a typical workplace. These challenges include changing ourselves, dealing with our pain, belonging in the world, choosing personhood, relationality as truth and choosing to embrace Interiority.

In Chapter 8, I describe the process of **Developing a Culture of Interiority**. In addition, I provide illustrative profiles of the core competencies of the Interiority-Powered worker and the Interiority-Powered organization. In presenting the material on Interiority-Powered workers and organizations, I provide illustrations of the effectiveness and productivity of workers and organizations powered from within.

In Chapter 9, I review key **Practices** aimed at behavioral changes that will improve the Interiority, productivity and satisfaction of the worker. I also offer ways in which organizations can support workers in the development of Interiority and also how beneficial Interiority can be for the stakeholders and society.

In Chapter 10, I review the **Programs** for introducing Interiority into an organization, including workshops, processes and opportunities for consultants.

In the **Conclusion**, I describe the impact of Interiority in the lives of workers and the importance of making the whole person the center of any organization.

This book may seem to be replete with programs, processes and positive-thinking strategies, but they are certainly not for the purpose of controlling our lives at work. The purpose of the book is to encourage workers to become communities of seekers who continuously respond to the call to fulfill their lives through work itself—while contributing highly productive results to the stakeholders and the community at large. Here I present Interiority as an ongoing state of growth and development that will not only prevent the loss of our inner resources but will offer opportunities to substantially increase productivity in our workplaces.

I attempt all this, secure in the belief we are not alone, actually never were or will be alone, for *something else* remembers and keeps score.

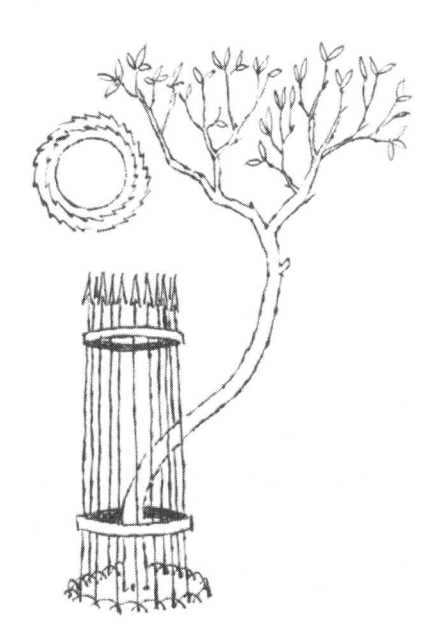

Seeking wholeness and being sought-after to make things whole

Chapter 1

Questions

"Wanderer, there is no road; the road is made by walking."
—Antonio Machado

Similar to the road Antonio Machado intones, there is no growth without questioning. *Legacies*, *Circumstances* and *Methods* are three key questions in this beginning Chapter on work. They refer to 1) the historical legacies about work that are mostly burdensome but reveal a progressive evolutionary trend toward meaningful work; 2) the present circumstances that allow fundamental improvements to take place and 3) the methods whereby those changes might be implemented. First things first, however, as I clarify the *Status Questiones* (state of the questions).

The Latin phrase, *Status Questiones* refers to the required first step in every philosophy class in college. By focusing on the status of the questions, the minds of the students are forced to be clear as they consider the subjects about to be discussed. For us that means clarifying "what we are going to deal with and what we are not." We begin by forming questions about work, especially the questions that workers ask themselves.

Questioning

Why should workers question everything? At a time when society already seems to have more questions than answers, an invitation to ask more may seem an odd way to begin a book. However, the rationale is twofold. First, what workers have been taught about the world of work has largely been done in the absence of questions. Second, by asking questions, workers begin to take responsibility for what happens in the workplace, in the world and, most importantly, in themselves.

Even with our long history, we know comparatively little about our humanity, the world we inhabit, the future and the real reason for work. Without inquiry, we run the risk of remaining uninformed and unfulfilled regarding the meaning of our work, neglectful of our potential productivity and dissatisfied with life in general. Questions allow us to gain knowledge and enlarge our sense of wonder at the beauty and variety of life.

With this process of questioning, we have the heritage of knowledge of the laws of nature, especially physics, which were developed by some of the finest minds ever to grace the planet. These laws offer us explanations that are useful until new information stimulates another round of questioning. It is in alignment with this iterative process of questioning and explaining that we develop our capacities of Interiority for the improvement of our work and every aspect of our lives.

Why should workers question *any*thing? *The core of Interiority is inquiry*. Workers don't need permission from anyone to search, question and adopt a stance toward their inner lives at work. Through thoughtful questioning in beginning the process of Interiority, we lay claim to increased productivity and personal satisfaction in the workplace.

Interiority deals with methods for gaining insight into our inner worlds while we work—that is, work in the external world. These insights can heighten wisdom, enhance creativity and improve productivity. For most people, however, the inner world is not entirely unexplored. Every time we ask "why," we open ourselves up to potentially new dimensions of the world.

Throughout history, questions have propelled people toward the expansion of knowledge. As we ask questions and find answers, we learn. Through learning, the human community has arrived at astonishing improvements in almost every aspect of life, most noticeably materially. But there have also been advancements in less quantifiable ways—within us. Consider the lives of artists, thinkers and scientists. Then again, there are spiritual sojourners in monasteries dedicated to silence, as well as mosques of solemn meditation and temples of devout prayer.

Civilization progresses not only outwardly, but inwardly. The historical record shows that civilizations collapse because they ignore the inner world of the citizens. Interiority affords us the opportunity to grow inwardly and access creative productivity while engaged in our work.

Out of the questions of the previous generations have come answers for the next. Not all the answers have been correct or complete because human nature and our own perspectives evolve within the paradigm of how the world works. For example, a statement attributed to Parmenides (540-480 B.C.E.) that "out of nothing, nothing comes" has been disproved because in our universe *nothing* does not exist. Today we understand: even out of a seemingly empty vacuum whole universes can emerge. So it stands, if nature by definition creates and grows continuously, we who are created of the universe are also creative by nature and are also on a trajectory of continual growth.

The history of man is about the development of higher level capacities for understanding and integration. The truth is, like our universe, we are also involved in a never-ending evolutionary process. Questions are fundamentally part of that evolution because *questioning is both a creative act and an act of creation.*

The possibilities unfolding through the interaction of humankind, the earth and the universe through ongoing inquiry is astounding. Even as we formulate questions, we are shaping the answers. And in shaping the answers, we are shaping reality. By focusing on certain aspects of the universe, we not only shape reality, but are ourselves shaped by reality. This is not to say we can control reality—at least not in a science fiction way—it is to say through the process of questioning and answering, delving and discovering, we unlock the potentiality of the world both around us and in us.

Big Questions

As the Bible begins its narrative with "In the beginning,"[13] so we start with the "big questions" formed when the first conscious being looked up at the night sky and wondered why it was there, where it came from and where it might be going. Out of those questions come others. Can we comprehend reality? Does a supreme being exist? And if it does, is it involved in human affairs?

These questions invite an even bigger question: So what? What is the meaning of our existence? Why are we alive and, in the context of billions of years of evolution, are our lives unique? Allied to the God question are questions of morality and ethics. Then there is the question about what happens after we die.

If you read these questions expecting to find the answers at the end of my discourse, I'm afraid I will disappoint you. I reiterate: *it is in the act of questioning and the act of searching that we grow*. Answers are not what matter most, but the process of inquiry itself. As each of us probes the fabric of our inner and outer worlds, we grow.

The quotation at the beginning of the Preface, "God is good," refers to physical and metaphorical *light*. "The devil's not so bad, either," refers to physical and metaphorical *dark*. Light and dark are two of the vital yet paradoxical elements of life. Both penetrated my boyhood imagination in ways that seem, from the vantage point of age and experience, lopsidedly out of balance.

I'd like to tell you a story about how I grew through the prompting of a power I describe as *soul*. You can think of this story as one episode with more to come. By way of introduction, once upon a time I believed the sole purpose of my life was to be good. Not a bad purpose in itself, but the way of being good taught to me was largely in terms of moral behavior. That became highly problematic for me. Being good, I was told meant *doing* good, all the time or else . . .

My Story – Losing the Dark

They say "the past is a foreign country" but hardly, to me. Happily I walk knee-deep down its grassy lanes disappearing along a narrow curve ahead, overgrown but verdant and quietly mysterious for I have come to terms many times with its beauty and its limitations. Like when I used to run down our yard, hurdling over the stones, gathering speed as I crossed the street and leaping upward catch the wooden electrical pole, puckered and gouged from the countless cleated boots of "electrical" men.

Then, with feet braced on the mortared stones of the railway wall, I shimmy up, monkey-like to swing out on railway lines that had swallowed many a rubber ball, high-flung from our street games, lost but not forgotten, locked in the inner room with the rest of the "strange things" that happened, seemingly for no good reason, until now.

The past is a place for climbing a pole, the better to view the rooftops of our town that also climbed and disappeared and for boys daring each other to dangerous stunts—until the call echoed insistently and I was back down that pole and running to the shop for bread and milk for the tea.

So much for my experiences in the *light* during the daytime hours of my "born to be wild" childhood; I will also share from the *dark* and the *something else like a prompt*, I remember.

> **My Story – The Dark . . . and Something Else**
>
> *In the gathering dusk, the shadows played on the hills. Shadows I knew were thrown there by clouds scattering before the errant winds that like me were playing in the moonlight—that much I understood. Wood splinters, skinned knees and frayed sweaters all spelled "no heed need be paid," for they were the price of living intuitively, of sorrows not-to-be-mourned, of youth's mindless run, recklessly grabbing, eating life's offerings whole and undigested; but also something else, like a friendly prompt, remembered while I had careless leave to live with mindless, nearly feral understanding of it all.*
>
> *Still, mysterious things piled up, more than I could remember until, in my budding manliness, I took for granted that memories with mysteries suffused were just useless sentiment when there was practical work to be done in the busy, grimy, smoke-filled family forge. Now I know those "shadows playing on the moonlit hills" were more and meant more. Something else remembered every detail and kept score.*
>
> *The shadows were messages to my imagination for a life to be formed by every head-covered, coat-sheltered ducking move against oncoming, rain-filled windy gusts, skipping over sidewalk puddles until lifetimes later, moments of meaning quietly dawned and subtly gave me pause. My times of conscious living happened between the pauses, but it was while the*
>
> **FIGURE 5: THE RAILWAY THAT ATE RUBBER BALLS**
>
> *pauses endured that any growing or evading occurred. Something else carried the youthful "growing or evading me" from pause to pause and anchored there scenes for later visits, times of wonder and engaging solitude, like this one.*
>
> *Daylight shortened, shadows deepened, dogs grew silent, crows flew churning paths through the fading light, bound for tree-top clumps of twigs against the darkening sky and settled cawing while milk-swollen cattle heaved into their stalls and the dark came down on people and land. Darkness then ruled the alleys, the eaves and the doorways; darkness ruled the fretful minds and flowed in veins*

> *of deep desire that sometimes ended in confessional whispers in the dark. Darkness stalked the graveyards, ran along the rustling hedgerows and lulled the fears that hummed on nerves strung taut—lest worse and dreadful things befall when eyelids closed.*
>
> *Yet, in circadian rhythmic repose, in the darkness, life quietly ruled and renewed the bodies of every living thing. Its healing touch brought calm to untethered anxieties that skittered from the ends of nerves and made them whole enough to face the dawn and day again. In the darkness, work was done below the level of conscious minds and still in darkness creative healing and integrating work continues to be yet done, hardly acknowledged as comparable to the kind of work done in the light. No matter, for there again, something else, below the surface of every natural thing, in shades of dark and light and of my whirling mind remembered and kept rhythmic time and score.*
>
> *Revisiting those memories, and that "something else", I can understand there is a power at work throughout my life and nothing—nothing at all—is without meaning. They say the past is a foreign country, but hardly.*

My Story – Reflections

From this story, I discovered the great loss of the power-filled dark from my life. It had been blasted away as blight, bane and blasphemy from my grinding mind, or else surely ending in a blistering burn, itself never-ending. Of course, I noticed the shadowy forms of the dark, but I was afraid of them because of the association of light with good and dark with bad. I tried to live only in the light, which effort counter-intuitively amounted to a disastrous incursion of the dark into both my conscious and unconscious life; causing me to experience a severely unhappy inner life, in spite of all appearances to the contrary.

For me, what connected with the dark was shameful, to be avoided, left unspoken and to be banished from my mind. I wanted only to be kind, good, happy, hopeful and generous. I did not want to be bad, unkind, pessimistic, deceptive, spiteful or vengeful. But, as you can imagine, darkness had a field-day in my inner world, precisely because I could not—nor should not—recognize it as legitimate. But I get ahead of myself.

What does it mean to have lost the dark? Just as light and dark are two aspects of reality that go together, to live only in the light means to disconnect from one half of reality and thereby invite the disaster of a bifurcated life. When

I lost the dark, I also felt diminished in my access to things physical and to the earth. This happened because of the juxtaposition of the light as the opposite of the dark, things spiritual as the opposite of the physical, the good as the opposite of evil, and the afterlife as the opposite of the concerns of this world.

When I lost the dark, I lost not only physical darkness, but also the metaphorical dark, which can manifest itself in uncountable ways. Briefly, the metaphorical dark refers to the erotic energies that drive new life, to evil in its so-called bad behaviors, and to the destructive tendencies of human nature. It carries with it the sense of great mysteries whose gravitational pull holds us simultaneously in thrall and in petrifying fear of the great unknowns, such as the pulpit-proclaimed alarming *powers of darkness and death*, and what lies beyond its portal.

The dark *is* something but it was the aspect of the dark identified with evil that presented the greatest loss for me. I was so afraid of the manifestations of evil within me, or in others, I ran away from the binding force of relationships, especially with myself, that depend on the sharing of what is real in life. For me, what was allowable for sharing was what was termed the good, the light and the warm, which left my relationships one-sided and bland.

My Story – Applications

To paraphrase a familiar saying, "the darkness will set you free, but first it will make you miserable." I was miserable, alone and isolated, but when I could, I was thinking and searching. The inner misery I suffered pushed me to search for answers in even deeper, darker levels of myself. Even though answers were emerging in complex ways, over time I was learning to integrate them into a self who was becoming whole. In the process, I discovered my past and the dark that figured prominently in it is not forgotten but energetically alive, requiring integration and seeking further insight and equilibrium. A key theme of this book is of me reconnecting with the dark, the earth, the world, my work and my own humanity.

Even though self-awareness dawns gradually, our lives are not merely accumulations of scattered pieces. We are always emerging as one whole. In addition, we can trust the intuitions of our souls as they do their prompting work over time, usually a whole lifetime. Aligning efforts with the sometimes disparate promptings of one's soul is the source of deepening Interiority. For me, I was gradually able to say the gift of the once-terrifying dark was a richer, integrated self. I take little credit for this integration but refer again to the prompts of that *something else* I call my soul.

One's soul has two infinite dimensions—the inner and the outer—and each influences us deeply. The soul keeps the thread of memory intact and ensures continuity of a person's story by streaming insights in intuitions, dreams and waking imaginations—oscillating through the sparkle and detritus of daily working, living. Embracing them all means accepting the mysterious self through which small miracles are made. I believe I am resourceful because I can bring all experiences to my work, and I can appreciate the light, the dark, the good with the bad and all the rest. How I learned this application of using my experiences makes for an interesting read, but that's another story. How I challenged the institutional authority that taught me and others about *good* and *bad* also makes for interesting reading but that's also a different story. Now, how about your story?

Your Story

What is your story of unusual experiences from long ago that may hint of *something else*, like a subtle prompt, and to this day remains vibrant in your memory for some meaningful reason? You may recall these experiences easily, but the ability to apply relevant insight to your work takes repeated practice and sustained effort toward wholeness.

If you take time for remembering, reflecting and applying your story and continue to do so throughout the book, then we will find ourselves on a journey together toward greater wholeness and benefit for all.

Pragmatic Questions

Many of life's questions are pragmatic and involve day-to-day living, and work. Over the centuries, work got a bad rap. Work is often associated with mundane sustenance—wages enough only to survive, earned by the sweat of our brows. Related thoughts about work are of being used and even abused. In the past four years, manufacturing in the U.S. lost 2.3 million jobs. Yet, since 2001, because of technological improvements and globalization, productivity is up 40%, while wages have increased only 9.9%.[14] The jobs lost, in manufacturing especially, will not return because of the requirements for highly skilled and better-trained workers.

The writing is on the wall for laid-off workers. Either we improve our own productivity, to qualify for employment or we will be permanently unemployable. We can qualify through online courses and training, but that is only half of the story. We have to knuckle-down and gain an edge in this hyper-competitive job market through buffing our unique credentials—and that begins from within ourselves.

We have been led to assume that work itself will not allow us to explore *meaning*, *mystery* and *wholeness*. As workers, it is difficult to consider that we can reach a mystical state so sublime as to surpass the greatest models of humankind—a level of productivity so astonishing as to outshine even the most talented, or a mode of service so altruistic as to approximate the most loving among us; yet my experience demonstrates that such heights are not only possible but within our reach. We too easily accept that the "business" aspect of organizations, dedicated to the provision of products and services, disallows the deepening of the soul.

Not surprisingly, my proposition in this book points to the opposite.

Historical Legacies

In dealing with such a subject as work, we must focus on the historical role played by philosophy. The roles of various philosophies in shaping work are fundamental and plentiful. Contrary to what we might think, it was not the products, the tools or the managers in any organization that established the current conditions of work and the attitudes toward workers. Rather, it was the *pivotal thoughts of influential people* throughout history that made work and the lives of workers what they are today. In other words, philosophical legacies influenced the deepest levels of our awareness.

In our time, major shifts occurring in every field of technology and the post-industrial global economy are influencing how work is done. Because these shifts are mainly helpful, the tendency is for workers to be swept along and adapt to them unthinkingly. However, if in similar ways, we passively adapt emerging systems of work to the philosophies of previous generations, we run the risk of adding "new wine in old wine skins" and suffering inevitable consequences.

We need a fundamental realignment between the philosophies and the systems that support the work being done. Unlike the physical sciences, which deal with basic and unchanging natural elements, if philosophical notions about work were adapted by people, they can be changed by people. Philosophizing is not to be considered only in terms of mental concepts, but should also include developing a new capacity for transforming the world. Whenever we philosophize, in a sense we change the world, and particularly the world of our work.

Since we are going to explore the impact of philosophy on work, we can do no better than to emulate the eminent Greek philosopher Socrates by using questions as our methodology.

Many philosophical concepts and subsequent organizational structures do not serve the interests of workers today. We should learn to recognize what to retain and what to let go. Of course, not all philosophical foundations are negative. Philosophers provided the foundations of many of the rights and freedoms workers enjoy today. On the darker side of the tradition, oppressive burdens on workers everywhere require that they release themselves to progress more freely and productively into the future.

Historical analysis reveals *legacies of deep anti-worker biases* in the workplace—and in society. The more obvious legacies: power flowing to the elite at the top of corporate structures and inequitable distribution of benefits. While the results of inequitable distribution are easy to see, the biases that hold them in place are difficult to discern. In fact, they are so well hidden—and yet so familiar. And because of the fears we attach to them with our learned habitual responses, they are practically inaccessible. Yes, ideas are powerful. As Napoleon said, "there are two powers in the world, the sword and the mind. In the long run, the sword is always beaten by the mind."

When we know the influence of historical legacies, we can choose to let go of what is past and irrelevant to our circumstances. There is no doubt that workers and organizations operate under the influence of historical legacies, particularly of philosophers, religious scholars and scientific thinkers. The question becomes: How can I manage the relevant—and irrelevant—legacies of philosophers and other thinkers on my work so I understand the forces that bear on me? That question opens the door to how I might fundamentally change the equation in favor of equality among workers, shared ethical responsibility with management for the organization's growth and sustainable use of earth's resources.

Undoubtedly accelerated by ecological anxieties, these latter questions are reflective of our generation's quest for meaning. If we are defined by an inability to confront the questions about who we really are in our time, we will suffer from what contemporary philosopher David Foster Wallace describes as a kind of *lostness*,[15] which I interpret as a *dearth of meaning*.

One of the symptoms of lostness is our devotion to distraction, reminiscent of the "bread and circuses" in the time of the Caesars that kept the Roman citizens happy, even if impoverished. In our time, entertainment technologies take the place of bread and circuses, too easily becoming distracting, dehumanizing addictions. Admittedly, such addictions are intensified by a desire for some fundamental ground upon which we can make choices. At the same time, modern humans suffer from a diminished sense of the sacred, which may leave us befuddled and in existential uncertainty.

So it is up to us to define who we are in the circumstances of our work, to retain what is relevant from historical influences and to make efforts to create the future of meaning. Most importantly, if we do not become aware of irrelevant historical influences, we may passively accept as reality what has been handed down from others.

What follows here is a brief historical overview to demonstrate what key philosophers, religious and scientific thinkers thought about life, work and workers.

Ancient Greece

"Wonder is the feeling of a philosopher and philosophy begins in wonder."
—*Plato*

Plato writing in Theaetetus (360 BCE) made the distinction between the philosopher and the banausos (common working man). In his meaning, the banausos was "uneducated, insensitive to art and with no spiritual view of the world."[16] The impact of this thinking on workers was to reduce their self-worth and the value of their work. This view was a reflection of the commonly held ideal that real life lay in the pursuit of philosophy, art and politics.

Aristotle (384-322 BCE) in *Politics, Vol. 4,* viewed work as burdensome in comparison to amusement and leisure, which was to be reserved for intellectual activities.[17] These views of two of the greatest philosophers of antiquity set the stage for domination and even enslavement of the "lesser"—workers who did manual labor—by the elite or the "greater," meaning those who used their minds.

In retrospect, one wonders how it was possible for even the most common kind of work, done by any worker, anywhere, to retain a sense of contribution to the whole. With difficulty, I think.

In Greek society (4th Century BCE to 30 BCE), there was a "gulf separating the philosopher/scientist/inventor from the farmer/craftsman/manual worker/slave."[18] The impact from the great Greek thinking traditions influences our places of work even today. In quoting briefly from these giants of antiquity, I am not intending to reflect negatively on their great contributions, rather to make a point about the roots of the conceptual legacies regarding the lack of dignity afforded ordinary work and workers.

Old Testament

The images of God presented in the Old Testament are male, creator, destroyer, protector, warrior, lover—and worker on behalf of the human race. In the minds of workers, this latter image established the altruism of God as a model regarding the importance of community-based work. Just as the prevailing image of God was as a worker who created the natural world, man was to be characterized as a worker who continued those creative acts through his/her work. Nevertheless, the key image of the Divine-human relationship, (God-Father-Lord) was a communication with male representatives of the human race (Abraham, Moses, David, Jesus, Apostles). Thus, power and authority was transferred. This became the dominant metaphor for hierarchical order in all social groupings.

In all probability, the biblical image of God as a powerful male personage exercising authority from on high helped establish male dominance over females by modeling social institutions as patriarchal. In addition, because God created everything from a remote place, the image intimated that "real growth" was a transcendence of the physicality of the natural world and, hopefully, someday an ascendance into an extra-terrestrial (heavenly) mansion.

The consequent loss of the possibility of Interiority was to have devastating effects on the achievement of maturity through work, especially that which was more physical in nature.

We also learn from the same Bible that in the expulsion of Adam and Eve from the Garden of Eden, humans had to "earn their bread by the sweat of their brow."[19] The concept of "The Fall" influences the perception of people as wanting and, therefore, needing guidance and management.

Furthermore, in being cast out of the Garden,[20] where everything was freely available, to earning their bread "by the sweat of their brow,"[21] the burden of toilsome work is laid on humans in retribution for eating the forbidden fruit. In this image, work is seen as a troublesome burden and a punishment rather than an opportunity to live in a productive way, and to grow and mature. Even though some images of God are of a creator, lover and helper of his people, the images of masculine authority, overlord, ruler and punisher established models for how management exercises authority today in a top-down, patriarchal and hierarchical chain of command.

Jesus

From the New Testament we learn stories about Jesus Christ, the carpenter's son, in his association with "sinners," fishermen, tax collectors, the ill and the poor. We also learn from how he interacts with housekeepers, shepherds, farmers, wine-makers, prodigals and others. The lives of ordinary people are elevated by sharing in a *kingdom* of love, in what might be termed the communities of the holy or sacred. This is a key insight. Although the words of Jesus pointed to the primacy of the Kingdom of God over the kingdoms of this world, his life pattern was to align himself with the poor and seek justice for all.

In this model, there is a tradition of seeing work as worthy of a just reward and workers as equals and collaborators in building a community on earth. In this sense, the perception of work went beyond the accomplishment of tasks and the gaining of results to building communities in which everyone's life was productive; all received a share of the goods and none were left out of "the kingdom of love." It was a consequence of this view that doing work came to have worth in and of itself. This was especially so when people were conscious of their work contributions and passionate about their roles in the building of the whole. In his words and through his example, Jesus shows that the source of the kingdom is within and the ideal way of living and working is in forgiving, accepting and joining with co-workers in building the earth. While these powerful messages still echo, the great traditions have become blurred by subsequent generations of Christian thinkers and leaders as the institutional aspects of the original gathering became more pronounced.

St. Paul

What did St. Paul (10-67 AD) Apostle and wide-ranging missionary of the early church, think of life, work and workers? The quotation from Romans 5:12 says it well: "Sin entered the world through one man, (Adam) and through sin death, and thus death has spread to the whole human race because everyone has sinned." In short, people are culpable for their own weaknesses and consequently carry a burden of guilt regarding their humanity. As a consequence of seeing human nature as *sinful*, a guilt complex has driven workers to agonize over mistakes or imperfections, and to carry the obligation to improve performance under the authority of a male boss (God, the father figure).

Later in his admonishments about work, St. Paul said "if anyone will not work, neither should he eat."[22] In this passage, there is an additional severity in tone that contrasts with the approach favored by Jesus toward the anawim (Hebrew for "the poor") and how he presented the kingdom of love and sharing the goods of the earth with all, regardless of performance or merit. In yet another passage, St. Paul exhorts his followers in words that might (only might) connect work itself with the holy: "Whatever your work is, put your heart into it, as if it were for the Lord and not for men."[23]

Monasticism

In the 3rd Century, newly forming monastic communities of Christian monks were obliged to work, as the work itself was considered both penitential and productive. Yet, they also considered work a daily cross that had to be borne because of the sin of Adam. On the other hand, early Christian views of the status of workers reveal that "both masters and slaves were considered as brothers."[24] This was a radical departure from the Greek and Roman attitudes that saw labor as of lower value than other occupations such as philosophizing or teaching. St. Ambrose of Milan (339-397 AD) taught "the worker must have his pay and it was a sin to defraud him."[25]

These early monastic communities contributed a relatively benign concept of work to historical legacies and a view of the worker as more equal to their masters than had been previously been considered. In the above examples, do we have an historical precedent for the consideration of Interiority as aligned with work and worker?

The Roman Emperor Constantine (274-337 AD) co-opted the cross—the major Christian icon—as a symbol under which his armies marched, and established Christianity as the official religion of his empire. This also influenced how work and workers began to be perceived. Just as the newly legitimized structure of the Christian church adopted a hierarchical form following the model of the empire's armies, so also the notion of the "divine right of kings" came to be associated with leadership in institutions. As a result, identifying the ruler with God began to weigh heavily on the shoulders of the workers as they began to see their masters having an authority sanctioned from above, and themselves with no other option than obedience to the so-called divine command.

St. Augustine

Even though St. Augustine (354-430), Bishop of Hippo in North Africa, theologian, philosopher, thought human nature was good, he elaborated on the thinking of St. Paul that connected sin (of which we are all guilty) with death (things having to do with the body, material goods and the earth) and salvation with spiritual things and the next life in heaven. Work itself was not so much honored because his focus was on the world to come. Even taking into consideration his enormous contributions, we must question whether this connection of sin (material things) and death contributed to a neglect of the earth and a negation of the fundamental interdependence of people with all things in the universe. In a similar fashion, throughout history, this connecting sin with death and earthly things provided a rationale for the misuse and even exploitation of the resources of the earth by those few at the top of organizational hierarchies. As a result, theology came to be established on an external kingdom. Heaven was ruled over by an autocratic manager, God, whose pronouncements allowed for domination of nature by humans.

The immanence of the sacred within the physical earth was lost and today, as a result, the human community is facing the destruction of the ability of the earth's ecological systems to renew themselves.

Medieval Period

Medieval Europe (5th to 10th Centuries) viewed work in a confusing variety of ways, including "a form of penance, a basis for charity, a defense against idleness and a sacred endeavor."[26] The Monastic (4th Century monastery practices) traditions viewed "work as beneficial but placed the emphasis on its ascetic value as the daily cross to be borne for the burden imposed on mankind due to the sin of Adam."[27] As a result of this thinking, workers continued to see work as a burden and sacrifice rather than as a way to grow, achieve satisfaction and contribute to the emergence of the whole. Nevertheless, the Rule of St. Benedict (480-547 AD), one of the early founders of monasticism, imposed work on all monks and did not undervalue work in comparison with prayer or other good works. This is evident in the popular Benedictine motto, "to labor is to pray," (laborare est orare).

Late-Middle Ages

The late-Middle Ages (11th to 14th Centuries) saw the rise of the guilds of stonemasons, carpenters, stained-glass makers and others, as well as the system of apprenticeship, journeyman and master in a trade. During this period, the great cathedrals of Europe pushed their spires skyward and men thrilled at the work of their hands—that symbolized something ineffably greater than the buildings themselves. Similar to the great works of stone, wood and glass, this period saw the creation of great compendiums of learning such as the Summa Theologica of St. Thomas Aquinas. He confirmed that work is a necessity of nature. Even though he recognized work as a natural right, he reasoned that the world is rigidly structured by God and everyone should remain within their allotted place throughout their lives. He advocated that the better way is to pray and contemplate God. In such a structured society, a hierarchy of three orders came to be accepted, namely *oratores* or priests, *bellatores* or warriors and nobles, and *laboratores* or workers—and do we not already know which order came at the bottom?[28]

Reformation

Martin Luther (1483-1546), who initiated the Protestant Reformation, "swept away the idea of the superiority of one type of work over another" and maintained "every variety of work has equal spiritual dignity" and "all work contributes to the common life of mankind."[29] For those who heard, his views must have elevated the value of even the most mundane work and contributed to a sense of liberation and meaning. Adriano Tilgher, who wrote about the subject of work in 1930, particularly the impact of Protestantism, said: "Protestantism is the moving force in the profound spiritual revolution which established work in the modern mind as the base and key of life, and in this matter, the first voice of Protestantism is Luther."[30]

John Calvin (1509–1564), an influential French theologian and Geneva-based pastor and leader during the Protestant Reformation, followed the Pauline (St. Paul) and Augustinian (St. Augustine) views of the fallen state of nature but refined their views by saying the only means of salvation was through the word of God as manifested in the Bible.[31] Accordingly, the view of work underwent a change of emphasis according to John Calvin's statement: "the necessity for hard work is a component of a person's calling and worldly success is a sign of personal salvation."[32] In these words, the equating of "success as a sign of personal salvation" introduced a differentiating new element into considerations around the impact of work. According to many commentators, this emphasis on hard work and thrift began to engage people in a rational work ethic that deeply influenced capitalism, entrepreneurship and diligence during the succeeding centuries. One potentially negative impact of Calvin's approach was for workers to act on the world but not necessarily to love that same world. This approach may have led to disaffection for and objectification of the natural world. Calvin's shift of emphasis in the direction of success at work as a sign of blessing, promoted the coming together of the middle and upper classes into a mercantile and landed elite. At the same time, in effect, the results of these actions removed peasants from ownership and deposited them into the sphere of landless laborers; and the dissolution of the feudal system led to what was to become a new class system of capital and labor.[33]

In examining the influence of the Reformation (Protestant - beginning in the 16th Century) on work and workers, I focus on the transition from symbols to words that came to characterize the Protestant revolt against the excesses of Catholic worship and its use of icons and symbols in liturgies. Nowhere was the revolt more evident than in the transition to "only scripture" (sola scriptura) and the iconoclastic rejection of liturgies, statuary and pictures that were sacramental symbols in the practices of the Catholic Church. What took the place of such sacramental symbols was the emphasis on *word* as the expression of *truth*, especially in the form of the Bible.

The following is a key example of the profound impact of these changes. Along with the removal of depictions of the body of Christ from the cross, came the loss of the connection with the holy that had been ineffable (unable to be spoken because of its reference to transcendent mystery). Now the holy became enclosed in words with merely literal meaning. Words became the means to control meaning, whether what they referred to was real or belonging to the realms of mystery. Thereafter what was lost to the worker was the value of the infinitely mysterious dimensions of the human at work, which had been accessible only through soulful intuition.

Enlightenment

Under the thinking of three important philosopher/scientists: **Francis Bacon,** (1561-1626) the founder of the scientific method that focused on laboratory-developed data as objective proof of truth, **Rene Descartes,** (1596-1650) who extolled the powers of reason over experience or religion – "I think, therefore I am," and **Isaac Newton,** (1642-1727) who formulated the laws of motion, life took on rational, scientific, mechanical characteristics. This further ordered and managed work and workplaces according to immutable laws and structures. The scientific age may have been ushered forward in exponential steps by these three, but at the same time an awareness of the dimensions of the mystery of life, and the inaccessibility of meaning through work itself, slipped unnoticed out the back door into the dimming light of history.

The diminution of mystery was hastened by the split between applied science and the traditional underpinnings of religion. It is not my purpose here to rue the exit of hierarchically-structured religious world-views and dogmatic formulations of "truth." However, I do lament the diminishment of our affinity for mystery, our sense of belonging to the natural world, and our allegiance to the common goals of the human community. Undoubtedly, during the advance of the scientific age, the development of mechanical marvels contributed to the improvement of the lot of many. Nonetheless, these advances also obscured the role of humans as constitutive participants in the natural processes of the earth's ecological systems. Humans as a constitutive element in natural ecologies became increasingly displaced in favor of those humans who assumed a dominant position and exploitative function over the natural world.

To this day, we labor under a false anthropocentric view of the natural systems to which we belong, wherein all things human take precedence over every other reality. Such a view of the earth's systems as being under the mechanical control of the human community brings with it an almost fatal imbalance that will probably prevent its (the earth's) recovery, or even an acceptable degree of sustainability. In the scientific/mechanical-uniformity approach to life and work that developed during this period, we lost a sense of the centrality of ecology and bio-diversity for the renewal of earth's systems—our sources of life. Today, we hurtle forward in a mindless rush for "more" material goods, consequently bankrupting the biological species and systems upon which we depend. According to this mechanical model of the universe, industrialism and colonialism also took hold of native populations of "foreign and savage" peoples. Consequently, the natural resources those peoples owned came under organizational systems managed, top-down, by powerfully ascendant elites.

According to **Thomas Hobbes,** (1588-1679) a rationalist-materialist-humanist philosopher and writer, "the life of man...is solitary, poor, nasty, brutish, and short. The condition of man...is a condition of war of everyone against everyone." (Leviathan - 1651). Hobbes also noted that "the way out of this desperate state is to make a social contract and establish the state to keep peace and order."[34] His thinking was that government was a human artifact and not something made by God. This served to further diminish trust in the relationship among co-workers and allowed for hierarchical bureaucracies to assume a dominant position and replace connection to the sacred. At the same time, his view of the selfishness of human nature led to a distrust of motivation in workers and furthered the establishment of the hierarchical order. His discounting of religion in favor of an empirical basis of knowledge contributed to work beginning to lose its spiritual dimension and become a more secular endeavor. His view that people should obey the sovereign established the kind of obedience workers must give to their supervisors—or to anyone placed above them in society or the workplace.

John Locke, (1632-1704) political thinker and writer, observed, "property ownership is legitimized by work."[35] By his statement "'tis labour indeed that puts the difference of value on everything,"[36] Locke established ownership of the fruits of one's work and of work itself as "worthy of a just reward" and also made the judgment that "if one man has more than another, it is because he is more industrious."[37] In this way, the rational/empirical dimensions of work entered the vocabulary and began to take precedence over the spiritual and ideal.

Even though Locke clarified the right of the worker to property through his labor, he also advocated maintaining labor discipline by means of a more severe poor law. "For the labourer's share, being seldom more than a bare subsistence, never allows that body of men time or opportunity to raise their thoughts above that, or struggle with the richer for theirs."[38] In this thinking, he also restricted the laborer's thinking about their plight because they were forced into subsistence living and "grunt" work. Even though Locke was said to "have espoused a universal and moral authority that all mankind was entitled to religious and social liberty," it was also true he recognized "people engaged in…accumulating wealth and property [that] could cause deprivation and denial to others."[39] In so doing, he paved the way for legitimizing a split in society between the haves and the have-nots that continues to this day.

There were other notable events that influenced the world of work during the period between the 16th and 18th Centuries. The modern corporation made its appearance at the beginning of the 17th Century, taking shape under "the confluence of Craft Guilds, Market shops, Trading companies, Modern Cities and Civil Service" structures, which were based on hierarchical order, empirical data and merit-based promotion.[40] Workers today still labor under these market values, administrative bureaucracies and management structures as if they were unveiled only yesterday.

In a historical anomaly, the French Revolution of 1789 freed capitalists and workers from the yoke of feudalism only to establish regulations that further curtailed the freedom of workers to think for themselves.

The Enlightenment (18th Century) put into place a secular view of the world rather than the traditional religious outlook and elevated reason as the primary source of authority. The contributions of **Immanuel Kant** (1724-1804), come to mind. His thesis proposed that the accumulation and processing of knowledge is work. It also created a new faith and, according to Adriano Tilgher "a religion of human society"[41] that surrounded bureaucracies with the aura of the holy, which perception has both positive and negative undertones from the point of view of the workers.

The positive undertone allows for a less absolute world-view that might have inhibited the workers' ability to make decisions for themselves.[42] On the other hand, the negative might augur a diminution of affinity for the transcendently numinous (pertaining to the spiritual and surpassing comprehension or understanding). A similar negative outcome would be to diminish a sense of belonging to the diverse ecological manifestations of nature surrounding workers in their workplaces.

The idea that knowledge is productive synthesis comes close to the main thrust of this book, which is to derive order out of the multiplicity of sense impressions by the exercise of our wills. This exercise of will to establish order through the processing of knowledge is a creatively human task and qualifies as work on a profound level.

Early Economists

In reference to **Adam Smith** (1723-1790), the Scottish moral philosopher and a pioneer of political economy, Herbert Applebaum writes, "in him we have the first formulation of a modern theory of work."[43] Because of Adam Smith's enormously influential 1776 book, *Wealth of Nations*, the recognition of the importance of the worker grew exponentially when he wrote, "labor, in addition to exchange, is the keystone of economic theory." Smith was said to have developed, "a labor theory of value…and considered that people who performed productive work, rather than gold, are the chief foundation of any society."[44]

Smith postulated that individuals act in their own interest from which evolutionary patterns of growth arise, as if guided "by an invisible hand." Out of Smith's principle, "society works best through everyone following their own self-interests by rational calculation,"[45] emerged a new set of values and ethics that led to all matters, including those of individuals being treated "in terms of quantification, profit and loss."[46] Calculations about the productivity of the worker thereafter became associated with economics and are expressed in the quote of **Jeremy Bentham**, (1748-1832), English utilitarian and social reformer, as "the greatest good for the greatest number."[47] Accordingly, this type of calculation of profit and loss led to work and the worker being perceived as a means to an end—unfortunately the losing end in the scramble for wealth. Even with his advanced economic theories, Smith still used the terms master and servants to describe employers and employees.[48]

Protestant Work Ethic

Hard work, thrift and efficiency in one's worldly calling were thought of as "the Protestant Ethic," which also included signs of individual blessing as a portent of salvation. In particular, Calvinism—based on a systematic theology, the ethic of hard work and thrift in the secular world—supported the rise of capitalism and the capitalist reorganization of society. Accordingly, profits and savings were to be plowed back into the expansion of business for the purpose of self-development and business improvement.

Again unfortunately, those latter aspirations became diluted and work tended to become an end in itself, as was money-making and capital accumulation through business expansion. In effect, the more idealistic dimensions of the Protestant Ethic became diminished over time as work tended to become a trap for the worker. In this context, sociologist **Max Weber** (1864-1920), in his book *The Protestant Ethic – 1905*, voiced a warning about materialistic capitalism becoming an "iron cage"[49] for everyone. Weber believed "bureaucracy is central to the rise of capitalism because bureaucracies make decisions that are predictable and, hence, amenable to calculation." Nevertheless, by his account "all of us—the wealthy and the poor, owners and workers—lead economic lives of quiet desperation." This "quiet desperation" of which he speaks presages the unquenchable thirst for things of the spirit or Interiority. Such words indeed have a contemporary feel with regard to the centrality of profit over all other considerations in our places of business.

Social Reformers and Work

In his idea of the working man as the true philosopher and in his banishing the idea of master and servant, **Karl Marx** (1818-1883) elevated work to a position of absolute importance and with it the dignity of the worker. It was Marx who saw the worker becoming alienated from his work because of the excesses of industrialization and capitalism. He was prescient in predicting that the machinery, technology and capital that contributed to the alienation of the worker would lead to the decline of the "work ethic." In an effort to dispel the influence of the "Robber Barons," Marx elevated the position of the worker, but also heightened the tensions between labor and management. He emphasized production for the sake of meeting men's needs rather than the making of profit. In retrospect, Marx' messages resonate today even more than they did when he was alive.

Albert Einstein (1879-1955) changed how we understand the world with his famous theory $E=mc^2$, which told us that all matter can be converted into energy. This theory fundamentally altered the way we view our relatedness to all things and our corresponding responsibility for sustaining natural resources. His thinking allowed workers to view their work as a creative relationship wherein both are changed. At the same time, his theory of relativity displaced static views of how the universe worked, which caused uncertainty to replace predictability in viewing how organizations, work and workers operate. If humans are part of complex adaptive systems, it makes sense that we should view management, leadership and organizations and the processes in which we do our work as less absolutist and necessarily more adaptive to the unique characteristics of the humans (workers) involved.

Hannah Arendt, (1906-1975), political philosopher, made the distinction between labor, work and action, which are three increasingly higher levels of what it means to be human. Labor means the *production* of consumables in order to maintain life and thus is cyclical. Work is the *activity* of man, the craftsman and maker of things, creating a stable and durable world for himself and his posterity.[50] Action initiates the *development* of something uniquely new and affords meaning to the worker. However, in her view, because of the ubiquity of technology, workers were losing the capacity for action and, in this way, had less and less ability to gain access to meaning at work.

Modern Pope's Views of Work

Pope **John Paul II** (1920-2005) in his encyclical *Laborem Exercens* (On Human Work), provided a sobering assessment of the benefits and potential weaknesses of technology when he wrote: "technology is an ally of work, …but when society exalts the machine and reduces man to a slave of the machine…technology can control human behavior, taking away any satisfaction in work." At the same time, his words struck a contemporary theme in support of work when he noted "everyone becomes a human being, through, among other things, work,"[51] and "by means of work, man shares in the work of creation."[52] By emphasizing "everyone becomes a human being," we learn that we, our co-workers and organizations are not static beings but works in progress. The assumption here is we, the community of human beings, are in charge of our development and growth toward wholeness and work is the key means toward that end.

Teilhard DeChardin, (1881-1955) paleontologist, scientist, Jesuit priest, wrote about the continuous unfolding of the material cosmos, extending from primordial particles to the development of elementary life forms, eventually to human beings and ultimately toward a point of convergence of consciousness in everything. He called this the Omega Point. In this theory, he describes the universe as being in constant evolutionary motion, an innate progress toward a goal of unity. As a consequence, he includes the life and work of each worker as a unique contribution to emerging consciousness in everything. In this way, every worker, every task, every organization is constitutive of what evolves and, therefore, elevates life (work and workers) to combinations of vital energy—from which everything is growing toward wholeness. When we examine Teilhard's vision, not only does the past weigh heavily on every aspect of work but the future weighs even heavier because of the difficult-to-imagine changes that are predicted to continuously and dizzily catch us unprepared.

Puritan Legacy

The Puritan legacy (16th and 17th Centuries) advanced questions about the constructive orientations toward work and workers that have been passed down through many generations of Americans to present day. The most obvious are the predilections for order, process and results that characterize the workplaces of America. This legacy, which can be traced to the example set by the Puritans toward work,[53] has triggered the extraordinary productivity of the manufacturing worker in the U.S. This productivity may be continuously increasing through the implementation of technological improvements, but it also holds a difficult-to-manage dark side.

In view of the successes of such large American organizations, the question arises as to when such powerful monopolies and conglomerates become too powerful for the democratic process to succeed. Is it when they wield their power to crush the reasonably protesting voices of the people at work? Or is it when bureaucratic institutions resist movements such as the Occupy protests? Just as important, when contemplating a challenging global future, if American workers wish to maintain a competitive degree of productivity at work, it seems necessary to apply the same constructive discipline to inner processes as to outer achievement. Thus, the more creative intuitions of one's Interiority can be made exponentially more accessible.

Be assured, the answer to all this is certainly not an exaggerated infusion of positive thinking. Not all of the Puritan influences were beneficial. One less obvious, but more problematic cultural influence was an irrepressible optimism that has since had a deleterious influence on American workers. Certainly, the optimistic can-do spirit has produced definite elevations of enthusiasm, energy and productivity—all necessary to motivate workers. On the other hand, the less desirable influences of relentless optimism spring from a lack of reality in estimating one's capabilities, coupled with minimizing the difficulties involved in actually doing the assigned work.

In addition, a resistance has emerged toward recognizing, as an opportunity for growth, the importance of one's mistakes and shortcomings in performance. One recent extreme of this kind of optimism is the "Law of Attraction," which promises if you think positively, positive things will come to you.[54] In her book called *Bright-Sided: How the Relentless Promotion of Positive Thinking has Undermined America*, Barbara Ehrenreich holds that the idea you can control the world with your thoughts is derived from the virus of positive thinking.[55] Her thesis asserts that Americans were blind-sided by the optimistic assumption of continuing prosperity that almost led to the collapse of the global financial system in 2008. Robert Reich, secretary of labor under President Clinton and professor of public policy at UC Berkeley, underscores this weakness in diagnosing what ails the U.S. economy as he explains, "Optimism also explains why we spend so much and save so little."[56]

Unrealistic optimism appears in the following ways in American workplaces:

- Over-estimation of one's competencies and resistance toward recognizing the realities of one's mistakes.

- "Multi-tasking"—because of the delusion that more activity lends itself to greater productivity.

- Over-dependence on motivational speakers who preach constant improvement... even in the face of glaring inconsistencies in performance.

- Overemphasis on "thinking you can do something means you are able to do it." An example of this thinking comes from the 1937 book: *Think and Grow Rich* by Napoleon Hill.[57]

- The practice of co-opting God into the mix of hard work, motivation and success with such slogans as "God wants you to be rich."[58]

- Extreme dependence on positive psychology, a.k.a. self-hypnosis, as a source of authentic happiness.

These examples of exaggerated optimism have led to a flattened, plastic culture that supports the perception that we humans are in control, can have anything we want merely by deciding we want it and can ignore the weaknesses to which we are prone. This thinking springs from a fundamental denial of the complexities of our humanity at work. Even if its purpose is a deepening of our spirituality, it creates a disengagement from the very source of our wholeness and maturity. As an antidote to these distortions in viewing reality, the honest engagement in one's life at work is a requirement for the building of authentic Interiority. Besides a copious implementation of the most effective aspects of one's cultural and historical legacies, it is necessary to retain a healthy skepticism about the potential vulnerabilities to which the citizens, workers and organizations might be prone.

The Uncertain Fortunes of the Labor Union Movement

In the western world, a great struggle for control of the order and productivity of the workplace took place between the 18th and 20th centuries. The capitalists, management and administrations of organizations were on the one side and expert craftsmen, industrial workers' unions (and the working class in general) were on the other. The sides labeled each other as enemies and adopted positions that suggested that they were dealing with unfriendly parties. This great struggle notwithstanding, the ultimate goal of both sides was to increase wealth and ensure survival. Lesser aims involved control of labor output and the enforcement of orderly behaviors by all involved.

Nevertheless, at one time or other, the behaviors of both management and workers were similar: scientific (mis)management, workplace legislation, personnel manipulations, alienation, sabotage, distortion of outcomes. Power and control passed back and forth from one side to the other as each sought advantage—often through violent means. This struggle for control came to be known as the union movement. It created a divide that widened and narrowed over the centuries, leaving a climate of suspicion and antipathy in its wake that remains to this day. Laws, workplace regulations and union rules were used to bind each other into consequent obligations, but volatility in the markets and emerging technologies swung everyone in cycles that peaked in prosperity, and ebbed in crippling unemployment, heavy-handed enforcement and poverty.

Even though the present day fortunes of the labor union movement have abated, workers can still make a point of resistance to excessive demand for increased output on the part of management. Nevertheless, for the unions and workers it is a losing game as management holds four trump cards. The first card is ownership of the means of production, which immediately earns the protections of the law that takes precedence over almost every other right. The second card is business competition based on profit margins and market forces, whose factors can be manipulated to exert control over the workers. The third card is based on the hierarchical structures of various social systems. One dominant hierarchical system is an educational approach that supports opinions, such as "expert" managers can be developed in classrooms. David Montgomery states this clearly in his book, *Workers' Control in America*, "The academic and industrial systems have been inseparable for half a century."[59] The fourth card was well played by President Ronald Reagan when he terminated the striking air-traffic controllers in 1981 and by English Prime Minister Margaret Thatcher when she broke the power of the trade unions in the miners' strike of 1984-1985. This card represents the ultimate coercive power of the government.

Against these cards, worker resistance, even supremely organized, will always be weak because it is usually based on external methods of recourse. The unions and movements share a proud history of being the voice and unifying arm of the workers. Nonetheless, the stress experienced through being locked into an antagonistic, reactive and one-sided approach to management is almost always doomed to fall short of victory.

Into this complex mix, I introduce the ingredient of Interiority. The goal of Interiority in the typical management/labor impasse is to reduce the traditional antipathy each side holds in regard to the other and lessen the stresses felt in managing mutual rights and obligations. Through Interiority, it is possible to focus on achieving the goals of the company *and* of the workers. Rather than adopting an either/or approach to management in the organizational hierarchy, Interiority allows for a strategy that includes both. The both/and alternative refers to adopting the view of management when appropriate and when the pendulum of circumstances swings to the opposite pole to adopt the view of the workers, again as appropriate. When the source of power is within and the worker draws his/her energies from the guidance of the soul, stress is reduced, insight is sharp and decisions are wise.

The aim of Interiority is to reconcile the sides in this great struggle by strengthening the inner worlds of both the workers and their organizations. The insight of Interiority is focused on attending to both the order and chaos, the movement and the stillness—working back and forth in great pendulum swings. This way, both workers and management, capitalists and free-wheeling artists participate in the evolutionary journey toward equitable treatment and concomitant consciousness. All sides are necessary to push the search for creativity and productivity forward, gain momentum, to slow down, then pick up the pace—in never-ending cycles of growth.

Through Interiority, all factions will look to deeper values than the accumulation of material goods and implement appropriate practices to ensure equitable opportunities for all citizens to achieve fair standards of living. Interiority stresses the awareness that we are all vital parts of that movement and each of us picks up the energy from the pendulum and makes a contribution through our work. (On this topic of polarity swings and the Labor Union movement, I provide more information in Chapter 6, in the section on Polarities and in Chapter 9, Practices.)

A Labor Tradition from the East

Japanese work culture differs significantly from that of the West. It is by now a cliché that we in the West are oriented toward individualism while the Japanese work ethos is group-centered. Upon digging below the surface of these differences, the question presents itself about what happened to make the institutions of corporate Japan models of group cooperation. Quite simply, the farmers did it. The successful corporations of Japan are overlaid by the millennia experiences of interdependent networks of rice farmers that evolved into a culture of group cooperation.

Second, the warriors also had a hand in it. In similar fashion, we must remember that the spiritual disciplines that strengthened Japan's international trading corporations emerged out of the traditions of Bushido (The Way of the Warrior – developed in Japan between the 9th and 12th Centuries).

Third, the Chinese Confucian traditions played a part. Building on the foundation of Bushido, the Neo-Confucian schools of the 16th to the 19th Centuries supported the contemporary feudal structures and gave rise to the loyalty ethic that binds workers and organizations today into lifetime commitments of service.

Digging a little deeper into what made the Japanese different from the West, two key orientations stand out. The Japanese had a predilection for *learning from experience* instead of learning from abstract concepts. When it came to achieving results over the long term, they also opted for *interdependence* and *fulfillment of obligation* among members of a work-group or community, over individual effort.

These two elements of experiential learning and interdependence shed light on where the West may have taken a rationalist/materialist/individualist detour on its journey toward productivity—which is now hampering its ability to plumb the benefits of Interiority for exponentially greater productivity.

Lessons learned from the Historical Review of Work

So what did we learn from this historical review of how work developed? My first response is that the concepts and practices of work, originally concentrated on survival of the clan, became progressively focused on self-absorption—which became a key principle that presently drives us and our institutions. This self-absorption emerged at the expense of the value of the common good.

In my opinion, self-absorption is presently the ethic that characterizes both individual and institutional behavior. Many workers are probably unaware of this ethic, as it was nourished, over millennia, within us and our organizations by the gradual diminishment of the standards and practices of sharing with others. The relegation of the needs of others to a secondary position should raise a warning flag to all: the counter-balancing ethic of relationality (connectivity) will only be restored by the work of Interiority, over a long period of time and with great struggle. (Relationality asserts that everything and everyone is connected and we are never objects, or totally separated, or autonomous individuals.)

The ethic of relationality is fundamental to Interiority and to sharing with our communities.

My second response reflects the astounding changes that modern science has shed light on regarding the nature of reality. In important ways, science has brought untold benefits to us all. However, along with marvelous discoveries came a scientific approach called scientism that treats all things as objects rather than as subjects, including workers. Managers have learned to take their cue from scientism that the only reality is what can be observed on the exterior of an object…or a worker. Because of the focus of scientism on exterior proofs and demonstrable results, an approach to worker management emerged that estimated performance on measurable and documentable behaviors and images.

Lost in this orientation were person-centered, intuitive, subjective, interpretive and dialogical approaches to worker management. Aspects of worker responsiveness, such as beliefs, values, feelings, insights, intentions and soul-guided decisions were judged to be non-measurable and, therefore, irrelevant.

The above two responses to the historical legacies that influence worker and worker management, set up key challenges that I intend to address throughout this book.

This does not mean that admirable efforts—and models—aiming at restoring the balance between the interests of self and community are not emerging in the marketplace. I immediately think of some examples of how we might restore the balance between self-interest and that of the common good. Some such movements and models are as follows:

- The Occupy Movement is clearly aimed at raising awareness of a disastrous gap in the ownership of material goods between the 1% and the 99%.

- Companies We Keep, *Employee Ownership and the Business of Community and Place,*[60] is a book that describes the transformation of a company based on the traditional organizational model into one that is employee-owned in order to preserve their livelihoods and their communities. Their Mission statement says it well: To enrich our community through our work.

- The World Café is a problem-solving movement that has arisen out of the need to focus on resolving local issues using local resources. Spurred by the ease of social media to inform, individuals assemble groups and experience spontaneous sharing. Guided by structured and facilitated processes, they are able to derive solutions to persistent problems in the community.

- Networked Science is a relatively new approach to solving intractable scientific problems, whereby globally-distributed scientists successfully collaborate on finding solutions together rather than alone.

However, while praiseworthy, these movements and models are, for the most part, based on external tools and methods of adaptation. All efforts based on external adaptation will fail if they are not nourished by energies driven from within, namely those deriving from the ideas and practices of Interiority—and throughout a lifetime of effort.

Having completed the questions about historical legacies, I now shift direction to explore questions about what is empowering change in our present circumstances.

Circumstances
(Questions that allow fundamental improvements to take place)

Empowering questions emerge from unexpected places. An example is, the worker who holds a disempowering fallacy about not having the opportunity for *development of the self* in the workplace.

The second question concerns *accountability*, which is similar to the previous fallacy in that it is assumed that workers do not have the ability to hold those in the hierarchical structure accountable for fulfilling their responsibilities.

The ubiquity and availability of information, through the Internet, for the development of the self and regarding the ability to hold others accountable, weakens if not disproves both long-held fallacies. Yet, while workers are capable of doing complex tasks in complex processes at work, they hardly consider themselves capable of engineering the changes necessary to maintain their freedoms, rights and developmental opportunities.

Just as workers are compromised by their legacy ideas, so is society compromised if its working members are not free to express themselves as whole persons. Undoubtedly, freedom is made inaccessible when the hierarchical systems are designed to benefit the few at the top at the expense of the many on the lower levels. In addition, legacy organizational systems became so powerfully rooted into hierarchies, they can prevail over the interests of those they are supposed to serve, and with impunity.

Workers have rights, but rights alone are not sufficient. Using Interiority as its base, proactive efforts to shape the future—its tools and supportive communities—is the key to effective change. Workers everywhere are needed to proactively implement change. Legacy limitations notwithstanding, everything necessary for us to develop ourselves through our work is available, if we but use those resources. Legacy systems that obstruct the development of self need to be let go. In this time of readily available resources, thinking of oneself as lucky or unlucky lacks credibility. Everything necessary is available and waiting for us to engage in change, beginning from within and lasting over the long term.

All this raises the question about our personal motivation for change or why we might let go of obstructive legacy systems. The most persuasive response is simple: we want to do what we can to realize a better future for us all.

Look how far we have already come. It used to be that we viewed work as an atonement for the sinful condition of humanity but now we are invited to see work as an evolutionary advance toward a beneficent future—culminating in unified consciousness. Empowering circumstances invite us to adopt a more nuanced stance toward the systems to which we belong so that we—and our work—are not defined by them. One consequence of not adapting a more nuanced stance is that interior dispositions (intuition, emotions, insight, soul-guided decisions and awareness of our accountability for the local community) are rarely afforded acceptance.

External Circumstances

Another question persists. What should be done about those legacy systems that remain prevalent in the minds—and hearts—of workers?

My response is twofold: 1) let go of what is dysfunctional and obstructive in thought and behavior and 2) adopt what will help one to succeed at work, and mature as a person.

When we become more aware of the ways in which our approaches to work—organizations and management—developed historically, we should be able to adopt a more objective and nuanced stance toward all of the systems to which we belong so we are not defined by them. Overall, this exercise of reflecting on our work experience, letting go of ineffective legacy systems and retaining those that are effective, liberates us to take ownership of what we want as workers and what we want to let go of.

The same kind of reflection helps us to understand the impact of our work on the environment and to choose to let go of any harmful eco-footprints. These exercises are not empty disciplines. On a deeper level, they challenge the *vital lies* (so-called by Daniel Goleman) we might passively endorse by thinking and acting as if what we don't know or can't see does not matter.[61]

Ultimately, this kind of reflection allows each of us to assume responsibility not only for our work tasks but also for our own growth and that of the organization to which we belong, our communities and society at large. This sphere of personal responsibility becomes all-encompassing, including those areas traditionally reserved for *the gods*.

These energies evident in Homer's *Odyssey* point to the influences of powers beyond human control on the destinies of heroes and villains on that epic journey. The proper relationship to the gods was to be in alignment with the flow of one's life by an attitude of gratitude, respect and awe. While we might acknowledge with gratitude how fortune has brought bounty to our lives or how misfortune might require appeasement of unknown destructive forces, we are not thereby relieved of the responsibility of our individual journeys. Like Odysseus *(Ulysses in Latin)*, we still have to slay the dragons—especially from within—and share the spoils (*of war or work*) as a contribution to our communities.

Things have not changed much since the times of Odysseus.

Inevitably, we arrive at a most compelling question in this book: Why is the ordinary worker assigned to be subservient in practically everything? I am not challenging the past 5,000 years of organizational and management development, but merely putting the focus on what might have been had the workers been central.

And I am specifically advocating the possibility of future generations of workers becoming central to their workplaces and to their organizations through self-awareness.

The question of worker centrality arises from the crises forming all around us as we step further into 21st Century. As an example, the organizational systems that worked tolerably well for most of the last century now seem to be incapable of resolving present-day challenges. This insufficiency alone sheds light on the need for workers who are grounded in Interiority, mature centers of workplace influence, capable of making decisions on the broad spectrum of issues at work and in society.

With this vast potential within, we begin to examine questions relating to our internal circumstances.

Internal Circumstances

For many of us, a most nagging issue centers around our productivity at work, or lack thereof, in the face of extreme competitiveness (often exacerbated by a fragile self-image). Such thoughts usually surface when we fail to accomplish what we set out to do. Swamped by endless tasks, we are tempted to reflect on our values (such as doing an honest day's work so we can feel good at the end of the day). But the deeper significance of our work too often proves elusive.

As workers, we are also plagued with questions about how we are perceived by our supervisors, with anxiety over the successes of our workplace competitors, and with the quality of relationships in our workgroup. Questions of competence periodically arise, mixed with fears about whether we have the confidence to succeed. Add to this mix concerns about the sustenance of our livelihood—pay grades, taxes, health benefits, vacation and retirement—these worries constantly drain our energy. We fret about business reorganizations, restructures and downsizing, imagining how we might pay the rent and buy groceries to feed the kids.

And then there are the related questions that nag us as we struggle for advancement in hyper-competitive environments…questions of achievement, performance reviews, recognition and advancement—or the lack thereof. Performance reviews can be terrifying because they link to issues of self-worth. We tend to perceive reviews as tests about our fundamental value as human beings and like it or not, our minds settle on what was not said or what score we did not get…and why.

Additionally, many question whether their achievements in the workplace result in worthwhile contributions to society.

Internal robustness founded in Interiority is vital for coping and overcoming these and other persistent work challenges.

Other nagging questions involve the ethical dimensions of behavior—both ours and that of our organizations. These questions speak to the consistency of our efforts to do the right thing, especially when the majority is more flexible about the moral aspects of their work. As Howard Gardner puts it, "What are my rights, obligations, and responsibilities? What does it mean to be a citizen of my community/my region/my planet? What do I owe others, and especially those who – through the circumstances of birth or bad luck – are less fortunate than I am?"[62]

These concerns include using the resources of the planet wisely in the fulfillment of work, for it is our responsibility to conserve resources and to raise appropriate questions about the sustainability of our products. This extends also to ethical probity in the employment of workers, especially where labor is considerably cheaper or where workers have few-to-no rights.

Further nagging questions refer to the values we live by at work. Is it that our workplaces are so depersonalized that we have no time to think our own thoughts, to feel our work-lives are real, to hold down-to-earth conversations with co-workers, to produce with satisfaction goods and services for which we are responsible—to act from conviction and a sense of making worthy contributions?

Are we so lost in the addictions of working, multi-tasking, following the rules and avoiding any relationships that threaten our positions that we lose all connection to soul?

Interiority not only finds us again but clarifies identity.

Have we settled for expediency in our decision-making, in securing our piece-of-the-pie regardless of the legitimate claims of those in our communities? Are we so enamored of those sporting the trappings of success that we join in the illusion that if we imitate them, we too can achieve materialistic fulfillment?

Nearly 5% of the U.S. population report being depressed[63] and many more suffer the symptoms. I do not make light of depression but many workers see depression as an excuse for self-pity, a resort to ravaging psychological dependencies, a ploy for self-abandonment or a means of escape. Or all of the above. This is important: through the application of Interiority these dark-side instances—the noonday devils (shadow tasks)—can be realized as potentially vast sources of energy for work and growth.

Are we so fearful of life's demands that we toil and fret over how we can be secure:

- *financially* by the accumulation of money and everything money can buy;
- *psychologically* by the accumulation of the emotional props of our so-called friends among the "beautiful people";
- *health-wise* by chasing the fountains of youth that sashay forth in every cunning garb;
- *fashionably* by dressing ourselves like the unblemished forms that lovingly gaze at us from glossy magazines?

Oh, the fears that rob us of our studied calm and cause nerves to jangle and tongues to jabber, to diversion, to distraction, unclaimed, mostly unnoticed by ourselves.

In view of this heritage of work theory and practice, is it any wonder workers have difficulty arriving at maturity and wholeness? As I ponder the inequities thrust upon the lives of workers, I feel a rage coming on and know I must turn these questions inward to examine the trajectory of my own life.

My Story – A Tattered Coat on a Stick

When I noticed him, he was standing in the lashing rain, with his back to the entryway, between the houses, beyond the telephone pole, at the end of our street. Of all the places to stand, the entryway was the worst, for the driven wind with its freezing blast would barrel between the houses and through anything unprotected, especially a wool topcoat full of rain.

From the shelter of our doorway, I watched as the rain, promising no letup, swept down in bucketfuls, flew in ragged sheets, spilling and flying from the gutters, causing a million tiny splashes to dance, flow and disappear on street-side puckered pools—relentlessly hammering the steaming backs of horses ready for sale or barter. Yet he stood there, motionless, desperately alone

FIGURE 6: **RAINY STREET**

or so it seemed to me. Hatless in his topcoat, streaming with water, he dejectedly held the reins of a nondescript horse that slumped, weary eyelids drooping, almost as dejected.

They made a forlorn pair.

He made no motion to get shelter or even turn away from the cruel winds, all but oblivious to the gusts of stinging, drenching rain as if attuned to an inner storm that also blew unreasonably, unfair...until the sadness, fear and rage were spent and no more could be done against him...or even imagined.

Unreasonable and unfair it was. Past his prime, over the hill, he still showed traces of the handsome man he had once been. Then tall, now gaunt, his coif of graying hair—doubtless supported by stiffening cream—withstood the blasts; but oh, how the light had dimmed from eyes once bright, now narrowed to a vacant gaze. His vigor had drained, the spark of daring withered, limp and hopeless.

My sadness raged at the desperate inequality of it all. Dylan Thomas once wrote, "rage, rage against the dying of the light." Yeats also had penned a lament for the fading trajectory of aging—save for a solitary sliver of life, swung aloft by soul-directed song: "An aged man is but a paltry thing, / A tattered coat upon a stick, unless / Soul clap its hands and sing, and louder sing."[64]

Upon a sudden impulse, I left the doorway, boiled the water in the kettle, buttered bread in the scullery, and carried him a mug of tea and sandwiches. My impulse was purely to warm him. He ate and drank slowly and silently, then hunched up his topcoat and after the ghost of a smile flickered across his face I don't remember anything else. Maybe I was grateful he hunched up his topcoat, but I never forgot him. Maybe he was one of those people you recognize out of the Great Caravan—horses, men and rain by-the-bucketful, on a Fair Day that didn't deserve the name—who were destined to never fade from memory.

And earn a mention here.

His standing there formed an early, enduring image that helped set in me a sensitivity for seeing oppression of any creature—whether from the blowing rain, repressive rules, obstinate bosses, rigid systems of control, fragile health or balky limbs. They draw from me a response to adversity, real or threatened and inspire me to bring something akin to tea and bread, a sympathetic word, a listening ear or just a silent presence.

Rainfall notwithstanding, I still feel sadness, fear and rage at the inequity of life, the suffering built into daily human existence, repeated failure without obvious gain, the inevitable decline and dissolution of our precious vigor and our mind-numbing inability to counter bravely the "slings and arrows" of adversity.

Inequity is not all I rebel against, but I feel it worse when the fated storms of life get the better of me—or anyone—and we can but stand in the blowing rain, drenched, cold and drained in the face of encroaching defeat.

My Story – Reflections

When I recall the man standing in the rain, I'm reminded that every underdog is still part of the human family. From that experience, I learned that I have the ability to put myself in the place of those who are suffering or are beaten down by the bitter tastes of life. I learned I would act somehow on their behalf.

When I ask myself what questions were predominant in my life and what emotion(s) prompted them, I can see how influenced I've been by my perception of "inequality and consequent dejection in anyone," coupled with rage against nature (or man or machine). Inequality-generated reactive anger and simple and predictable responses just about explains the trajectory of my life. I don't know what made me line up on the underdog's side, but from early on I have found myself there, and often. Admittedly, not all of my reactive anger had its source in empathy for the desperate condition of all creatures, great and small. I also acknowledge a combination of aggravated impatience, a lack of confidence and plain old guilt for all my inadequacies and sins, but that's another story.

I do not deny that life's inequities can purify one's inner life and focus one's aspirations on what is of real worth, but tell that to the poor and desperate parent hovering over a sickly child. To my eyes, inequality defined life. Almost everywhere I looked I saw its consequences and I was not unresponsive, even if powerless to help. No great legacy of activities has characterized my life and my life's work, but simple, charitable responses—without need for compensation—followed me through the years. I would see the downtrodden and feel rage at the oppressors, in any form, but especially those who exercised unrighteous dominion for profit or power.

Of such is the ultimate oppression made.

Your Story

What then is your story of adversity? Adversity may have visited you in the shape of the cruel side of nature, an illness that drained your strength or the oppressive behaviors of the demanding boss, domineering organization or unreasonable working conditions that stretched you beyond your breaking point.

Take time for remembering how you were affected, how you survived and how you moved on. What vivid memory remains to this day that gives you pause, strength or insight?

Methods (for implementing change)

Just as it is necessary to learn and implement various methods for updating one's knowledge and skills at work, so it is necessary to acquire the knowledge and practice the skills of Interiority for adapting and renewing the philosophical legacies that shape our work and present-day social systems. The deep resources of Interiority provide incentives qualitatively different from external incentives such as money, status, position and authority.

The methods for implementing change—specific to Interiority—are the only sure means for developing habits of adaptation and renewal for ourselves and the various communities to which we belong.

These methods include everyday minutiae and as such are not the exceptions in our lives but are a constitutive part of our human makeup. The energies flowing from the dynamics of inner dialogue (our self-talk) have the potential to enliven our communities and generate more adapted ways of working, new forms of social interaction and workplace productivity. From simple story-telling episodes that spark youthful imaginations to sophisticated exchanges in global video-conferencing sessions, the sharing itself already shapes the participants.

Dialogues between members of communities are the key dynamics by which transformational forms emerge. It is incumbent on all workers to engage in such exchanges in whatever community they find themselves. It is an unwritten rule that the deeper and more authentic the interior dispositions of the community members, the more innovative and effective will be the evolving forms that result. These dynamics make the case for robust Interiority from which innovations arise, and they also argue for constructive involvement with co-workers in resolving ongoing workplace issues.

Does Interiority matter in today's organizations and, if so, by what methods might it be implemented? There is a surprising dearth of answers. I recognize that much is written about work and all the associated dynamics. What is missing, however, stands out more than what is there—namely, the *inner world of the workers*—in a word, Interiority. In our inquiry, it is not that we are looking for conceptual knowledge about ourselves at work. We are looking for the wisdom that comes from the kind of reflection on our work that leads to wholeness. As Helen Keller put it, "The best-educated human being is the one who understands most about the life in which he is placed." Certainly there have been attempts to uncover meaning at work, but those efforts too often intimate aspirations to a higher plane of awareness, especially in the area of spirituality.

Perhaps, what we need in the workplace is something a little less lofty and a little more organic.

Method 1. Interiority more than Spirituality at Work

Of late, there's much ado about spirituality at work. Surprisingly, many treatments of spirituality at work do not approach the subject of the sacredness of work itself or the depth of the union of our work with the universe. Treatments of spirituality at work span a wide range of variations:

- exhortations to use the insights or practices of a particular religion
- personal experiences of the authors that proved transformative for them
- ways for using spirituality to make a profit, be promoted or succeed in competitive scenarios
- quotations from well-known personalities, reflections on preferred values at work
- lists of the beneficial effects of spiritual practices and interviews with CEOs of workplaces with spirituality programs.

In short, spirituality at work is usually a rehash of traditional ritualistic approaches to managing emptiness or dearth of meaning. All of these efforts notwithstanding, a certain nervousness is exhibited by workers in approaching these subjects that reveals a lack of an inner life at work, a general distrust of the area of spirituality and avoidance of anything to do with religion. Perhaps the subject of attaining wholeness through work is too private or simply may be the mixture of the intangible with the tangible most people resist.

The major difference between spirituality-at-work and Interiority-at-work is in the origin of the initiatives. In the former, the initiatives come from outside oneself whereas the locus of Interiority-at-work begins within one's experience. The Interiority-based path leads to *growth through reflective practices* and *encounters that enrich our relationships* with work, co-workers and communities.

The practice of living in order to work begs to be changed into a practice of living as a whole person who works and matures through the same work.

We must debunk the idea that people should not bring their whole selves to work and that they should leave their inner lives at the door. Statistics about sports, theories about political conspiracy, scuttlebutt about the latest fashions and up-to-the-minute celebrity gossip are all seemingly acceptable in workplace discourse, but questions of mystery and meaning run into trouble. Do we think if workers were prompted by their inspirations and intuitions something terrible would occur?

To top this off, we hesitate to consider conflict at work as a potentially abundant method of growth, but it is nevertheless important to think of its possibilities, as I do in the next section.

Method 2. Conflict and Growth

When conflicts erupt in the workplace, energy is being consumed. It's entirely possible to re-direct that energy into supportive, positive work and improved work relationships. In the same way, depression can be a source of profound self-understanding and wisdom. Even those unsavory encounters with unpleasant co-workers can be sources of inspiration in becoming a whole person.

Just as important, if I suffer self-criticism when I make the odd mistakes at work, I can use those situations to help me become more human and more balanced in everything I am and do.

Conflicts introduce opportunities to grow. Growth through conflict first involves awareness of the conflict itself. Following that awareness is one's reactions toward the *other* and the recognition of the source, and only secondarily the action that became the tipping point. Finally, one must release *self* and the *other* from blame by using non-judgmental listening skills. By this method, one becomes centered, resourceful and responsible. This is the basis of energy rejuvenation and restoration of wholeness.

Perhaps a story will better illustrate the process. The main characters are a headmaster perhaps too long in the job, me at nine and a delayed release from an early memory.

> ### My Story – The Man (and the gift that came with the smack of a stick)
>
> I was sitting in the back row of a classroom packed with boys. Our regular teacher was absent that day. There were three classrooms in the school and ours was separated from the senior boys' room by a thin partition. Naturally, without supervision the noise rose and the headmaster came in and warned us twice to keep quiet and learn our spellings. This didn't stop the noise which rolled up 'til it fairly bounced off the walls. Suddenly, the door flew open and the headmaster tore to the front of the room and stood there glaring. His eyes lit on me and he beckoned me to the front. He and I were facing each other as the class looked on.
>
> "Tell me who was making the noise," he growled as he whipped his cane against his trouser leg.
>
> I answered, "Please sir, I can't tell you."
>
> His voice rose menacingly. He said slowly and clearly for the straining ears to hear, "Tell me who was making the noise"
>
> Again I answered, "Please sir, I can't tell you."
>
> He repeated a third time in a more threatening tone, "Unless you tell me who was making that noise, I will slap you."
>
> I answered, "Sir, I won't tell."
>
> "Hold out your hands."
>
> I did.
>
> He lifted his cane high above his head and came down on my hands as hard as he could; six times . . . on each hand.
>
> Then, "Go back to your seat."
>
> As I walked back to my seat more than my hands were burning. I knew I had just been abused.
>
> I labeled him and all like him as 'the man'. Thereafter, it was easy for me to recognize 'the man' as one who abuses his (or her) power of position. I didn't realize it at the time, but deep within me was born strongly a resistance to those

> *in authority. There were exceptions, but as I experienced problems with those in senior positions, I sided with those whom I saw as victims.*
>
> *And so the question arises about whether to remain in the grip of victimhood or to choose release by taking steps to maturity. The method of release from victimhood is to become aware of one's inner state, acknowledge it openly to a friendly ear, forgive oneself and the other and choose to behave in ways that are not reflective of victimhood. When I forgave myself, I was empowered and growing. When I forgave him, or any of the many who represented 'the man', they had no power over me.*
>
> *The method sounds simple but it was only after years of reactive patterns of conflict with those whom I perceived as 'the man' was I able to let go of the illusions I was a victim forever. That's the real challenge—letting go of the illusions that devour us and permitting ourselves to grow.*
>
> > *"We would rather be ruined than changed.*
> > *We would rather die in our dread*
> > *Than climb the cross of the moment*
> > *And let our illusions die."* W.H. Auden[65]

My Story – Reflections[65]

What a fearsome truth is given voice in these lines about our willingness to sacrifice even our most precious and emerging self rather than change and grow. The method of growing through conflict is an inner process. It is the basis of Interiority. Not only can we grow through conflict with others but through disaffection with life, nature, health, everything. Just as everything can be a stumbling block, so can everything be an opportunity to become whole. That is why I titled the above story: The Man (and the gift that came with the smack of a stick).

Your Story

What experiences, seeming negative at the time, have afforded you the opportunity to free and shape yourself? Was there someone like "the man" of my story who took advantage of your age, weakness, innocence or other fragility? What was your reaction then? Was it to swallow the hurt, try to forget it or overcome it by distractions or addictions? Did you later become aware of your flight from the hurt and did you stop running and face "the man"? Or are you still running from your hurt and trying to be better than you judged yourself at the time of that bitterness?

Only you can look back and reflect on what went on and how you handled it, but maybe it's too difficult to do so all by yourself? Perhaps you need some professional help to get a hold of the event and finally dislodge "the man" from your life—and let that undeveloped part of you come to life.

Method 3. The Good Worker

A third Interiority method is about being a good worker. In becoming a good worker the task is to increase awareness of and integrate the different energies of our inner worlds into our working styles—with the result being greater productivity. To do this, we must have an *interactive relationship* with work. We must maintain *good health* to be able to produce the highest quality work of which we are capable. We must strive to continuously *find joy* in it. We must be faithful to work demands so we can cultivate a *spirit of inquiry*.

Good work emerges if we remain open to the messages that come from work itself. Like the artisans who shape wood and iron so the inner properties of the materials are drawn out, so must workers find delight in the design, efficiency and utility of the products that flow from their interactions. The good worker is one who establishes a rhythm in seeking the needs of the job, applying mind, heart and body in virtuous cycles of productivity.

As for the organization, the key attribute of what constitutes good is the contribution the worker and the work make to the enterprise. If we are motivated only by external rewards, our interest will eventually flag, our need for diversion will increase and the level of fulfillment will diminish. To ensure we make a quality contribution, one must *deepen his/her inner core* to flow in alignment with the growing complexity of all business processes.

Simultaneously, we must be able to sustain ourselves at work in the midst of every kind of irreconcilable contradiction. (As an example, irreconcilable contradictions face politicians every day between budget availability and promises made to the electorate.) Reconciling the irreconcilable requires the constant balance of *inner discipline* toward work with the need to *keep pace with disruptive change*. These efforts are further complicated as we strive for continuous improvement.

Regarding co-workers, we must afford attention to the *interests of colleagues*, different though they may be from our own. Certainly, we can maintain ourselves as good workers if our awareness is allowed to expand through the meaning of work, but it is just as important to engage with each other, ultimately furthering the social contract we all share.

And regarding the needs of society, we must feel the struggles of all the people—for in their own way, they are working and striving alongside us.

The challenge is to arrive at the place where we truly listen to what we are doing so the process of engaging in work becomes as much a meditation as it is a contribution. Just as our work has its own integrity, so must the relationship with our work become an opportunity for truth. Being truthful means we do not evade the difficult tasks and pursue only the easy parts. It means not allowing slipshod performance merely because no one is around. It means not covering up weaknesses of which others are not aware.

In essence, our integrity should be the same if the whole world was looking on and judging us…or if no one took the slightest notice.

Every encounter with every task becomes a reflection of the story of our unfolding lives, which hold within the seeds of the unfolding cosmos. When we engage with the ominous, unbidden pressures rising from shadow consciousness, we are fashioning the person we have the potential to become. Regardless of the ill-defined realities of the workplace, the work itself should draw us to a place of deep contemplation.

As we move from phase-to-phase in completing our tasks, we are reconstituting the powerful influences of parents, siblings and communities—so their work continues through us, even in their absence. In engaging this way, we turn our work-stories into narratives that will guide us in the workplace.

This third, powerful method lets the work teach us, so work and systems are shaped through our experiences in accordance with the needs of workers, everywhere.

Method 4. Connecting with Meaning through Work

If our experience of work is of increasingly bureaucratic, boring formulas, we need to find our way into normally inaccessible realms of *mystery and meaning*. Ages have passed since charcoal drawings first graced remote cavern walls. Those charcoal drawings echoed with meaning, reflecting the world, the work and even the soul of the artist/worker. Obviously, much more than prehistoric charcoal drawings have influenced how we see our work and the lives of workers, but they invite us anew to contemplate the deep, arcane world of work.

In modern times, the ever present need for meaning is heightened because of the diminishment of the place of God and other frameworks for belief. The need for meaning is further exacerbated by the emptiness and boredom that has replaced concepts and images of the divine. (We stop short of the nihilism that says the search for meaning is futile, because humans cannot have certainty about anything, even uncertainty.)

The only recourse is to focus on inner experience to generate contemporary meaning that is authentic and worthwhile. Much of that meaning lies in what we produce from within—especially by creating the emerging future of work.

Method 5. Meaning through Creating the Future at Work

There are many reasons why we must connect with meaning. The common denominator amongst them is an inner desire for a participatory future. Presently, we are experiencing a rapidly accelerating sense of progress and productivity. The developments that recently took 100 years of evolution are now compressed into the space of 10 years or less. To keep pace, we need to create an ever-compressing future by intentionally connecting with meaning from the inside out.

In this age of hyper-speed, we can augment meaning even as we are forced to take charge of change all around us. We *stay current* and *adapt* to present conditions. To withstand the accumulating stresses of the modern workplace, we can utilize methods of stress release—buoyed up by deep, profound energies rising from within. Today, when the latest discovery outpaces the last at dizzying speed, we can find meaning in envisioning a future emerging from our inner capacity for infinite adaptation.

Meaning is made real when we manifest the truth of ourselves through our work and recognize the authentic truth of others as revealed in their work.

Meaning can also be found by preparing for a future that will surely encompass the whole of the planet. Meaning emerges from the awareness of belonging to the whole and in the reality that we either grow in that inclusive image or we hasten the demise of the human family by consuming at the expense of future generations.

Meaning also emerges from the potentially destabilizing impact of billions of new customers coming online. Regarding this fact, I tend to respond with gratitude for the always-connected Internet and other astonishing technologies shaping our age.

Method 6. Lessons from Emerging Terminology

Undoubtedly, we are being taught by the contemporary terminology that describes our changing circumstances. One of the clearest indicators about the need for Interiority at work comes from the terminology used by business and management consultants in fields related to work, as well as the terms referenced in the written and digital media—not to ignore the reflections of workers themselves.

Central to the emerging vocabulary are terms describing the *content* of work such as: the hunger for *meaning*; *humanizing* work processes; belonging to *communities* of concern; *interdependence* to support solidarity; *sustainability* in the use of resources; *emergence,* as in innovation in complex patterns deriving from simple interactions; *holism,* as in seeing connections with the whole; *evolution,* as in the adaptive capacity of workers to overcome challenges; *uniqueness,* as in nothing being repeated - ever; *unpredictability,* as to the unknowable future and *teleology* (from the Greek *telos*, "end"; *logos*, "discourse"), which means "everything being directed toward an end or a purpose."

Distinct from the content of the work but central to the emerging *methodological* vocabulary are such words as *relationality,* as in everyone and everything being interdependent; *openness,* as in avoiding being locked-in to pre-defined ways of thinking and working; *authenticity,* as in acting truthfully from one's center; *centering,* as in the practice of living and working from the center of one's awareness; *complexity,* as in understanding the depth of decision-making; and *ambiguity,* as in necessary tolerance for *paradoxical* situations (which necessitate growth through both light and dark, health and illness, success and failure, the obvious and the incomprehensible).

It seems the solutions to the challenges of the future lie in the direction of Interiority. A major consequence of Interiority is in reclaiming responsibility for oneself, one's authority and becoming the change one wants to see in the workplace. In considering *responsibility* on a wider scale, every worker is a *change agent*. Every *tension* of opposites is a call for tolerance of the ambiguity and paradoxes, for seeing the *whole* (workers, management, customers, suppliers, resources and society) and not just privileged individuals, for understanding the preeminence of *networks* of trusting relationships and responsiveness to *community* concerns.

In the table below are two columns that show a comparison of characteristics of our present state (*right-side column – rational and left brain*) and those that arise from an Interiority-blended (*left-side column – Interiority and right brain*) in the context of work. The right column outlines characteristics of the present state with a one-sided, rational, bureaucratic context. The left column indicates the more complete context, in terms of human wholeness, and, therefore, a preferred emphasis. The positioning of these columns is not intended as an either/or comparison because we need the inclusion of both sides for full personhood and as a way of working that focuses on the interdependence of all things.

Interiority-Blended Context *Right-Brain Orientation*	vs.	The Present State *Left-Brain Orientation*
Inner *(orientation)*		**Outer** *(focus)*
Respect *(for others)*		**Subservience** *(to authority)*
Human *(limited & infinite)*		**Mechanical** *(model of work)*
Ecological *(diverse)*		**Hierarchical** *(structure)*
Communal *(belonging to all)*		**Authoritarian** *(rules)*
Intuitive *(core response)*		**Rational** *(approach)*
Imaginative *(wide-ranging)*		**Measurable** *(quantities)*
Dialogical *(interactive)*		**Rule**-bound *(regulatory)*
Unique *(expression)*		**Standards** *(measurement)*
Cyclical *(round as in nature)*		**Linear** *(processes)*
Natural *(experience-based)*		**Manufacturing** *(industries)*
Spiritual *(beyond category)*		**Material** *(substance)*
Numinous *(of the spirit)*		**Explainable** *(by concepts)*
Communitarian *(wider impact)*		**Bureaucratic** *(organization)*
Metaphorical *(unspoken message)*		**Real** *(phenomena)*
Complexity *(stance-adoption)*		**Analytical** *(problem-solving)*
Spontaneous *(inimitable)*		**Structured** *(step-by-step)*
Whole *(inclusive)*		**Partial** *(fragments)*
Mysterious *(entrancing)*		**Observable** *(sensory)*
Experiential *(lived)*		**Theoretical** *(abstract)*
Relationships *(connections)*		**Tasks** *(isolated & specific)*
Multi-Dimensional *(values)*		**Monetary** *(financial)*
Infinite *(ongoing impact)*		**Temporal** *(time-bound)*
Wisdom *(ultimate value)*		**Knowledge** *(factual)*
Justice *(rights)*		**Expediency** *(pragmatic)*
Quality *(of personhood)*		**Performance** *(of tasks)*
Person *(treasure)*		**Product** *(goods/services)*
Personal *(attached)*		**Impersonal** *(detached)*
Sacred *(all)*		**Secular** *(worldly)*
Subjective *(belonging to you/me)*		**Objective** *(tangible)*
Being *(acceptance of life)*		**Doing** *(activities)*

At a glance, we can see the imbalance that has emerged regarding work and workers. As a result, aspects of experience that lead to wholeness and maturity have become inaccessible to workers. For too long, the emphasis has been primarily on the *doing* side of work. It is time now to push the pendulum toward a more inclusive and human context, to put the focus on *being*.

It brings me back to a summertime hilltop, one late afternoon—the beginning of my questioning journey that has lasted a lifetime.

My Story – The Shotgun

Seven years old, standing among trees bunched together on a hilltop that overlooked our town, I tied a shotgun to a fence with its barrel angled upward. Then I secured a length of string to the trigger and blew a hole through the branches of a tree. I was unhurt, which had been my overriding concern. In one fell swoop, I received a hillside of information: the cattle took off in full flight from a grazing posture, tails flying, and the crows lifted in protest, indignant until, in the ensuing silence and unnatural stillness, all things great and small once again resumed their routines of life, me included.

In my meandering searches through the ruins of our 500-year-old town, I had resurrected the rusted shotgun from its hiding place of yore, under the eaves of a timeworn barn wall. The stock was half-eaten from woodworm, but when a dollop of waste oil earned a solid click from the ancient hammer, I knew I was in business. For me, this old weapon was not part of a fanciful legend of some marauder on the run. No, this was my opportunity to learn practical lessons about gunpowder, cartridges, firing mechanisms, safety steps—and killing power. Killing power that might deal horrible death or disfigurement too horrible to the unwary.

It was not in my mind to be among them.

One blast was all it took to deliver a shower of shredded leaves and torn branches, but they would never tell their tale of rude disturbance. One blast was all it took to scatter the cattle, disturb the crows and silence the buzzing flies, but neither would they disclose this escapade, of that I was sure. And one blast was all it took for me to get the message, to trigger a preoccupation-with-mortality, a deafened silence at the dinner table that evening.

And I was surely not going to tell.

I remember little more of that daring stunt when I was seven, but I had learned my lessons, and I was grateful that no one was any the wiser. Like other kids, I

> *sought to solve the acute questions of life and death in the physical world around me. I've hardly touched a weapon since that blast on that hilltop long ago.*
>
> *Life is fragile and easily brought to death or disability; that much I understood as I absorbed—and absorbed again—the lessons from the blasted tree branches of my early hilltop experience.*

My Story – Reflections

What did I learn from this early hilltop experience that I carried with me to this day? Was it that I took the risk of the rusted, woodworm-eaten shotgun blowing up and in that way learned something worthwhile? In taking the risk of a misfire maybe I learned I could plan for unforeseen happenings and take cover. Did the hole in the branches foreshadow blowing holes in philosophical theories to allow for new theories to emerge according to the needs of the times? Is creative destructiveness what I learned? Did the flight of the cattle presage my being left alone on the hilltop with the smoking gun and no explanation except I was there and so was the shotgun that needed to be tested? Did I discover meaning in finding myself in those circumstances just as I find meaning in being here, at this time, with this legacy and with the need to create our future?

Besides understanding I was someone who learned from doing, reflecting and adapting to the prevailing circumstances of my life, I learned I was a risk-taker, someone who searched the edges of what had been done before, looking for a better way not just for myself but for all those with whom I would come in contact. In its own way, such an early hilltop experience may have been my first efforts at clarifying meaning.

Your Story

What questions have shaped you the reader, sending you on your path, step-by-step along your evolving story? Did an early, out-of-the-ordinary experience leave its message on your questing mind—and inner self? What questions do you ask yourself today that emerge from a time when "anything was possible?" (Analogous to the "walkabouts" of the original inhabitants of Australia, the rites of passage, the "dreamtime" of adolescent discoveries when "things magical" could occur.)

Most important, how do you still use the answers to improve your daily tasks of work and life?

Take time to ponder again the mysteries of how you quested and what you've learned from life's enduring experiences and unremitting questions, especially regarding Interiority. What is there to discover about your style of learning? What is so unique about your experiences that they deserve to be integrated into your life and preserved forever? How have you incorporated this knowledge into your life—if indeed you have?

If not, why not?

Method 7. The Great Work of Becoming the Self

I have used the major questions about work to highlight the themes and practices I will discuss throughout the rest of the book. And yet, I have barely touched on the greatest of all questions, the question that concerns the most challenging work humans can perform. I refer to the great work of becoming the unique self that each of us is called to be. This is the real aim of life and will not be accomplished without our hard work. (I am referring to the 2nd level engagement with the tasks of Interiority as presented in this book.)

Most of us assume that the processes of fully becoming our unique selves will just happen naturally and without conscious involvement. In that context, first level engagement refers to the normal investment in *thinking*, *reflection*, *behavioral change* and *maturation* that accompanies our progress through the stages of life.

Second level engagement has two areas of concern. On one hand, it puts the priority for becoming one's unique self on personal initiative. On the other hand, it recognizes the imperative challenge of cooperating with the soul energies that lead us towards holistic fulfillment acknowledging the needs of everything else that supports this life of ours.

Popular opinion maintains that our greatest endeavors resolve some intractable problem that besets the human community, such as the eradication of a dread disease or the reversal of global warming. But it seems that such great works can only be done by the extraordinarily talented and powerful. Not to belittle noble achievement, but I suggest that perhaps the truly great work is the becoming of self in each passing moment of one's life.

This greatest work is available and accessible to all. It requires some degree of self-knowledge, skills at listening to and dialoguing with one's soul, the intention to respond to the invitation for wholeness and finally the diligence to do the never-ending work of *reflection*, *centering* and growth-ful *adaptation*.

This work of welcoming and receiving the gift of one's maturing self is the source of our productivity and satisfaction at work.

In Chapter One, I have tracked the history of the perceptions of work. At one time, work was perceived as a *curse*, then as a *blessing*, then an *atonement*, then as a means of *separating the masses from the privileged classes*, then as a means of producing *wealth*, and finally, an *objectively measurable output* and, in my estimation, a key means of *human maturity*.

In Chapter Two, we shift our focus toward *growing through the dynamic tensions* in which we participate—especially as they have become clear through present-day discoveries.

The powerful dominate unless we hold them accountable

Chapter 2

Context

"Nothing worth doing is completed in our lifetime; therefore, we must be saved by hope. Nothing true or beautiful makes complete sense in any immediate context of history; therefore, we must be saved by faith. Nothing we do, however virtuous, can be accomplished alone; therefore, we are saved by love."

—Reinhold Niebuhr

The context in which we live and work constitutes who we are and what we are called to become. Context is the historical period wherein we make our contribution. Because that context includes ubiquitous and powerful forces that shape our lives, we must become aware of the *major trends* that influence us at work and *adapt our behaviors* accordingly. We must *learn from the patterns of nature* and allow ourselves to be taught unanticipated lessons.

These dynamics point the way towards achieving Interiority through the work we do. We lead an astonishing existence in the workplace because, through the outer and inner contexts in which we exist, we are at once *solitary beings* and yet *connected to everything*. On one hand, we are seemingly inconsequential agents of influence; on the other, we affect everything that happens. This bifurcated reality is difficult to grasp, but by participating actively in those two related contexts we allow the future to be shaped through us. The future is full of unlimited possibilities and through our choices we influence what emerges. So, it is essential that we periodically look to the horizon and learn from the context in which we live and work.

We must look out as far and as often as we can to the natural world, to be filled with excitement at the gorgeous, endless firmament, to marvel at the genius of human art and technology, and at the same time, to soberly encounter the daily dross of injustices roiling the earnest aspirations of the people—woeful reminders of our humble origins and challenging conditions.

From solitary thoughts, we must look to the exterior context for connection to current events, to join—by voice, through labor, in celebration and mourning—with others (to discover they are earnestly doing much the same).

We must stretch our hands so we are not done in by fear of the unpredictable and we must steady ourselves for another day. We must look out to the exterior context, for in that action we are *building bridges to our interior* where we mostly live.

We need the bridges between the exterior and the interior so healing can take place when pain invades either space or both. From the integration of our whole beings, we can take our place in the larger order, which requires proportion and humility. Similar to the Zen Koan, there is no absolute solution to the riddle posed and therein lies the answer to all riddles. Thus, we must look to our exterior context with tolerance. At work, we need to acknowledge the harshness of the tasks still undone—a witness to the disorder, a reminder to get working.

In looking outward, we must acknowledge the drumbeat of silence that sometimes meets our morning greetings and signals a less-than-happy prospect to that workplace day. We must endure the difficulties that leave us cold, at the same time responding with compassion. The exterior context reminds us that we are contributing to its emergent possibilities in ways that are growth-producing and conducive to wholeness.

When we awake to the magnificence of the world around us, we are prepared for the journey inward. That is the essence of Interiority.

Context is like the covering of the cradle that established the parameters of an infant's world, until that baby stepped into the darkened night and drew its finger upward in amazement at the uncountable stars twinkling in the sky. In such revelatory moments, context changes drastically and our minds never revert to the same understanding held a moment before. Context is only what we know within the present moment of understanding.

Context for me, when I was young, derived from our kitchen walls and the saints they knew.

> ### My Story – I Grew Up with Saints
>
> I grew up with the saints. From the living ones who tramped the furrows of dark-brown earth, to the butchers, bakers and horseshoe makers along our street. Their work alone made whole-cloth out of their lives, not merely trailing strands tethered to the shuttling loom of painful days, whole cloth they made out of their lives at work.
>
> Then there were the so-called holy ones, who by pulpit reputation earned a place on our walls, looking out from ornate frames. Their untiring eyes following me 'round the kitchen. Before the worn, chipped, oft-patched, shelf-based plaster ones, many a fervent prayer was said. I knew them all, for they helped create my childhood context when the world was new and I was too. Whether they served me well or poorly, they were my context and erstwhile source of meaning.
>
> We all have our youthful contexts against which we measure our realities and test for meaning, truth and viability as survival guides. In my youthful context, one saint stood out because his 4th Century AD dictums provided the foundation stones of morality over which I often stumbled, causing me no small pain. I was familiar with St. Augustine because his moral teaching pervaded our town in dark and dank confessionals. According to his dualistic distinctions between this world and the next, which for him were real places, I felt myself caught. My body and imagination were definitely of this world, as I simultaneously tried to observe the rules to make sure of the next (presented as beyond the "pearly gates").
>
> Considering the pressures of that divided context, it is no wonder I left our town early.
>
> In my imagination, I actually left years before. I visited foreign lands and the possibilities I invariably found there promised greater things than were available in the place I called home. I finally left the familial, social, cultural contexts and the vibrant heritage of Celtic myths and images. They had provided me with comfort and confusion, darkness and light, wings and anchors, but I thought the new and unfamiliar context would allow me to be different—meaning I would wake up to an improved version of myself. I didn't realize that no matter where I went or what generous opportunities presented themselves, I would always be no more or less the self that departed those emerald shores. I would always remain

so, but time and again—while shuttling between dreams of an improved self and shattered delusions—the new context taught me I had not fundamentally changed, but would mature inwardly if I accepted these realities.

To that extent perhaps, because of the demanding context, I came to recognize the process of human development etched in my own struggles and, in that way, I matured and became somewhat less delusional.

Your Story

What then is your story of an early life context you changed as you moved away from home? As you learned about life in the new context, what was the realization that told you things had changed very little because you had changed very little?

As reflected in the contexts in which you lived and worked, take time for learning about yourself. What learning emerged as your unrealistic expectations were unfulfilled and cherished delusions came to naught?

Bound as they were in gilt-edge frames, the saints who populated our kitchen created a context mostly static or unchanging. Their God appeared static in being only on the side of the *good* and so the saints were statically inhuman, the truth was statically dogmatic; they were surrounded by a comparatively static society and the institutions and philosophies that supported that superstructure were static.

If I were to describe the context of today, I would use terms like change and fluidity—nothing static—so perhaps the way we see reality has adjusted. In the context of today, not only is change central but the pace of change itself has accelerated. We merely adapt as best we can and resolve to remain open to changing ourselves, even as change engulfs us. Needless to say, the saints of my current context are of a decidedly more secular, scientific, and philosophical bent, and they have influenced my life—and the world—to become more human, complex and infinite than could have been imagined in the days when their somber counterparts looked down from the frames on our kitchen walls.

Key Principles

There is Only the Dance Itself

Plato, Thomas Aquinas, Isaac Newton, Albert Einstein, Carl Jung and Peter Drucker all had something in common. Besides being geniuses who deeply influenced their periods of history, they developed frameworks for viewing reality that made the world a more comprehensible place. But even these giants suffered the limitations of historical context. They spoke or wrote necessarily about reality limited to the knowledge available during their periods of history. Yet, rather than cursing the darkness in the limitations of such frameworks, through their contributions they became examples for us to follow.

Though we are products of our time, the message for us is that we do not really come to know the needs—and wisdom—of our contemporary world until we experience them in the context of work. Like Fritjof Capra (physicist and systems theorist), we can say we come to an awareness of whatever is evolving only when we actually do our work. He says, "There are no dancers, there is only the dance itself."[66] In other words, whatever insights are going to happen will surface within us during the moments of our engagement with work. Moreover, we will not even come to know those needs until we pay attention to our inner worlds.

Evolution of the Cosmos Depends on Us

The worker is central in organizational life and it is incumbent on each worker to allow his or her self to grow according to the changes taking place in and around us. Jung taught that every person's great life-work is in becoming his or her own self. He urged us to not underestimate the inner resources we have for such a task when he said, "we all walk in shoes too small."[67] A further comment on the importance of individuation is given by James Hollis, "The evolution of the cosmos depends on the individuation of each of us."[68]

Interiority expands this approach, both on a personal and an organizational basis. To ensure that the outcomes of Interiority might be achievable and not merely talked about, let us examine what is changing in the biggest possible scheme-of-things. Many writers have addressed organizations and workers in terms of structures, processes and methods for productivity improvement. So many have done so, it begs the question, "What is uniquely characteristic of the context of work in our time?"

In posing this question, we examine what sets our historical context apart from all other periods of history. Two characteristics immediately come to mind. The first stems from the discovery that we are *part of an expanding universe*. The second submits that *our consciousness is expanding* in line with the consciousness of the universe—because each of us is a part of the living organism known as the universe. Distant and inaccessible though it may seem, this emergent universe is in itself a source of consciousness. As cosmologist Brian Swimme explains, "Each of us is at the center of this expansion of the universe."[69]

In light of these two expansive characteristics of life, new areas of creativity and deeper satisfaction in the performance of our work become possible. The immediate conclusions: we do not live in a static world or even a cyclical one. As Swimme and Berry explain in their book, *The Universe Story,* our universe is "a self-organizing cosmogenesis, a cosmic process expressing itself in a continuing sequence of irreversible transformations."[70] The main implication is we are also living and working in the context of irreversible transformations in our own lives.

The term *cosmogenesis* also refers to the "ongoing, developing reality"[71] that is one self. This statement is stunning in its implications. Each of us is the subject of this ongoing developing reality that continues across generations of workers. The universe can be observed in our irresistible attention to the details of our work and in our choices to fulfill our tasks, to grow and to allow transformation to take hold. This does not mean that all workers intentionally focus on the details of their work and participate in their own growth to an equal degree, but only that all participate in the emergence of consciousness. The transformation involves mastering the arts and skills of doing one's work perfectly, increased consciousness through individuation (as referred to by Carl Jung) and the evolution of more complex forms of life from single-celled organisms.

This transformation is already taking place in and through us in incremental steps as we become mature and whole human beings.

Somewhat disconcerting is the realization there is no point at which we can say we have arrived. The maturation process often takes place without our knowing it. It makes sense then that the quality of our work, on both the external and internal levels, becomes either facilitative or obstructive to our maturation. When we become aware of what is possible through Interiority at work, we can either "get with the program" or we can resist at every turn. We can either see our work as a blessing and an opportunity to expand our lives and make a contribution, or we can see every aspect of our workdays as a cursed imposition. In the former case, our growth proceeds; we learn from our context and are taught by it on the road to maturity. In the latter case, our potential maturation stalls; we descend into patterns of getting through the day by various escape mechanisms, distractions and addictions.

This emphasis on work does not mean people cannot develop deep inner lives outside of the workplace. Many do, but because work occupies a major portion of our conscious lives, there is a great need for Interiority happening in the workplace. This does not mean any aspect of our lives is of lesser importance than any other in terms of growth. Just as the foundation of cosmic consciousness lies in connectedness to and rootedness in the earth, the extension of our spiritual aspirations to fulfill the most human of ideals— individuation—is also evocative of our coming to maturity through that most cherished extension of ourselves, our work.

Similar to the tree, which cannot grow toward the sun without its roots taking hold of the earth to steady and nurture itself, so too, we cannot deepen our maturity without steadying and nourishing ourselves through the soil of our work. Even now at seemingly mundane tasks, we must take hold again of all we did not leave behind when we struck out in early youth. James Joyce wrote in his *Portrait of the Artist as a Young Man*, "I go to encounter for the millionth time the reality of experience and to forge in the smithy of my soul the uncreated conscience of my race."[72]

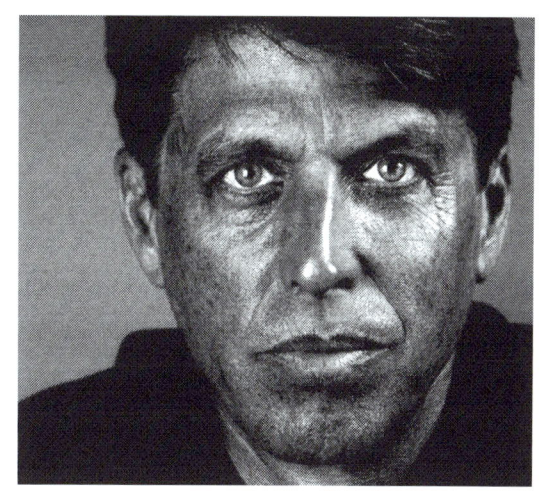

FIGURE 7: **A MINER'S EYES**

What is it then, that holds workers back from embracing the wholeness within them? A key reason, as noted earlier, is the thousands of years that workers have labored under hierarchies through which power was distributed from the top and acted upon by individuals in tiered levels below. So much has this pyramidal model taken over our societies that workers do not see themselves as anything other than the tools others wield so work gets done—with some reward doled out to them, usually a pittance. For workers, the burden of this negative self-image of perennial underdog is a barrier to seeing themselves as centers of creativity and productivity, shapers of the emerging future and, therefore, of inestimable worth.

However, in a present-day response to multiple economic and political crises in our global context, reality-changing scientific discoveries and almost immediate access to knowledge because of communications technologies, a new awareness dawns. Workers are beginning to see in themselves the *source*—and the *goal*—of work energized from *within* rather than from without. Workers are becoming aware of themselves as self-organizing producers with ever-expanding capacities. When we lend our strength to the task with an intense desire to see it done, each one of us is at the center of the universe, in each moment creativity erupting through us and through our communion with the work we do.

Whether we intend to or not, our lives have an impact on the universe.

A further characteristic of this astounding creativity is its uniqueness in each succeeding moment.[73] Scientific revelations about the natural world are potentially prophetic regarding the emerging issues that workers must grapple with. If the sequence of irreversible transformations in the natural world is able to be applied to work, then we are not too soon in projecting incipient forms for how the worker will survive and flourish—with hitherto un-achievable productivity—at work and in the community.

The story of the self-shaping universe is written across the vast curvature of space. We are privileged to know it, and it is up to us to raise into our awareness the evolving story of the human at work. The emerging narrative of the worker attending the tasks of our time will follow the same increasingly complex trajectory of the universe itself. Since we have become aware of Earth's fragile and interdependent ecologies, our worldview personally matters to us, as it does in the workplace and in the wider community. Not only that, but the mental context we hold about the work we do and its consequences matters exceedingly.

At this point, the reader may ask, "Of all the possible things to pick for inspiration about the future of work, why choose the universe?" Simply said, the story of our ongoing transformation is already prefigured in the sequence of dramatic changes that characterize the 13.5 billion years-long story of the universe. At work, we have to constantly struggle to avoid thinking that the result of our work is merely the product or service before us and nothing more. Just as the universe is being transformed by the deepening progression of human consciousness, we can affect much more by expanding our perception of what may be taking place through us.

For eons, we have underestimated ourselves…scrunched, cramped into benches or cubicles, taking orders, fulfilling expectations, passively accepting skimpy monetary rewards, lurching along in "shoes too small." Fortunately, in this task, sometimes we raise our eyes upward and take our cues from the patterns and evolutionary steps of the universe itself.

Of course, the tendency is to think of the universe only as the vast expanse of space that can be glimpsed through the Hubble Telescope, but there is also a universe in the context of our daily work.

My Story – Adapting

Most mornings, early enough to see the first light creeping across the hill beyond our house, the trees on our street looked down on me busily readying myself to face the day. Over time, I've noticed nature around me does the same, that is, get ready for the dawning of the day. The leaves of grass drink the dew off their backs so they can work the sunlight's rays into rivulets of energy. The daisies spread their petals and turn their heads sunward in a generous display. The bushes, swaying in the rustling wind, strengthen their sinews. Birds, with gimlet eyes, bobbing beaks

> *and finely balanced tail feathers, flit unerringly from limb to spreading branch, aloft and away.*
>
> *Everything is adapting to the day—and to everything else. Doors swing open and people, purpose-driven, move to the car and the road, tune to the radio, merge with the traffic. Or they are seeking the blessed parking spot, backing in with bags loaded from the night before, rapping along with the greetings of the day, bright or filled with gloom.*
>
> *All are adapting, endlessly moving, changing as is everything else.*

Your Story

What then is your story of adapting your behaviors to your context, your surroundings in nature, your workplace, your family, community and society?

Take time to see yourself easily adapting—or perhaps experiencing some difficulty aligning yourself with your surroundings. How might your ability to adapt to the emerging circumstances of your life afford you confidence in going about your work?

Scientists describe nature as an adaptive system of things working together to sustain life. They further say nature is a "complex adaptive system"[74] and each of those words is important as only scientists can make them: complex, adaptive, system. That description feels right, and so it should because we humans are also complex adaptive systems. From the extraordinary flexibility of workers' brains that keeps them doing their jobs effectively, to the beautiful and indeterminate collaboration of jazz musicians, humans are indeed complex adaptive systems.

No wonder we find the hierarchical, linear, silo-ed, matrix-ed, logical organizations and concomitant ways of managing often ill-suited to contemporary places of work. How might we make our work patterns more effective?

We might begin with the realization that the source of effectiveness lies within ourselves, our teams and organizations and, more than likely, streaming along neural pathways, mimicking nature's adaptive models.

For understanding nature's adaptive model, there are few equals to Janine M. Benyus' book on Biomimicry, *Innovation Inspired by Nature*. In its pages, she presents in astonishing detail laws of nature, its strategies and principles, such as:

- Nature runs on sunlight
- Nature uses only the energy it needs
- Nature fits form to function
- Nature recycles everything
- Nature rewards cooperation
- Nature banks on diversity.[75]

Not all of the above are self-explanatory. Perhaps a few practical examples might show us how we have learned from natures' apothecary. We have learned how to make Velcro by studying the grappling hooks of seeds. We have created powerful adhesives from the glues mussels use in adhering to underwater rocks. We have developed swimsuits that mimic sharkskin and allow swimmers to break world records. We have weaved bulletproof vests from spider silk.

FIGURE 8: **NATURE'S ENERGY SOURCE**

The most obvious display of nature's creativity is the ubiquitous event of photosynthesis that turns the sun's light into energy in leaves, grass and grains, to name just a few. Case in point: *nature is our primary teacher* and learning its lessons and adapting our behaviors, especially inwardly, is our *contextual project*.

It took the universe 13.5 billion years to arrive at the level of consciousness it has attained by means of human development. But in that journey of evolutionary development is a story replete with examples of how we can tap into the creativity that lies within ourselves, our co-workers and our organizations. Based on similar patterns in the universe, the following five examples of creativity at work have been well explored by Margaret J. Wheatley in her seminal book, *Leadership and the New Science*.[76]

Self-Organizing Structures According to Need

- *Translation*: Teams of workers organize themselves intuitively and spontaneously according to the needs that emerge. A spontaneous re-formation happens in the group to allow it to respond to emerging circumstances. For example, threats to computer data that might be corrupted by invasive viruses, cause employees to converge, communicate and use protective measures to isolate and destroy the invaders.

- *Requirement*: With the understanding of managers, in teams that suggest themselves, workers must cultivate the freedom to recognize what needs are emerging, and the knowledge and skills to move across inner and outer boundaries.

- *Example*: Assume I am an expert in anti-virus software. While my co-worker is describing the virus shapes and impact, I already know what needs to be done before they do and I am immediately developing solutions to meet the need.

- *Application*: Business leaders potentially derive greater productivity through allowing workers the latitude to see emerging needs, resolve immediate problems and shore up or adapt parts of the system that might be unraveling. We are made to be self-organizing creatures according to need.

Interacting Living Systems Eventually Arrive at Order even out of Chaos

- *Translation*: Workers will feel driven to continue the problem-solving process until some solution is reached. The destructive chaos of hurricane Katrina drew forth extraordinary feats of cooperation that fed, clothed, housed and re-settled the people of New Orleans.

- *Requirement*: Intuitively, workers will recognize the evidence of order in the middle of destruction and accommodate themselves to turn that order into workable solutions.

- *Example*: In every ward, many houses suffered destruction beyond recovery, but the consequent demolition exposed new opportunities for development, renewal and ways to manage hurricanes and floods that will surely come again. In every problem lies the suggestions of solutions; we only have to move methodically through them to select the most appropriate one.

- *Application*: We have to trust that in the dissolution of some parts of a system, rather than holding on to the way things were, we might more profitably look for evidence of the emergence of greater order than existed previously. *Interacting living systems eventually arrive at order.*

Participation and Relationships are Fundamental to New Discoveries

- *Translation*: Workers will be prompted to discover new things by somehow joining others and working together.

- *Requirement*: They will be prompted by the activities of each other and even inspired to join forces and uncover formats, structures and products that emerge.

- *Example*: Every organization matures to the point (with technology, production, etc.) that they need to generate viable options that all employees can support and commit to. The simple act of brainstorming allows the group to use individual inspirations to generate solutions that might not be possible without the help of all. In so doing, the impact of the whole working together is much greater than the sum of the parts. A diverse group of workers answering the question, "what would inspire action in everyone" almost always does better than if they were working alone. James Surowiecki illustrates this phenomenon in his book, *The Wisdom of Crowds*, when he writes: "every week, *Who Wants to Be a Millionaire* pitted group intelligence against individual intelligence, and … every week, group intelligence won."[77] *Relationships are Fundamental to New Discoveries*

  Application: The architectural designs of newer workplaces emphasize the use of spaces for workers to gather in interest groups. Similar to the way Mastermind groups effectively use the resources of its members to resolve issues, so too, the free flow of information and resources in informal settings allows creative solutions to emerge.

Large Systems Remain Vital when a Variety of Potential Options are Available in the Environment

- *Translation*: When there are open-ended options, the larger group or community generates energy for the task of selecting and implementing options.
- *Requirement*: Energy that will expand the potential in the workers to keep the organization focused and productive.
- *Example*: When the vision, goals and means are unclear, the energies of the group devolve into conflict among workers, which might even lead to disintegration. The way to ensure a resurgence of collaboration is for people to coalesce around a common good that can be achieved by working together. Just having this common good energizes the group to move in the direction of attaining it. Then it is a matter of working out the practical details of some of those possible futures for that good to happen.
- *Application*: The fragility of globally interdependent economic systems can be the occasion of devising new visions of what the future will look like. We cannot depend only on our imaginations for inspiration to envision the future. More often the vision is apparent in the experiences of the people who are

drawing on the genius of the unique cultural resources of that particular group. The culture usually holds the vision of the future in embryonic form and traces of that vision are constantly in evidence in the experiences of the people, if they only take the time to reflect and see. Then it is up to the entrepreneurs to take that vision and turn it into products and services for the emerging market.

Everything is Always New and Unique to Us

- *Translation*: We do not do or think the same thing exactly as before but are always in some evolving process.

- *Requirement*: Even in the most obnoxious, mundane and repetitive tasks, workers can find newness, uniqueness and make important contributions.

- *Example*: The life of a security guard or a hotel doorman can be merely a long interminable wait unless they find ways to be of service to the residents passing to and fro. In that case, every shift is potentially a new experience of helping people. All workers must cultivate a fertile mind so if the circumstances of their work are not compelling, in themselves, they can have recourse to their inner resources for relevance and satisfaction. As John Milton wrote in his Sonnet XIX: "They also serve, who only stand and wait."[78]

- *Application*: Even though it is said that history repeats itself, the emerging event is never exactly the same as what happened in previous times. Everything around us has a message about the future if we are able to hear and incorporate it into our activities at work. We can never exactly anticipate that message but we are assured that it will be of value sometime, someplace for someone.

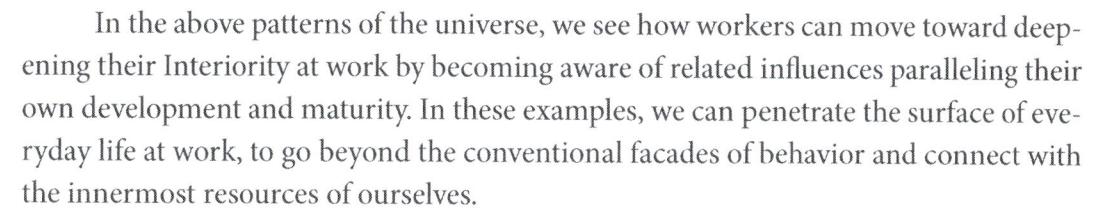

In the above patterns of the universe, we see how workers can move toward deepening their Interiority at work by becoming aware of related influences paralleling their own development and maturity. In these examples, we can penetrate the surface of everyday life at work, to go beyond the conventional facades of behavior and connect with the innermost resources of ourselves.

Besides looking to the universe for examples of creativity, two other accessible paradigms appear to characterize the organizations of the future and, by extension, have relevance regarding why workers must depend more and more on their Interiority. The paradigms I refer to are the Protean Corporation as described by Michael S. Malone[79] and Network Culture as described by Tom Hayes in their books, *The Future Arrived Yesterday: The Rise of the Protean Corporation and What It Means for You*, and *Jump Point: How Network Culture is Revolutionizing Business*.[80]

The word *protean* is derived from the figure in Greek mythology, Proteus. "Proteus is the most transient of creatures. Yet whatever form he takes, he still retains his self."[81] The protean corporation will be essentially different from our hierarchically structured organizational models.

Malone describes the protean corporation, which will have up to one million employees, as having the following unique characteristics:

- An *amorphous external form* that will *rapidly adapt* to market, customers, finance and even ownership, and
- A *slowly evolving center* that maintains *identity* and *continuity*.[82]

He suggests rather than the traditional, rigid pyramidal structure, the protean corporation will more accurately resemble the acceleration of particles around the core of an atom. As support, he cites the new discoveries of particle physics to emulate how the protean corporation will be structured and operate in concentric rings of constantly shifting parts.

Thanks to Planck, Heisenberg, and a whole squad of particle accelerators around the world, we now see the atom as a comparatively solid nucleus composed of a myriad of subatomic particles, surrounded by a probability "cloud" showing the likely locations of the orbiting electrons at any given moment.[83]

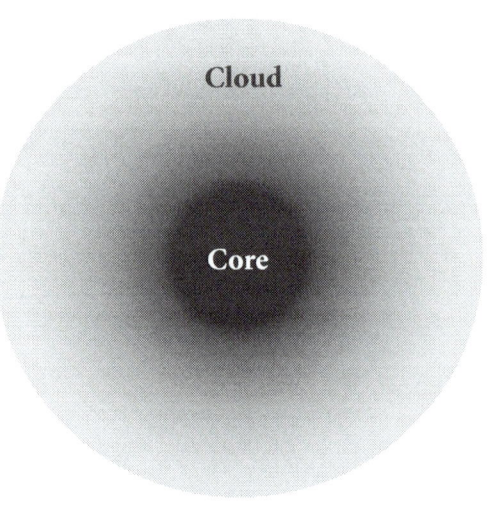

FIGURE 9: **THE PROTEAN CORPORATION**

Malone uses the terms *core* and *cloud* as analogies to illustrate how the emerging organization will function at the relatively stable core and at the relatively volatile level of the shape-shifting cloud that forms the outer rings. Such an organization will be massively decentralized and constantly reorganize itself with the fluidity of cloud formations around our planet. He cites Google and Wikipedia as examples of such protean corporations[84]

According to Malone, organizations that resemble the protean corporation will be necessitated by extraordinary increases in computing power, Internet accessibility for all, an entrepreneurial style of business and social structures and the arrival of three billion consumers in a global marketplace.[85] My interpretation of a protean corporation is one where the worker will always be on view. There will be no place to hide. Therefore, personal integrity—in the face of constant change—will be paramount for maintaining credibility in the eyes of co-workers and stakeholders. It takes little imagination to further project extraordinary degrees of complexity in managing one's work, coping with changing relationships and dealing with the demands on one's inner resources (or Interiority). Now, we proceed to Hayes' theories and the networking paradigm.

Tom Hayes defines *jump point* in his book of the same name as "the moment when an emerging culture becomes the dominant culture and we all move forward a little bit together." He posits that the "culture of the network is rapidly approaching its crossover as the world's dominant view."[86] What we are interested in is his description of the fifth (out of five) *discontinuities*,[87] which he calls the primacy of trust caused by the emergence of the network culture. His very persuasive argument is: "In a global network economy where billions of impersonal and anonymous interactions take place daily, trust is everything: every breach is a crisis."[88]

To anchor home the point "trust is everything," we reference two of his six cultural forces driving the Millennial Generation (those born from 1995 onward) or in his term, the "Bubble Generation."[89] Those two cultural forces are:

- *Angst*[90] (collective anxiety) over environmental, economic and social connectedness threats (social bonds weaken) in our society, and
- *Authenticity* meaning "the Bubble Generation expects transparency and abhors artifice."[91]

My interpretation of a networked culture is one where workers need all the qualities afforded by Interiority, especially the quality of trust that will sustain collaboration in work-teams and communities. The networked culture will be characterized by *inclusivity, horizontal coordination, distributed leadership* and *mutual accountability*.

Inclusivity features every worker contributing according to his or her abilities, regardless of diversity of background. *Horizontal coordination* revolves around a flat structure that replaces one hierarchically organized and work done in teams of workers who are accountable to each other. Instead of one center of control, *distributed leadership* makes each worker a center of control of outcomes for which he/she is responsible. The team, functioning as a unit and as individual members will require that each member be accountable for results to which they committed themselves.

Much of the technology needed for horizontal coordination in the networked organization is already available but such items as clear personal identity, values-based decision-making and integrity in performance and relationships are not necessarily guaranteed. Clear personal identity is necessary for continuity on one's journey toward maturity. The capability to make values-based decisions is necessary to keep one's balance in an increasingly materialistic and consumption-oriented society and workplace. Integrity is necessary because of the lessening of direct supervision and the dependability of each worker to produce expected results.

For our purposes, the implications of such emerging organizations (protean and networked) point to an ever-increasing need for each worker to have well-developed Interiority. Every worker has the basic capacity for Interiority but many opt not to develop theirs to a self-sustaining degree. To succeed in future organizations, a worker must develop their Interiority to the extent that it will anchor them against any storms and enable high productivity—despite the most complex issues at work. Otherwise, due to lack of self-care, the tendency may be to overwork and burn out, live in a self-absorbed workplace bubble that shuts out the rest of the world, or gradually atrophy inwardly and lose the ability to taste life in all its wonder.

As we face this daily contextual project of Interiority, we can look to the birds for inspiration.

Complexity vs. Coordination

If interiority seems too complex to achieve, consider the example of flocking birds that hints at simplicity at the heart of complexity. No one who has watched flocks of birds swirl through the sky can fail to be impressed by the precise coordination of the flock as a whole, as hundreds of birds swoop and turn in unison. The feat of coordinating the motion of hundreds of individuals in so precarious an environment seems complex and daunting and

FIGURE 10: **"THE BOIDS"**

looks as if someone (boss bird?) must be imposing central control. In fact, complexity theorist Craig Reynolds discovered that the complex behavior of the flock emerges from a few simple rules of individual behavior. Wryly, he called his computer simulation "boids."[92] In the model, each boid obeys just three rules: 1) fly in the direction of other boids; 2) try to match the velocity of neighboring boids; 3) avoid bumping into things.

The computer simulation begins with the boids placed randomly in space, but quickly the individuals form themselves into a flock that behaves just like real birds, wheeling and turning together, and avoiding obstacles in their path. This display demonstrates the complex behavior of the system as a whole. The coordinated motion of the flock emerges from a few simple interactions among individuals, not from a single leader. This has been called distributed control (each boid as a center of control), in contrast with central control (single leader), which is what many CEOs try to achieve when they follow a mechanistic model of management.

The example of the boids illustrates both learning from context and allowing context to shape our behavior.

My Story – Hooping Cartwheels

This is a story of water, cartwheels, iron hoops, willing blacksmiths and me. There was a well dug deep into the hillside outside our forge. It was my responsibility to keep the well clean and flowing for a special task that could only be done by working together. I did my job by periodically getting into it, stopping the flow, emptying out the water, scrubbing the stones on the floor and walls till they were free from grime, moss, hapless flies and other creatures. After I whitewashed the walls and waited until they dried, I restarted the flow and soon the well was full of clear, cool water—and that was just the beginning of my work in preparation for the hooping of cartwheels.

My job was in the hooping. I couldn't shift the heavy wooden cartwheels by myself because I only stood as high as the axle. The wheels stood tall and white against the barn wall. All twenty-four of them leaning there, a dazzle of spokes and fellows and axle shafts like sunbursts piled together. They were missing the final hoop of steel that would make them useable. That was where I came in. The task sounds simple but nothing is simple if you don't have the wherewithal and the all-important know-how.

Not everyone could fit a blazing hot steel hoop to six-foot-high wooden wheels so they would stay tight and run true when fitted on the axle of a cart. Not everyone had a measuring wheel by which you could cut the right lengths of flat steel bars for the hooping. Not everyone had a coiling machine to form the hoops. Not everyone had machines to weld the bars into precise hoops that would fit the wheels. Not everyone had an outside seven-foot coal circle of fire for heating the steel to a red-hot glow. Not everyone had the tools for carrying the red-hot hoops. Not everyone had a massive iron wheel, dug into the ground, upon which the blazing steel could be laid around the wooden wheel. But we had. We had all of these things. Even more, we had the know-how to make the hoops tight but not too tight, flat and not warped, round and not oval, square to the rim of the wheel and not overhung.

> *We had a team of men who knew their jobs in the hooping of the wheels. Men like Benny who could judge the placement of the hoop for greatest strength in the join; men like Jemmy and Barney who could swivel the hoop in the blazing coal fire to get an even heat; men like Jack who kept the wooden wheel spokes and fellas tight, straight and true and ready for the hoop; men like Tom who could swing the sledge and with well-placed blows and taps shape the circle till it was perfect; men like my father who knew the whole operation and when the hoop was brought to the right heat, would give the word for the lift and guide the placement of the hoop. And then there was me.*
>
> *I was assigned to carry buckets of water from the well to cool the blazing rim so that it would shrink onto the wheel in a tight and lasting fit. Lest you think I was doing a meaningless task, the second the hoop was settled on the wheel, you would find out soon enough from the shouts for water. Men could not pour or cool or tighten or circle without water. My job was to make sure that they had it in bucketfuls at exactly the right place and time. My strategy was to fill a large barrel with water near to the fitting wheel so that I could get a jump on the demand. That didn't stop the shouts of "Where are you? Water over here, now! What are you doing?" Such comments flew, but with smiles and jokes and teasing to lighten the seriousness of the job.*
>
> *I ran between the blazing hoops of steel, handing over the slopping buckets, filling the barrel again and keeping a wary eye on the hissing, spitting, clouds of steam as the fellas and spokes cracked and eased into place under the pressure of the cooling, shrinking steel. When the newly hooped wheel was stood up and spun and tested for smoothness of the circle, it was declared done, wheeled away and stored for the finishing touches. The pressure didn't let up, for 24 cart wheels had to be hooped while the fire was ready and the men available. That meant a wheel every 20 minutes and no mistakes.*
>
> *What a work is teamwork. What a sense of worth remains when men who know their jobs bend their backs and minds together, muscles straining and sweat glistening in the sun and steam and excitement of the job. The payment is, of course, the money earned, but nothing beat the satisfaction of belonging to the job so that something worthwhile got done.*

Reflection

What I learned from the hooping of the cartwheels was *how to work*. Learning how to work is not a specific skill but a general orientation for *seeing a task* needing to be done, *taking ownership* of the work and *finding a way* to do it efficiently and effectively.

Learning how to work is an enormously valuable *mindset*: actually doing the work, each task, in turn, in rhythm; adjusting to new and unanticipated tasks; sticking with them until satisfactory results appear.

Learning to work means having a ready *attitude* to pull into the effort; not standing back or searching for excuses, but joining in the exchange of mind, muscle and application till the results are achieved.

In addition, I learned the way in which each of us did our work influenced all to pull together for the completion of our common tasks, great and small, immediate and in the future. These are the patterns I learned from wooden cartwheels, blazing-hot iron hoops, willing men and buckets full of water. When we did our jobs, the farmers had their carts for every job imaginable around the farms that ringed our town. The crops got saved and drawn to the barn, grain got carried to the market, creamery-cans of milk got carried to the creamery, dung got carried for spreading on the fields and the people even got carried to church on Sunday.

The lesson of this story holds whether it is in the design and fabrication of a billion-gate integrated circuit in Silicon Valley, building a mile-high skyscraper in Dubai, wheeling boids or building the minds of students in classrooms everywhere. What commerce, what bustle, what excitement, what ingenuity binds the communities of species, to do their parts in the great work of life, in the stupendous unfolding of the cosmos?

Your Story

What then is your story of learning how to work and in due course, the multiplication effect of working together on common tasks? What contextual conditions left a lasting influence on how you chose the kind of work you do and how you approach its fulfillment?

Reflect on how your work patterns derive from models that made an impression on you in your early formation. How might you continue to dip into that formative resource as you continue in your work so it is done well and will continue to influence how work is done in the future?

In applying the above stories to our theme of contextual influences on our inner worlds at work, what may have appeared too complex to even consider may turn out to be manageable if workers utilize Interiority by following simple rules. Similar to the examples of the cartwheels and the boids, hopefully, the apparent complexity of Interiority will be reduced to simple rules later in the book.

Recognizing that our contemporary context requires inner tasks different from those of previous generations, we turn our attention to how we may actively participate in becoming the change we wish to see in our workplaces and society. Just as public demonstrations may have characterized previous generations of workers who railed against injustice, so the contextual project of Interiority serves the same purpose, but according to an inner dynamic.

Key Tasks

Here we examine the key inner tasks related to the contextual aspect of Interiority.

- The Question of Meaning: *Clarifying purpose*
- Revolutions in the Sciences: *Accessing the dynamism and unity of everything*
- Reinterpretations of the Sacred: *Describing the three spheres of the sacred—the life-bearing universe, inner centeredness and loving actions*
- Making a Contribution in Terms of Inner Connectedness: *Working for healing and fulfillment in everything*
- Subjectivity in Viewing Work and all Things: *Understanding personalization and productivity*
- Resisting Repressive Systems: *Embodying desired reforms*
- Work as Responsible Use of Earth's Resources: *Producing sustainability-based work*
- Work as Accountability in Global Economic Systems: *Utilizing interoperability of workers and management*
- Workers Implementing Accountability: *Creating Internet-based accountability systems*

For the remainder of this Chapter, I examine each of these nine tasks in detail.

The Question of Meaning – The Most Sought-after Pearl

"What does it all mean"…"Why am I doing this work?" However voiced, these questions have surely been asked by all our predecessors at work and are increasingly relevant. We can add, "Why does the question of meaning matter?"

It matters because immediately upon uncovering some kind of meaning we are faced with the responsibility of pursuing that meaning and of making our contributions accordingly. For example, if I find personal meaning in having a vibrant inner life, then the thrust of everything I am and do moves in the direction of such fulfillment. Likewise, if I am aware of the imperfections in the natural and man-made systems of life on earth and I long for their healing, I am compelled to *become the changes* for which I long. If I assume such a stance, then I am prefiguring in my being the health and fulfilled possibilities of everything. This stance is not inconsequential because at the deepest level of the consciousness of which I am capable, I am effectively working for and hastening the next stages of transcendence in everything.

In many cultures, this is known as *prayer*.

In connecting to the deeper meaning of work, we need practices for cultivating our inner worlds that will allow for the unfolding of personal stories. Our inner worlds depend on the stories (including myths, beliefs, cultural legacies) we tell ourselves about who we are as individuals, groups and organizations. We need to know our stories because they include some myths that constitute the realities that we need to let go and some we need to keep.

Examples of present-day contextual myths we *need to let go* include: The *male-dominance* model of organizational governance, and equating a *high position* in an organizational hierarchy with *power*, *knowledge* and *greatness*.

Examples of contextual myths we need to *hold on to* include: The importance of *working toward personal transformation* in harmonious complexity, and the equality of community and relationships with individual personhood.

We need myths to support our stories of how things hold together, and if we continue to reflect on those stories and adapt accordingly, there is a great probability we will not return to ineffective or unhealthy patterns that previously characterized work behavior. Eventually, one becomes confident in his/her story, which has been in the process of formation throughout the life-journey and as part of the greater journey of the whole.

To conclude the question of meaning and why it matters, the emergence of our stories through our lives and especially at work is constitutive of the emergence of the story of everything. In this way, the clarification of meaning is an essential part of our contextual project of Interiority.

Revolutions in the Sciences

As we cultivate Interiority, we are influenced by revolutions in management practice, the physical sciences and psychology, but let's initially focus on *cosmology*. In ways different from the physical sciences, cosmology treats the greater meanings streaming toward us at the speed of light, throughout the billions of years since the formation of our cosmic home.

If we doubt the continuing emergence of meaning, consider this: until Galileo's telescope experiments in 1609, the earth was considered the center of the universe and all meanings about the nature of things were deduced from that contextual premise. Cosmology tells the great story of how, during the billions of years since the Big Bang, we arrived at our present condition. It reminds us that if the patterns of evolution continue, humans will be able to project the future shape of everything throughout the universe, including consciousness. We can make this projection because the shape of the universe is already prefigured in the orientation of matter and in the progressive complexification of the human community and its aspirations. If there is any task worthy of our imagination and spirit, it is to capture the emerging shape of our cosmic home so we can align ourselves with those energies.

Hans Jonas (professor of philosophy at the New School for Social Research in New York City from 1955 to 1976), in his book, *The Phenomenon of Life*, reflects the idea that "matter reveals a tendency toward inwardness."[93] Elsewhere, he provides this description: "The organism is possessed by an always latent, *ceaselessly emerging living future*."[94] This notion aligns well with nature as a complex, adaptive system, which we have already examined.

In an earlier passage, I referred to a key definition in cosmology that explains the cosmos as a *cosmogenesis*. This term refers to the *cosmos* as an *emergent entity* and consequently *at work* we need to consider ourselves as *coming into being*. Considering the ecological threats to our planet, we are also driven by an abiding urgency to evolve a new consciousness as *conservators of our heritage* in the natural world and *arbiters of accountability* for our common resources.

Reinterpretations of the Sacred

Many think the *sacred* or *holy* refers to keeping the rules of religious institutions and the patriotic memories of those who gave their lives for their country. The *sacred* or *holy* properly means *knowing the self* from the inside out, following the soulful promptings and connecting with the sounds reverberating in everything. What is sacred is the *power of love at the core* of the human and in some form or other at the core of everything.

At one time, theology was thought of as the science of the holy. To my mind, what constitutes the sacred or holy requires redefinition and reapplication concomitant with advances in contemporary knowledge and consciousness. Such fresh expressions of the sacred will ensure that the deepest creative energies of our inner cores are brought to bear in our most intimate work relationships.

As the first reference point for a new theological expression of the sacred, I use Thomas Berry's explanation of the evolutionary process of the universe from his book, *The Great Work*. In regard to the data of evolution, he writes: "We need merely understand that the evolutionary process is neither random nor determined but creative."[95] All of us, at one time or another, have become aware of the seemingly spontaneous and continuous creativity of the universe when we have experienced the recuperative energies at work—such as the recovery of grasses, plants and wildlife after devastating fires or natural disasters. Life is made up of living systems creatively generating new life in life-death-life cycles.

On a deeper level, we become witness to the all-nourishing fertility of life, as the universe in its psychic manifestation reflects on itself through the medium of human consciousness. In this way, the universe can be understood as a subject that heals and renews the *other* (that which is the subject of our attention). Berry continues, "As physical resources become less available, psychic energy must support the human project… we must now celebrate the sequential transformation moments in an emergent universe and as a result…the story of the universe is now our dominant sacred story."[96]

Consequently, we have moved from a dependence on physical energies that are diminished by use—into a concentration on psychic energies that expand with use. People are responsible for carrying forward the evolutionary process of the universe… a sacred task. In a way distinct from this evolutionary process of the universe toward consciousness, we now examine the *inward search for the holy at the center of the self*.

A second reference point for a new theological expression can be found in contemplation of the heart of the human, or the realm of the sacred. The assumption here is that at the center of self is a spiritual energy that is loving, creative, healing and a source of *wholeness* (holiness). The advent of wholeness involves an inward search for the sacred in *wisdom* (focused on ultimate concerns), *ecstasy* (mystical state), unified consciousness, or enhanced awareness. This inner state of union with the sacred arrived at through this inward search is different from the method of searching.

According to William Johnston, S.J. in his book, *Silent Music*,[97] searching begins by initially going beyond thoughts, concepts, images and reasoning into a place of *profound silence* which may progress to enlightenment or mystical experience and which is an intuitive encounter with total reality.[98] According to the various religious traditions, this state is called *sanmai* in the Japanese Zen tradition, *contemplation* in the Christian meditation tradition and *Samadhi* in Buddhist Sanskrit terminology.

The method that restricts the stream of ordinary consciousness and pushes the mind into expanded consciousness varies according to tradition but most often includes an exclusive focus on *breathing* or a *mantra* (sacred words such as OM or maranatha), a *Koan* (an insoluble phrase from Japanese Zen tradition), a *mandala* (a visual image upon which the attention is fixed – from Tibetan Buddhist tradition), or *Gregorian chant* or *rosary* recitation (from the Catholic tradition). The results of this expanded consciousness include:

- arrival at a state of union with the sacred at the center of oneself
- healing and integration of the personality
- allowing oneself to become more truly human
- development of interior senses that parallel the outer senses of seeing, hearing, tasting that allow for a new dimension of intuition as well as a deep and simultaneous tolerance of paradox such as "light is dark, nothing is everything, joy is suffering"[99]

"It is only with the heart that one can see rightly; what is essential is invisible to the eye," Antoine de Saint Exupéry.[100] A third reference point for a new theological expression of the sacred can be found in the *love of self, others, community…all things*.

Love is the focal energy key to meaning in life and deserves to be called sacred. Love is so central in the human and communitarian context its energies are traditionally identified with the deity. "God is love, and he who abides in love abides in God and God in him." (1 John 4:16). Yet, because love has been identified with deity, the concept has largely been confined to an inner core of people, to human relationships and often to the exclusion of the loving energies that animate all matter.

This duality is unfortunate because the energies of love are always tending toward higher and more complex manifestations in all natural phenomena. This is especially true with regard to humans who are profoundly impacted by giving and receiving love… in their beings, in their lives and in their work.

Love is popularly thought of as warm feelings of romance, but in fact love has many practical manifestations. *Love at one's core* is therapeutic and a source of healing with others—and the community. The love that ensures the *continuance of life* expresses itself in sexual energy and also celebrates *caring* in the relationships involved. *Compassionate love* for humanity generates the desire to continue loving others and to be a helpful presence.

Love is so powerful that without it, societies become alienated from themselves. Loving behavior between two people leads to expanded awareness and eventually their communication goes beyond words into intuitive understanding.

Love might also be described as the "strange attractor"[101] (as referenced by Margaret Wheatley in her book, *Leadership and the New Science*), that consistently moves all natural things toward *unity*, drawing *order out of chaos* and ultimately arriving at *consciousness* in all. No wonder the energies of love can be termed sacred. If we can deepen our understanding of cosmology and theology, this area we consider 'the sacred' will strongly enable work itself to become a source of meaning, innovation and creativity.

In a brief recapitulation of the foregoing section, the contextual project of Interiority invites us to re-interpret the sacred as the story of the universe and to see the heart of the human as the source of wholeness (holiness).

Called to Contribute

Another characteristic of workplace context appears in our longing for meaning inside organizations and in the publications of management "gurus."[102] Here, we refer to the insights presented by Hendricks and Ludeman in their provocative book, *The Corporate Mystic*. In their reflections, they point to a growing aspiration for creative response at work that will allow us to reach beyond ourselves, our product or service to make a contribution for the sake of the wider community. This desire for creative response through work allows access to the unique mystery of self. Thus, we open to the expanding flow of energy because we are aware of our place in the natural order of things.

Associated with these aspirations for meaning is a deep desire for transcendence… which is part of the worker's responsibility for self-liberation and a key component of the contextual project of Interiority. It is particularly difficult for us workers to consider that in our individuating selves, we are the contribution…but we definitely are.

Because of the absence of Interiority and the lack of community in contemporary workplaces, many workers feel alienated from themselves, resulting in an inability to be at ease within. The enormous pressure in the modern workplace to consistently produce excellent results at top speed, or face termination, often leaves workers feeling frazzled, drained and fragmented. When there is no time to unwind, recollect oneself and enjoy the work, workers tend to lose touch with how they feel, often hardening themselves against human weakness in order to survive. In reaction to this increasingly complex and depersonalized world of work, it is not surprising that a deep desire emerges to transcend the product or service we provide so we can belong to ourselves as whole persons and to the greater community of living things.

This deep aspiration for Interiority, transcendence and wholeness provides the impetus to seek meaning and purpose in everything we are and do, especially in our places of work. Simply put, we want to work for more than a paycheck. Tony Hsieh,

CEO of Zappos, puts it more succinctly in the title he chose for his book, *Delivering Happiness, A Pathway to Profit, Passion and Purpose.*[103] We want to work in an organization that attempts to provide for wholeness in the lives of the stakeholders and allows workers to engage in personal and professional growth through the work itself.

Eventually, the challenge for each worker comes down to self-management. This ultimately means taking responsibility for personal and professional growth, especially in our interior lives, while at work. What we are interested in here is how workers will be liberated through self-management in the deepening of their inner lives, at the same time fulfilling the organization's business purpose with great productivity. To help us arrive at such productivity while achieving balance in the use of natural resources, we must consider ourselves as related to the whole.

The best way to describe this emergence of our relatedness to the whole is in the term *subjectivity* used creatively by Thomas Berry in his book, The Great Work.[104]

Subjective Perspective

A vital aspect of the contextual project of Interiority lies in how we view all things as either being in relationship with each other or in a relationship of subjectivity. Initially, subjectivity can best be understood in contradistinction to the term objectivity. For the past three centuries, we have been living in a world where all things, including people, were thought of as discrete objects with no connection to each other (objectivity). Modern science has revealed that we are made up of energy that at its core is interrelated. This includes our inner lives and all natural things.

Due to these scientific insights, we are no longer able to describe things as discrete objects...instead as belonging to the flow of constantly changing forms of energy—us included. This reality weakens the perception of the world of work as being filled with separate, distinct objects upon which we can act according to our whims. At the same time, this reality strengthens the perception that, as part of the whole, we can exercise an influence even if we are not conscious of doing so.

The result: when we are speaking about anything we perceive as different from ourselves, we are actually describing part of our subjective reality. This perception alone fundamentally changes our relationships with everything in the world. If we accept this perception as valid, we can no longer treat others and the natural world as separate from ourselves but as an interconnected part of the whole to which we belong.

The implications of subjectivity in terms of how executives might adapt their behaviors regarding the workers and stakeholders are potentially enormous—but, of course, this depends on each executive's decisions.

Even if this adaptation was possible, most of us do not yet fully comprehend the implications of subjectivity. What we can say is this: we are living and working on the cusp of a *powerfully transformative consciousness* wherein workers are becoming aware that the *psychological*, *spiritual* and *intuitive* dimensions of their inner lives are constitutive parts of *what matters at work*. Formerly disdained as non-objective, non-measurable and non-productive, these resources are becoming enormously beneficial for enhancing productivity at work and effecting unique contributions in the human community.

Nowhere are these resources more valuable than in the worker's relationship with the customer. This one relationship clarifies why we need workers with the ability to *self-manage*, who practice the cultivation of *Interiority*, who have an appreciation of the *sacred* and the *unknowable* and who participate in the phenomenon of *subjectivity*. What a customer (like you or me) needs is to work with a human being who is *knowledgeable* and *skillful*, who has a *sense of self*, who is engaged in the process of *becoming whole* and who can *listen*. We appreciate someone who is *empathetic* with our human situation, who can *respect* our *values* and experience and who can *understand* our *needs*...so together we can fulfill them.

In other words, as customers, we are looking for someone not unlike our best selves.

Realistically, most managers and workers focus on the externals of the product or service. This means if they make a sale, develop a new product, hire an excellent worker or add to the bottom line, they consider themselves successful and usually they will be rewarded for their efforts.

There is nothing really wrong with this. The problem arises because they do not go far enough in considering such activities in the context of subjectivity. The whole person of the worker is typically not taken into account. The relationships between managers and workers usually begin and end at the externals. Rewards are usually material, which serves to fulfill one's needs momentarily, but could possibly end up as distractions. Most often, the result is depersonalization, alienation and bitterness at the lack of sensitivity to one's deeper needs.

Peripheral interests serve only to distract and have little to do with what is real. What is real touches the worker at the core where the genuine work happens. As Steve Chandler and Duane Black write in their book, *The Hands-Off Manager*,[105] "The real change happens internally, not externally. Change becomes visible only in the external world. Our access to destiny occurs earlier than that."

As yet, subjectivity remains an ideal, but in the meantime, workers can exercise an influence on oppressive organizational or management systems.

Resisting Repressive Systems

Another vital aspect of contextual Interiority is its counter-balancing influence on oppressive systems—so they become oriented to collaboration and equality. A relationship of reciprocal influence exists between our work and our lives in society. On the positive side, when we do our work with respect and care, it pays us back by guiding us on the journey toward maturity and wholeness—as individuals and as a human community.

Such reciprocity is important for moving our own development forward and adding momentum to the renewal of historical legacy frameworks. This is important for our human evolution because, as I have referred to before, in the western world our organizations and institutions have been dominated by a quasi-stationary legacy of classical dualism, romanticism, rationalism and humanism —all of which tend to rigidly imprison us within the ideological parameters of previous historical periods.

Because workers tend to get stuck in a particular historical era, all of these legacies are necessary precursors for nurturing the kind of transcendental humanism to which the majority of people aspire at the beginning of the 21st Century. Nevertheless, while recognizing the importance of those legacy systems, it is our responsibility to forge new and creative ways for workers to grow personally and professionally.

That is our contextual project of Interiority. It is our responsibility to regenerate all the traditional institutions so they can support us in this current period of history.

In this work of regeneration, we are not alone.

The work we must do will potentially teach us what we need to know if we listen closely, keep our minds open, our hearts courageous and hopeful spirits ready to act. The kind of systemic reforms we are thinking about are never easy. They are possible when individuals embody the reforms in their lives and especially at their work. We cannot wait for others to lead in these reforms. We already have the sanction to implement them by virtue of the truth of ourselves—which is the supreme foundation of all real change.

It must be borne in mind for everyone who aspires to personify those reforms, there will be ten thousand who are pulling in the opposite direction. This kind of systemic change is lonely and challenging, and it can require doing over and over again to the point of extreme tiredness. But in the exhaustion, we will narrow our focus and find firm footing and encouragement to pursue the fulfillment of our call.

With regard to changing the extreme abuses of the earth's resources, we can begin by becoming aware of our carbon footprint.

Responsible Use of Earth's Resources

Continuing with contextual Interiority, now that each of us can individually measure his/her carbon footprint, we must admit that we have arrived at a time of inescapable responsibility for the health of our natural systems. The human community is being forced to face the fact that our way of working and using the earth's resources has driven us to an almost irreversible breaking point. Sad examples abound, such as the dying oceans' inability to renew themselves and the destruction of the world's forests and ecosystems.

Belatedly, we have realized that the speed of consumption of the earth's resources has outstripped the ability of the earth to renew itself. We need new models for how those *resources* are to be effectively *used* and *conserved*...and *we definitely need new models for how work is done*. Because we habitually look for solutions through establishing more bureaucratic structures, most efforts focus on reducing greenhouse gases and developing geo-thermal, wind and solar power to replace coal, nuclear energy, oil and the like.

Even though it is the most accessible model, what is usually bypassed is the vast *untapped inner resources of the ordinary worker*. Those resources could be enlisted to bring needed conservation to the limited physical resources of the natural world. For this unprecedented task, we have only impoverishment of language, practices, models, sanctions, direction, consensus and structures.

And, if we are going to ask workers to hold themselves accountable for the conservation of resources, it is reasonable to expect they have the capacity to reciprocally hold global economic systems equally accountable.

Accountability of Global Economic Systems

An essential component of contextual Interiority is self-education...so we can take part in holding global economic systems accountable. A tall order for one person, but in cooperation with others of like mind gathering for serious discussion and systemic changes in global economic systems, it might be doable.

Over the past several years, we have experienced the difficulty for global economic systems to recover from recession—a result of the baggage of hierarchical governance models and privilege for the few on the backs of the many. The notion of free-market capitalism being able to manage common resources foundered on the fallacy of self-regulating financial markets. This was painfully evidenced in the collapse of Wall Street investment banking companies during the Great Recession of 2008-2009. Consequently, we are facing the demise of the traditional notion of capitalism and the weakening credibility of the American brand of democracy. Whatever system replaces what has been lost in this economic downturn, it will not depend on western capitalist ideas alone or on one supposedly impregnable bastion of monolithic trust in the markets.

We are facing the arrival of the *global financial marketplace*, the possibility of a *financial cold war* and the *quantum* (uncertain) view of everything. This is especially true when we consider what we are learning from experts, such as Joseph P. Quinlan in his book entitled The Last Economic Superpower, *The Retreat of Globalization, the End of American Dominance, and What We Can do about It*.[106] The title tells it all. The *U.S. is deeply in debt*, the *rise of the rest* (of the economies of the world) is well under way and the *West must change* the fundamentals of how we perceive our roles in the world.

Deregulation of the financial markets, particularly on Wall Street, has been one among many of the root causes of the economic downturn. The damage has already been done and trillions of dollars of savings and 401k plans have evaporated from the accounts of ordinary workers around the world.

From the point of view of the ordinary worker, fixes to issues of this magnitude cannot only depend on re-regulation and managing financial meltdown by increased government and treasury department liquidity. These are short-term fixes—and the negative fallout affects the lives of people around the world for a long time.

Re-regulation attends to *external fixes for an internal problem*...and we intuitively realize that it *will not work*. When a problem arises from an inner cause in an individual or organization, it cannot be resolved by the mere application of external solutions. A problem that arises from an inner cause can only be fixed by an inner-generated solution. Here, I refer again to the long-absent ethic of *accountability for the common good*. This ethic is based on the moral principle of *relationality* referred to previously—in contradistinction to the ethic of self-absorption.

Again, the issues are systems-wide, which include both inner and outer forums and call for systems-wide solutions, both inner and outer. With the passage of the bailout packages, those who were responsible for mismanagement of the systems most likely will not be held accountable. In many of the systems upon which our communities depend, this deficiency—this lack of accountability—points to one of the most common causes of the economic meltdown.

Seen from this perspective, the best way to ensure stability in global economic systems is to establish accountability in those who manage common resources. Here, the two operative terms are *accountability* and *management*. In the organizations of the future, these two functions *must belong to all workers*, regardless of where they are working. Those who manage others and those who are managed must have the *same levels* and the *same tools* of accountability at their disposal. A proposal in this context was made by Vineet Nayar in his book, *Employees First, Customers Second and Management Third*. The title alone tells us what we need to know.

Let's be clear. We do not want "the foxes guarding the chickens." So we need ubiquitous eyes, ears and hands that know the behaviors of those in positions of responsibility and hold them accountable for their actions. Historically, those in positions of holding managers of financial institutions accountable—such as *politicians, courts,* and *oversight boards*, including the *SEC* and the *rating agencies*—became themselves compromised and failed to do their jobs. Oversight systems whose very purpose was to ensure accountability in the systems upon which the citizens depended also failed in that task.

Just as happens now in worker performance, it is time for worker involvement in management accountability. When workers can hold co-workers accountable and be held accountable themselves, then we will have the basic mindset—and the skills—to hold larger systems accountable for doing their tasks.

Implementing Accountability

An important part of our contextual project of Interiority is the commitment to accountability. The management of common resources must be arranged through the development of a *covenant* that spells out the obligations of the managers and the managed, as well as the methods by which such accountability take place.

The most ubiquitous resources for making authority figures responsible for their actions are workers imbued with Interiority, knowledge and the means of managing such accountability. This is a most pertinent and practical reason for the development of Interiority in our times.

Is this notion of Interiority in the ordinary worker too far-fetched? Framed another way, the question is: Is the concept and practice of Interiority a practical possibility for the ordinary worker? The answer lies in the following three reasons:

FIGURE 11: **HIGHLIGHTING THE NEED FOR ACCOUNTABILITY**

- The possibility of reaching *maturity* and *wholeness* for any person does not depend on learning, wealth, position, health or any other life circumstance. Indeed, those of us who have been deprived of any of life's good things have the highest probability of arriving at maturity and wholeness—precisely because we have (or had) little and must *focus on what is of lasting value*.

- If workers perceive *their* work as their *mission* in life and *invest their energies* in doing it with integrity and to the *best of their abilities*, they potentially reap great *satisfaction* from that work and become very *productive*. No less an authority than Abraham Lincoln attested to this matter when he said, "Every man is proud of what he does well; and no man is proud of what he does not do well. With the former, his heart is in his work; and he will do twice as much of it with less fatigue."

- If workers come to appreciate what is *important* and of *lasting value* in life, they will be in a better position to view work and work relationships as continuing opportunities to *grow* and *mature*.

If we accept that workers are capable of interiority and of holding each other accountable, a brief consideration of the consequences of not making efforts at accountability will help recall the periodic cycles of ballooning consumption through easy credit and sudden evaporation of savings and investments by bursting bubbles. These events should alert us to the reality that the financially weaker members of society are left holding an empty bag, while those who make unconscionable profits are free from pursuit and ultimately unaccountable. Accountability is the most effective solution to workplace and social inequities and it must be exercised by the workers in organizations and communities everywhere.

Regardless of the opportunities afforded any individual to gain education and knowledge, it is every worker's responsibility to nurture his/her own authentic voice and reveal his/her truth whenever a real need surfaces because of injustice. This kind of system-wide accountability presupposes investment in and the development of interiority in workers and organizations. One thing is certain, none of this accountability will happen without interiority as a base in individual workers, teams and leader/managers. This is because the prevailing culture of self-preservation has too great a hold on the mind of the people. On the other hand, for the norms of accountability to prevail, interiority must provide a strong identity and values-based choices that require integrity in all situations. In the age of the knowledgeable worker, who can make enormous contributions to overcoming systemic problems and organization-wide cultural issues, the possibilities for rebalancing opportunities for all are real and practical.

In support of the possibility of accountability throughout an organization, I cite the experience of a previously mentioned, employee-owned company on Martha's Vineyard, Massachusetts, called South Mountain Company. Their story is told exceedingly well in a book entitled: Companies We Keep, *Employee Ownership and the Business of Community and Place*. The main theme is about "designing and creating self-accountability among the people who share in the life of a firm," as stated in the Foreword.[107]

I quote the company Mission: "To enrich our community through our work."[108] That statement captures the ethic and practice of this forward-thinking organization. The *workers* and the *community* are the *core* of the company.

What attracted me to this organization as a model of community priority is the identification of the worker with the totality of his/her commitment: to the *work*, to the *community*, to *each other* and to *self-accountability*. This company would not have become a model of employee-ownership without the efforts of the original owner, John Abrams. In relating his experience in helping the company become employee-owned, he states "It's the company we nourish, the company we test and challenge, the company we hope will endure and continue to enjoy the opportunities conferred upon us by this place. This is the company whose care is entrusted to us, and whose success requires our relentless dedication. This is the company we will keep."[109]

Above all, transparency and integrity must characterize the communications of leaders and managers to the workers. If we commit to the investment in Interiority in the workers, there is no doubt they will further be able to understand and make decisions about suspect behaviors of leaders/managers. However, if there is doublespeak, obfuscation and impossible promises, the game is over before it has begun. By then, the leader will have lost the trust of co-workers and only by the recognition of fault, due contrition, recompense and renewal of effort can the leader restore that bond. Leaders who strive for authenticity must break through all barriers to speak directly to the workers' minds and hearts to let them know the relationship between the organizational goals and the work assigned to them.

Again I ask the question, "Is this notion too far-fetched?"

The worker with deep Interiority who accepts his work as his *contribution* and makes all his *resources available* for the achievement of that work is powerfully *ready to perform*. But workers generally have been kept in the dark about information vital to their livelihoods. This information-gap enhances the case for open organizations that not only make financial data available to workers but make information available on all key decisions regarding the organization...and the methods whereby those decisions were reached.

In addition, managers generally underestimate the ability of workers to understand and commit to work that is in their own best interests. Too often, workers do not have the knowledge, the inner resources or the means to hold their leader/managers accountable for their actions. Nevertheless, because of manipulations of those standing to make untold profits and even with high levels of transparency, the most financially sophisticated observers are potentially deceived. Gary Gensler, chairman of the Commodity Futures Trading commission, addressing the Libor case in the New York Times of August 7, 2012, writes, "*The Barkleys' case demonstrates that Libor has become more vulnerable to misconduct. It's time for a new or revised benchmark-an emperor clothed in actual, observable market transactions - to restore the confidence of Americans that the rates at which they borrow and lend money are set honestly and transparently.*" This situation—too little information available to those who depend on it for decision-making—must change. Moreover, it is important to not leave information communication to the spin-meisters, those who market information with the purpose to keep things as they are, i.e. concentrated in the hands of the few who make disproportionate financial gains.

There is a practical reason for giving prominence to the possibility of influencing the global economic system: the *Internet*. With the Internet, the workers have at their disposal the most empowering influence on potential global awareness ever invented. It's potential as an unsurpassed medium for accountability has not been plumbed fully, but it is in progress. Witness the Arab Spring uprisings of 2011; the overthrow of the despots could not have happened without Internet-based media—texting, Linked-in, Twitter, Facebook, and the like. Similarly, the Occupy Movement has been organized through the spontaneous disaffection of the dispossessed. This alone should send an unmistakable message to those seeking the anonymity of the impersonal corporation.

The foregoing nine tasks form the contextual project of Interiority through which we come to fulfill our key roles as workers in this time. When we deepen our awareness of these tasks, our stories, our energies, our consciousness—in collaboration with the energies of the universe—gives definition to an emerging framework of reality, now and in the future.

In Chapter One, I tracked the history of the perceptions of work. In Chapter Two, I focused on emerging, present-day scientific discoveries. In Chapter Three, Foundations, I review how the experiences of any life can become the grist for growth and maturity.

Unlock your mind with your heart key

Chapter 3

Foundations

….like a foolish man who built a house on sand.

—Matthew, 8:26

One of the more practical Biblical quotes concerns "sand" as a foundation. Sand crumbles easily and so does a house upon which it is built. If a house is only as sound as the foundations upon which it is built, what does that say about the foundations upon which interiority might be built? Since interiority is a characteristic of the inner state of a person, the foundations must be set in the sturdy depth levels of the innermost heart's core. The four foundations of interiority that make up this chapter are presented on the right. The title of each foundation may be unfamiliar but the topics are vital. To help in understanding the topics, I will a accompany each foundation with a story. It is fitting that I begin with a love story. For me, one of those foundations was set in an unanticipated relationship that was so powerful it was as if I was reborn from the experience.

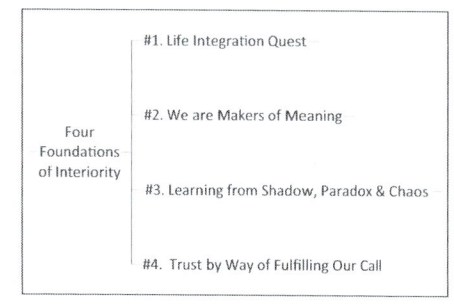

Four Foundations of Interiority:
- #1. Life Integration Quest
- #2. We are Makers of Meaning
- #3. Learning from Shadow, Paradox & Chaos
- #4. Trust by Way of Fulfilling Our Call

FIGURE 12: **FOUNDATIONS FRAMEWORK**

My Story – Unschooled in Love

Because of the 2011 earthquake in Japan, the resultant tsunami and reactor meltdown, the word Fukushima entered the vocabulary of the human community and its impact will, like Krakatoa, reverberate forever. For me, the impact entered long before, for it was in a Fukushima valley, on a hillside of long, dappled grass, slender saplings and waving maples I shared a kiss and fell in love for the first time.

She was a woman who was as unschooled in love as me, yet it took us but a moment to learn we had the power of creating each other, again and again. I had fallen in love. Like a fish without water, I flopped around. She was quiet, deep, smart and willing to risk getting close. She was also unsure, unaccustomed and searching, just like me. We made a pair.

Those precious moments came as they did after years of knowing each other—a threshold between imagining what the embrace would be like and a reality that was infinitely better. Her touch was gentle and generous as we were enfolded into each other, matching breaths and heartbeats.

It was a moment of becoming known as we set out to cross a valley infinitely wider, deeper and more fertile than the one in which we lay. We stepped from being acquaintances to being lovers and the realization changed us utterly.

It was a moment of belonging that could not be repeated.

It was a moment that invited the wonders of ourselves to be explored and known as never before.

It was a moment of seeing the world around us take on a glow we had never seen before or imagined. A moment that could not be taken for granted for it was full of risk, anticipation and responsibility.

It was a private moment of our own, and upon which society could not intrude, but nature would.

Nature spoke to us. The rivers—spilling, falling over mottled stones, scattering spray from far below—waved at us, two shadowy figures away up there on the bridge, so close we seemed as one, so far above that the sounds of the flowing waters were out of reach. But we were one with the flow, above, below and in-between.

The gorges, strewn with lichen-covered boulders, lent their surfaces to our exploring feet, and led us through the slenderest, greenest canopies of saplings—who told us tales of running sap that fed the spreading leaves, in cycles, just like us. The waves already knew us; they knew we would be there as they gathered themselves *in whorls of waters that pushed ahead to greet us and fall over themselves, to pull at our toes as the sand slipped backward to erase our footprints.*

The delicate leaves of autumn trees surrounded us, cushioned us underfoot. Green branches invited us to be steady and secure and to lock arms around and around each other—and we did, often. The plum, pear, cherry and apple blossoms sprinkled us with tiny streams of fragile petals and pushed around us the breath of perfumed air—along the parkland waterways that made our vision full of promise, full of a timeless future.

The winter snows floated over and around us in soft drifting veils, enclosing us deeply into each other, to a place where we were unaware of the world about.

The moment stretched beyond that day, that week, that month, that year and brought with it other moments of time. The sunlight shone and made a brighter path, the crowds parted because they somehow knew, the trains ran as if on cue, the subway doors opened to welcoming, vacant seats, and all things worked together for us—until they could not hold together anymore.

And there came a time when nature did not speak to us. It was a time of wrenching breakups, long periods of absence, of rules broken and obligations toward the priesthood reinstated…only to be disregarded. It was a time of inner conflict and troubled conscience, of fears of discovery, decisions enforced by systems that recognized no hearts like ours. It was a time of cultural misunderstanding, where sacred vows, repeatedly explained, were not convincing.

It became a time when monastery meetings evoked tensions of a divided life, when protestations of love competed fiercely with commitments to the church and the mission. It was a time of depression for me when the best counsel sounded reasonable but could not reflect the heart-centered reasoning of my realities. Eventually, we could not bear to hold each other, as our bodies protested the divided messages echoing from within. Reality intervened. We could not sustain the relationship and we had to part or be splintered within forever.

We were no longer the same people who had met, kissed and loved on the Fukushima hillside. Our initial lightness was long gone and the pain was deep in our hearts. Nature no longer spoke to us in the way it had. No consolation flowing on the warm breeze could soothe the ache, the incessant longing. No summer warmth could quell the involuntary shivers or sighs. No future scenario beckoned with its promise of better times. Instead, it warned of futile hopes and dreams filled with unending disappointment.

> *We parted, but for months, years and even until today sightings of her in the distance flip my heart over. Involuntarily, I see her walking away from me in the familiar movements of unknown women on the street. I suddenly see her reflected in a window as I pass and when I turn she is not there.*
>
> *Though imaginary, it is nevertheless real.*

My Story – Reflections

That love was truly pivotal in my life. I came in from the cold of the world where I did not have a counterpart, someone who responded to me as I did to her. By the power of that love, I was pulled into the depths of me and I knew what it was to build my own foundation for living. I opened up to the secrets of life that, for me, in my dedicated state, was taboo even to imagine and a breach of sacred trust. Yet, the sacred was there in our relationship, of that I am certain. Illicit though it was according to the rules, at its core that love was not illicit but holy. It led me to myself in ways that I had previously no inkling. Through that love, I found my core…and I still pursue the world that was opened up to me on the Fukushima hillside of the long dappled grass, the saplings and the maples. I have no regrets. It was beautiful.

My Story – Application

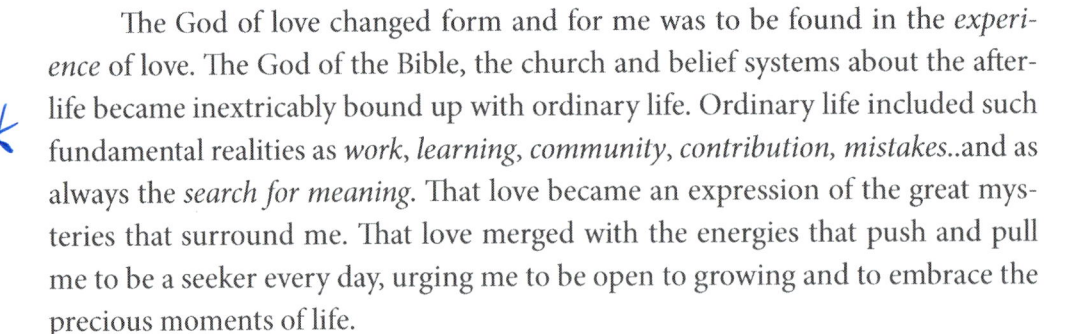

The God of love changed form and for me was to be found in the *experience* of love. The God of the Bible, the church and belief systems about the afterlife became inextricably bound up with ordinary life. Ordinary life included such fundamental realities as *work, learning, community, contribution, mistakes*..and as always the *search for meaning*. That love became an expression of the great mysteries that surround me. That love merged with the energies that push and pull me to be a seeker every day, urging me to be open to growing and to embrace the precious moments of life.

Your Story

Reader, what then about you? In building the foundations of your life was there a grounding experience that left you utterly changed? Can you recall a pivotal experience that moved you from an objective and idealistic view of the world into a more complex and human appreciation of life's mysteries? How did that experience begin to show up in your work? As a result of what you learned from those experiences, what practices of mind or behavior did you put in place at work?

So it is for all who live and work in lives distracted, divided and unfocused, life inexorably invites us to affirm ourselves. Inevitably in the turbulence of the turning world, each of us hears an invitation to lay out our foundations on which we build our lives, and whether we do or not, we become aware and are no more innocent.

There are **four foundations for Interiority**. These foundations are the dimensions of human nature that allow for re-thinking the connection between work, personal wholeness and productivity. Each of the foundations is a pivotal turning point in personal growth through our work.

Foundation #1: Life Integration Quest

The first foundation of Interiority is life integration through work. Life integration is a quest because it is a *never-ending journey* of growth. The importance of becoming oneself through integrating all of our capacities through work cannot be overstated. Basically, the more we become integrated into the person we are called to be, the more our lost energies will be restored and released for greater productivity at work.

However, this process of integration does not take place without intentional involvement. We must choose to deepen awareness and actively implement the practices of Interiority. The key method is to make our *inner dialogue* (self-talk) *conscious*. We do this through reflecting on our experiences and by learning from them. This inner dialogue usually takes place without conscious effort. But when we make the process conscious, we gradually diminish or lose any reactive and dysfunctional behavior patterns and become more inner-directed. These reactive behavior patterns are barriers to growth; they drain energies and deflect us from integration and eventual mature wholeness.

Furthermore, when we actively engage in self-integration through the practices of Interiority, we become more *self-aware* and have immeasurably more of our *energies available* for increased productivity. As reflected in my story of returning to myself through the experience of love, this was a turning point for me on my way toward integration of my life and it began with me saying to myself, "stay within." When I remained within myself, I was calmer, less reactive, more balanced in my decision-making and more capable of creative and productive work.

But that inwardness was not always there. I had been an outward man moving away physically and psychologically from intimacy. My reactive mode was to go outward to what I thought others needed from me.

As far back as I can remember, my motivations have derived from somewhere outside of myself. I responded to the real expectations of others and also to the expectations I projected onto them. I was living on the outside of myself and acting because of what I thought others wanted. It was truly a lonely place to be.

I came back inside myself because of being loved. It was also because I could no longer sustain the façade or endure the pain of loneliness. Nevertheless, I gradually began to live within myself and I worked hard at remaining within. This proved very difficult because my instinctive reaction was to revert to my old pattern. The old practices of acting because of the expectations of others died hard. To change the habit, I got used to saying to myself, "come within" and "stay within," especially in times of stress. In that way, I gradually began the occupation of my inner self and initiated the work of the integration of my life.

Integration is derived from the term *integer*, which means whole. The process of integration begins in *constant reflection* on our experiences. It also includes the *learning* and *wisdom* derived from those experiences. Bringing learning and wisdom together within us results in wholeness, but gradually. The integration takes place when our inner and outer lives are formed into one authentic, continually deepening self-expression. The sense of being whole does not remain constant but must be maintained and nurtured through the process of integration each time we go through a significant experiential transition.

Truly being whole is fully occupying the person you are and acting out of your core with all of your knowledge, skills, experiences and insights. This is a constant challenge. The feeling of being whole is akin to the feeling of *belonging*, the feeling of being who we are and doing what we are supposed to be doing in life.

At work, we come closer to being whole when we are aware of acting with *integrity* in response to the needs of the customer, our co-workers and the world. This aspect of being whole is expressed well by Frederich Buechner in the phrase: "the place where your deep gladness meets the world's deep need."[110] Through the repeated process of reflection, we arrive at a style of integrative learning that is most suitable to our individual needs. The process of integration is as important as the end result because we cannot achieve the ultimate in personal integration at any one time. Neither can we achieve the fullness of being human all at once, but we can begin in the moments we assuredly can claim as ours.

When things come together in a product or service because of our presence and efforts, our style and insight, we can validly claim the results as our own and relish the accomplishment. Genuine appreciation of self often derives from the work we completed in spite of obstacles and obstructions. Recognizing one's contribution is different from the *self-absorption* that comes with *exaggerated pride*.

Since information is one of the defining characteristics of our historical era, it makes sense that the **first element** in the re-definition of what it means to be human derives from the *information revolution* itself. Its most immediate manifestation is its *abundance* and ubiquitous *availability*,—so much so that we feel we are being inundated by information and have difficulty coping with all that is available to us.

To maintain our humanity in the face of such a deluge of information, it is helpful for us to have new kinds of processing skills. We must be able to manage the uncertainties of so much data by *tolerance for uncertainty* and *balanced judgment* to cope with the practical demands of life and work. To manage ourselves in the era of seeming contradictory evidence, we need the *open-mindedness* of being connected to the whole while steadily retaining our *ever-expanding awareness*. To manage any potential chaos that might derive from the constantly changing informational vortex of work requires *intuitional skills*, which enable our growth and survival and allow sound decisions to be made—without having to process each piece of data separately.

To remain in touch with our inner source of values and practices, we must be aware of the potential for *unethical distortions* in any system in which we participate—and be ready to name the distortion so it does not go unnoticed. If such distortions are undetected, they become Trojan horses that lead to injustice and oppression. We must become both *searchers for truth* and *seekers of insight*. To stay current with the newly emerging information, it is necessary to see ourselves as learners and practice learning continuously. *Continuous learning* does not mean merely accumulating new information. It is an openness to new meaning coming directly into our consciousness as if we are always beginning again.

A **second characteristic** of our era is the *dizzying pace of change* that threatens to engulf us in constant activities so we lose both our capacity for and the practice of reflection. To gain the wisdom necessary for personal growth, we must master *self-reflection*. To cultivate our inner lives, we must exercise a discipline that sets aside time and energy for the practices of Interiority. To hear the messages sounding forth from the inner voices of our evolving stories, we must become used to *silence, stillness* and *solitude*.

In an era marked by incremental as well as fundamental change, we must be ready to be transformed so that we—and the systems in which we participate—are made constantly new.

A **third characteristic** of this age is a growing awareness of our responsibility for the collective or the *human community*. To manage the sense of belonging to the whole, it is necessary to creatively respond to needs as they are generated in the collective.

For example, we need to *pool our resources* constantly to take care of the multiplying populations of refugees from political unrest and natural disasters. To avoid seeing ourselves merely as controllers of specific outcomes in the workplace, it is necessary to see ourselves as *servants of the emerging whole*. To manage interrelatedness and interactivity, we must become adept at *networking* in our workplaces and at cultivating social networks for solving the problems which require the resources of the collective. This kind of networking is not merely exchanging information with others. Real networking means making our unique contributions available so that we can form communities of concern that respond to real needs around us.

To become adept at networking, we must learn from the *macro* and *micro* universes, which reveal dimensions of interrelatedness.

It is a simple, but far from easy, step to go from talking about belonging, to acknowledging the astonishing revelations of *present-day science* regarding how all things depend on one another. Almost daily, we are confronted with the seemingly infinite proportions of the natural universe. Distant, near and immanent worlds are moving around cataclysmic explosions and the re-emergence of fields of energy from which we and everything else are constituted. The Hubble telescope reveals the macrocosmic enormity of space and the electron microscope reveals microcosmic worlds at the levels of quarks and gluons. Yet both views are intertwined. Our minds reel at the implications of the recently—verified yet elusive Higgs boson—that is described as an energy field that imparts mass to elementary particles, thus enabling the universe and ourselves to exist.

This tension of being pulled outward to examine the billions of galaxies and then drawn inward to revel in the mysteries of the nano-level world engages us in both *embracing our own humanity* and in *being embraced* by the interdependent energies of the whole.

Nevertheless, although science has opened up the macro and micro universes to us, we are barely cognizant of its implications for meaning at work and the interdependence of all things. So taken are we by these revelations—which so often defy logic—that words fail us. We are left grasping for images to comprehend the vastness of these interdependent energies. Yet, we are confident there are applications of all these mysteries to our work.

At least, we should be confident in our inner resources because we have in our Interiority a capacity to comprehend and engage with it all.

For this, we need to fundamentally rethink the relationship between the human community and the rest of the natural world. Simply put, we must attribute to all things the same rights to existence as we attribute to human beings. This practice may be difficult for us to accept until we remember the words of Chief Seattle (1786 - 1866) of the Squamish tribe in Washington State: "The Earth does not belong to man; man belongs to the Earth. This we know. All things are connected like the blood which unites one family. Whatever befalls the Earth befalls the sons of the Earth. Man did not weave the web of life; he is merely a strand in it. Whatever he does to the web, he does to himself."

So, for the attribution of the same rights to happen, we need a new *story* or myth we tell ourselves about interdependence.

The traditional version told the story of an earth to be used by human beings, who saw themselves as *above* all other things and who might appropriately use or misuse the earth's resources as they saw fit. The operative word in that traditional story is *use*.

The operative word in the new story is *gift*—we *are* the gift, and we *receive* the gift from everything in our environment. We must take seriously the idea that humans are part of all natural things and we came at nearly the end of a long line of evolutionary changes that made our very lives possible. In that sense, we are the ultimately dependent beings. As the recipients of life-supporting environments, we are responsible for stewardship of the earth. Everything we have is gifted to us. We ourselves are part of the giftedness in which all things participate.

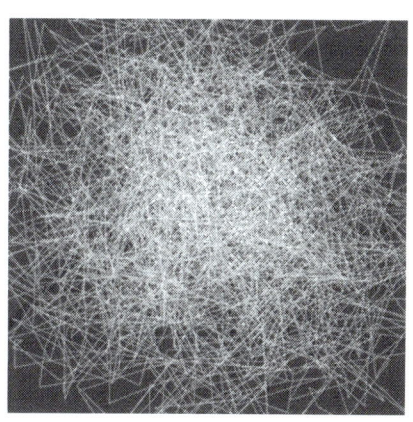

FIGURE 13: **WE ARE A STRAND IN THE WEB OF LIFE**

The reality is stark: we either cooperate and live mindfully in unity or we continue to abuse all other life forms in a seriously degraded natural environment—and eventually perish together. For our purposes here, the definition of what it means to be human in our time centers on the acceptance of the *fundamental interdependence of everything*. That sense of interdependence applies to all that surrounds us in the accomplishment of our work. Further, the awareness of this interdependence is necessary for us to apply all our resources to the fulfillment of that work.

The Resources of Interiority

The major resource that encapsulates Interiority is *the Soul*. I describe soul as the *intuitive capacity to align one's life with the great mystery*. Soul, as intuitive capacity, searches beyond the rational discursive mind for immediate *connection* with the ineffably transcendent and immanent dimensions of our existence. Soul allows us to become *renewed in our inner lives* and to productively *connect* to all things *through our work*.

Aligning one's life with mystery means to engage and raise awareness through *prayer*, *belief*, *ritual*, *ceremony* and especially through the *contributions* we make in our own *lives* and *work*. The soul is the ultimate guide for us. More than any external institution, code, regulation or belief system, even those that purport to be the voices of the gods, our soul's code is the arbiter upon which we can depend.

The agenda which the soul has in mind for us extends over the long term, includes every experience, expresses itself through multiple means and focuses on our health and wholeness. The *language* of the soul includes *dreams*, *intuitions*, waking *imaginations*, *patterns* of thought and behavior, prompts of our *conscience*, *interactions* with others, *turns of events*, the *journeys* we take and the work that is done on and through us.

The human capacity of soul means that a *benign energy* moves at the core of *reality*, which engenders a greater *complexity of consciousness* and *new forms of life*.

The second resource of Interiority is *Heart*. Heart describes the capacity to be *fully human*, to *love oneself and others*, and *commiserate* with those who suffer, to be *hopeful* for better things to happen and to bind relationships into communities of *common concern* and *action*.

The third resource is *Emotions*. Emotions refers to the capacity to *rejoice* over good things, *be sad* over unfortunate happenings, *feel fear* over impending danger, experience *anger* over injustice and *desire unity* with loved ones. Emotions are the human capacities for experiencing the diverse offerings life brings our way.

A fourth resource of Interiority is *Imagination*. Our capacity for imagination allows us to *picture a range of possibilities* in any situation. Imagination *allows us to choose* from those possibilities some alternative courses of action. Imagination also allows us to *explore the outcomes* of each of the possible actions before we make a choice or decision.

A fifth resource of Interiority is *Intuition*... the capacity to *sense* what is happening and, without fully using our thought processes, to *move into action*. Intuition is useful in *protecting* us in cases of potential danger or of going along with an opportunity to gain some benefit.

The first way of making these resources of Interiority effective is to *act from the center of self-awareness*. When we act from our centers, our energies are not wastefully dispersed reacting to outside stimuli. Acting from the center means we choose to be grounded in self-awareness while we are doing work. When centered, we have all our capacities available to respond effectively to whatever needs arise.

Another way of acting from our center is through *authentic self-expression*...which is avoiding communications-related behavior that smacks of self-deception. Self-deception is a subtle way of distorting reality. Unseating it requires committed and continuous self-reflection in order to fully understand the biases that distort perception.

Taking full responsibility for our actions is another way of acting from our center. Even though we may be greatly influenced by others, we stand fully accountable for what we do. This ensures that we act according to our values while making decisions and we do our work in the way we know best. In addition, if we reflect on these experiences, we understand ourselves as *learning, changing, growing* and *integrating* while in the process of doing our work. In this way, we affirm our *contribution to* the *stakeholders* and *society*.

At the same time, there is a dimension of soul that is characteristic of the organization. When an organization is founded, the driving force is usually the desire to make *profit*. Another driving force is often to remedy a need in the world by way of *products or services* the organization would supply. These energies can be experienced as a spirit that characterizes the organization. Workers can continually draw inspiration and energy from being connected to that spirit as it pervades the organization's activities.

At best, such a spirit emphasizes *service*, *collaboration* and *achievement*.

This core element of spirit can also be called the soul of the organization. Soul strengthens identity, makes room for change, guides innovation and provides stability to the organizational culture. If we identify with the soul of the organization, we tend to take responsibility for personal and professional development for co-workers and for the impact of the organization on the world.

In assuming responsibility for our own inner worlds and for the soul of the organization, we are creating meaning in the work we do.

Foundation #2: We are Makers of Meaning

We are makers of meaning. This is the second foundation of Interiority. This is in contradistinction to the idea that meaning comes to us as an adjunct characteristic of doing work. "A maker of meaning" derives from an *emphasis on* our *choices* in life, our *behaviors* at work and in terms of a kind of productivity reflective of who we are. In that sense, we make our meaning by putting our unique stamp on the work we do, how we do it and the lives that we live.

Of course, meaning is also an intangible but real aspect of work that provides depth, energy and direction to the worker. However, historically, workers did not always have the choice of being makers of meaning. Traditionally, the impact of work was almost immediately evident from the environment in which we worked. For example, as a baker, I would be able to find meaning in baking loaves of bread so people might be sustained. The transition of workers into becoming *makers of meaning* took place over several centuries, beginning in 17th Century England. Prior to that, people believed the world was an orderly place and everyone fitted into a naturally predetermined structure. As Joyce Appleby pointed out in her book, *The Relentless Revolution*, in the year "1520, in order to produce food, 80% of the people worked the land.[111] One hundred families could produce enough food in a regular season to feed 125 families."[112] By 1850, "the farming population dropped to 25 % of the whole." This meant famine would be overcome; people could feed themselves and take risks with their savings in the development of commercial activities.

In this agricultural revolution, the image of human nature changed from being *fated to work* in a predetermined structure to being *in charge of one's life* and choosing to work in a certain venture. Not only did the notion of a predetermined orderly world fall, but the idea began to rise that people could claim their own destiny and make their own meaning. Again, according to Appleby, "among the welter of revolutions in the early modern centuries, that (which occurred) in agriculture is the one with the most profound consequences."[113]

Today, most of us find meaning, not so much in work itself, but in paychecks. But not all workers can connect to either the traditional kind of meaning or our modern meaning (money for consumption of goods). And it is most dispiriting that certain kinds of work are so structured as to be dull, repetitious and endless—and seemingly devoid of meaning.

We can easily imagine what happens to those workers whose work lacks meaning. They lose interest and begin to dislike working altogether. In which case, one would hope they would either make personally creative efforts to find meaning in their work or find other work meaningful to them. In other words, it is up to us as workers to discover meaning in our work by our own efforts.

By uncovering worth or by investing it in our work, we make our own meaning.

In the usual discussions of what is meaningful at work, *we say we are seekers of meaning*, as if the meaning comes from outside. But we are not merely seekers. *We are makers of meaning* when we enter into a *personal engagement* with our work. We make meaning every time we connect because, as Margaret Wheatley says, "everything is always new and unique to us."[114]

Workers becoming makers of meaning is the opposite of having the meaning of our work defined for us by others. Becoming a maker of meaning entails doing the necessary reflection so we can *uncover meaning for ourselves*. In this way, we take responsibility, not only for our tasks in the workplace but also the integration of that meaning within our consciousness.

To help us in becoming our own sources of meaning, we need to create a fresh and correct *vocabulary* for naming things, especially in the context of work. As the Chinese say, "The beginning of wisdom is to call things by their right names." With *words*, we *make meaning*. With words, we also *communicate meaning*. The words of our conversations enable our relationships. Words can also confine people within narrow boundaries of thought and action. Words can even imprison people through descriptions that drain them of their humanity. Rather than imprisoning or confining people, we need to create a new vocabulary that allows for the expansion of the inner world of the worker and the meaning of work.

The first place to uncover deeper meaning at work is in the work itself that we might call *good*.

We do not usually consider the work we do as something good in itself. However, *work becomes good* when it provides an *effective solution* to someone's real need and when it *leads us deeper* into our inner selves. We usually consider our work to be a means of achievement, a means of earning a living and supporting a family and a means of gaining status in society. However, when we think of the work itself as something that is good, we are probing below its usefulness to examine how we are changed by it. It is there that we discover much about ourselves by analyzing our strengths and weaknesses as they appear in our performance. We realize that much of our growth happens to us through doing the work.

One's work can be a *contribution*, a *connection* with others and an *expression* of one's deepest self. Work can elevate us, help us build our communities, engage us in the mysterious energies that move us all and generate energies within us for our unique contributions.

Work can be considered a sacred endeavor as it adds to the good that is done in the world.

The good achieved by us in our work is a *spiritual practice*. In fact, the act of working is a spiritual practice. In these times that seem to lack meaning, we hear much about spirituality in the workplace. This usually means the observation of beliefs or the practice of rituals or routines in the workplace. These practices aim at connecting workers to a major religion or to non-faith based concepts that go under the name of spirituality. But such externalization into ritual seems to sidestep the point of the *engagement with the work itself as a spiritual act* through which we are fulfilled "in our essential being," as described by Karlfried Graf Durckheim.[115] As such, work requires awareness more than ritual, discipline more than explanation and appreciation more than acknowledgment of pragmatic functionality.

Work requires respect for our practical situation, leads us to gratitude for the opportunity and satisfaction when the product is effectively used or the service is satisfactorily performed.

Everything we touch receives our stamp, carries within it our imprint and manifests to the world that we came, worked, left our mark and moved on. In our work, we can see our shape in our unique approach and character stamped on the results. In our work, we are revealed in all of our *magnificence* and *flaws*, *creativity* and *fatigue*, alive with *expectations, frustrations* and *times of near-destruction*.

Three psychic links between oneself and one's work suggest themselves for examination:

Involvement, Alignment and Appreciation.

Involvement

Being involved with our work means our energies are focused on the fulfillment of the need that requires attention at work. The kind of involvement necessary for good work is that which absorbs us completely during our work and in some way before and after we complete our assignments. Involvement with work does not mean merely doing it but *joining* with the work as it is being accomplished. Even though we physically leave the workplace, we bring our work with us at the end of the day—not as a distraction but as an opportunity—so when inspiration happens, we can frame it for retention and later implementation in our work.

The first psychic link, *involvement*, is subdivided into *six elements*:

- **Presence** is a requisite element of good work and means I am here and available to the greatest extent possible in the circumstances of the workplace. Physical presence is only the first requirement, for good work is necessarily followed by the orientation of my intellectual, emotional, psychological and spiritual energies on the work at hand.

FIGURE 14: **ENGAGING CUSTOMER SERVICE**

Physical presence requires that I maintain my body in a healthy way so that when I am at work I am aware of when my physical being feels comfortable and when it might be overstressed and in need of rest and recovery. When I am present in this fashion, the work opens up an infinite universe of possibilities so who I am has an *infinite character* as well as a *practical impact*.

- **Attention** means bending all my faculties toward an understanding and a comprehension of what is involved in the work. Paying attention means I constantly choose to attend to the needs of the work and avoid becoming distracted by peripheral concerns. Attention is particularly necessary at the beginning stage so I notice everything and consider everything I must do to accomplish the work completely and with the requisite quality. Taking time and paying attention to the planning of my work ensures I do not overlook any important factor and I proceed with each task in the proper order. When I pay attention to the key details, I am entering deeply into the flow of energy that infuses every aspect of the work and everything. When I am paying attention, I am not wasting time, playing games or otherwise engaged in trivial distractions.

- **Awareness** is remaining alert to the aspects of my work that continually reveal themselves at different levels and at different times. During the moments of unimpeded awareness, *inspiration* tends to strike, take shape and suggest itself as a possible solution. Inspiration can happen at any time, in any place and from any source. I must maintain sufficient awareness to retain that inspiration so it can be applied when needed. Awareness also includes not working with undue haste to get the job done as quickly as possible, instead allowing me to be used in the service of achieving quality.

- **Interest** in my work arises from the *perceived value* of the work itself and of the customers for whom the work is a necessary good. Being interested in my work means I commit to it, am willingly engaged in doing what is required and in expending the energies necessary for its completion. When I am interested in my work, a bond develops that allows me to do that work in creative ways, to push the boundaries of how it was previously conceived —and to do that without becoming tired or stressed.

- **Caring** means I have a deep *respect* for the work I do; I am sensitive to its demands and I form an emotional bond with the work and the results I achieve. Caring also means I actively invest energy in framing and prioritizing tasks so I can effectively complete each task in turn and finally, the whole work.

Caring such as this is visible to all who see the results or are the recipients of my services. A caring approach is palpable, especially when my performance seems to flow from a place deep within me, from beyond the framework of my rational mind, aligning itself within the flow of all other natural things.

- *Identification* is about positioning myself within the work so I see and act from the same need for completion as the work itself. Identification means I do what is *necessary* and avoid what is superfluous. When I identify with the work, in moments of encounter, I can see not just from the point of view of the end-user. I also identify the *past circumstances* that led us here and with the future people and events that will be influenced because of what I do and how I do it.

Alignment

Being aligned with my work means I adopt the *values*, *goals* and *processes* of the organization to which I belong and which generates the work I am assigned. This does not mean I force myself to be in constant agreement with the organization's management, but even in my disagreement I make my energies available for the fulfillment of the work. The kind of alignment necessary for good work is that which absorbs me in some way before, during and after completion.

Alignment, the second psychic link between me and my work, is subdivided into five elements:

- *Responsiveness* means I adapt my mind, my skills, my actions and my attitudes so my work gets done in the way only I can do it. Responsiveness is using all of my resources, holding back nothing that might be useful in the fulfillment of my tasks.

- *Receptivity* deals with the urgency that flows from the work itself that tells me what needs to be done. If I am receptive, I will realize everything is waiting to draw my attention to the tasks, to the tools, to the challenges and clues unfolding the story of my work.

    Receptivity means I am open to the messages that randomly flow from work (or from any source) and that I receive them with respect. Being receptive keeps me sufficiently silent and observant about the requirements of the work so that I can maintain myself free from distraction. Receptivity also means that I keep open the communication channels for absorbing information and intuitive warnings about potential mistakes. An attitude of waiting helps me to not rush to the first solution that suggests itself and to constantly consider the variety of possible futures. If I persist in my efforts, out of this variety will eventually come a solution that succeeds.

- *Flow* means I enter smoothly into the first step, then the next and so on. Flow is the mark of work that is well ordered and proceeds from beginning to end with an outer and an inner integrity. Flow also includes leaps of inspiration that have no obvious connection to the logical steps of the usual work process but emerge like the notes from a jazz musician's strings, unbidden but arranged harmoniously as if by invisible fingers.

- *Creativity* means I constantly seek new approaches to my work, test options that suggest themselves, apply new tools and eliminate unnecessary steps. In a sense, creativity is less technological than it is artistic, finding its artistic form when it is of *sensual rather than rational* origin. Creativity seeks a truth that cannot be expressed in logical sequences but in what pleases the senses and the intuitive connection between the self and the task. Art in work derives from that which is essentially human such as deeply-felt *harmony* in form, color, design and utility.

- *Expression* is a check on emerging results so I can appreciate the integrity that exists between me and my work. If I work from what is true for me, I will easily see that truth reflected in the results and such integrity contributes to making the work a useful product or service. This integrity serves to ensure the work is done with the quality required by the work itself.

Appreciation

Appreciation is a stance of being grateful to the organization and the stakeholders for the opportunities afforded to me in my work. This attitude of gratitude supports a constructive and positive climate in the workplace, and goes a long way toward smoothing out differences that may crop up.

Appreciation, the third psychic link, is subdivided into these four elements:

- *Impact* is a keen sense that I am in the process of changing all things through my work and being changed in myself—even if the quality of my participation is minimal. Growth-producing changes that happen within me while I am at work are as important as whatever I can accomplish through my workplace achievements. These changes have an enduring impact on how all things evolve while my practical achievements at work contribute to the progress of the human community.

- ***Participation*** in the specific tasks of my work allows me to contribute to the practical results, to cooperate in the development of all natural forms and to align myself with the great ongoing mystery of life. Through my work, I influence the shapes of everything that happens, even if my immediate awareness of that impact is non-existent. Workers influence each other through the performance of work and on subliminal levels by their attitudes—whether those attitudes are positive or negative. My work carries my influence into the next generations.

- ***Satisfaction*** happens when I have completed a specific work and experience a sense of gladness in that accomplishment. Such deeply felt joy comes from my contribution to the fulfillment of some need in my community by virtue of the work I have done.

- ***Growth*** takes place when I am shaped by the doing of the work in such a way I become aware of myself as belonging to this evolving world full of mysteries revealed within me. I grow through my work when I learn something at which I could never have arrived had I not been present and involved. I grow when I *appreciate my own being* and *more fully occupy the space that is myself* and when I am grateful for the opportunity to be of service to the community in the way unique to me.

After reviewing the specific language of the psychic links and elements of good work, we might assume that we have named everything possible about what constitutes good work. However, we would be remiss if we did not recognize the work of *animate beings* in whose community of workers we can count ourselves. All animate beings have a life cycle that includes doing the work of maintaining life. As you know, many animals hunt to get food, mate to produce young, nest to rear their young and when they come to the end of their lives they die and return to the earth from which they came. When we become aware that we are doing our work as part of a larger community of living and working beings, it assumes a greater meaning. We take our place among all species as equals, at least from the point of view of working to sustain our respective lives.

The activity of work provides us with a sense of comfort in belonging in the community of all animate beings, busily at work. Otherwise, the context of workers can feel empty and without inspiration. But when we become aware of the marvelously and intensively busy panoply of species in the natural environment around us, we might be prompted to become more productive and creative. By naming their contributions, we afford them the respect that is due.

Finally, we need a *language* of the heart, of our physical beings, of our emotions, our relationships, morality, society and all the stakeholders that eloquently describes this important dimension of the great mystery of our lives: Our work. Developing a new vocabulary presents the opportunity to define our lives in terms of openness to transformation. If we use a *transformative vocabulary* to describe the human, then the organizations that form around those words will reflect these processes. Not only are we and the organization open to single transformations, but our creativity will become more fruitful when we have the consciousness of participating in a series of, in Swimme and Berry's term, "sequential transformations."[116]

> *When the wise man learns the Way*
> *He tries to live by it.*
> *When the average man learns the Way*
> *He lives by only part of it.*
> *When the fool learns the Way*
> *He laughs at it.*
> *Yet if the fool did not laugh at it,*
> *It would not be the Way.*
> *Indeed; if you are seeking the Way*
> *Listen for the laughter of fools.*
>
> Lao Tzu

My Story – I Grew Up with Iron

I grew up with iron. From the rust-colored water that flowed from washing my hands at dusk; to the ponderous, grinding racket of the girder meeting the plates on the stanchion tops; to the striking of the blazing arc where molten steel ran from the welding rod, I knew the sounds of them. I knew, without looking, the sounds of tin, cast iron, aluminum, copper, brass, galvanized plate steel, which of the anvils was being hit by what hammer, on what iron, whether it was blazing hot or just coming in from the rain and cold. I knew the sound of a ballpein hammer and the sledge as they alternately beat a rhythm on the white heat of a horseshoe being formed on the anvil face, the muffled hammer beat shaping the heel-caulks on the step and the rising timbre ringing all the way down the tapering horn.

I knew the sound of rust that slowed the wheels on a mowing machine, that had almost welded the nuts on the mowing bar, that promised skinned knuckles

> before it budged, that shook like red chaff dropping from a harrow. I knew the sound of rust when it was ground into speckled grime that built little mounds on the bench under the whirling grindstone or blasted abroad 'til it hung wavering in the sunlit air and formed a black paste in your nose that you only discovered in the sudden silence when the roaring of the sandblaster stopped.
>
> The touch of the steel was enough to tell me what strength it would take to bend or break it or if there was a weakness or a crack in the bar, making it useless. Growing up, I knew iron just like the shoemaker and the saddler know their leather, the draper his cloth, the farmer his animals. Each of us knew our medium because it meant work and work meant sweat from dawn to dusk. It also meant trouble as sure as the day was long, sighs of pride, frustration and grunts of "never good enough"—but always worth enough to draw you tall..no mean lie unworthy of the task or blemish on the name.
>
> Still I sought the wonder beyond the iron thing. I was drawn beyond the scrolls and curlicues, past the punchers, ploughs and pruning hooks, the drills, cutters and welding rods, the latticed fence, scaffolds climbing tall, and tools of all description 'til meaning unfolded in the seeking itself. I sought that which was missing in me until I knew the state of seeking was what was missing. I was going on a journey in life and realizing that the journey is the teacher, the lesson and the pupil taught. When I gradually became aware, the seeking did not stop but enlarged my scale of endless knowing and of being taught by life.
>
> One cannot learn or be taught something until the pre-conditions for knowing have been experienced and then the insight dawns. The Chinese saying goes, "When the student is ready, the teacher appears."

My Story - Reflections

This is a book about work and the question I pose again is: *what will provide work with meaning?* The answer is in the *doing* of the work. Not just any doing but doing with an eye to what is missing and constantly sought. The Japanese have a word for what is missing in us. The word is *sukima*, meaning space. When we don't have it, we know it. When we don't have that space within us, we have no way of growing.

Jungian psychologists have their own word for the thing that is missing: *shadow*. It is what is repressed—and no more than a shadow—because it is the integrated shadow that provides us with the golden means of living. Lovers have many words for when the beloved is absent. They wax poetic, yearning for the one who is missing because the loved one is part of them, closer than the marrow of their bones, than the sight of their eyes, than the breath to be breathed, than the song unsung.

Loin-clothed holy men, stand one-legged at Ganges' edge, needing no distraction, contemplating, contemplating, desiring only what fills them with wonder. Still, they share a sense of what is missing, and in the desiring, the contemplation itself makes them whole.

We have so much at work and we are *still missing the important pieces*, that which connects what is deep within us with everything else. The search is soul-driven, an insatiable thirst, an itch that does not give way to any amount of scratching—and its unreasonable demands drive us to do the unreasonable.

The search is *not the same for all*. Everyone is attracted to a different treasure and searches in different ways. We must search for that which speaks to an inner need. The search is endless and the more serious and inward it becomes the less comprehensible it appears. It is like the descent into the nature of physical things. At the level of quantum mechanics, logic and reason are no longer applicable, but the experience is nonetheless more than valuable. When you reach the point where you hear the laughter of fools, even if not reassured of the goal, you might take heart that you are on the right road.

Work is there in front of us but what will it take to turn the work into wonder?

Your Story

What then about you, the reader? For greater understanding of your life-direction, what was the home environment that provided your growth? What attitudes, beliefs, values, behaviors and relationships did you absorb from your family members? How have you lived that early programming in your work? In what ways has that environment been a detriment to your development and how did you work at overcoming its influence? In what ways has that environment been a benefit in your development and how did you work at increasing its influence?

Foundation #3: Learning from the Energies of Shadow, Paradox and Chaos

The Energies of Interiority

As explained in Foundation #1, Life Integration Quest, the human characteristics of soul, heart, emotions, imagination and intuition (Resources) are available to us, in varying degrees through Interiority. A more specific way of connecting Interiority and wholeness is through the energies available from within. Briefly, these energies can be divided into three types, namely: (1) **Familiar**, (2) **Unfamiliar** (3) **Existential**.

(1) **Familiar:** These energies, which are generally known to us, are: *physical, mental, emotional, psychic, relational* and *communitarian*. These energies are readily available while we work but they still require effort for effective use.

(2) **Unfamiliar:** Among these energies are those that are blocked, inaccessible, lost, depleted in distractions and addictive habits, denied, or consumed in reactive behavioral patterns— all lodged in our shadow area. Here, I provide a brief explanation of each of these unfamiliar energies.

Blocked: As the name suggests, we cannot use these energies because of unhealthy habits of thinking, feeling or behaving that effectively blocks usage. An example of a blockage might be the belief that I do not have some capability, such as a particular type of leadership, which in fact I do possess. However, my belief acts as a blockage to its usage.

Inaccessible: As the name suggests, we cannot gain access to these energies, perhaps because we have repressed them. It may be that we associate them with what is taboo or evil…anything that nullifies their usage. An example might be that I identify sexual fantasies with what is forbidden to me and, therefore, potential energies of creative imagination might become unavailable.

Lost: As the name suggests, because we have learned that the expression of certain feelings were disallowed or merited stern reprimands, we have denied their existence and they have become as it were, lost to us. An example might be that I learned that exuberant play was not allowed and, thereafter, I found playful curiosity very difficult.

Depleted: In this case, I find that I am without energy because I fill up my time with distractions and other activities that draw me outside of myself. The result is that my energies are drained away and generally go un-replenished. For example, I might be so distracted by playing with gadgets and games that I have no energy for serious work or potentially growth-ful pursuits.

(3) **Existential:** These are the energies that are associated with limitations in our daily existence. We are human, which means mortal, limited in capabilities, subject to mistakes, prone to pain and to what eventually happens to all living things, namely, decline, death and dissolution.

Counter-intuitively, none of these existential conditions are without meaning. Moreover, if approached realistically, these conditions can be wellsprings of energy. I emphasize the term *realistically* because our orientation is to see life through rose-tinted glasses or to not accept these realities. Naturally, our tendency is to avoid thinking we might become ill, suffer or die. The potential energies are those that arise from acceptance of limitation. Gruesome as it sounds, that is why ancient monks placed a skull on their desks with the inscription, *memento mori* (remember death). The idea was that they would be motivated and get busy. "He who is not busy being born is busy dying," warns Bob Dylan.

Nevertheless, because of our non-acceptance of such realities, we have the *unused energies* of the *shadow, paradox, chaos, pain, suffering* and *life-death cycles*. From here on, I will be discussing this foundational aspect of how we can liberate these energies from within and enable ourselves to become whole through our work.

This is the great work of our lives, the foundation upon which all other great work is done.

Shadow

Here, I discuss *the shadow, shadow material* and *shadow integration* at some length because of their importance in providing a hitherto untapped reservoir of energies for achieving a vibrant Interiority and creativity at work. Initially, this section focuses on the interplay between two dimensions of our lives, namely, the *ego*, which is concerned with doing and the external world, and the needs of the *self* (soul), which is concerned with being and our inner world.

During the *first half of our lives*, we are primarily concerned with ego needs and doing things in order to achieve work goals and establish a place in society. During this period, the ego is concerned with self-presentation, power, control and order. When we advance in some organization or in society, we usually assume a position of responsibility. Through the power afforded to us in that position of responsibility, we attempt to achieve targeted outcomes in a predictable and controlled world and by and large we are able to do so.

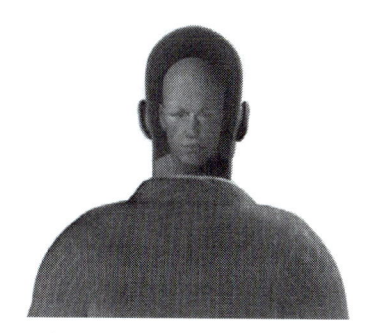

FIGURE 15: **THE INNER PERSON IS ALWAYS PRESENT**

During the *second half of our lives*, the world becomes less predictable because of our growing awareness of limitations in life (including menopause, passages and the resurgence of shadow material). During the second half, we discover that the once predictable tends to change in disconcerting ways...and keeps on changing. During this august time of life, we find ourselves paying more attention to the balance between the ego and the needs of self. Indeed, one will seek a kind of psychological adjustment through the physical changes of life (menopause, male and female) that usually happen to people around the ages of 40 to 50 and onwards. Those transformations can be thought of as a *coming to consciousness* and entering the stage of finally growing up.

The transformations that usually happen during this change of life are not tasks that can be done in quick linear steps or in a controlled sequence but often involve doing the opposite of our previous pattern of behaviors. What is much more interesting for our topic of Interiority is that this passage to a more mature way of living and working signals the rise within us of hitherto inaccessible energies that have great potential for our growth. Because of the passage journeys, these energies, which were probably repressed during the first half of our lives but which never went away, become more readily available to us. Harnessing these energies is known as shadow work. Carl Jung coined the term *shadow* to refer to repressed energies that seek expression during the second half of our lives. As he pointed out, "the underdeveloped side of our selves (shadow) seeks recognition and integration so that we become more fully whole in our shadow humanity."[117]

During the emergence of shadow material, enormous energies are potentially released for the second half of our lives. The emergence of the shadow then offers us new opportunities for fulfillment of the tasks of maturity, wholeness and integration. If, during the first half of our lives, we were drawn to achievements in the external world and then realized that the real life-work is only half complete, the shadow allows us to turn inward to engage with becoming whole as a person. However, this task is far from easy.

Because shadow material has been repressed, when the energies of the shadow rise within us, we usually become uncomfortable. These energies and expressions are unfamiliar to us and threaten our ego that usually seeks refuge in habitual patterns. Furthermore, there were good reasons why we repressed those feelings in the first place, and when they emerge in later life, they remain as difficult to face as ever. For example, during childhood, in order to be perceived as *good*, it is probable we had to suppress risky behaviors and feelings, but in that suppression we may have lost touch with the feelings themselves. In becoming re-acquainted with them, we discover they are no easier to manage.

In order to be whole, the challenge is to restore and integrate the lost parts of ourselves. When we separated from those good but risky elements during childhood, we find ourselves on a journey of re-integration with them during passage periods—and thereafter. Even though we may be intimidated by the integration process, our ever-trustworthy soul remembers and pulls us toward integrity. We have to trust the promptings of our souls. The soul's quest is aided by forces of which we are mostly unconscious. Some of those forces cause disequilibrium in us, but we need that imbalance to eventually come together.

For this integration to take place, we may need to come out of a cocoon of inherited idealism, belief and admonishment to more fully answer our own call.

In the early part of our lives, it is usual that our patterns of behavior—in living and working—have been predicated on the assumption that there is no such thing as shadow in our lives. It may be we have lived in that awareness for so long we only look outward for opportunities to grow. We don't expect the kinds of inner tensions that accompany the emergence of shadow. But, the fact is everyone has shadow material, and most of us are not aware how those energies influence us. Therefore, it is no surprise that we resist the encounter with the repressed and unacknowledged parts of ourselves that has come to be called shadow work.

If we are not overly intimidated by these energies, we can use them to *turn inward* to *deepen self-awareness* and *self-acceptance*. We can uncover new and *creative expressions* of our work. We can *consolidate key relationships* through a higher quality presence. We can assume more active *responsibility* for the wider communities to which we belong.

In other words, if we do our shadow work well, we assume a deeper level of ownership of the work we do and of the world of our times.

However, there is one further complication in working with our shadow energies, which is that *not all shadow material is constructive*. Much of the shadow material can be destructive and generate behaviors and outcomes that we might call evil. This material is generally termed *dark shadow*. Such evil can happen when we *do not acknowledge* our shadow material and *project onto others* that which we refuse to take ownership of in ourselves. One example of this is the "angry person" who sows discontent wherever he goes. You and I know this person.

My Story – Code of Silence

I met him during the first spring of my Seminary formation on the stretch of ground that served as our playing field deep in the New Hampshire woods. We were playing touch football. For an uninitiated Irish recruit, this meant that merely touching the man with the ball would end the down—and there would be no "rough" play. On offense, I was instructed to take my place on the line and stop the oncoming horde from getting to our quarterback. I found myself face-to-face with a burly senior seminarian, but rather than tackling him I had been instructed to drop in front of his legs so he would fall over me. Dutifully, I did so and it worked. Down he went and our line moved well forward.

This being a Seminary, lessons about Christian politeness were the order of the day, so I did not anticipate a counterattack. But, on the next down it came in a ferocious assault of fists, elbows, knees and shoulders, so now I was the one who was truly flattened…and our line moved backward. As we regrouped, I was moved off the line and became a decoy end. The burly one proceeded to notch up other victims, but as others learned from their own experience they gave him a wide berth.

The burly one was big and well-muscled. He was a good athlete and an excellent academic, but his manner was intimidating. Most everything he did seemed to be an invitation to conflict, not un-reminiscent of a bully. People were on guard around him, but he could put on an amicable display of good behavior when the occasion called for it. Eventually, some sharp-eyed clerics took note of his displays of aggression and tendency to violence. Shortly afterwards he was gone. His reputation for violent outbursts was the cause of his removal.

As we gathered for meditation the next morning, the seminarians breathed a collective sigh of relief when we noticed his empty seat. The Rector had words of warning for us. In brief, he said it was not charitable to allow such behavior to continue unreported—it was our duty to report such behavior patterns. He said that it was the opposite of kindness to become so tolerant of bad behavior that a code of silence might grow around members of the group. If it were left unacknowledged and untreated, he said such behavior would become a danger to the rest and to the individual in question.

My Story – Reflections

You might expect in exceptional circumstances, as in a Seminary, such individuals would be eliminated in the testing grounds of the Novitiate. But the truth is, they show up there just as they do in any workplace. Individuals with unhealthy attitudes and un-integrated behavior patterns often slip past the usual safeguards and they can contaminate workplaces, rectories and monasteries. The usual pattern is built on finding fault in others and arguing that the causes of their own discontent derive from the behaviors of others. In actuality, the cause of their discontent is actually within them and most often derives from conflicted, immature and un-integrated shadow material.

Generally, we can understand and accept a certain amount of tension in people that simmers from leftover resentment due to ethnic persecution and discrimination, as well as unresolved family issues. We can learn to cope with such patterns in ourselves while we make sure that they are not openly destructive of others.

This is another reason for becoming aware of the *ethnic oppression* and *negative familial patterns* that are part of our own history. These histories require us to reflect, understand and let go of the dysfunctional habits.

Your Story

What then, dear reader, about your *experience* of angry or even violent people? Was your life perhaps marked by the anger and violence of others? Can you recall how your *encounter* with an angry person influenced your relationships? What *explanation* do you give yourself about the reasons some people are angry or violent? What *approach* have you developed toward expressions of anger, especially in someone who is expected to know better?

How has anger or reactivity *figured in your own life*? Have you suffered from *your own difficult-to-control surges of anger* in your work (and workplace)? What have you *learned* about yourself from feeling deep anger? In what ways have you *come to terms* with your anger or displays of violence?

Perhaps nowhere is the shadow presence more evident than in the repressed lives that we live because somehow, we learned not to express ourselves in ways that might upset our parents—or others. For example, we didn't yell wildly because parents or neighbors didn't like it. The result: in pleasing parental figure(s), we suppressed our natural effervescent energies. For repressing those innate energies, we paid a price. Unfortunately, for many of us those repressed energies morphed into feelings of guilt, shame, anger, sadness, depression, exhaustion and the like.

We paid the price in three ways: first, by *losing contact* with some of our *naturally expressive energies* (because of the negative feelings associated with them). Secondly, the *guilt, shame* and *difficult-to-manage emotions* we adopted as a cover-up. Thirdly, in our *workplaces*, the early childhood dramas of repression and projection that play out over and over again in all our relationships—with self, with supervisors and with co-workers.

When we don't recognize those difficult-to-manage feelings or when we deny them, we often project them unto others. In a workplace where conflicts abound, our repressed shadow material can be projected onto our supervisors and co-workers. We see in their behaviors or attitudes what we *do not like in ourselves*. For example, if my supervisor reminds me of my father, I may project complex feelings of wanting to please him/her and at the same time experience rage or resentment at his/her instruction to do a particular task. Who has not, on some occasion, allowed feelings of resentment, jealousy and anger to boil over into behaviors subversive of authority figures?

We can easily recognize that even mildly irritating behaviors in our supervisors can trigger major negative reactions toward them. Such feelings are not evil in themselves, but if they turn into destructive behaviors toward others, we can wreak destruction all around us. Imagine a workplace where repressed shadow material finds expression in continuous cycles of conflict between workers and supervisors.

Acrimonious relationships are often evidence of *un-integrated*—and *projected*—*shadow* material in individuals and groups.

The question is then, how do we handle shadow material that is potentially destructive of ourselves and others? The following steps for integrating shadow energies are valid whether we are dealing with constructive or potentially destructive shadow material.

Awareness is the First Step

It is not easy for us to become aware of what belongs in our shadow material because we have denied or repressed those energies for so long. One sample method is to ask: How am I carrying on the *unlived life of my parents*? The answer might reveal that I am living according to their agenda. Perhaps they wanted me to become a lawyer and so I became one even though I wanted to be an artist.

I may also be acting out their unfinished agendas in the workplace. I might find myself behaving as a good lawyer should, even though I am angry at having to do so... and feel drawn toward artistic wood products, for example.

If we can do this kind of reflection, we can at least become aware of how our shadow material is influencing how we behave. For example, if we find ourselves striving to achieve educational goals our parents always sought but never achieved, we might discover our motivations were to fulfill their longings and in doing so we might have missed our own goals and calls. If we can become aware of such misplaced motivations at work in ourselves, we can make choices that clarify our own agenda in life and work and how we might live more authentically from that base. Such choices and integrative work is referred to as *bright shadow material* because it is usually derived from experiences of things that were good but incomplete.

Obviously, apart from our relationships with parents, there are many other ways in which shadow material may have been formed within us. In any case, it is part of being responsible for our own growth to continue to examine instances in which our shadow may be operative, whether that might be as a result of our bright or dark shadow. This is a never-ending task but is made easier by having a deep respect for the light and the dark in us and in all things.

Such *deep respect* is the *second key* to handling shadow material.

Awareness of and respect for the shadow dimension of our inner lives can lead to the release of enormous energies for creativity and wholeness in us. This possibility is the subject of the illustration in Figure 16, which depicts these energies as a golden flower in the darkness of the surrounding shadow.

FIGURE 16: **GOLDEN FLOWER IMAGE DRAWN BY PATIENT OF CARL JUNG**

Embrace our Own Humanity

Respect for self is an important part of living comfortably with our inner selves. Robert A. Johnson says it well in his book, *Owning Your Own Shadow*, "We must come to a full-blooded embrace of our own humanity, not a one-sided that has no vitality or life."[118] Embracing our humanity means respecting and accepting everything about ourselves—including the light and the dark aspects. Johnson continues: "wherever we find ourselves, we need to honor the part of life that lies in shadow. We are presently dealing with the accumulation of a whole society that has worshipped its light side and refused the dark and this residue appears as war, economic chaos, strikes and racial intolerance."[119]

Inner Dialogue – Based on Requesting Guidance from Our Soul

The third key in working with shadow material is to establish a *dialogue* between our two parts, namely *ourselves* and the part represented in the *shadow image*. For example, if I find myself in conflict with someone with whom I have only a passing relationship, such as the person at the checkout counter, I can examine whatever is operating in me that triggered the conflict. The easy part is acknowledging that whatever the other person did or said *triggered a response* in me, which was out of proportion to the nature of the event or to the relationship.

It becomes a little more difficult to proceed to the next step: understanding for example, that what was triggered in me was the conflict I had as a child with my father.

> **My Story – Drawing Wrath**
>
> I considered myself a dutiful son, diligent, hard-working and helpful in the forge, the house and at the church, helping the neighbors and anyone who needed assistance. No matter, however innocent, incidents such as the one I am about to relate can sometimes turn awry and undo hard-earned respect.
>
> One Sunday afternoon, I came running down the yard and out into the street, right in front of our car. It was an unthinking act but it drew my father's wrath. I didn't know it but he was about to drive off with some guests and was startled to see me suddenly in front of the car. His perception was I might have been hurt and mine was I was only being playful. He shouted loudly at me and I was chastised severely for what I thought was merely exuberant play. He promised me that when he got home I would be in for more of the same. At that time, I was deeply fearful, but I was also shocked at his severe reprimand and I felt very angry. I was dismayed that such a seemingly innocent behavior would eventuate in a broken relationship.
>
> I was never able to express that anger toward my father and I repressed those emotions into my shadow which I carried with me from that time forward. I think I lost my ability to be open with my father from then on. I showed him what I thought he wanted to see. At the same time, the loss of the father I thought I knew left me lonely and without hope for the intimacy I wanted badly. In addition to covering over my real self, I began to doubt myself and my judgment. My world darkened considerably and I became less open and carefree—and overly cautious not to offend or to make mistakes that might draw someone's wrath.

My Story – Reflections

Since that incident, insignificant as it may have appeared, I have periodically come to grips with why I have experienced great difficulty in managing my strong emotions when I feel misjudged and unfairly criticized. So it should be no surprise that when I meet someone whose behavior reminds me of some aspect of my father's, the same emotions get triggered and expressed out of proportion to the nature of the experience.

Besides becoming aware of the original incident and how it played out in my life, it became necessary to work with that *repressed anger*. The final step was to constructively use those energies through an *inner dialogue with the shadow* material that was so much a part of me.

On a much different plane, the dynamics of losing my freedom of expression with my father was unsettling. As I experienced this loss, even though it was just in how I felt, I think I searched for a father figure for a long time. I realize it was a fruitless search and the father figures that came into my life never really filled the gap.

Proceeding to the next step, I can enter into an inner *dialogue*—not with the other person who is a peripheral presence in this case—but *with the shadow side* of myself. The dialogue method calls for me to take the part of my shadow side and engage in a dialogue with my usual self. For example, as the shadow side I might say, "I realize this person triggered my repressed emotions left over from that incident with my father. In this case, those emotions exacerbated my relatively shallow annoyance into an extremely angry expression. Now that I am aware of this potential in me for extreme reaction, I can recognize potentially similar situations before they happen in the future. I can channel the emotion into more positive expressions and thus be free of unsettling consequences."

This is a rather straightforward example of a dialogue that almost never happens in such a simple manner. However, this inner dialogue becomes the occasion of a healing process within me. The healing is not only for me, but potentially for the relationship with *my father* and with *others with whom I work*.

When I engage in that inner dialogue, I am acting as a responsible and mature adult using my emotions in positive ways. I can choose to channel those emotions into expressions of positive regard for the other person. In that way, I show them respect and care...and, at the same time, do the healthy thing for me. By having this kind of dialogue between my two sides, I can prepare to manage potentially negative situations between myself and others and thus promote my own growth toward maturity and wholeness.

Another way of working with shadow material is to *ritualize the relationship* with our own shadows. A useful ritual for managing shadow material is to stay grounded by periodic or even daily centering practices. When we engage in daily centering practices, we can learn to fully occupy personal space and be comfortable, as it were, in our own skins—influenced by material from the bright and dark shadow within.

Your Story

Your turn. What difficult experience have you had that might have led you to deny or ignore some unique part of self-expression? Even though it may come with complex emotions, are you able to bring such an experience into your awareness? If you can do so, then perhaps you can move to the next step of examining how, thereafter, you were *inhibited in expressing* yourself because of the earlier *denial* or *self-repression*. If you can also accomplish this examination, then perhaps you can *engage with the repressed part* of you and *let go of* the habit of *being inhibited*. Then, maybe you can allow yourself to *expand your self-expression* to include that repressed energy that never found sufficient expression before. In this way, you may *recover* some *lost capacity* and *feel more comfortable* because of the release.

Activate Our Best Qualities

Another method for working with our shadow material is to activate our own best qualities in the achievement of work. If we can *release our shadow material* into the *fulfillment of work*, energy will flow through us into *creative productivity*. In this way, we do not project our own best qualities onto others as *hero worship* and give too much of our own shadow energies away.

When we project onto others our own best qualities, we are choosing to not see those capacities in ourselves and thus lose access to them. Certainly, I might recognize the leadership capacities of co-workers, in their ability to lead teams, make decisions, provide insights and deliver strategies. But in my concentration on them, I might not recognize my own capabilities for understanding the latent needs of the group, the organization of resources and the administration of activities leading to the same goal. The reason for not recognizing those capacities in myself might derive from poorly thought out notions of humility or reticent behavior patterns or an over-emphasis on the virtues of restraint.

The Enlargement of the Soul

The great truth is that an *unlived life of energetic expressions*—in the form of shadow material—is *bottled up* within us and is *seeking expression* in all aspects of our *lives*...and certainly in our *work*. Becoming conscious of that great wellspring of energies is part of the work of becoming mature and whole. The integration of carefully selected energies requires deep awareness and Interiority in order to proceed in a psychologically healthy manner.

Shadow work is vital to the development of the *soul*, the securing of true *identity* and the establishment of sustainable *relationships*, especially at work. This brief reference to shadow integration is sufficient for our purpose of identifying learning opportunities that arise spontaneously from the inner world of our shadows, especially while we are at work. But, there is still the matter of practical examples of how I experience and attempt to manage latent shadow energies so I, myself, might mature.

> **My Story – Accumulating Shadows**
>
> *The Catholic Church happens to be the largest organization in the world and has been in place longer than any other. Within the church are many smaller organizations carrying out the many functions needed to ensure the fulfillment of the Church's mission.*
>
> *In my role as a consultant, I had conducted an intervention in one of the Church's sub-organizations. The leader of the organization was on my case from the beginning of my work. In his eyes, I could do nothing right. I was not to be trusted. I was being paid too much. I was biased in my judgment. There was simply no winning with him and yet I was lured into playing his game.*
>
> *Others told me to pay him no heed. They said it was his way to be difficult. I didn't take the bait he cast at the first go-around but about the sixth time, I swallowed it whole. After he persistently pushed all my buttons, I reacted. I gave him a vicious tongue-lashing, calling him a negative, tiresome, puerile, SOB and then some. I immediately knew I had made a mistake but the damage was done and to cement the damage, I didn't apologize.*

My Story - Reflections

Upon reflection, my wrath was not truly directed at him. I realized the fault was not so much in him as it was in me and in the accumulated shadow material I had never processed or integrated. Once I accepted that the source of my reactivity was in me, it was comparatively easy to focus in a more detailed manner on the deeper origins of the shadow.

The object of my repressed shadow energies was the Catholic Church, which has been my faith affiliation by virtue of my birth. My unresolved anger was piled high at the legacies of shame and frustration, and a disbelief at the obduracy of an organization that generally chooses its own security, authority and power before anything else. It was that anger that I let loose and became the cause of this reflection.

So how did I manage to pile up those shadow energies. They accumulated, unconsciously, little by little, with a mixture of positive and negative affect that began when I first heard the bells of the local church from the confines of my pram.

With the Church, I realize that the communitarian nature of the *holy* is contradicted by a tradition that presents even the most sacred reality as *hierarchical*, *dominant* and requiring *subservience*. This is reminiscent of the medieval kings on whom the Catholic image of God is modeled. The Christian message is basically a simple story that reveals a beautiful human life. I have slim expectations that the institutional Catholic Church will lead the charge to confront the shadows that are its *legacy*, its *burden*—and its potential *release*. Nevertheless, I have a responsibility to confront those shadows in my own life.

In this regard, my main step was to *replace the institution with a personal relationship*. Today, my faith-based allegiance is to a person rather than to an organization, its laws, practices or ceremonies.

My second step was to *let go of fighting against* and *reacting to the structures and traditions* of a church that located the holy outside of me and all other things. Such reactivity only lent credence to the image of the holy as above, remote and controlling. In healing this construct, I was bidden to turn my energies to cultivating whatever was of *love* in me to greater *kindness* so my heart was available as solace.

In this way, I freed myself from supporting and giving credence to shadow material so I could *focus my energies on creative work* in the community.

Your Story

What then is your story of some reactive emotional expression that was not caused by another person—or object of your attention—but arising spontaneously from within? Did the reactivity occur because it was generated by a person in a *titled position* or had the appearance of institutional *authority*? Were you able to reflect on the real *cause* of your reactivity pattern? Were you further able to *reconcile* with the source of such reactivity and find both *release* and *comfort*?

In reconciling with the reactive pattern in yourself, perhaps you may have been able to redirect the energies of those patterns into some creative and productive outcomes or enhanced relationships.

Paradox

Another potentially fertile learning opportunity for deepening Interiority is paradox. Life and work are full of paradoxical material. A paradox can be defined as a seeming contradiction in a statement or situation that is (or may be) true. For example, while daydreaming during a meeting we discover valuable new insights. Paradoxically, studies show daydreaming can lead to problem-solving in unrelated areas around half of the time.[120]

Paradox can also reveal the *two-sided nature of reality*, and while we would prefer to choose one or the other, that is not reality. Some examples of this kind of paradox are day and night, male and female, north and south, to name just a few. We cannot choose day alone because day is only day until night comes along. North is only north because there is a south. The Chinese call this dual nature of reality *yin/yang*.

FIGURE 17:
YIN/YANG

If we try to have only one side of reality, such as happiness, we can suffer the most profound grief because such an effort will certainly turn out to be fruitless. When we apply this type of paradox to our lives, we see that life brings happiness and sadness or suffering and they are intertwined. When we mature, we realize we cannot have one without the other. As Jung notes, "Suffering is not an illness; it is the normal counterpole to happiness."[121]

Many people spend their lives in headlong pursuit of endless pleasure or fun, but this is an empty quest. This kind of pursuit of one side of the paradox of life can cause us to use tremendous amounts of energy in trying to sustain it. We cannot have only joy in our lives because the greatest joys sometime come from the most profound suffering, and the challenge is to accept both joy and sadness. In work, we understand that without some mistakes, toil and drudgery, we do not develop *expertise* or arrive at *creative* and *productive* results.

The secret of including paradox in our lives—and work—is to embrace both sides. We really produce creative results when we embrace the toil and reward, the mistake and learning. When we do this, we are using a faculty of soul called *healing* or *bridging* because in essence we are bringing both sides of the paradox together. The ability to deal with paradox depends upon our openness to the results we seek and also to the results we stumble upon (seemingly without conscious intention). This flexible openness to paradox ensures that we change or are changed as we engage in work.

Learning from the paradoxical nature of reality is an important aspect of the Interiority of the worker. Some other examples of paradoxes are:

- We arrive at the truth through our successes and failures.
- We reach an enriching or troublesome destination although it was not part of the original plan.
- We complete our work by recognizing that individuality and the uniqueness of our workplaces are sources of creativity.
- We come to deeper understanding of the special qualities of each person when we move through the conflict and tension between us.

When we embrace the paradoxical nature of reality, we open ourselves to the insight to be found in enduring the duality of things. Insight blossoms in our embrace of the ordinary at work, such as when we work as individuals and as part of a team, when we succeed and when we fail. Out of the tension of success and failure, we can potentially come to greater wisdom about ourselves and become even more productive at work.

Chaos

Disruptive energies occur in both natural and man-made phenomena...as if we needed any reminding after the earthquake and tsunami in Japan. As evidenced by scavengers and microbes, the forebodingly dark side of reality is replete with *dissolution* and *disintegration*. Think of the chaos brought about by the emergence of new technology. The auto replaced the horse and buggy, email has all but replaced hand-written communication and the great manufacturing companies largely gave way to service and knowledge-based industries.

Chaos happens.

The poets described the instability of life as "The best laid schemes of mice and men gang aft aglay" (Burns[122]); "When I have fears that I might cease to be" (Keats[123]); "Things fall apart, the center cannot hold" (Yeats[124]). At work and in life, what we think is dependable can suddenly and utterly change. The harder we try to hold on to the way things are, the more futile our efforts appear. What increases the difficulties of chaotic change is we lament it, deny it, resist it...struggling to prove we can control desired outcomes.

My Story – Horseman, Pass By

The glowing red sun appeared to evaporate in wavelets of steam as it dropped below the horizon of a picture-perfect ocean. I walked on a secluded corner of a beach piled high with driftwood, stacked in disarray against the bank of earth eroding mournfully away.

> *As I walked, a tall, slender black bird stood stock-still, crouched in a wind-sheltered nook. The stillness of its bearing was unnerving—I expected some fluttering attempts to escape as nervous, flighty birds are quick to do. Still and quiet, it remained motionless at my approach, vacantly staring at me out of an unblinking eye, its head cocked sideways. I stopped and looked as if to understand. It looked back at me with a penetrating vision that seemed to take in the beckoning beyond, way beyond my sight or mind.*
>
> *To me, its quiet, waiting stance was imposing...a purposeful and distinguished acceptance of an inevitably encroaching death. But by miracle of re-forming life, the death of one means life renewed for others. Quite literally, microbes, worms, slugs and termites transform dead matter into that which brings life. The waiting bird was content to follow nature's path of dissolution.*
>
> *Only humans have the added burden of knowing the inevitable end. The unblinking eye of the bird brought home to me a somber message of my mortality and of the swift-moving shuffle of this "mortal coil." I moved further up the beach and the epitaph of Yeats' tombstone came to mind, "Cast a cold eye on life, on death. Horseman, Pass by!" Even from his tomb, Yeats was urging the passersby not to linger but get on with the business of living. But how?*
>
> *The how of letting go is familiar if it includes a daily dose of dying and dissolution as part of creative work. Creativity requires letting go of the way things were conceived, known by us and used by us in the ways they were designed, yet which were susceptible to the march of progress.*

My Story – Reflections

The dying bird reminded me of the fragility of my own life and my eventual death. The aspect of dying that affords me comfort is that my passing is the occasion of new life being born. The business of living further suggests sober consideration of my mortal condition. Such considerations, rather than being morbid, tend to enrich my consciousness of being in the moment. If I can move through a moment-to-moment letting go of what is already past, I can appreciate everything else that shares this moment with me. Remembering my life cycle, I am buoyed by the thought that nature is inexhaustibly fertile and I am part of that fertility, as energy and alas as fodder.

Your Story

What then is your story of being reminded of the fragile hold that you have on life? Was it in a moment when your brakes did not slow you down and you came too close to the vehicle in front? Was it when another vehicle suddenly merged into your lane and you gasped with fright? Have you been present when people or animals were dying? What sober thoughts drew you to appreciate the passing moments all the more?

So what is the relationship between shadow, paradox and chaos and how do all three relate to creativity and productivity at work? In coming to terms with the realities of shadow, paradox and chaos within us, we become aware of the ultimate vanity of ambition and move through ego-driven action to mature growth. When we shift from our ego-centered motivations to working according to the requirements of the work itself and in the service of the community, dynamic energies are released within us. Each of the three states of shadow, paradox and chaos hold dynamic tensions of opposites, which also generate energies that can be directed toward creativity and productivity. We cannot arrive at the place of binding together or embracing both sides of a paradox without somehow recognizing and embracing our shadow.

Organizations are in a period of fundamental change requiring a deeper capacity of Interiority in the worker and in the organization itself. We are presently moving out of a period of hierarchical control and linear activity, that has been in use for the past 100 years, into a transitional period that provides a more holistic, self-organizing, interdependent structure and working environment. Some examples of holistic organizations are Linux, Google, Zappos, Wikipedia and Linked-in. These organizations are characterized by inclusive processes which highlight the need for balance between ego and soul in the worker and organization.

The ego and soul are usually seen as opposites. The implication is the presence of one cancels out the other. However, modern psychology has revealed both these inner capacities actually complement one another. We need our ego to support our decisions for survival. We need our soul to be the source of connection with all that is non-material.

Now, we might question why we need to balance the ego and the soul. Here we return again to the answer that all of reality is made up of both the energies of light and dark, positive and negative. In using all of these elements of shadow, paradox, chaos, ego and soul in our orientation toward inclusivity, we become more aware of our innate drive toward wholeness and trust.

Foundation #4: Trust by Way of Fulfilling Our Call

Trust is the fourth foundation of Interiority. The elementary dimensions of trust are to know one's self and to be known by others as dependable and trustworthy. I cultivate trust by repeatedly choosing to complete my work according to the highest standards of which I am capable. Trustworthiness is earned by repeated behaviors that are beneficial to others, productive for the company and affirmative of self-respect.

On the other hand, I entrust my fate to the energies at work in all things so that through them I will reach a level of productivity that is worthy of the call to which I am summoned. The basic shape of that call is discernible in how I am equipped to respond to the needs of my time. Yet, the true emergence of my call only becomes evident in my incremental engagement with immediate substantial tasks.

The cultivation of trust in oneself is a lifelong task. We learn first to trust our physical selves. Then we learn to trust our mental capacities to know, act, learn and work. We trust ourselves at work that we will be able to produce the necessary *results*, nurture vital *relationships* and generate sufficient *compensation* to live comfortably in this life with which we have been entrusted. Through a spontaneous inner dialogue, we learn to trust that, in our relationships with all other things, we will do more than merely survive; we will grow and enjoy the journey.

Trust must be intentionally cultivated. Initially, when we become aware of the outside world, we must trust in the dependability of the natural context, such as the sun rising each morning and the air we breathe refreshing our energies. And even though nothing of nature's bounty is guaranteed, we trust we will have enough to survive in some degree of comfort. In spite of the difficulties, failures and trials of living, *trust motivates* us to strive to succeed. We trust the processes of life to bring us through numerous cycles of effort, failure and learning to maturity and wholeness.

We come to know our work as the tasks with which we have been gifted. Then we learn to trust the relationships we have that act as the fulcrum of our growth. It bears repeating that trustworthiness is earned by repeated behaviors that are beneficial to others, productive for the company and affirmative of our self-respect.

The question of how to motivate workers towards excellence often perplexes managers. We know some things for certain: Each worker is responsible for the execution of his/her assigned tasks. Yet, between the assignment of the responsibility and the execution of a task, many factors come into play. First, the *assignment must be imagined*, *accepted* and *done* within the *worker's inner world* before the work is begun in the external forum. "The game is played in the mind, first and foremost and language is the critical instrument," writes Rayona Sharpnack in her book, *Trade Up.*[125] Upon the assignment of the task, a dynamic interaction involving trust plays out "inside" the worker. The worker with deepened Interiority is able to accept the tasks and trust his/herself to complete the work satisfactorily. The worker who is imbued with Interiority can trust in the confluence of energies in everything that is driving toward wholeness through the completion of the tasks.

David Bohm, renowned physicist, presented the view that in all things there is "an unbroken wholeness at a level we cannot discern."[126] Thomas Merton, the contemplative Cistercian monk said, "There is in all visible things …a hidden wholeness."[127] Such wholeness is not immediately evident to us but must be uncovered by reflection and integration. Wholeness is not the result of a one-time event but of a series of events, usually recurring in a cycle throughout our lives, which ends in a new state of personal integration. The life processes of the human follow the cyclical life processes that take place in every living thing in the universe. As opposed to a linear process from birth to death, these cyclical life processes are recapitulated many times over during our lives.

As each specific cycle happens, we become more whole and participate more fully in the universal whole. Each completed task highlights some dimension of our emerging call to contribute. Only gradually do we come to know our unique contributions.

Each of us is offered multiple opportunities to develop awareness of this cyclical development process through our work. This means that when things seem to be falling apart we realize we are going through another cycle that has the potential for greater wholeness. I use the term potential here because it is only through *repeated acts* and *completed cycles* that *we become whole*.

Encounters with these apparently disintegrating processes force us to go deeper into our inner cores. Through them, we gain an even greater appreciation for complexity—the reconciliation of divisions, harmony of opposites and compassion for the fragmented. As we participate in such reconciliation, we can say we belong to the emerging whole. As we reconcile these apparent divisions into one whole, we begin to comprehend this life with which we have been gifted is the *best path to greater life*.

This is the task of Interiority in workers.

We have to learn how to live with the challenges and find ways to reconcile, harmonize and even love all of the seemingly disruptive cycles of life we experience. Even though the cycles may happen in the physical dimension, wholeness takes place in the inner dimension. For integration to occur, it is necessary to go through the three stages of the cycle outlined on the following page and graphically shown in the illustration. These three phases parallel the Hero's return, popularized by Joseph Campbell in his work, *The Hero with a Thousand Faces*.[128]

During the first stage of the hero's return, the hero sets out on a journey. During the second stage, the hero slays the dragon. During the third stage, he/she returns to share the spoils with the community. Likewise, every worker *sets out daily on a journey*, encounters and *learns from the challenges of work*, and *returns to share the benefits* of expanded awareness and maturity with the family and communities to which he/she belongs.

Cycles of Integration

The cycles of integration consist of three periods:

- *A period of disintegration:* any time we leave a previous state (1 below)
- *A period of transition:* any time we cross a critical threshold (2 below)
- *A period of integration:* any time we experience a deeper sense of self (3 below).[129]

Our Work Teaches Us in Cycles

The nature of work involves both our inner selves and the task at hand in cycles of interaction. When we switch on the machine, package a product, analyze a research subject, dig furrows in the earth or interface with a customer, a change results in ourselves and in our work. We are constantly taught through our interaction with the tasks in front of us. Through them, we learn and make the benefit of our learning available to all, as others share their learning with us.

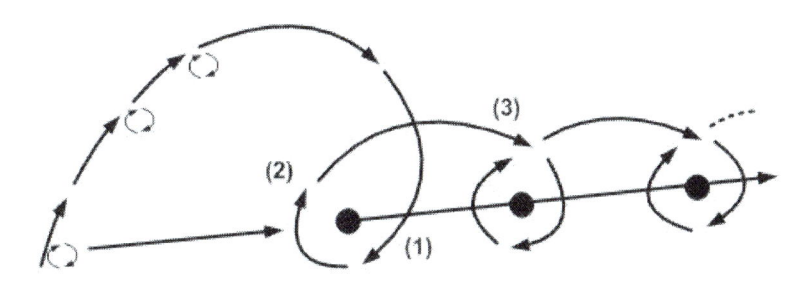

FIGURE 18: **CYCLES OF INTEGRATION**

When I engage in writing this book, I am doing so on a desk that is the result of effort by other human workers. It is the same with the computer I am using, which was made by the work of countless collaborating people. The energies expended in those efforts are an essential part of the desk and the computer. In turn, if I creatively engage with my work, I will be created in the process and the energies I expend will remain in the results I produce. At the same time, if I maintain myself as an open system, the work itself (this book), will teach me about life, about myself and others—that is, if I pay attention to what is going on within myself. The teacher is also taught by what he/she teaches; the artist is created by what he/she creates. A necessary part of being taught lies in our openness to discover what has not yet dawned upon our awareness. It is the stance of an open mind that is able to see the potential in the work itself more than the difficulties of performance.

The lesson is rather than engaging the work in a controlling fashion, we may be better off engaging with the work as a partner. For example, when I am doing ornamental iron work and bending the bar by hand into a scroll, the beauty of the shape depends on the pull I exert and the keenness of my eye, as every delicate move gives the finished work its character. The degree of heat in the iron, the placing of the bar in the turning tool, the purity of the metal and the pull of my hand are all part of the communion in which we are all changed. Each of us is fulfilling our purpose in the moment as well as providing a beneficial result. As we engage with the work, we begin to see ourselves, our patterns, our values and our preferences as a statement from our lives about life emerging through the work itself.

Another aspect of engagement in our work is of being partially consumed by the effort. For example, the actor on the stage is consumed by the expenditure of energy to bring the part to life. In turn, the part being played becomes consumed by becoming part of the life of the audience. In the consumption of such energy, the actor becomes part of other emerging systems. As we become part of other systems, our respect grows for the other, the role, the product and the earth. If we pay respect to the other, it will reflect a concomitant respect for us and provide nurturance for our lives. The result of work done in such a way is a sense of gratitude for the opportunity, the fulfillment and the oncoming day.

On one level, we grow to be ourselves by passing through the stages of self-knowledge, maturity, productivity and contribution to the society. However, on a much deeper level, we grow to be ourselves in recognition that we are forever part of the main that has been changed because of our involvement. In our daily preoccupation with the minutiae of work, many of us fail to realize our ideas or practices are a part of an enduring process of evolution. Our energies remain an active part of whatever is growing, dying and re-emerging in different forms. If we fail to realize those dimensions of our contribution, we deprive ourselves of the fulfillment that is part of belonging to something greater than our individual life. Any organization worthy of its employees tries to make sure its workers grow by their contribution, but also by recognizing their particular contribution is a part of the enduring whole. Workers who are worthy of their organization collaborate by contributing the results of their work but also by the quality of their teamwork and character.

Commitment to Personal Development

To sustain the drive for personal development at work, we need a fundamental commitment to being the kind of people we aspire to be and to implementing the practices of Interiority that will ensure continuous growth.

To develop, you must continue to choose to build on the previous stage and embrace and commit to the task of the next stage. While you cannot relive any previous stage, you can be carried forward in your commitment to the great work of building your own life. Thankfully, you are not dependent only on the commitment of your will but you have a stable ally in the energies of your soul.

- **Our Souls Urge Us Forward.** Our souls urge us forward by raising the opportunities of each stage and they will not let us rest until we have come to some kind of accommodation to the great work of our lives. There is a work that is ours to do and we will be urged to do it by promptings from within because it is *necessary for the good of the whole*. There is no escaping these prompts because our souls are prompters par excellence. Similarly, there is no escape from the necessity of a daily commitment to the work of our lives.

- **Working Because of a Calling.** Throughout history, we have assumed that the execution of organizational policies belong to those in executive positions. However, as Drucker suggests, if every worker were to take ownership of his/her work *and* the organization—which means to think and work as if he or she was an executive—then the execution of the organization's tasks belong to every worker.

If we go one step further to explore workers' motivations that provide energy for work, then we encounter the element of vocation or calling. One's calling comes from the whole community and connects further to meaning and purpose. It derives from the belief all of us are called to fully become the unique beings we have the potential to become. By responding to the calling we hear within us to serve (work) in a certain way, we can arrive at more satisfying levels of meaning.

When we have a sense that we belong to something greater than ourselves, it is easier to believe we have a *reason to be alive* and to be *doing this* work, *at this* time. That reason has much to do with our calling. I recall the time I spent in discerning my own call, during the year-long period called a Novitiate.

> ### My Story – The Value of Mistakes
>
> *Once upon a time, I was a novice. That means I entered the Novitiate of a religious order of Catholic priests. The Novitiate is the beginning year of a long period of discernment regarding whether an applicant to the priesthood is worthy of the calling. The Novitiate year consists of simple routines of prayer, silence, work (usually manual labor) and study. The location of the Novitiate itself is usually a monastic setting, away from the enticements of the secular world, and novices are supposed to remain within the confines of the monastery perimeters. Facing a life of asceticism, they are expected to try their best to be good in every way. Being good in this context means to obey the rules, pray diligently, be kind to others, study, reflect on one's call and work hard. In my case, the objective was to engage in the practice of perfection and Christian virtue, about which we heard lectures daily from the Novice Master. Since it was a time of discernment, I had presumed it would be plain sailing…but I was about to be convinced otherwise.*
>
> *About six months into the year, in the early spring of 1959, I was sailing confidently along, immersed in ascetical practices in the North-Midlands of Ireland. One day, the Novice Master asked that I "take out" the well-worn cast iron troughs from an old cowshed slated to be rebuilt on the same farm location. I agreed and he went back up the hill to the monastery. Then I got a large hammer and proceeded to "take them out."*
>
> *When he returned, the troughs were in a pile of mangled pieces on the floor. I was expecting praise for a job well and quickly done, but I knew immediately from his face I had made a major mistake. He was so furious he muttered something under his breath that included "stupid," turned on his heel and stalked away. It dawned on me he expected the troughs to be carefully removed and then able to be used somewhere else or perhaps sold to some dairy farmer. Because of my hammer, haste and lack of clarity about the task, it was not to be. There I was, in utter embarrassment and shame, all my good intentions shattered, tripped up not least by my confidence that I was doing the correct thing.*

My Story – Reflections

Oh, the lessons life teaches when we think we know it all; and yet we can't stop striving to know as much as necessary for our work. Nothing to be done but get rid of the pieces as quickly as possible, try to learn the lesson and get on with life. The admonition I had heard often from my father in the forge, "The man who never made a mistake, never made anything" was of no consolation whatsoever.

As an obedient novice, I had been so intent on not making a mistake I had blundered badly, blind-sided by thinking I knew what he meant when he said, "take them out." All the prayers, study, lectures, acts of kindness and hours of manual labor were no match for my harsh encounter with the reality of human limitations.

I have been learning humility ever since that day in the cowshed on the hill when the muttering Novice Master turned on his heel and stalked away. No wonder I was assigned to remove tree stumps for months on end at the far end of the monastery farm during that year of Novitiate.

Your story

In your experience, was there some mistake that remained in your awareness and taught you many lessons about your calling in life and work? Assuming there was, what impact did that mistake have on the emergence of your calling? Has your call clarified during your life's journey? How does your sense of calling influence your behavior at work? Are you appreciative of the trials, the mistakes, even the enemies that have guided you in the fulfillment of your call? Without those experiences, what might your call, your life and your work have been?

The Road Less Traveled Has Made All The Difference

While I am on the subject of Novitiate and discernment of calling, and speaking from this vantage point of many years later, I consider that I responded to the call of the priesthood out of some unresolved inner set of complexes, rather than from an invitation by the holy, or my soul, or to be of service to the human community, although these latter were also part of my intentions. Yet, all of these made up the muddled context of my response to the call. Even from that muddle, and with all these years and experiences under my belt, I have come to vindicate my living out of a call that took a "road less traveled," which "has made all the difference."[130] I am so glad I followed that call to the priesthood and after 27 years in religious life, took the roads that led me to where I am today.

I can say this now: real discernment can only come about over a lifetime's worth of experience, reflection and decisions. For even while I am constantly making choices, I am being brought to an awareness that *something* is choosing me for a certain work, which brings its own challenges and compensations to my doorstep.

The Struggle with Discernment of One's "Call" is Part of the Discovery. In a number of places, I have referred to *something* like a friendly prompt *that triggers either recognition or hesitation when confronted with a choice about one's call.* That *friendly* *prompt is the intuition of the soul upon which we* acutely *depend in* the *discernment* of the call. The discernment process requires that each of us make our own meaning out of the patchwork of our experiences. Trust in Interiority at work ensures that something like quilts of exquisite design will emerge to form the people into which we have grown.

This inner certitude is cyclical: from doubt...to anxiety...to painful reflection... and back again to trust and certitude on a deeper plane within. Importantly, it is what provides the drive that *increases* our *productivity*. That is why the struggle with the discernment of one's call and eventual arrival at this certitude is a necessary condition for increased productivity at work and in the things that really matter.

In the case of the cast iron troughs, the necessity for struggle came home to me as I pondered my mistake. Coming to terms with life's limitations is a hard lesson to learn, but a necessary one for the cultivation of Interiority. A one-dimensional approach to life and work, such as thinking the world will fulfill all our expectations, can never cut it. All too often, life comes around and delivers a swift kick in the pants. We eventually learn, if we can endure and move to a deeper appreciation of life, in the end it is all beautiful, good and meaningful.

At this point, it might be helpful to review what we have considered in Chapter Three, The Foundations. To the right, you can see the framework of the four foundations of Interiority. In Chapter Four, we will turn our attention to the more practical consideration of an organization that is in "trouble."

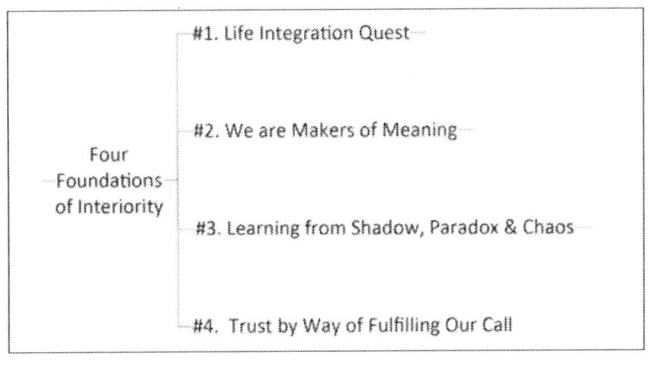

Four Foundations of Interiority
- #1. Life Integration Quest
- #2. We are Makers of Meaning
- #3. Learning from Shadow, Paradox & Chaos
- #4. Trust by Way of Fulfilling Our Call

FIGURE 19: **FOUNDATIONS OF INTERIORITY**

The Butterfly Will Come To Rest On Your Shoulder.

For most of us, work is the place, working is the time, worker relationships are the occasions for us to come to higher levels of trust in our lives—and to decipher life's meaning. No doubt, we can easily give our time and energy, learn trust and gain a modicum of meaning in outer domains. Deeper meaning derives from the inner domain of our lives at work and the trust of the circumstances and demands we find there.

Most often, the lessons worth learning emerge from the hard *mistakes*, enemy *encounters* and abject *failures*. At an even deeper level, we arrive at meaning when we engage with the *mystery of ourselves at work* that is completely beyond comprehension and accessible only by some form of belief and consonant practice. We only notice such a mystery when we are conscious of being enveloped in its silence, stillness and oneness and when we assume a quiet, collaborative stance toward its presence in our lives.

We often chase after butterflies to catch them—but it is often when we stand still that they will come to rest on our shoulders.

The foundations of Interiority remind us again not to be "like a foolish man who built a house on sand." Matthew, 8:26.

Stay ahead of the alligators

Chapter 4

A Troubled Organization

Does the road wind up-hill all the way?
Yes, to the very end.
Will the journey take the whole long day?
From morn to night, my friend.[131]
—Christina Rosetti, "Up-hill"

The Intervention

I was hired as an external organization development consultant for a 200-member division of a large corporation whose identity cannot be disclosed. The executives saw the organization as spiraling into chaos after what they believed was a communications snafu during a re-organization. The tipping point had been reached when headquarters restructured the organization so nearly all the workers were transferred to new locations and reassigned to new jobs. All this was done without consulting either the workers or the clients. The division was in an uproar and most were resisting the transfers and new assignments and, of course, inadequate communications was trotted out to me as the presenting issue. Typically, there was plenty of blame to go around but nobody took ownership of any fault. Everyone was in defense mode as it became a classic case of CYA, (cover your a…). My task was to enable the organization to adapt to the restructuring and recover from the dysfunctional spiral.

As it turned out, what was going on in the division was mirrored throughout, as almost every dimension of the organization was somehow caught up in conflict. The executives were distant from management. Management was misunderstood by headquarters and workers. The workers were in conflict with management, each other and the customers. The customers were in shock at the disarray, yet desperately needed the products the organization provided.

As background, the organization was an important player in the telecommunications industry. The total number of employees was about 30,000. Most of them had been recruited *en-masse* from various pieces of the old Bell system and other newly sprouting organizations. New fiber optical technologies, fast processing circuitry, miniaturizing of everything and exploding markets for telecom services were transforming the industry. Venture capitalists smelled opportunity and sent in turnaround experts to create the new organization, streamline it for efficiencies and make sure management was focused on grabbing market share. Everything was being done at hyper-speed. Not surprisingly, glitches showed up when the first iterations of organizational restructuring were not tested for viability and everything was reorganized, again. It turned out, however, that no sooner was one re-organization completed than it was obsolete and another one was being implemented. Meanwhile, workers were trying to maintain their professional expertise and increase productivity while doing their jobs.

Management explained, in memos and videos no one looked at, that new forms of organizational structure were being introduced so workers might have more autonomy. They promised that participatory decision-making would be the order of the day. The problem: no one knew or cared about participatory decision-making. In reality, the organization that emerged was the good old hierarchical model based on a command-and-control system of decision-making and communication. The business model focused on capturing market share in the service of rapidly transforming global corporations as quickly as possible; then flogging a raft of products and services at the clients as fast as they could absorb them.

A Profile of Dysfunction

In the Operations department of the division into which I was called, there were severely dysfunctional areas. Planning decisions made at headquarters regarding how operations were to be conducted were not considered effective on the shop-floor or by the field-sales representatives. It seemed obvious that the plans had been drawn up by Ivy League graduates, now in management functions at headquarters, who had never gotten their hands dirty in making the products fit the needs of the clients. Experienced field service technicians scoffed at the theoretical directives and refused even to read the manuals.

Furthermore, there were conflicts between management and workers. Local management was not able to implement the directives from headquarters because of the resistance from the field. One of the main barriers was that the supervisors supported the line workers, rather than management. The workers had been recruited along with the supervisors in intact teams and the V.P. and managers were recruited individually. The management group was accustomed to a command structure and to following orders coming from headquarters.

That system had worked well in a manufacturing plant environment but this was a knowledge and skills-based industry and every issue was new and every solution had to be creatively developed and implemented. There were almost no standard processes to follow. Beyond those gaps, a more serious element involved what I had not been told about the V.P. in charge. To complete the picture of the challenge that I faced, I will continue by describing my experience of a series of interviews, starting with the V.P.

My Story – Embattled

As she walked toward me, what caught my eye was the sharp cut of her tweed business suit moving in time with the clacking of her boot heels on the tiled floor. Formidable was the term that came to mind. Curt greeting finished, she turned and, clacking forward, led me to her office. Little was memorable in that dimly lit space except for the files piled to the side of her desk. We sat and she began, "I don't know what you have heard but I want to give you my side of the story of this workplace, which I believe is accurate." Without breaking eye-contact with her, in my yellow pad, I wrote, story - accurate.

She moved a file from the pile to the center and said, "Albert's a trouble-maker. For some reason, perhaps because he wanted this job, he has had it in for me ever since I arrived here. I've tried to work with him but he's too far gone to revive and he is bitter that he has not been promoted. The lies he tells to make himself look good are just that, lies. He is in competition with me, whenever he gets a chance. I tell you now that he will wait a long time for any promotion to happen under my watch." I took a deep breath and wrote, Albert - trouble-maker. She moved another file into the center and continued.

"Helen's a slacker and addicted to her own version of reality. You can't believe a word that comes out of her mouth. She told me that she sent a letter, marked urgent, that I had given her and I found it three days later in her desk drawer. When I confronted her, she made up some excuse that it was a duplicate for her records. Now, I'm not dumb but I played dumb just to move on. She'll get her comeuppance one of these days." I found my stomach growing cold and wrote, Helen - slacker.

"Now Pete has promise but he has misrepresented his qualifications for the job he was hired to do. I don't trust him at all. I'm trying to find a position in another division so that I can ship him off. I know someone who can do his job and do what I tell them. I will replace Pete by writing a glowing reference so that I can get rid of him out of my sight." I wrote, Pete – misrep.

"Chloe spends her days in rounds of attending to her makeup, chatty phone calls, endless visits to the bathroom and shopping for fashion on the Internet. I don't know how she got in here but if I can help it she also is heading for the door, ASAP." I wrote Chloe – makeup, out.

I knew I would not write any more. She said, *"Now, I'm only telling you these things so you will have a realistic picture of what is going on here."* I already had a picture and it was different from what she was painting. It was not in her favor.

She touched another file and laughed lightly as if contemplating a happy scene. *"Now, there's Mark. Oh Mark - the snark. That's what I call him. He is so bright and if only he would do what he is supposed to do, he would be a brilliant performer. But he is so dammed snarky, so cynical, so know-it-all that he thinks the work is beneath him and elects to be bored all the time. And his personal hygiene is dreadful. I'm going to load him up with so much work that his head will spin. He won't possibly be able to do it in the given time frame. I'm going to cure him of his big-headedness if it's the last thing that I do."*

She did not move any more files but she leaned forward over the desk, looked me in the eye, steepled her fingers and continued.

"I know my job. I have experience, a track record of success and qualifications that equip me to do this job, even blindfolded. I know these people, you meet them everywhere and they make me sick. I know what they need. They need to straighten up, stop blubbering and do their work. If they would only do the work that they have been assigned and get it in on time, everything would be okay. I'm the boss here and I'm a reasonable person but I expect compliance with the rules and the processes of this office. There are reasons why we have those rules and processes in place and I

expect that they, (the workers) will deliver and not complain. That's why I am here. That's it in a nutshell. I expect 100% compliance. Our clients expect the best quality, the keenest prices and timely delivery and that is what I expect of the workforce. Now, I know that you've been sent here to do an organizational assessment. But, you know, I don't believe in those things—assessments. They're a waste of time and money. But then you need to earn your consulting fee, right? So I suppose I'll go along with it. Assessments are only done when the top executives can't manage things by themselves.

"Now, I hope you don't think that I am trying to persuade you about anything. I'm a very ethical person. Anyway, thanks for coming. Agatha, my assistant, will see you out and if there is anything that you need, just call Agatha. Aagathaaa!"

She stood and I was out the door and on to the interviews with her staff, for which I had to travel to a hotel that was several miles away. After my first interview experience, I was not surprised that the workers had requested the meetings be held in a remote hotel. It came out later they thought she would have spies posted to hear what was being said if they were done at the office. Paranoia unbound!

They came into the room, one-by-one according to the order listed. I could see from their shifting eyes that they were nervous and hesitant. I told them why I was there, reassured them of confidentiality and gradually they opened up. Behind their stories, I detected cries for help. I could feel the emotional wounds sustained from cutting comments, their fears of possible reprisals for speaking up, creeping dread at the sudden disappearance of co-workers and hopelessness from the barrage of malicious innuendos about them as workers—and as people.

One by one, they shared their stories of dashed hopes and withered ideals— as their bodies told of the wretched treatment they endured in the workplace. As they related their anguished experiences, I pondered the possibility of workers doing any work at all in such repressive circumstances. I marveled at their ability to carry on, when, at the same time, I'm certain they just longed for the day—and the week—to be over.

One told of abuse from having to change whole documents over and over for using commas instead of semicolons. Another one related incidents of harassment to get tasks done…even as they were not allowed bathroom breaks or lunch. Another one described continuous criticism that had been directed at her by the V.P., because of inconsequential mistakes. Their stories told of withering criticism for appearing different. "Why can't you be like so and so" was the contemptuous refrain.

> *Some related stories of the boss playing them one against the other. For example, they were forced to answer loaded questions, the answers to which they feared would be lodged like missiles of doubt at co-workers so she could gain leverage. Others were accused of dishonesty and having their integrity put under suspicion. Most dreaded coming to work and a few told of looking for jobs elsewhere, anywhere, as long as it was away from here.*
>
> *Story after story came out of crushing workloads, impossible deadlines, and unclear tasks as well as threats, rejection, manipulation, and not surprisingly, lack of appreciation, recognition and respect. They talked of sleeplessness and nightmares. Some said they both dreaded speaking out and the continuation of hostile management. Some were so shaky that they feared for their sanity under the workplace conditions. Some were trying to hang on to threads of decency amidst the barrages of intimidation and threat.*
>
> *They admitted that they were not enjoying their work and were unable to do their best. They confessed to having submitted sub-par results because they were unable to focus their energies.*
>
> *Embattled they were.*

My Story – Reflections

Workplaces are supposed to be places where people can work, gain satisfaction and develop competencies. In truth, workplaces can have the most efficient systems to produce desired results, but if the manager does not model people-friendly behaviors, over the long term the desired results will not be achieved. Workers emulate the behaviors of their bosses. When workers are manipulated, they turn against each other and do not realize they have become puppets. This is especially true if tensions arise over productivity. Most managers and workers are not equipped to manage the tensions between them to avoid descending into chaotic interactions that drain and embitter. Conflict resolution tactics usually only scratch the surface and raise awareness of what compatible relationships look like.

During diagnostic interviews, I realized that every interviewee told not only his or her story but added nuances for greater credibility. While discounting stories padded in such a manner, I generally reported what I heard and let the experiences of the workers tell the tale.

My Story – Application

I did my job well enough to have a steady flow of work. However, in such a conflicted context, I did not escape blame and I too became a target for displaced anger. I often found myself caught in between management and workers, which often occurs in such interventions. I learned to withstand the pressures and tensions and focus on getting the stories straight and building solutions based on the real issues.

Your Story

What then about your experience of less-than-skillful managers who may even have had a toxic influence on your workplace? Was your work life marked by interactions with a manager who took a dislike to you and made things difficult? How did you manage such encounters and what awareness and skill did you develop because of that experience? How have inadequate managers figured in the places where you have worked?

In general, what kind of impact do such managers have on the workers? In your own function as a manager, what has been your approach to getting the best performance and highest productivity from those for whom you are responsible?

As if the above scenario was not enough, there was severe dissension between co-workers over accountability for completing tasks, divergent communication styles and inconsistent problem-solving. There was significant dissension between administration and the field-sales and service representatives. To complicate matters further, 30% of the new workforce was ethnically diverse and many had serious issues with each other over historic squabbles, language and cultural differences.

External stakeholders were frustrated with the changes in field-service procedures—which were considered far from dependable. Predictably, sales people had oversold the products and services and made promises of quality and dependability that could not be sustained.

Notwithstanding these areas, *not everything was negative*. It was clear that the services provided to the customers were important and in demand. For example, automotive clients depended on the telecommunications services to arrange for training their sales representatives on new products. E-Learning was in vogue and each dealership was trying to get ahead by using the new systems. Another positive was that the workforce was professionally qualified and highly trained. Since the workforce had grown up in the telecom industry, they knew its protocols and were able to straddle the divide between analog and digital media.

It was also an advantage that the workplace was well equipped and workers had advanced technologies and tools to do their work. Driven by the competitive necessity to capture market share, venture capitalists spared no expense in providing excellent facilities and other resources. The final positive was compensation: the workers were comparatively well paid and opportunities for advancement were available. The economy was expanding and the "war for talent" was real among the telecoms. They paid well to ensure retention of talent for high productivity and demanded results—or else.

In Figure 20, I present the wider context of the organization to highlight the underperformance of the workforce. The inner oval represents the inner life and culture of the organization. The smaller ovals around the outside of the inner oval represent the status of its key systems. The outer oval represents its business context.

Note the bell curve of productivity is at 25% due to multiple tensions occurring simultaneously.

According to the above scenario, the managers have largely absented themselves from their responsibilities, the workers are demoralized and productivity is low. This was nowhere more evident than when I began the intervention and tried to get the management group to engage with the workers in adopting common goals and processes. It turned out the managers came from a more traditional command structure and the workers, who were weaned on newer technologies, were more attuned to operating independently to get their work done. The two sides had different goals and neither wanted to support the goals of the other. I discovered the managers had developed serious reactive patterns to anything the workers suggested. They seemed to take suggestions as an affront to their authority. Their reactivity, in turn, caused the workers to be more resistant to following orders.

The element of Interiority was almost completely absent in this organization and only present on an individual basis in a few of the workers. Workers were reluctantly doing what they had been pressured to do; they were uninterested in productivity, habitually finding fault with co-workers, obsessed with covering up their own mistakes and disconnected from relationships with the stakeholders.

Sadly, this situation is not uncommon in many corporations today. Sometimes, ruthlessly driven executives can create *high productivity*—with by-products of *low morale*, a general *disregard for the rights of workers* and outright *abuse*. Like a computer that needs defragmenting, these troubled organizations are in dire *need* of *regular main-*

tenance. The problems of a computer in need of maintenance are often hidden from the visible eye. When a computer becomes fragmented, data on the hard drive gets scattered, resulting in slow processing. The drive requires defragmenting in order to be restored to normal performance levels.

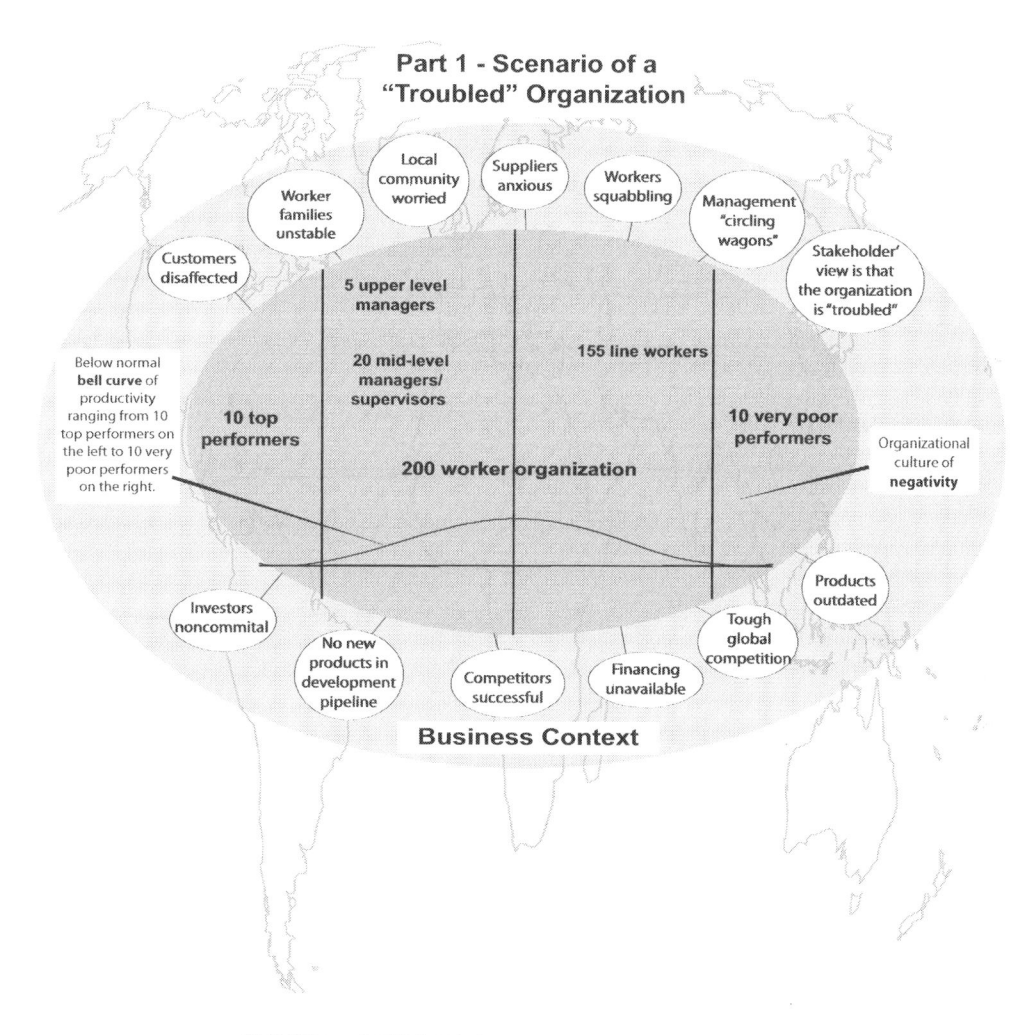

FIGURE 20: **SCENARIO OF A TROUBLED ORGANIZATION**

In a similar fashion, organizations become fragmented, the data becomes disorganized, the capacity to process tasks is overwhelmed, productivity declines, management (the user) becomes intimidated and exerts its authority by using pressure tactics. In all of this, the major issue is that the workers, and their work relationships, become brittle, caustic and often toxic. The energy needed for productive tasks is used up, stalling forward momentum.

The defragmenting work that has potentially the *most powerful effect* and is *most often neglected* is aimed at the cultivation of the *inner life* of both the workers and the organization.

The parallel between computers and organizations ends here. Just as individuals need the integration of shadow energies and adapt to paradox and chaos to become whole, so do *organizations need their troubles to grow and mature*. Surprisingly, in those very troubles lie the energies that can make the organization more productive. However, the default option for fixing organizational issues is by legislating more rules, becoming more rigid in the application of existing rules and treating workers as if they are parts of a machine. This approach all but ensures stalled productivity.

In the case of the intervention I was leading, the necessary component to unify the organization was *heart*—but it was missing. The CEO was extremely bright, energetic and a workaholic. He expected others to mold themselves after him. However, without the glue—the heart—to hold them together, they fragmented, made mistakes and began to lose vital customers.

As odd as it may seem, heart is critical to the health of any organization, which is a lesson I learned long ago in the woods of New Hampshire.

My Story – The Heart of the Matter

I spent six years in a seminary located deep in the woods of New Hampshire. We lived in an old wooden building and made use of army surplus supplies for almost everything. Because we, the seminarians and priests, were very poor, we had to do everything ourselves—cooking, cleaning, building and all of the things that went into keeping 120 young men focused on their education and training for the priesthood. That meant lots of bologna and salami sandwiches and bundling up in jackets and blankets to keep out the winter cold. It was tough going, but we had something that held us together.

That something was a religious Superior who had a heart the size of himself, which was quite considerable. He was no paragon of virtue or religious decorum. He invariably struggled to be on time for morning meditation in the chapel, arriving after everyone else, straightening his habit and rubbing the sleep from his eyes. Without looking, we knew he had arrived when he flopped onto his kneeler...which groaned in protest at the added weight. He usually flubbed the opening prayers, he forgot where he was in the mass, he put on his vestments backwards, but none of that mattered. What made the difference was that he was loved.

> *He was funny, good natured and laughed at himself and his inadequacies. He lifted our spirits. He paid attention to us so he got to know us and what we needed. He was kind and he kept track of the small things. I remember well the new ice hockey skates I got for Christmas. It was a great surprise as I had been expecting an extra piece of fruit. He got a kick out of it also; I knew he was watching when I put them on for the first time. Somehow he found the money to get them. I was happy to get out of the battered racing skates I had been using to chase the puck during lunch break.*
>
> *He had heart and we were all ready to do our parts and more to overlook his shortcomings and even to take advantage of his needs to provide what was necessary. We worked to keep the place running. We often did without necessities. We fixed everything so it would do the job and we had a great time doing so. The whole thing worked because we had heart.*
>
> *He was always looking for ways to give us treats such as ice cream or broken shards of chocolate he bought as leftovers from the chocolate factory. He endeared himself when he went on the defensive in protecting the seminarians from his boss, who was a strict disciplinarian. That boss was always taking away our privileges—such as television—or he would insist we could only watch Lawrence Welk reruns. Our Superior found ways to restore what had been taken away and then endured the reprimands from his boss for corrupting the seminarians by letting us watch the news. We even had to get special permission to watch President John F. Kennedy's funeral after his assassination.*
>
> *Ours was a boss with a human touch. He was human himself in his disheveled appearance, his untied shoes and new cigarette burns (from the ash that dropped in the middle of his white habit).*
>
> *For me the lifetime lesson: because he had a heart we could all take heart. We found heart in our common tasks. His heart enabled willing community.*

My Story – Reflections

Tasks themselves are usually not the most difficult part of work. They can be done bit by bit as we apply our energies to understanding what is involved, setting goals, assembling the needed resources and getting on with the job. In the process, we learn better methods, improve our skills, become faster at completion and grow more productive. We become more willing and skillful when we feel supported, acknowledged and respected for our efforts.

In getting key tasks done, a crucial component is a lightheartedness and comfort in doing our work. Work gets done smoothly when leaders, who enjoy their own work, laugh at their foibles and human limitations, are comfortable in their skins and spread warmth around themselves. Such heart-filled leaders are the key to creating a work environment in which workers can enjoy their labors, take joy in the uniqueness of their workplace and grow in a culture of support and collaboration.

My Story *(Intervention)* – Application

The obvious problems are only the beginning step in any intervention. Clarification of the so-called hard issues is only a preamble to going below the surface to determine what is going on in the inner core of the workers...and in the living heart of the workplace. If the heart is cold and demanding perfection, then the workplace is tight with tension and *lacks* the human touch of *failure, restoration,* and above all, *appreciation of the opportunity to contribute.* If the heart is warm and *understanding of imperfection* and *still pursues constant improvement,* then workers are buoyant with enthusiasm for themselves, each other and the work of the day.

Getting to a place of warm-heartedness is the *ultimate aim* of any intervention. If this is a given, then any hard issues can be resolved.

Your Story

What then about your experience of working with those who had large hearts in the workplace? Has your life at work been made positive by interactions with caring and loving people? Can you recall experiences of generosity and concern by your co-workers? What explanation do you give yourself about the reasons some people are generous and caring? How has showing love and care for co-workers figured in your own life? Have you suffered from your own experiences of showing generosity and care for co-workers in your workplace? What have you learned about yourself from feeling deep care and concern for co-workers? In what ways have you come to terms with your tendencies to express deep positive regard for others in the workplace?

Diagnosis

In diagnosing this troubled organization, I was not so much trying to put solutions in place. I was trying to help the organization become *aware* and begin the *journey toward wholeness*. When most CEOs realize what issues are besetting their organizations, they reactively develop solutions, implement them quickly and move on—as if to outdistance the reappearance of the same troubles. By doing so, they actually truncate the growth process and are surprised when the same issues crop up later. The trick is to become mindful of the *angels and demons* beneath the surface levels of the organizational culture—meaning, the behaviors, relationships and systems. And then, to use the *tools of Interiority* to set the related energies free to increase *productivity* and *satisfaction*.

With this distressed organization, I helped facilitate awareness by interviewing a cross-section of the workers and providing feedback to the assembled workers on what I observed. When I gave feedback, I emphasized, "This is what you are saying about yourselves." I also emphasized that the intervention should be thought of as a journey they were setting out on and it would require both working together and as individuals to grow to a fulfilling place.

Let us leave for the moment the discussion of this "troubled" organization, suspending them in Part One of their journey, *becoming aware* of their troubles. We will return to this organization in Chapter 6 (Intervention) and examine the process and results of the intervention.

When feelings flow, empathies grow

Chapter 5

Patterns and Issues Influencing Productivity

In this chapter, I treat a range of behavioral patterns and issues that influence the improvement or the reduction of workplace productivity. The issues are important because, if neglected, they tend to dissolve into a dysfunctional malaise—which infects many present-day organizations ranging from the financially powerful to the politically connected, the educated and the religious. Clarification of the *deeper* and *more complex causes* of these issues will allow us to consider how the practices of Interiority might be applied to implement greater productivity.

I begin by drawing from the more intractably conflicted behaviors that characterized my own early adult experience. Looking back, I was a walking case study in internal reactivity, alienation, escapism, fear and conflict while on the outside I came across as a hard-working, talented, creative and generally all-around okay guy. I was not unaware of my double life, but I was more concerned about pleasing others and meeting their approval than resolving my duplicity. Regarding the work assigned to me, however, I knew how to do it and I was very productive. What I didn't know was how to handle growth and maturity.

As I think of it now, my basic issue was that before I could even begin to grow up, I had to contend with barriers built up within me that were the emotional equivalent of small mountains. My way of coming to maturity was painful. In terms of the intricacies of the issues I experienced in my work, the saying, "The mills of the gods grind slowly but they grind exceedingly small" definitely applied to me. The mills also ground slowly when you consider how long it took me to become aware of myself as something other than a victim…and finally beginning to choose personal growth in a painful process.

Along the way to early adulthood, I survived many hurts, resentments, fears and doubts. But I did survive and that signals other powers at work in me. Certainly I was no paragon of Interiority. As most do, I stumbled my way along as best I could.

In the various workplaces where I toiled, I found abundant issues—struggles for control, colliding ambitions, manipulation of information, warring cliques, hyperactive rumor mills and everywhere, a lack of communication. These were only the surface level manifestations that pointed to a lack of Interiority. Those of us who considered ourselves as workers tried our best to resolve issues—by personal reading, talks on the subject, retreats, conferences and endless training workshops…as well as committing to changing ourselves. The efficacy of those efforts at renewal and self-improvement was minimal and engendered chagrin in those with whom we worked. That was the case in the following example.

My Story – Reactive Complex

It happened when I was in Japan as a member of a missionary Order of Catholic priests and brothers. Each missionary was working according to his own inspiration but with the general goal of promoting the Christian message to the mostly non-comprehending and resistant Japanese. This resistance was the reason I tried a variety of innovative ways of being a missionary.

It was the mid-1970s. I needed funds for my book-publishing project—the theme of which was, of all things, communication and relationships as the basis of personal growth. I took my proposal to the assembled members of the Order and made a request for funding, that I intended to pay back from the sales. I had some trepidation about the request because the subject of the book only obliquely mentioned the Christian message.

My fears turned out to be well-founded because the validity of my project as a missionary venture was questioned. During the meeting, the arguments questioned whether there were not projects more worthy in terms of Jesus and the Japanese. As I listened to the discussion, I could feel my trepidations quickly turning to anger, so

> *I peremptorily took umbrage and withdrew my request. My withdrawal ended the discussion—to the chagrin of some of my supporters. [As a side note, I later raised the funds on my own and published the book.]*

My Story – Reflections

As the meeting progressed, I kept relatively calm on the outside. Inside, I was livid, embarrassed and conflicted about how to proceed. When I withdrew my request, I was in the grip of a *reactive complex*.

Everyone experiences reactive complexes to one degree or another. There is nothing abnormal about them. A reactive complex is a pattern of responding in life situations according to emotional behaviors based on childhood decisions made in situations of stress or trauma. *Reactive* refers to an emotional response triggered by circumstances similar to those in the original experience. *Complex* refers to the group of highly charged energies that are the source of the reaction.

I had reacted to the direction of the discussion about my project, but the fires that stoked that reaction had been set aflame many ages and memories before. Only later was I able to learn that my extreme sensitivity, which triggered my reactive complex, was in fact a gift I might use to work with others who suffered from similar complexes. I could understand what they were going through and allow them the space to work through their issues to some reasonable accommodation.

Admittedly, I am a living repository of the issues that bedevil our contemporary workplaces—and society—both on the surface and underneath. As in my case, it is not the manifest problems that get us in trouble in our workplaces; it is our lack of awareness of the legacies of *unresolved issues* and *complex selves* that provoke dysfunctional situations.

Your Story

What then about you, reader? Have you experienced something like a reactive complex in yourself? Can you recall the pivotal experience that exposed your weakness and left you raw, hurt and angry? How did reactivity show up in your life as a recognizable complex and cause problems for you at work?

Alternatively, how did your weakness help you to work with those who might have shared the same weakness? As a result of some difficult lessons learned, what practices (of mind or behavior) did you put in place?

A Framework of Recognizable Patterns

There are six patterns of behavior in the workplace, which we must understand before we can get beneath the exterior manifestations. They are as follows:

- Response 1: **Responsible Engagement** refers to the characteristics of a productive and dependable worker.
- Responses 2 and 3: **Passivity** and **Escape** refers to poor performers and the negative impact they have on the other workers.
- Response 4: **Exploitation** is characteristic mostly of management behaviors and directed toward mismanagement of workers.
- Response 5 and 6: **Fear** and **Conflict** can affect and debilitate all workers.

Responsible Engagement

The first type of responsible behavior in a worker is to embrace the objective perception of all reality as a primary and personal responsibility. Basically, this means letting go of illusions, empty myths, unrealistic assumptions and illogical beliefs that might support an unproductive work style. Some may argue we can never reach total objectivity in our perceptions but only arrive at a biased version of reality mediated through our eyes and other senses. Nevertheless, with a heightened awareness of those biases and a dedication to integrity and responsible judgment in assessing situations, we can arrive at a close approximation of reality. An example of this response might be a worker who is sufficiently self-aware to be able to listen to all sides of an argument, consider the implications of each course of action and opt for action based on values, principles and best results for all stakeholders.

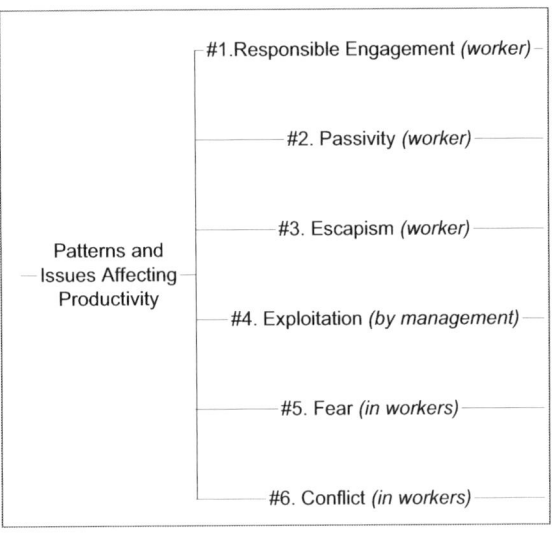

Patterns and Issues Affecting Productivity:
- #1. Responsible Engagement *(worker)*
- #2. Passivity *(worker)*
- #3. Escapism *(worker)*
- #4. Exploitation *(by management)*
- #5. Fear *(in workers)*
- #6. Conflict *(in workers)*

FIGURE 21: **POSITIVE OUTCOMES & TYPICAL ISSUES**

The second type of responsible behavior is to adopt a *socially responsible lifestyle* through serious engagement with reality as a whole. We can do this by using our own experiences at work as the primary reference points for choosing our values, actions and contributions. You see this in the workers who try to improve the conditions of all workers and organizations, societies and communities of which they are a part and who speak up about the inequities in their organizations. They would then lend their energies to improve the systems themselves.

The third type of responsible behavior is taking *ownership of community needs*. Community needs are different from those addressed in social action, which targets the achievement of specific goals within a certain timeframe. Community needs are those intractable issues belonging to the wider human citizenry, which will never be resolved but must be shouldered by all. Examples might include exclusively using renewable resources or the maintenance of peace between people of contrasting belief systems.

Taking ownership means: I take the initiative to be responsible for the issues of which I am aware and I am doing something about them, even if it is just giving them shape. Examples of responsible engagement to community needs can be seen in the behaviors of social entrepreneurs who attempt to resolve some major issues among a disadvantaged demographic population through entrepreneurial activities.

Case in point, Muhammad Yunus founded the Grameen Bank in 1976 to provide microloans on easy credit to poor men and women in rural Bangladesh. He saw a systemic need, took responsibility for it and made a solution happen. As Head of the Rural Economics Program at the University of Chittagong, he did more than his academic work by demolishing a vicious cycle of usury. The virtuous cycle of self-improvement that he established became a model of responsible behavior in rural Bangladesh—and throughout the world.

Likewise, as every organization is part of a community, so does the requirement of *responsible action for the whole* belong to every worker. This assumes that because we are part of the human community we have some ownership of the conditions of society and have a proportionate obligation to do what we can to bring about beneficial change.

It must be noted that the longer a person continues to act in responsible engagement at work, the easier it becomes to mature and make a positive contribution. Conversely, the longer workers persist in negative and unproductive behaviors that produce poor quality results, the more difficult it becomes to make constructive contributions.

Passivity

Characterizing the second set of responses (negative), passivity can be classified as emerging from the following types of behavior: *indifference, boredom, resignation* and *agnosticism*.

Indifference. The *indifferent* type of passive behavior is a *neutrality toward* or *removal from* events or circumstances at work. Workers who choose indifference are avoiding the need to perform according to expectations. They are not interested in their work, their co-workers or the organization. They have learned how to avoid work and they excel only at hiding their non-performance, covering their tracks so as not to be blamed for mistakes, avoiding supervisors so they can work on their private tasks with impunity. Usually, the rest of the workforce leaves them alone as they can turn any call to accountability into a vicious counterattack.

These people are not indifferent to their pay and benefits package and can lead any action to gain their "rightful" compensation. Often those who seem indifferent are using this kind of persona to mask a manipulative approach to getting their own way. They trump up complaints against management and exploit legitimate protections of workers to their own advantage. They spend their time thinking of how to use the system for their own benefit. They do not concern themselves with the interests of others and see sincere and hardworking workers as deluded and naive.

Boredom. Passivity is often caused by *boredom* with assigned tasks or lack of commitment to the work, to their co-workers or to the organization. Bored workers are not engaged because they have developed mental and physical habits of *avoidance*.

Bored workers fall somewhere between the not-engaged and the actively-disengaged at work and together they make up *71% of the workforce*. The reasons for such boredom in workers derive from some combination of the following causes:

- Feeling that their jobs do not suit them and they are under-stretched
- Never learning how to work productively; developing poor work habits
- Having no goals to strive for and consequently finding no meaning in the work[132]

Resignation. The third type of passive behavior is a disconnection from any circumstance that might lead to favorably influencing one's reality. This resignation can be seen in workers who do not believe in their unique capabilities to do any more than obligatory tasks. They are restrained by poor self-image and prefer to avoid any controversial activities potentially risky to their position. They take whatever comes along, whether beneficial or detrimental to their well-being, which may even extend to their pay and benefits. They do not do the thinking necessary to understand the potentially negative results of their own lack of involvement, and if they did, they do not bring their observations to the attention of the representatives of management.

Agnosticism. Perhaps the most common type of passive behavior is the agnostic approach. This kind of worker ignores questions of meaning, purpose, ethics or contribution. They may work effectively and produce results, but the reason for such industry is merely self-interest. They are taken up with their own lives and work with sufficient diligence to be comfortable and secure by acquiring money—for themselves only. This approach can be seen in people who often refrain from thinking about questions of ultimate meaning or purpose because any answers may present uncomfortable options. They work hard to gain position (power, reputation and material goods) and, in some cases, make a considerable contribution to society. However, on a deeper level of connectedness to the whole, they are tone deaf to the unethical aspects of their activities.

In an opinion piece in the *NY Times* on March 14, 2011, Paul Krugman related the activities of a certain bank which sold mortgages to populations of people who could not possibly repay them. To further compound the unethical behaviors, they packaged those mortgages as collateral for securities and sold them on the market. These unethical activities contributed to the collapse of the financial system throughout 2008-2009. After the government (citizen's taxes) bailed out the banks and tried to support those mortgage holders who were "underwater," this and similar banks further took advantage by using that largesse to the detriment of mortgage holders.

Talk about being tone deaf, they do not know because they do not want to know or recognize the depredations caused by their activities. They have so hardened their consciences against the ethical dimensions of their activities, they become *habitually agnostic*.

My Story – Just Plain Crazy

The fact that they did not work but remained employed for 30 years made no sense...except to the two of them. In their own minds, they were excellent and experienced workers who deserved every penny they got—and more. They created an art form out of avoiding work. Together they made common cause in not working, avoiding work, looking like they were working and providing alibis for each other when they were away from the workplace without permission. They had evolved ways of threatening and intimidating their managers and co-workers, so they were left alone. Due to their longevity with the organization, their higher-ups were loath to terminate them. Their managers were fine, well-intentioned people but long-suffering—far too long.

I was called in to help resolve the situation. When I interviewed them (and some of their co-workers), I concluded that their arguments made no sense. These two did not do any measurable work; they had built a façade of being overworked and even claimed abuse by anyone who had the temerity to question their productivity. No one could build a case against them because they had defensible alibis. They could not be reprimanded by their supervisors because they consistently lodged complaints against them that seemed on the surface to have some merit. Moreover, they claimed all kinds of discrimination based on the flimsiest evidence. Their reputation was so widespread that the EEO (Equal Employment Opportunity - administration) knew them by name and their record of submitted claims.

They conducted a campaign of innocence and self-defense to the point where their co-workers gave up and did the work of the complainants, as well as their own.

Even though they were assigned specific tasks, they managed to do work only of their own choosing. They left everybody guessing about what they were actually doing. No one saw any results. To make up for the lack of results, they had ready a stream of excuses about being called away to do other priority jobs. When they used the "other priorities intervened" excuse, everyone smiled knowingly but no one was amused. They moved around so much in the workplace no one could keep track of them. Reports on sightings were so baffling that when they were reported in several places at once, people just shrugged and walked away. When they were called to account for their lack of productivity or absence from the workplace, they produced letters from medical doctors about the precarious state of their health caused by being overwhelmed by the amount of work they had to do. They were periodically at their desks but all anyone could see were documents being shifted, seemingly serious phone conversations and assurances of reports being almost delivered. Discussions with them were impossible as they shifted from topic to topic, used non-sequiturs that boggled the imagination and waxed eloquently on irrelevant subjects.

Pity the manager. Pity their efforts to corral these two into some semblance of order. Pity their sleepless nights, days of wasted energies and exhaustion from inconclusive discussions. Pity the managers who questioned their own sanity when they were baffled by the unbelievably nimble contortions of two workers, who claimed they were highly productive but who showed no results. Pity the manager who was cornered by thinly-veiled threats to expose his/her weaknesses, to make claims of discrimination or injustice. Intimidated, the managers backed away from encounters with the terrifying two and gave them a wide berth.

Yet, they drew their salaries and used whatever benefits to which they had access. No sooner was some benefit announced than they handed in their completed documents for the next one. One had to stand aghast at their temerity and bedazzled at their footwork. This is the astonishing situation into which I was called to do an intervention.

My task was to sort out the impasse, find out what was going on and make recommendations for a course of action. Dutifully, I conducted interviews, put together

> *an intervention and did my best to come to a reasonable solution that would ameliorate the situation, but it turned out to be impossible. In my report, I emphasized the unsolvable nature of the impasse. I made it clear the individuals had extremely poor work habits. This was shorthand for "just plain crazy."*
>
> *The upshot was that the upper-level management eased them out.*

My Story – Reflections

Every workplace has its share of poor performers about whom much is tried with no success. Every manager has nightmare tales of pursuing workplace miscreants only to have the tables turned and every strategy defeated—so all tactics became more trouble than they are worth. And every manager faces the task of what to do in such unclear situations…before they ask for outside help.

My Story – Applications

It is often the burden of highly productive workers to carry the workloads of the less-than-productive members. The hard-working members learn that no amount of guidance and support will supply what is lacking—in nature or habit—or is plainly derived from ill-will. It is an inescapable fact that not every worker is similarly equipped to be productive. And, up to a point, it is also inescapable that the better-equipped worker is often forced to help those who are less equipped. Eventually, a time comes when *termination* is the only option. When work patterns such as those described above are carried on for a long time, it is impossible to change the mindset or value system upon which they are built.

At times, the situation is "just plain crazy."

Your Story

What then about you, the reader? Has your life been marked by interactions with less-than-productive people in the workplace? Were your efforts to work with these people frustrated with lack of results? Did your own work suffer because of their lack of productivity? Was your willingness to cooperate perhaps taken advantage of by unscrupulous or insensitive co-workers? What explanation do you give yourself about the reasons some people are not productive? How have you learned to work with such people?

[handwritten note: Scott Peck: "People of the Lie"]

Escapism

The third set of responses is escapism and can be classified as three different types of behavior: *denial*, *distraction* and *submersion*.

Denial. In the first type of escapist behavior, the workers deny difficult realities by getting angry and *reacting in destructive manners*. They are usually over-reactive to feedback and typically have short fuses. Co-workers tread lightly in their presence and only the most secure and courageous dare do anything that might incur their wrath. They are either openly or passively aggressive and overtly obstructive to anything with which they do not agree. They can intimidate everyone around them to the degree that even supervisors become afraid to call them to account. As in the previous story, managers oftentimes allow them to remain in the system.

Distraction. This is the second type of escapist behavior. Distraction characterizes the workers who, similar to those in denial, are *shutting out reality*. They do not want to take their work seriously. They see the workplace as an opportunity to be preoccupied with matters unrelated to the work, such as sports, entertainment and social media. If they are pressed to work, they make sure they do work that amuses them, satisfies their cynical side or does not identify them with any serious matters.

This behavior can be seen in those who are addicted to chemical or other dependencies. Such addictions might include games played merely for the purpose of being distracted or to repress ideas, personal feelings or connections with people whom they find distasteful.

Submersion. The third type of escapist behavior can be seen in the submersion of self in the *external world*—to the point that the person is wholly enveloped in exteriority. This kind of worker is most evident in the workplace today. They are consumed by spectacles of so-called *heroes* and *heroines* and the ways in which the *beautiful people* comport themselves. They are attracted by images of the physical and all of the ways in which the physical body can be ornamented for display. These workers are preoccupied by being consumers of elegant lifestyles and chase after each emerging fashionable accoutrement. They are so immersed in external displays that they continue working just to avoid the feeling of being alone. This response can also be seen in workaholics, who are in constant motion around events or people who are external to themselves.

Exploitation

The fourth set of responses, namely exploitation, can also be sub-classified as three types of behavior: *taking advantage of human diversity*, leveraging *undue competitive advantage*, and *obsessing over wealth, power and position*.

Taking Advantage of Human Diversity. This first type of exploitative behavior includes those who take advantage of the normal imbalance between diverse people (social groups and societies). History books are filled with examples of taking unfair advantage of indigenous peoples, for example, by purchasing natural resources from them at a fraction of the market value. The practice has not stayed in the past. Even though there are many laws against the exploitation of people at work in so-called advanced societies, there is no shortage of organizations abusing the rights of workers—especially oppressed minorities.

Undue Competitive Advantage. The second type of exploitative behavior focuses on maintaining competitive advantage with the exclusive purpose of maintaining wealth, power and position. This can be seen in the selective positioning of oneself or one's organization so there is only engagement with people seen as sources of authority and influence.

Obsessing over Wealth, Power and Position. Similar to the second example above, the third type of exploitative behavior can be seen in individuals or organizations whose sole goal is *accumulating* wealth, power and position. This is seen in behaviors that focus on grasping opportunities exclusively geared for the accumulation of wealth, associating with those who are seen as powerful and being perceived as holding positions of power.

Fear

[handwritten note: at root of all anger - what am I afraid of?]

So far, I have been discussing some milder forms of soul-deadening experiences at work. I will now take a look at two of the more toxic forms of oppression that workers can experience, namely fear and conflict.

Fear is ultimately the *basis of conflict*. Fear is also a personal emotion and as such we must cultivate a dialogical relationship with it before we can learn to manage it. In other words, because our fears will not go away, we must *accept* and *work with* them in an ongoing dialogue through which they become our friends. Thus, the key practice becomes one of developing a trusting relationship with our fears.

In short, when our fears are *faced*, *understood* and *accepted* as our partners in dialogue, they become our friends and supporters.

Most workplaces have some form of tension among employees. In fact, most people recognize that a certain amount of tension heightens energies and sharpens focus. However, where the normal amount of tension deteriorates into states of fear and conflict, teamwork and productivity decline drastically. Fear and conflict are alike in that *both debilitate the energies necessary for productivity* and *generate cycles of mistrust* between the parties involved. These cycles of mistrust tend to stay around and become even worse if they are not treated thoroughly by the practices of Interiority.

All workers arrive in the workplace fully loaded with fear. They bring entire histories of fearful experiences—all of the fears of the individual as well as universal unconscious. Because we are distracted by immediate tasks, we tend to lightly dismiss these histories as *manageable* and *controllable*. We assume our egos are strong enough to move us beyond any of our past and present ghosts.

In truth, our egos are usually not that strong. In the workplace, workers encounter legacies of their own fear as well as the fears of their co-workers. Add in: the boss's fear, the immanent fear in the system, in society and the media (which markets itself on the basis of fear), and indeed you have a fearful mix. "Be afraid, be very afraid" is the darkly muttered mantra of the nightly news we readily consume as must-have information.

Fear is the emotion most often manipulated by the media so viewers will consume advertised goods (and be no wiser). Fear is the goad used by those who exploit their positions in organizational hierarchies to frighten workers into doing what the manipulators want.

What you and I bring into our workplace amounts to an *enormous energy source* with which we have learned to contend every moment of every day. Fear is presented to us as something to be *avoided*, *fled from* and *hidden* because it is considered a *weakness*. We have been taught that fear is a *negative* in our lives. Truly, fear can indeed rob us of the energy we need when it manifests itself in anxieties, agitation, self-doubt, procrastination, nervousness—and many forms of avoidance.

So what should we do about this ever-present emotion of fear?

What if we viewed authentic fear as a *positive*, even as a *gift*, that helps preserve us when real danger is around…and as our *constant friend*? First, let's differentiate *authentic fear* from inauthentic or neurotic fear, such as free-floating anxiety. Authentic fear alerts us to the presence of *danger*, especially with regard to those who do not have our interests in mind. In the context of Interiority, fear is to be *faced* and *grown through*. Eventually, it is our lot to embrace omnipresent fears and turn them into our friends.

The following experiences are among those commonly recognized as *inducing fear* in a worker or group of workers.

- having one's credibility questioned
- being left out of decision-making
- being criticized in front of others

- not getting the information necessary to succeed
- having a key assignment given to someone less deserving
- not getting deserved recognition
- having suggestions misinterpreted as criticisms
- getting poor performance ratings
- getting fired
- hearing rumors about the possibility of layoffs
- proliferation of un-discussable subjects (which leaves many guessing about key activities)
- having one's legitimate work efforts undermined or sabotaged
- receiving threats to one's person or position
- being threatened with severe retaliation over speaking up

The list is intimidating, especially when you consider that this is an abbreviated treatment. Besides these commonly recognized external causes of fear, there are *internally-generated fears* that drain the vital energies needed for higher productivity. These include:

- harboring negative feelings about oneself, such as lack of confidence
- suffering extreme self-criticism
- holding on to negative feelings regarding one's work
- loss of trust and pride in oneself as a valued group member
- extreme rumination over mistakes.

Then there are the *fears induced by the systems* themselves. Every organization has ways of doing what it does and these develop into normative systems accepted by the majority as the culture or "the way things are done around here." Those systems become oppressive when they include:

- instructions that are unclear and/or contradictory
- political pressures, which are the basis of promotion rather than performance excellence
- bosses who send out ambiguous messages (by saying one thing and doing another)
- roles that are duplicative and unclear about who is doing what and how

- workers who use vicious methods to compete for promotional opportunities
- communications which are spotty, confusing and disempowering
- insufficient resources, which devolve into constant struggles for scarce items
- norms of workplace behavior which are unclear and unevenly applied by supervisors
- unethical conduct that is covered up and becomes an un-discussable item at meetings.

Then there are the fears that are induced by the system, as a whole. In the face of such systemic cultures of fear, workers might lose heart and just go along because they are threatened by the system. Or they might move against the system.

When workers see the organization as a fearsome influence on their lives, they tend to demonize the whole system. They fear the system because they sense they have no control over it; its influence is everywhere and yet that influence appears to be located in no particular position of authority that can be held accountable. Workers fear the system when they are left out of the decision-making process but are held responsible for whatever decisions are made. As an example, I remember appointing my successor in a group for which I had responsibility in Japan. I did so without consulting the group members and the ensuing firestorm caused severe disruptions in the group's activities and their relationships. It was a severe lesson in consensus decision-making and I was forced to back-pedal and mend fences to continue the group's forward momentum. This is an insignificant example but makes the point of worker-resistance if they feel excluded from the change process.

On a larger scale, even though the system may be oppressive, workers often resist changes to what they have known because they distrust the perils of continuous disturbances and opt for what is familiar—"the devil you know." When such *distrust of the system* penetrates the workplace, *three identifiable reactions* become apparent.

The *majority tend not to react* because they fear that the system will somehow get back at them and their situation will become even worse.

The second type of reaction is from a *vocal minority* intent on *sabotaging the system* by exacerbating its weaknesses, draining its resources and sometimes by outright disruption of its targeted outcomes. Sabotage activities can either be active and purposeful or passive and scattershot but the results are the same, as the systems turn against themselves and the organization quietly implodes into irrelevance.

Conversely, a *vocal minority* with *constructive intent* might try to *reform the system from within*. They might evolve a new vision of how the system might work more effectively, set achievable goals, connect with kindred spirits, devolve manageable change projects, highlight what is worth saving, implement models of the changes they aspire to and communicate about the status and the beneficial changes to all concerned.

They can only do these things over the long term if they remain loyal to the system as a whole while actively working toward the preferred organizational state.

Little of the above can be achieved without robust practices of Interiority. To paraphrase JFK, "*We shall never negotiate* out of fear, *and* we *shall never* fear *to negotiate...*"

I add my thought that we shall sometimes act out of fear but we shall not fear to act.

> ### My Story – Shooting the Messenger
>
> *Just in case you think consulting is easy, I have been fired more than once for doing my job. Surprising as it may seem for a consultant, just doing your job as it is written in the contract is no guarantee of immunity from being let go. It happened to me when I was doing my best and, in my view, saving the client's bacon. The basic problem is that no one likes to receive negative feedback even if it might save his/her hide. That factor is increased in proportion to the ego involved, such as the one by a hugely successful V.P. who received accolades for excellence in his area of expertise.*
>
> *After six years of sterling service, I thought I was on safe ground with a particular client in the airline logistics services area. Their major client was a major Japanese air cargo corporation. I was providing consulting services as a go-between, promoting the business relationships between the two. My consulting strategy was based on the provision of excellent quality services to the Japanese client. I believed success in this project would lead to enormous follow-on business for my client, with interconnected organizations in Japan that belonged to the Japanese client's conglomerate. I had effectively provided many different kinds of consulting services and my reputation was solid. In particular, my advice was followed regarding the quality of services expected by the Japanese.*
>
> *Nevertheless, I began to get anxious when my client took on too many obligations to provide similar logistics services to organizations other than their Japanese air cargo client. The problem centered on the V.P. in my client organization. He was an excellent salesperson but oversold their services thinking they could provide the same level of quality to fulfill the increased obligations. It quickly became apparent they could not, but he did not recognize the impasse and continued on, leaving the harried service technicians to try to maintain the necessary quality. As the support*

for the technicians dwindled, some of the key workers saw the writing on the wall and left for other opportunities.

At this time, I picked up the message that the Japanese managers were increasingly dissatisfied with my client's services. They felt they did not have dependable service technicians with whom to work. I reported the impending crisis to the V.P., who nodded and promised action. I tried to have the V.P. meet with his Japanese counterpart to apologize and explain how he would ensure continuation of excellent services. The V.P. dismissed my suggestions by saying he was too busy to get into such Band-Aid™ measures. He assigned new staff to the Japanese client and urged them to maintain quality. It was immediately evident that his response was insufficient and too short term to do any good. Immediately, signs of problems appeared when he refused to provide the new staff with adequate resources.

Soon several major service glitches showed up and headquarters in Japan became involved, threatening to withhold payment for service. I knew that this Japanese client was a linchpin in my client's business strategy. I also knew losing their business would be disastrous for my client.

Time was running out. The Japanese were losing patience. I requested a meeting with the V.P. and presented the crisis in plain language. I explained the consequences that losing this client would bring about. I repeated the advice that if one Japanese client has experiences of poor quality my client's reputation would be ruined in the wider Japanese business community, both in the U.S. and Japan. The stakes were huge.

To my chagrin, he refused to change his plans and now I was facing the danger of losing face within the Japanese business community. I redoubled my efforts and focused on the strategy of maintaining high quality to ensure long-term financial health. He wouldn't budge. As a last resort, I told him that his own direct reports had lost faith in his efforts to maintain services and he had the reputation of having poor overall judgment. As I related these facts, I could see he was wavering and I was skating on thin ice. However, I felt under an obligation to save their business and so I pushed the same arguments again. He relented, but as was soon to become apparent, it was a pyrrhic victory. He acknowledged that I was right and he had to support the Japanese client and ensure top quality. The upshot of that decision was to retain the Japanese client and to gain enormously increased business. I knew I had saved the day.

But I was politely paid for my services and not invited back. The messenger had been shot.

PATTERNS AND ISSUES INFLUENCING PRODUCTIVITY

My Story – Reflections

As a consultant, I always serve at the discretion of my client. Regardless of my insights, if I offend the sensitivities of the client by making reference to his less-than-effective behavior and poor judgment as being the cause of the problems, from his point of view I have crossed a bridge too far. I had been correct to exert pressure to save my client's business, but I had forgotten the adage that "shooting the messenger" might apply in my own case—and that whistle-blowers have a poor record of survival.

My Story – Application

You live and learn. As an alternative tactic, I could have arranged a meeting between my client, the V.P. and the Japanese client and allowed the Japanese spokesperson to communicate the possibilities directly. I learned to soft-pedal the message when it conflicts with the self-image and ego of the client.

Your Story

What then about you, the reader? Have you been at the receiving end of a vengeful supervisor, co-worker or clique? Were your efforts at working productively unsuccessful, even a waste of your energy? Did you suffer from upper management's failure to notice how you were victimized? Were your pleas for help ignored? Was the culture of the organization one that allowed all kinds of inappropriate discriminatory behaviors? What explanation do you give yourself about why people get stuck in organizations that are toxic to well-intentioned and behaving workers? What have you learned from such people—and organizations—that you can bring to your next place of work?

Conflict

Because of many changes in today's workplaces, people feel tremendous pressure to *perform* at a *high level...all the time...under all circumstances*. These changes include: layoffs and downsizing, increased work volume coupled (with diminished resources), constant demands for new knowledge and skills, and weakened staff loyalty.

It is little wonder conflicts arise with greater frequency than ever.

In this section, we will examine a fundamental cause of conflict known as *divergent perceptions of reality*. This kind of conflict usually results in *spirals of negativity*. The remedy for resolving the conflict and changing the result is in the inner forum of Interiority.

Most of us willingly accept that it is normal to perceive reality according to how it presents itself to us. The truth is, there are many elements in our human makeup that alter what our senses pick up. Among others, Neuroscience points this out, as does the influence of one's unconscious. The result is that each worker in the same workplace may observe the same circumstances but *interpret* its message *in dramatically different ways*. One worker may perceive the situation as benign while another may see it as dangerous and requiring an aggressive response.

One example, that derives from the distant past of the human community (when people were hunter/gatherers), is the perception of nearby noises as coming from dangerous animals or enemies—generating a fight-or-flight response. Today, because of the Internet, Twitter, texting, Google, et al, workers are hyperaware of the latest news, juicy rumors and general scuttlebutt. In the workplace, good news draws only passing attention but news of upcoming changes precipitates defensive or aggressive maneuvers to protect one's position. In the outside world, Wall Street gyrations precipitate scrambles for suddenly scarce resources.

The end result: tensions, exhaustion, declining health—and an elevated temptation to take illicit advantage while one is able.

All of us are familiar with workers who react to perceived threats with their own threats. Such aggressive stances are evident in muscular tension, constricted voice, rapid breathing, injurious words spat out with hurtful intent. So begins round after round of vicious fault-finding, demonization of others and denial of one's own issues.

Beyond the physical manifestation of workplace conflict, there is also an all-too-common *passive-aggressive conflict* which can be seen in behaviors such as:

- resistance to compliance
- working-to-rule
- the silent treatment
- hostile body language (such as throwing things and slamming doors)
- avoiding eye-contact
- non-cooperation in teamwork
- flinging statements indirectly at others—while smoldering with resentful innuendo
- sarcasm and other denigrating activities

The problem with passive aggression is that because the protagonist's anger is repressed and appears in body language, it is often unfocused and misdirected, so the anger is felt by many in the work environment. Workers whose conflict management skills are limited to passive aggressive behaviors often suffer greatly because of intrapersonal tension. They are often lonely, given to extended, brooding silences, begrudging participation in any teamwork and rumor-mongering. For these people, even coming to work can be a distasteful and draining experience. Work itself becomes an unpleasant affair to be endured impatiently until the clock shows it is quitting time.

Both active and passive aggressive behaviors are forbidden by workplace regulations, but that does not prevent such cycles of negativity from happening among workers. Before long, there is a widening gap of negativity that contaminates cooperation and drains workgroups of the energies needed for productive work. (See the illustration).

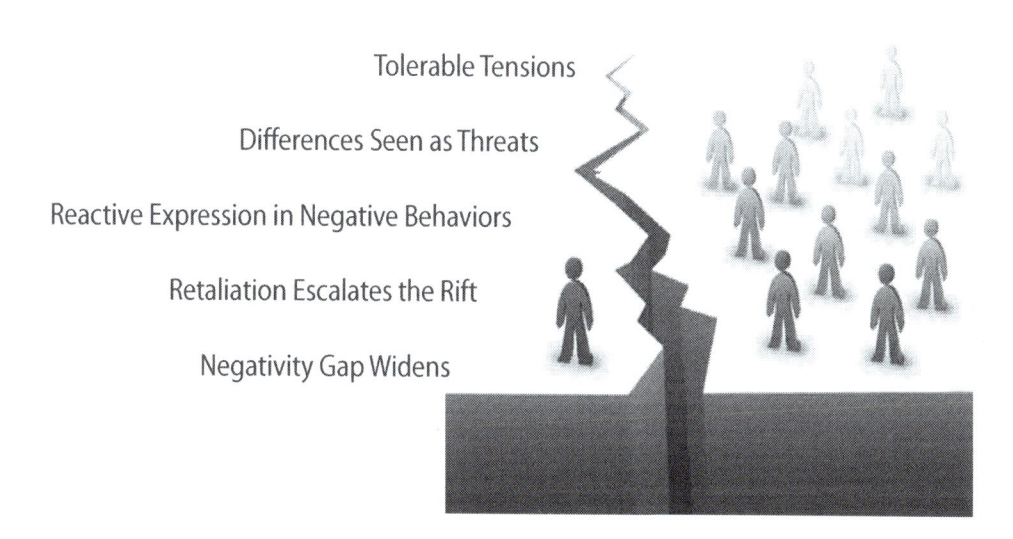

FIGURE 22: **WIDENING THE GAP OF NEGATIVITY**

Even with this kind of contaminated work environment, all is not lost; it is possible to break the cycle of negativity by changing aspects of oneself in the forum of Interiority. Especially those employees embroiled in conflict need to cultivate and practice Interiority. Most conflict resolution strategies involve getting both parties together for negotiation and, perhaps, amelioration of differences. But more often than not, differences are papered over and both sides smolder until the next tension breakout. The *only viable option is to go inward* and redirect the energies into a positive vein.

The rest of this book will be devoted to the development of these optional practices of Interiority that may free workers from negative cycles of conflictive behavior and habits of overwhelming fear. Replacement of repressed conflict-management habits with practices of Interiority can provide relief for the individual and prevent conflicts from spreading and decreasing productivity. The following chapter continues the treatment of the "troubled" organization that we encountered in Chapter 4. In the chapter, I explain the impact of the intervention that I conducted, which resulted in an increase of awareness of the issues—but realistically, the organization still remained weak.

Petrifying projections may prevent passion's play

Chapter 6

Intervention

*And how am I to face the odds
Of man's bedevilment and God's?
I, a stranger and afraid
In a world I never made.*
—A. E. Housman, *The Laws of God, the Laws of Man from Last Poems*

Reflecting on Housman's poem, in our fear we sometimes prefer to disown the bedevilment of work that is not of our making. We imagine we could be happy in some world where people are all working comfortably together with no mistakes. Most of us, however, make the best of our lot at work and resign ourselves to thinking, "This is just the way things are." Even when we try to figure things out, we get bogged down in complexity and end up thinking that there's not a lot we can do to change things to our liking—yet we try.

Here, I continue my story about what I did over a twelve-month period in the process of intervening in the system of the so-called "Troubled Organization" in Chapter Four. I will concentrate on two aspects of the intervention, namely: <u>awareness of the issues</u> and the <u>still-missing pieces</u>.

Awareness

For any system to change, it has to become aware it has a problem. When it discovers and takes ownership of its problem(s), it can begin to change. To continue to change, the organization has to understand that real change is a long-term project and not based on a one-time intervention activity. Here, I review the steps I took to resolve the issues as well as the positive and not-so-positive results from the intervention that I conducted in the organization.

The Intervention

As a consultant/trainer/coach, I was deeply involved in almost all aspects of the intervention. The intervention was a 13-step process which included interviewing, feedback, skills development and implementation planning.

Interviews

As explained in Chapter Four, I interviewed a cross section of the employees to get their views, see how they felt and what they would like to see done more effectively. Not all interviewees had been able to state what they did or didn't want, so I had to sort through disconnected comments, examples, feelings, sporadic accusations of blame and even reticence to address the interview questions. My approach was to regard each interview as revealing something significant about the workers and the workplace. It didn't matter how the information was communicated to me. I was there to listen.

I recall sweeping statements from management representatives that conveyed ultimatums, such as "People are here to work and, considering what they are getting paid, we want work done." In a similar vein I heard, "I want people to do their work regardless of their past experiences or in spite of what others are doing." Again I heard, "When I call people on their lack of productivity, they don't like it. Liking or not liking is not my concern. I am simply focused on getting results."

Some workers spoke only about their own experiences of mistreatment, such as "This place is full of hostility both overt and repressed. Nothing is getting done; styles of supervision are completely non-productive; relationships with customers are cold and employees snipe at each other, constantly. My real feeling is that I want out of here." Similarly, regarding a supervisor I heard, "She is insulting, demeaning and derogatory toward her subordinates. Who does she think she is—acting like she is better than us? She holds onto information we need for our jobs just so she can manipulate us." Again, "You can't even go to work every day without being stressed out for fear of having your character or your work attacked. When I come into this workplace, my heart starts thumping so badly, I feel like I am going to have a heart attack. This is no way to come to work. Can't you do something?"

Another interviewee came really prepared, or so she thought. She had a foot-high stack of folders bulging with documents. She immediately began to make her case by lifting the top sheaf of papers. Dog-eared as they were, I surmised it was from heavy use as she began reading. She read rapidly and breathlessly but since I had no context, she had to interject extraneous material. We made little progress. I urged her to put the folders down, briefly tell me the story in her own words and focus on what and how she experienced her situation. In spite of her copious documentation, her story emerged in a convoluted series of anecdotes of the *he said – she said* variety. I made connections as best I could, but it was the emotional context of her immediate working relationship in which I had the greatest interest. When all was said and done, she hated her supervisor. From what I deduced later, the feeling was mutual.

After I collated the information from the interviews, I assembled a report and then provided feedback on what I had heard—that is, how they (the workers) perceived themselves and their organization, its issues and possible solutions. I did not distribute the report except to the top executives, but I provided the key messages contained in the report at the beginning of the intervention during a feedback session for all the workers. In providing the feedback, I had to be careful to protect the privacy of individuals and, at the same time, provide a clear picture of the issues and possible solutions that faced the organization. This feedback fulfilled the need for the workers to hear what they were saying about various dimensions of their work/life situation.

Interestingly, it was as if they had come to confirm or take issue with what they were saying about themselves.

At the beginning of the workshops that were part of the intervention, I established the condition that all discussions were confidential. Everybody nodded—but nobody paid attention. Confidentiality smelled like conspiracy and was good because everyone wanted in. I recall standing in front of the assembled workers to review the feedback results. I posted two bullet-point lists: one for positives and another for negatives. Excitement pulsed around the room; tensions rose as their eyes flipped back and forth between me and the screen. As had happened in the past, what they wanted was for me to be an honest broker. If I respected their interview comments, I would be okay and if not, nothing I did thereafter would regain their confidence. I read each of the points slowly and kept an eye on their reactions. Conspiracy makes for good sauce.

Some were scribbling fiercely since I had not given them a handout detailing the feedback. Others had their eyes glued to the screen as if to make mental copies of what was written there. Some critical items included the following from the worker point of view:

- "XX manager adopts a command approach and is unable/unwilling to take a team approach."
- "Upper management is taking a hands-off approach and letting the division go down the tubes."
- "People are paid to work for ABC but little work gets done relating to ABC."
- "Numerous complaints and grievances are lodged that signal evasion of responsibility for results."
- "We let those things go for quite some time. But enough is enough and now we need to insist on compliance and results."

While many of the comments seemed general enough, they were loaded for those "in the know."

I had summarized a number of the comments so they could not be accurately connected to any particular worker. Even so, some were knowingly making eye contact with their buddies, signaling approval. As much as possible, I connected the feedback statements to specific issues for which solutions might be able to be developed and implemented. Management certainly wanted this to be the approach of the intervention. Subordinates wanted management behavior patterns to change and accountability attached. Managers wanted work done; subordinates wanted accountability for their managers.

Reactions to the feedback were mixtures of surprise, approval, disapproval and fervent agreement. They understood that they had not only been heard, but now they had a cogent voice with which to address leadership, management and cliques of co-workers alike. The effect was as if they had collectively said, "This is what it feels like, this is what we think and this is what we think you should do." Some were disappointed that names were not identified, only functions.

After commenting on each of the points, I could feel the excitement and energy for change surge around the room. The explanation part of the feedback took 30 minutes. The excitement stemmed from the possibility of positive change, at last.

Then I opened it up for Q & A. Not surprisingly, the interest focused more on the negative comments than on the positive. The negative was where the pain was concentrated. I allowed a substantial period of time for the debriefing and a "taking ownership" process. Some were deflated that there was no complete indictment of those who had made them suffer. Some were philosophical in critiquing the feedback as the best that could be expected in the circumstances. A few took advantage of the opportunity to vent further and loudly, as if to resolve the issues right then and there.

In addition, I provided an analysis of the data; what I perceived as the underlying causes of the issues and possible solutions. I used this approach as a model for seeing the data and approaching its messages. I wanted to establish a pattern to improve the functioning of the system; to encourage behavioral and attitudinal change; and to promote participation in personal and organizational improvement. No instant change was possible.

An important part of my feedback strategy was getting participants to take *ownership of the issues* from the beginning to the end. Taking ownership meant more than being responsible for resolving the issues. It meant becoming aware of their own behaviors that caused the issues to emerge. It meant examining the systems, norms and culture that had formed around those behaviors.

The feedback factor was more than information; it was a teachable moment. I wanted to anchor the message that, if it was a mess, it was their mess. I reminded them not to squander the opportunity to improve the functioning of the system to a manageable state and then monitor it for continuous improvement. The crucial part was for them to take *ownership of their own ineffective behaviors* in the workplace. I linked everything to the process of the workshop, so what they were going to be asked to do made sense. It meant work would be required for them to improve. But I also held out hope for achieving the targeted improvements. That process is called *buy-in*. Inevitably, some eyes rolled, shoulders shrugged, sighs were breathed heavily for effect and belts were hitched up noisily. Job done, we took a break.

During the break, I checked my observations with some of the co-facilitators. These co-facilitators had been chosen from the organization in a secret ballot procedure by the whole group. They were to assist me in conducting the small-group interactions and act as a sounding board for any adjustments that might be needed to the intervention design. After hearing their reflections, I felt I was on target. Good, now onward to the practical issues. From my point of view, all organization development workshops were focused on the resolution of real-time issues. As much as possible, the workshops reflected actual conditions in the workplace. Real time stuff mattered.

I had designed and conducted the workshops for the whole workforce, including all the executives, management staff and workers as a group. The purpose was to allow the representatives of each level to hear what was being discussed and to participate in problem-solving together. For the purposes of the intervention, the workforce was divided into diverse teams. For the resolution of the key issues, the workshops included structured exercises for problem-clarification, skills development and decision-making.

The solutions to the issues were decided upon by small—and large—group consensus. This was a key part of the intervention. Because the decisions were by consensus, the process became complex and time-consuming. However, I used all of those extended discussions in the small-group interactions to practice related skills and then implement them in the consensus decision-making process. It was agreed that the small-group facilitators were to act as worker representatives who, along with management, would see to the ongoing implementation of the solutions. In this way, learning and applying skills would be more useful in the long run.

Closure

In a planning session, I brought the intervention to a close by having all involved—the executives, managers, supervisors and workers—agree and commit to the changes and implementation methods. The planning session was conducted on several levels. On one level, the original issues were revisited, progress in implementing solutions was noted, areas of weakness were reviewed and adjustments made.

On another level, I arranged for individuals whose relationships had been strained to come together in private dialogues. I provided the participants with both processes for letting go of past difficulties, as well as for healing. For healing of relationships to take place, individuals had to recognize their fault(s), make restitution, (restore reputations) ask for forgiveness and be willing to let go of past inappropriate behaviors. For those whose feelings had been hurt in ways beyond immediate reconciliation, I arranged for symbolic ceremonies of belonging in which all could participate and not have to confront each other directly. Both time and healing opportunities matter.

Finally, everyone in the division came together for a concluding session. All implementation plans were reviewed. The V.P. in charge sanctioned the vision and goals and also dedicated the resources needed to complete the job. Symbolic closure was invoked in a ceremony that included awards for significant achievements. The co-facilitators were given special awards for their service to the whole group. In this way, I brought closure to the process. I had one final meeting with representatives of management, during which I reviewed the whole process and agreed on ongoing responsibilities and accountability measures. Closure on a high note speaks for itself.

Positives

In retrospect, the intervention was successful as management, both at headquarters and locally, became aware of the situational complexities involving the workers in the division.

The major positive for the workers was being heard by management, and in response arranged for the intervention. In turn, workers became aware of the constrictions that influenced management decisions. Throughout the intervention, skills for self-presentation, issue clarification, problem-solving, feedback and decision-making around real-time issues were practiced—in individual cases, in small groups and in the whole assembly. Opportunities for participation in decision-making were made available to all workers and many major adjustments to organizational life were implemented.

During the small group discussions, more reflective individuals became aware of their biases and adapted their behaviors. One worker said, "I was able to see my pattern of expression as oriented toward action only, and avoiding the building of necessary relationships. That awareness made me pay more attention to listening to others." Another said, "During the small-group process-reflection, I learned I came across as only pointing out the negatives of the group and not appreciating the positives."

Negatives

Inevitably, there were limitations to the success of the intervention because realistically *no intervention fully satisfies everyone*. Below, I outline those limitations:

- ***Lack of follow-through by top leadership***: Headquarters had been exceedingly accessible and involved during the contracting and start-up phases of the intervention. Ironically, they were equally as inaccessible when it came to following through on their commitments to the workforce. This became one of the weaknesses of the intervention because, as a consultant, my leverage was only as effective as the backing that I had from top management to pursue follow-up. The basic problem here was twofold. One, management expected the intervention would resolve all major problems. Interventions usually can resolve *some* system issues; however, unless management engages in ongoing coaching for themselves, their own behaviors will not change. Subsequent lack of management behavioral change is usually not lost on the workers who quickly lose motivation to change themselves.

Another area was lack of accessibility of managers to workers. The mantra "I have an open door policy" wears thin when the manager is never in the office or never walks around the workplace. The lesson: management must either, "walk the walk" or avoid talking about "walking the walk." Always assume that workers know the difference.

- *Lack of follow-through by local management*: In the same way, local management was going through the motions of cooperating in the activities of the intervention. As became evident later, they lacked commitment and hoped for a return to the way things had been prior to the intervention. They perceived the empowerment of the workers as a diminishment of their authority. They made a brave face of participation, but they were in waiting mode—that is, waiting for the intervention to be over. What enabled that attitude of waiting and withholding commitment were the signals coming from headquarters that the intervention was over. The net result: little of the authority or promised empowerment of the workers happened as it should have. This drained the implementation plans of their impact.

  An additional negative impact was felt by the workers who had spoken up during the intervention. They had taken the risk of advocating solutions that diluted the authority of some management staff and were now in the position of being sidelined and disempowered.

  A serious word of caution: in the wake of non-fulfillment by management of promised changes, *cynicism might grow* among the workforce and *reduce productivity in the long run*.

  In spite of this lack of follow-through by management, the workers had become aware of their own *power*, their unique *purpose* and the possibilities of *concerted action*. The workers had become personally empowered, understood workplace dynamics much better and were able to act positively in their own regard. Empowered workers cannot fail.

- *Lack of financial commitment*: Money talks. In this case, there were severe limitations on the financial resources available for continued implementation of solutions. The financial cost of being responsible and accountable proved too much for leadership and the easier option was to return to the way things were, although not completely.

My Story – The CEO Who Wasn't There

I had been contacted by an HR manager about an intervention project that involved two aspects: 1) coaching for a division manager on workforce leadership and management, 2) skills development for a workforce on effective relationships with said manager.

There had been considerable conflicts between the manager and his workforce. The reason given: a lack of leadership skills on the part of the manager. The word from the office of the CEO was that they did not want to lose the manager because he was an expert technologist in his field. In other words, they would not consider removing him from his post. At the same time, they feared without some kind of coaching intervention they might lose key individuals from the workforce, which also had a high complement of technical experts. To further complicate the task, the HR manager was on the East Coast, the CEO was on the West Coast and the division in question was located in the South—so access to the key players was difficult. Nevertheless, because the manager in question had accepted the intervention, I agreed to do the work and began the process of interviews, report generation and submission of recommendations.

In my investigation, I found out that the manager was technically very capable but he expected the same or higher levels of skills and performance from his workforce. It appeared that he was highly informed in his area of expertise, but he was dictatorial in his decision-making. While he was also energetic and persuasive, he was ultimately dismissive of others. The general assumption was that he was aware of the deep-seated reasons for his issues but was terrified of losing his position and the post-retirement benefits that would accrue. Further problems arose because many in the workforce complained that his goals and directions were unclear and often contradictory.

Inevitably, many did not measure up to his expectations and suffered his verbal castigations, threats of dismissal, demotion or hints of reprisals. The result was a demoralized, fragmented workforce and plummeting performance.

Nevertheless, the picture I got from the manager was that he was amenable to one-on-one coaching and also agreeable to a series of conflict resolution and team-building workshops. I organized the coaching sessions and workshops to make the best use of the time and resources available. During the workshop series, the manager was present and, on the surface, working well with his workforce.

But all was not so lovely behind the scenes.

> *In our one-on-one sessions, he proved to be most difficult as a coaching client. He refused to accept the results of a 360° assessment of his leadership. The results of the assessment revealed a pattern of most damaging behavior, and for that reason alone, a case could have been made for his removal. Because he refused to accept the major reflections of the workforce that he lacked skills in communication, empathy, decision-making and support for the workers, he would not accept development in those areas. No amount of persuasion would convince him otherwise.*
>
> *Because of this impasse, I decided to contact the CEO but was told by his office to work through the HR VP in this regard. After many discussions, I discovered the HR VP did not have any leverage over the manager in question, or on the CEO. I began to see myself with several defined tasks but without the required influence that might motivate the manager to face his own issues.*
>
> *However…all was not lost.*
>
> *The workforce was being held together by several supervisors who were the un-appointed leaders. They stepped up and led the employees through difficult relations with the manager. They continued to be respected throughout the whole intervention project. But because they also were not able to make representations to the HR VP, they were gradually being worn down by the stress and were considering leaving the organization.*
>
> *I redoubled my efforts to coach the manager through face-to-face, phone and other media contacts. Since he was proving to be un-coachable, I decided again to call the CEO. I was thinking that I needed leverage to put pressure on the manager to accept the coaching or be demoted, transferred or relieved of his responsibilities. I got no response from the CEO's office. I tried e-mail messages to no avail. I even composed a performance improvement script for the CEO to use in working with the manager, but still no response. I resorted to getting the best intelligence on what was happening with the CEO, but ran into cryptic inferences that politics were involved in keeping the manager in place.*
>
> *I did what I could to complete the project by coaching the workers on how to work effectively in those circumstances.*

My Story – Reflections

There is nothing more frustrating than working with someone who is not present. In this case, because of political influence and poor selection of managers, the freedom of the CEO to act in the best interests of the organization was compromised. His solution to the issue was to absent himself. The situation with the manager should have merited at least his transfer to another division or his release from direct contact with the workforce. In spite of my best efforts, I admit to having had only a limited impact on the situation. In effect, I was powerless because I could not work with the CEO to influence the situation.

Over the years, I have come across many CEOs who are not there to take the heat when bad things happen in their organizations. They become inaccessible, speak only through spokespeople and wait out the storm away from influences that might hold them accountable. To be clear, I am not referring to CEOs who might have broken laws or engaged in other damaging activities. I am referring to CEOs who have become entangled in pursuing profit and business expansion or chasing those who have powerful connections. In doing so, they have so compromised their own integrity they are unable to act.

Technical expertise alone does not equip a worker to be a supervisor. *People skills are an absolute necessity* for anyone in a leadership function, especially when working with highly professional technologists. Workforce development can be carried only so far and without guidance from a trusted leader, the energies of the workers will begin to dissipate and work relationships will fragment.

My Story – Application

I resolved that after the previous intervention I would avoid projects that would prevent me from access to the top decision-maker. Access is vital, even though by itself it does not guarantee that problem-prone middle-managers will be open to influence from anyone. Openness can only be ensured by the commitment of the individual manager to engage in the necessary tasks of Interiority. Only then, through a step-by-step process, can a leader widen his/her perspective and develop the necessary attitude and skills.

In addition, in putting forth these ideas on Interiority at work, I am hoping decision-makers will act not only from positions of expediency but also with inner integrity. In this way, they can be guided from a solid foundation in their decision-making to opt for truth and justice for all those who have a stake in their organization—and for all the affected communities.

Your Story

What then is your story of being maneuvered into a dilemma in the workplace? Was it a conflict so constricting that no matter which option you chose you would lose something of value? Was it a predicament of speaking out as a matter of conscience at an obvious injustice? Would speaking out have triggered possible retribution to one or more workers, turning them into victims? How often have you confronted such dilemmas? What has been your pattern of response? What lessons have you learned that have served you well?

Below the Surface

On the surface, the above-mentioned intervention was moderately successful, but beneath the surface of the organization's culture, strong forces were exerting a regressive influence. The adage, "old habits die hard" succinctly summarizes the retrenchment that took place inside the culture of the organization and in the hearts of the workers, albeit unconsciously in both cases. I would describe the results of such retrenchment in two ways: 1) a distinct *disengagement from self,* and 2) an *unhealthy co-dependency* between the worker and the organization. Herein I make the case that such rapid retrenchment was in great part due to a lack of Interiority.

Disengagement from Self

In our time, we are all aware that workers are encouraged by managers to do more with less—and do it faster and cheaper. In addition, long-standing habits in the world of commerce require that we define ourselves by what we do and by what we have achieved, especially in terms of financial worth and by our status in society. Consequently, in our workplace relationships, it is considered normal if the workers do not engage in deep inner reflections with each other except to the degree necessary for the fulfillment of work.

In other words, because of this diminished access to their inner resources while at work, workers experience a *crisis of self-management*.

Due to increased workloads, workers today have greater responsibility for self-management. However, if no time is available for the practices of Interiority, they tend to live on the surface. External symbols, such as the achievement awards and the hoopla that goes along with reaching longevity milestones, just add to the distraction. In the workplace, the new normal is to maintain a façade of upbeat, energetic well-being, regardless of what is happening in our inner worlds or workplace relationships. In this high-pressure environment, we tend to put on our *we're-having-fun* faces. Upbeat façades like this and high-energy choruses of team support ring hollow…and good feelings quickly fade.

As in the case of this client, responsible self-management is unsustainable without robust Interiority. Driven by discomfort with our inner lives, we race from activity to activity, distraction to distraction and never find the time to be in solitude and quiet reflection. If I never take the time to be with the one person that matters most, namely me, I will experience deep discomfort within. This is as a result of not being in dialogue with my inner energies.

At the same time, relationships with our circle of meaningful connections are diminished. We are thereby deprived of the nourishment that could make us stronger and more mature. (I will make more specific references to this disconnect in Chapter 9, Practices.) In seeking technology as a way to cope, we get caught in ever-greater demands for learning, discarding new iterations of technical tools along the way. This is the anomaly of our technological age. There are so many methods available to manage the complexities of our work, we are forced to multi-task, using many media. In the case of my client, too many workers were attending too few tasks and arriving at incomplete results. Workers were flitting from one incomplete task to another. With distractions getting in the way of worker output, the organization failed to gain expected results.

In the small group interactions, I noticed that the majority of workers didn't listen well, argued opinions from ill-considered or inflexible positions and discoursed on peripheral issues. They did not give personal views or emotional responses on anything. They kept their observations directed toward externals only. This orientation to externality seemed to keep them from knowing themselves—or each other—on a deeper level. In their anxiety, they seemed to participate defensively in the small group discussions. Perhaps they were afraid of mistakes or being called to accountability. As a result, the workers were shallow, distracted, unproductive and apprehensive.

They needed the grounding that would have come only from Interiority. Workers who are unaccustomed to thoughtful reflection tend to stop growing and even regress into immaturity.

And finally there is *outer conformity* to the policies and rules with *no inner commitment*—resulting in habitual behavior patterns detrimental to relationships with self and others. Outer conformity is sustained when workers are taught the organization's required rules of ethical behavior. The real meaning of ethics is inner commitment of the whole person to a truthful lifestyle. Nevertheless, even with training on ethical rules and policies, some resort to an outer façade of conformity or develop chemical dependencies (or other addictions) to dull the pain of emptiness. In which case, they try to lessen the guilt burden by dumping problems on family members or close ones. Maggie Jackson asks the question succinctly in her book, *Distracted*: "Consumed by the vast time and energy simply required to survive the ever-increasing complexity of our systems of living, are we missing the slow extinction of our capacity to think and feel and bond deeply?"[133]

There is a big picture in all of this disconnect. We fail to belong anywhere or to anyone. While we find ourselves living in a world of superfast connections, *we fail to connect to what really matters.* Like orphans, we do not know from where we came, how we got here, or where we are going. Because we do not see from the point of view of the whole, loneliness passes from one to another and gradually pervades our culture. Our world is one of beguiling but scary, isolation.

Our *natural state* is *interconnectedness* with all other forms of life, each with its unique purpose on this great, evolving journey. Without this living interdependence, we inhabit a world of lifeless things that fail to satisfy. Making matters worse, an air of desperation pervades our loneliness when we glimpse ourselves as victims in *co-dependent relationships with our organizations*. In the case of my client, I also noticed the topic of unhealthy co-dependence was a non-starter or an un-discussable topic. Non-starters usually signal lack of awareness, or denial.

Unhealthy Co-dependence

One of the least recognized but ubiquitous areas of dysfunction between worker and organization is co-dependency. Dependency comes from being held fast by some habitual behavior pattern that inhibits inner freedom of choice. For example, workers can perceive their bosses as parent substitutes and transfer to them needs and expectations that cannot possibly be satisfied; so they are doomed to be disappointed.

Co-dependence also includes workers who do not challenge the dysfunctional behaviors of others, or collude in hiding inappropriate behaviors of their bosses. Co-dependence derives from joining together with others to keep some system, such as a family, team or organization in place. From a therapeutic angle, co-dependents are people who are locked into a system of *supporting one or more addictions*, while both sides derive some kind of *perceived benefit*—even though in reality it is *injurious* to all concerned.

An example of co-dependency in an organization might be the existence of a serious flaw in a manufacturing system which produces defective products harmful to consumers, but which neither employees nor management want to admit for fear of losing jobs. A case of this kind actually happened in Japan where workers in a large auto manufacturing company concealed serious faults in the braking systems in order to retain their jobs. Neither did the management inquire about the concealed issues for fear of being forced to fix the problems at great expense. In this case, the issue was *co-dependency of criminal proportions.*

In most situations, co-dependency does not reach a level of criminality but appears in subtle ways. Examples of co-dependency are everywhere and are difficult for us to examine because they are part of what we have put in place to support some weakness in ourselves, or in the systems to which we belong. We usually fear our co-dependencies more than other kinds of habitual difficulties because in order to heal them, we are required to acknowledge their presence. We don't want to acknowledge the flaw in our thinking or behaviors that protects us from facing an unpleasant reality. In the case of my un-coachable client, it was as if the manager's supporters could see no shortcomings in his behavior. Their denial was so complete I was tempted to believe them. I suspected that they had so convinced themselves of their beliefs regarding the manager, they were not able to see any other reality. In their eyes, their manager was one of the good guys and that was that.

Manifestations of Co-dependency

Co-dependents in the work situation often make more of the organization than it is; assigning to it greater value than is merited by the facts. Even in the face of widespread management malfeasance, workers often believe the system will protect them because they believe management represents the *good guys*. The logic of such thinking is that they (the managers) must be *good* to have acceded to their elevated positions. In the case of my client, the perception of management as good guys amounted to a misreading of their behaviors; since they so obviously failed to fulfill the changes promised to the workers.

As we examined this particular scenario, it was evident that many workers assigned the accolade of "good guys," to managers who were *seriously deficient*. This was symptomatic of habitual ways of thinking by workers who judged managers on the basis of their "*good intentions*." Regardless, intentions—no matter how sincere—are not persuasive when behaviors are inappropriate.

Only integrity based on deep Interiority would equip workers to alter those impressions. Not only did management shortchange the workers, they also weakened the organization because of unproductive management/worker relationships.

The acceptance of the good-guys phenomenon is usually connected to other self-deceptions. It is possible the workers might even support the malfeasance of the management by offering them the kinds of gifts that implied that they were actually good guys. Witness the case of Bernie Madoff, who for almost 20 years had the confidence of investors, his employees and family before he admitted that his scheme was a big lie. Over the years, the investigators assigned to look over his books missed obvious clues to the deception—in spite of numerous warnings by investment community watchdogs. Of course, the management (Madoff) inevitably plays along with this self-deception and co-dependence on the part of everyone involved.

Co-dependency can become insidious in that it may be hidden under the mantle of righteousness. Co-dependent workers may avoid discussing acts of injustice or oppression by managers by maintaining quiet, dutiful conformity to rules and obsequious behaviors toward their abusive managers. On the other hand, under the guise of being balanced in their behavior, managers can justify oppression by awarding promotions, recognition and privileges to overtly dutiful employees. Nonetheless, neither of the above patterns of behavior can camouflage the underlying co-dependency that is in place for the sake of such things as preserving jobs.

In times of great economic stress, employees might be forgiven for co-dependent behaviors. However, at the expense of an inner life of integrity, the benefits must be bittersweet.

Missing Pieces as Indicative of the Need for Interiority

Interventions are usually successful up to a point. That point involves recognition of Interiority (or what lies beneath the surface) as a legitimate part of work-life. In the case of the above-mentioned intervention, the still-missing piece I could not broach was Interiority. This was partially due to Interiority being lumped together with religion and politics as among the *verboten* (forbidden) in the workplace.

Part 2 - The "Still-Missing" Pieces
Organization

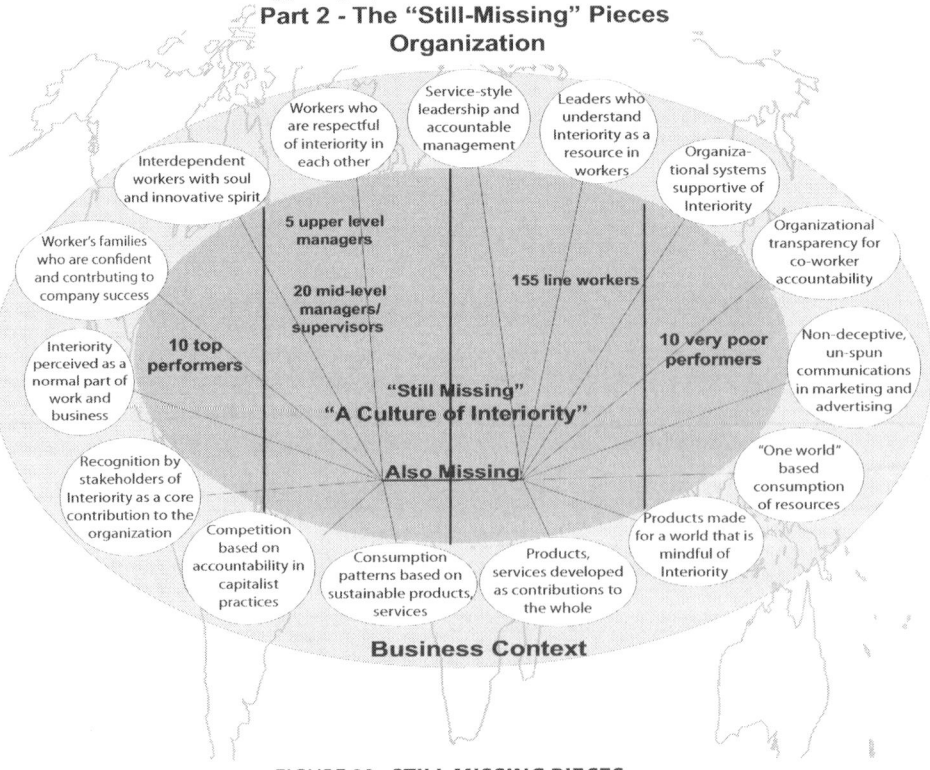

- Workers who are respectful of interiority in each other
- Service-style leadership and accountable management
- Leaders who understand Interiority as a resource in workers
- Interdependent workers with soul and innovative spirit
- Organizational systems supportive of Interiority
- Worker's families who are confident and contributing to company success
- Organizational transparency for co-worker accountability
- Interiority perceived as a normal part of work and business
- Non-deceptive, un-spun communications in marketing and advertising
- Recognition by stakeholders of Interiority as a core contribution to the organization
- "One world" based consumption of resources
- Competition based on accountability in capitalist practices
- Consumption patterns based on sustainable products/services
- Products, services developed as contributions to the whole
- Products made for a world that is mindful of Interiority

5 upper level managers
20 mid-level managers/supervisors
10 top performers
155 line workers
10 very poor performers

"Still Missing"
"A Culture of Interiority"
Also Missing

Business Context

FIGURE 23: **STILL MISSING PIECES**

In this section, I am going on a search for the missing pieces and what might be made available through robust Interiority. Fortunately, we have clues in the workplace as to the whereabouts of those missing pieces. Please review Figure 23, for clues to what is still missing. Further clues include incivility in behaviors, lack of ethics, lack of accountability, escape from freedom, paralysis from counteracting force-fields, choosing exclusion over inclusion, countering the bully and being flummoxed by the dynamic tensions of polarities. We begin with incivility in behaviors.

Incivility in Behaviors

During the intervention, a curious phenomenon took place: the *positive aspects* of some of the worker's behaviors were *not replicated* or even *encouraged*. It was as if management could see their value, but they assumed it was impossible to encourage them across the workforce. One the other hand, incivility and coarseness was more characteristic of worker interactions than kindness and cooperation. The obvious question is: Why? Was it because the workers were so accustomed to negative feelings in themselves that they expected and tolerated negativity in others? Perhaps they were so accustomed to abrasive relationships they could not deal with kindness.

It was as if the workers could see the detriment of those negative behaviors and attitudes but they assumed it was not possible to demonstrate the opposite patterns—or even courtesy—as a matter of course. Particularly during open discussion sessions, certain participants would demonstrate abrasive behaviors, which were shockingly tolerated by the group. Not being able to name those behaviors as inappropriate struck me as a **missing piece**.

With the workplace in question, it seemed there were unspoken taboos against mature interactions. It is as if the presence of responsible and whole persons would militate against good order in the organization. Of course, the workplace is where work is done, but it should also be a setting and occasion for the growth of workers into people who might demonstrate mature interactions. When civil behavior is decried, the coarser options become acceptable.

Lack of Ethics

As long as people are not at the center of organizational life, there will be a lack of ethical *decision-making*. Decisions based on organizational functionary-type response will be made mostly in terms of *profitability* and *investor relations*. Only workers who have an inner-directed ethical compass are able to hold themselves, co-workers and the organization accountable to the values to which they are committed. An ethical compass

ethical compass

is based on a series of ethics-related questions that workers must ask of themselves to ensure probity in decision-making. On occasion, when the voices of the workers are raised together in protest against some egregious injustice, many organizations give lip service to the implementation of missing values, but provide few resources for such action.

Additionally, all members of the organization need an ethical compass to guide their decisions about the communitarian way to conduct business effectively and ethically.

Historically, Enron provided an outstanding example of a lack of ethical direction. Enron was a major organization, headquartered in Texas, which collapsed because of illegal manipulation of the electrical energy markets. Strange as it may seem, out of all major organizations, Enron had the most advanced ethics-in-business training programs on the shelves. As history was to become a witness, they neglected to implement those programs—with disastrous results.

All of us recognize the power of mechanistically-oriented organizations to control outcomes, often at the expense of the freedom of the individual workers. To counteract this tendency and to maintain the balance between the organization and the individual, it is incumbent on each worker to *make up his/her own mind*, *cultivate a* voice based on ethical and human values and be able to *share it* when the opportunity comes along. Only workers who value their own humanity will have such motivation. An Interiority-based ethical compass provides direction.

Lack of Accountability

As part of the intervention, I made sure the participants included certain criteria for accountability and processes for holding each other accountable in their planning. Nevertheless, accountability requires inner commitment, courage and skills to implement, which in this case were lacking. Accountability is a wonderful principle because it binds workers together in a compact for the *benefit* of each *individual* and the *enterprise*.

Unfortunately, accountability is more recognized in the breach than in the fulfillment. True accountability binds all those who belong to the organization *to do and be what is required…by working together*. This element can only be acquired by the cultivation of Interiority.

Escape from Freedom

During the intervention, I was constantly aware that there were areas of immense potential for increased productivity. Those areas went largely untapped. The inner resources of the individual workers and organizational systems were blocked. The result was that no one was free to realize their potential. The reasons they were not fully free were twofold:

- For the individual *worker, freedom is difficult* because of the *responsibilities* attached to becoming fully in charge of oneself.
- For the *organization, freedom is hardly allowed* because of the *hierarchical structure* of authoritarian systems and because of the perceived threat to the managers who are pressured to collude with each other to hold the system in place.

In essence, workers did not choose freedom, nor were they empowered with freedom by managers.

Erich Fromm, renowned psychoanalyst, in his book *Escape from Freedom*, recognized the forces that pressure people to seek some kind of dependence on authority in the face of their own increased freedom. He wrote, "*Powerful tendencies arise to escape from this kind of freedom into submission or some kind of relationship to man and the world which promises relief from uncertainty, even if it deprives the individual of his freedom.*"[134] Fromm's message is that the perceived "*relief from uncertainty*" holds more weight than the possibility of being filled with creative energies that come with being free to be responsible.

Freedom to be responsible makes choices more difficult unless supported by Interiority.

Paralysis Due to Counteracting Force-Fields

During the intervention, it seemed that many workers had the vision, goals, knowledge and skills necessary for innovative productivity. What they lacked was access to the energies of their inner worlds. This was primarily because their immediate frame of reference in the workplace was business productivity, profit, employment, a salary and the ubiquitous relief from uncertainty. *Force-fields* of energy (see figure 21, below) were at work, some of which *moved them forward* while others *held them back*. Many workers were paralyzed into inaction because the energies they might have used for positive action were drained away by similar amounts of opposing energies. To the extent they missed out, so did the organization and all the stakeholders.

Mature levels of Interiority would have raised awareness of these force fields and perhaps this knowledge would have released the blockages and turned the tensions into energies for individual and organization improvement. Release of blocked energies magnifies productivity. Does the illustration look familiar? It should. Similar scenarios are played out every day in bureaucracies around the country.

Force-Fields of Energy

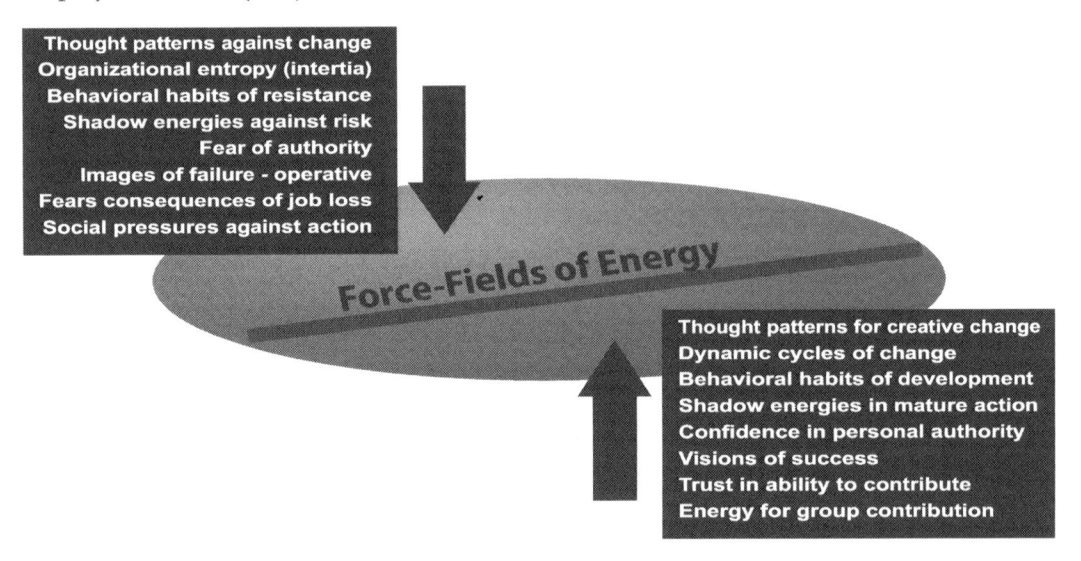

Thought patterns against change
Organizational entropy (intertia)
Behavioral habits of resistance
Shadow energies against risk
Fear of authority
Images of failure - operative
Fears consequences of job loss
Social pressures against action

Thought patterns for creative change
Dynamic cycles of change
Behavioral habits of development
Shadow energies in mature action
Confidence in personal authority
Visions of success
Trust in ability to contribute
Energy for group contribution

FIGURE 24: **COUNTER-ACTING FORCE FIELDS**

Exclusion over Inclusion

In our time, we are learning again that all humans are bound together much more than we are separate. However, because of preoccupation with our individual selves and our immediate needs, we seldom take into account all those who have a stake in our circles of work. It is as if, since we do not see them, they do not exist. This is true of the stakeholders of the organizations for which we work. Their contributions are missing because we have not learned to belong to the wider community of our work.

It is the *responsibility of leadership* to constantly raise the expectations of the community of stakeholders (those for whom the organization is in place), so workers make the connection with all of those constituents even while they are doing their particular tasks. We become exclusive because we tend to associate only with those who mirror our own thinking. The negative side of this tendency is a lack of depth that comes from a variety of experiences and networks. Difficult as it is, we must *join in diverse groups* that will allow us to expand our frames of reference, our range of knowledge and interests. Only by expanding those networks can we become more inclusive of those who are radically different from ourselves. Interiority is a key driver of inclusion.

I've met many workers who qualified as bullies. Some used their positions of power, some their aggressive behavior, some by gathering a support group of like-minded workers into voting blocs and some by passive resistance. The common denominator: they all tried to exert some undue influence over their co-workers.

Usually co-workers are intimidated by these tactics and need to break out of the pattern of giving in; but most often they don't know how. The following is a story of breaking the pattern of the dominance by a bully over a group. (In order to avoid identifying an actual group, this story is assembled from different examples of bullying I have observed.)

As the facilitator of dysfunctional workgroups, I am used to challenges coming to me, so I was not taken by surprise. I am also aware of the conflicts that simmer behind the scenes and how individuals might bring their own pet issues for resolution through the medium of a workshop. In this case, prior to conducting the workshop, I had done thorough interviews and submitted a report to headquarters about the issues facing this group. I had a good understanding of what I was walking into.

As usual, at the beginning of the workshop, I began by checking out whether the group accepted the conclusions of the report, adjusting the wording accordingly so we might have a clear basis for proceeding with skills development. I also made sure I had the understanding from headquarters that allowed me to focus on certain issues and solutions.

My Story – Countering the Bully

As I prepared to address the participants, I suddenly heard a voice saying, "Why do we have to have this workshop in the first place?" Everyone's ears picked up and I clarified the issue I thought was being addressed. The individual then said she thought the resources of the group might be better used for other deeper issues that confronted them. In other words, she wanted to deal with issues that were significant to her and her sympathizers. The issues she identified as "real" were the organizational restructuring that had recently taken place, the switching of field service functions and the consolidation of the various groups into a distant location; none of which she agreed with.

She continued by challenging my position as an outsider to know what was really going on with them and not being in any position to help. In other words, she wanted to take over the group and run its activities. Again, I tried to clarify what I was hearing from her and adapted my hypothesis about what she wanted to have happen during the workshop. She further contended that the structure, instruments and processes of the workshop I had prepared were a waste of time. A third time, I tried to reflect what I was hearing as her key issues and again adapted my hypothesis about what it was that she wanted to take place. For clarity, I identified her preferred issues as the "new" issues.

I turned my attention to the whole group and began to poll their opinions regarding the three issues I had established from her statements. Immediately, she intervened by asking the opinions of two others who were seated close by her. This was her effort to divert the wider group from asserting their opinions. I allowed the two supporters to state their poorly concealed iterations of her positions. I knew then this opposition had been orchestrated before the workshop had begun. After I clarified their positions, I went back to systematically polling the group regarding the issues that should be dealt with in the workshop. Some aligned themselves with her statements about the new issues, others mumbled what amounted to a neutral position and some were clearly in opposition to what she wanted.

Finally, I made my position clear that her proffered issues were outside the purview of the workshop, and since we were already behind schedule due to her statements, we should continue to do the pre-determined work of the workshop. I assured her I would come back to her new issues in due course.

The group was non-committal to the proposal, so I continued with the process I had planned. It was not to be. At every turn, she blocked what I was doing by asserting no one was interested in my process and issues; and for this she got support from her bloc. I was in danger of losing control of the workshop. I had a situation that was reaching a standoff and as is usual in such a case, we took a break.

During the break, I consulted with the manager of the group and his deputy. During the exchange, they had both been strangely silent and seemed intimidated. The manager was not clear on what should be done and was halfway between agreeing with my program and their new issues. I knew it would be up to me to deal with the situation. I told them my hypothesis: the bully and her supporters wanted to take hold of the workshop as their means of persuading the group about their positions on the major issues of concern to them (hereafter to be known as the "disaffected" group). I told the manager and deputy I would have to partially allow the discussion of the new issues, but I would gradually shift the main discussion to focus on the behavior of the individuals involved—that is, of the disaffected group. I warned them that this might mean an escalation of the tension between me, the bully and her supporters, and the rest of the group members, but I hoped it would end in valuable learning for all concerned. They were reluctant and fearful of a wholesale conflict but they agreed. We reassembled.

I told the group that since the new issues had been raised we would focus on clarifying them, examining possible solutions and using the process of the discussion and the behavior of the protagonists as learning opportunities. I also mentioned that the group did not have the authority to make final decisions regarding the new issues. The group agreed in general to the strategy. I could sense the atmosphere had changed and most of the members were willing to see a good fight. On the one hand, I had capitulated to the consideration of the new issues, but on the other hand I had shifted the focus to include the process and the behaviors of the disaffected.

I got the group to agree to keep all discussions and interactions of the reorganized workshop confidential. I also capitulated in agreeing to not disclose to headquarters any of the ensuing discussion. In a sense, I was empowering the group to discuss the new issues and in gaining their approval, I was co-opting them into a learning opportunity—through which they might carry new attitudes and skills into the workplace.

My job was not simple. I had to make sure we only raised as many new issues as we reasonably could handle, given the time and energy limitations of the group. I also had to model the kind of behavior that others could emulate in resolving conflict situations. I had to respect the individuals in the disaffected group even though I would be questioning their behavior. I realized I was an outsider and if I did not show respect toward all the members of the group, they would close ranks and I would be helpless to do anything. Then I would really be on the outside.

I did my best to clarify the new issues, spending considerable time polling the opinions of even those who were least vocal. Time and again, I went back to the group to clarify the main points of the new issues and to make sure no other substantial issues were left untouched. Then I made my move to name the behaviors that had been made manifest in the raising of the new issues. Naming was crucial and obviously not what the bully and her cohorts intended. The three resisted strongly but in doing so illustrated the inappropriate behavioral styles that caused dysfunctions in the group.

Nonetheless, I persisted in polling the group regarding what they saw as inappropriate behaviors in raising the new issues. The behaviors included: disrespect for the established processes of the workshop, dismissive attitudes toward the less vocal participants and taking over the workshop for their own purposes. I did not get as much data on their behaviors as I wished, but it was evident from the comments: this behavior pattern had been going on for some time in the regular workplace.

I then proceeded to my next step, which was to examine, in the group context,

> the problems caused by such behavior. Long-repressed emotions came to the fore as participants who had been cowed by the bully for so long found their voices. They expressed anger at the bully's arrogance, impatience with the management for countenancing such conduct and shock at the possibility of the continuance of such bullying; and what it would do to their workplace.
>
> Again, I led the group toward explaining what they wanted. I made sure they differentiated between the experience of the oppressed workers and what they hoped for in the future. I was not done yet. I also led the group toward methods of implementation of desired behaviors in the group. Then I led the group toward clarifying the criteria whereby they would know that acceptable behaviors had been implemented, and if not, why not. At that point, I had empowered those who had for so long been oppressed by the bully. It was enough for me to return to the new issues and consider new solutions.
>
> I worked as thoroughly on the new solutions as I had done on the new issues. By involving the whole group, we finally arrived at solid solutions, completed some action planning and assigned who was to do what actions, and when. At the end, I quickly tied the process of the workshop back to the original, predetermined objectives. I did so to make sure they agreed that the objectives of all had been achieved even though we had taken a detour. I conducted a round-robin poll of the group at the end. The majority agreed the workshop had been successful.

My Story – Reflections

Upon reflection, it is difficult to manage bullies in a group except to call their bluffs. Doing so during an intervention is no exception. In the foregoing example, I used the time and energies of the participants to make sure they got done what they needed to, while enabling them to deal with a bully. In my own mind though, it was the process of doing that work from which the group would learn. Such learning would prove useful in the long run in the interactions of the workplace. Through the process, the silent workers had found their voice and participated in stating the kinds of workplace behavior they wanted. They had struck a blow against the bullies and in doing so had struck a blow for themselves and their dignity.

All workplaces have bullies. Not all managers or supervisors have the interests of the workforce at heart or the necessary skills to manage bullies. Not all workers have the opportunity, or are equally able to assert themselves in confronting the bullies. That is the nature of workers and workplaces. We all learn in different ways how to get along with others. Most often, the culture and practices of the workplace are sufficient to establish and observe standards of interactions. Behaviors can change and the behavior of bullies can change. That is, if they are made aware of the negative impact of their conduct. Sometimes we must follow such a countering-the-bully process to ensure the most equitable behavior for all.

My Story - Application

It is necessary for all workers to have ideas of what is acceptable behavior, know how to name it and also be able to name what is unacceptable. The crucial distinction is to identify the unacceptable behavior while respecting the person. *Even bullies deserve respect.* Equally important is to have a mechanism for requiring the behaviors which are acceptable in the workplace. Again, naming those behaviors is important. Arriving at an agreement on what are acceptable behaviors and implementing an action plan is a most necessary step. Developing a way for holding all workers accountable to that accepted standard is the final step.

Your Story

What then is your story of encounters with bullies in the workplace? How did you manage in those encounters? Was your approach to capitulate to his/her obnoxious behavior or attitude? Did you name his/her reprehensible behaviors? Did you let him/her know the impact such conduct had on you? Did you inform him/her of the behaviors you wished them to show? Did you come to an agreement as to the way forward? What lessons have you learned from those encounters, which have served you well?

A Culture of Interiority

In the context of the intervention, what was definitely missing was an organizational culture that recognized the importance of the inner lives of both the workers and the organization. The worker's common frame of reference was mainly external, which provided only limited recognition to their inner lives. A culture is a combination of beliefs, values, behaviors and practices that characterize an organization or group. For a culture of Interiority to take root and grow in an organization, it is necessary for leadership to nurture these attributes in the workers and all stakeholders. As the culture is formed and fostered, it is not just the leaders who contribute to the culture, but all the stakeholders as well.

Organizations generally miss the developmental insights of workers—who are continuously passing through cyclical stages of growth and discovering themselves anew at each new stage (cf., Cycles of Integration, page 147). Workers themselves are seldom aware of these cycles and thus do not take advantage of the opportunities for letting go and adopting more mature attitudes. All cycles of growth have value, but organizations tend to focus on youthful energies and creativity; as if other cycles in the lives of more mature workers are not creative in unique ways.

Flummoxed by the Dynamic Tensions of Polarities

In Chapter Three, I discussed three kinds of Interiority energies: Familiar, Unfamiliar and Existential. I suggested that we come to terms with the energies in the Existential area because they involve limitations such as the birth/life/death cycle. In a similar manner, we must come to terms with the dynamics of polarities.

The term polarity derives from the familiar "pole" as in North or South; or the positive (+) or negative (-) poles on the battery in your car. These "poles" cannot act independently of each other. Rather, because of their electro-magnetic properties they exercise a *dynamic attraction or repulsion* with regard to each other.

This dynamism is the source of energy that we harness to drive our electrical tools.

Now that we have established this dynamic tension between the physical "poles," it is pertinent to apply this model to workers and organizations. Take, for example, the worker and organization polarity (energies flowing in dynamic tension between the two); a worker can perceive his awareness moving back and forth from one to the other in endless motion. His objective is to avoid getting stuck on one side of the polarity (worker) or the other (organization); instead to align with the flow of energy between the two.

Now, work and workplaces are chock full of such polarities. Some familiar polarities are: competition vs. collaboration, marketing vs. operations, central vs. regional and capital spending vs. cash flow. *Flummoxed* is an appropriate self-description when we align only with one side (pole) or the other, and find ourselves in conflict with the dynamic flow of energies toward the opposite side. However, when we *align with the flow*, we are in business. Aligning ourselves with these flows of energies is a prime stance that is

Individual / Organizational Responsibility	
L+ Individual	Organization **R+**
Not waiting for permission to act Taps own initiative and creativity Organizational support increases	Organization gets needed feedback Organization can respond and improve Individual support increases
Individual	Organization
Does not give organization needed feedback Organization cannot respond and improve Individual resistance increases	All are waiting for the organization to improve Does not tap into own initiative and creativity Organizational resistance increases
L−	**R−**

FIGURE 25: **POLARITIES AND LEVELS**

ultimately guided by our Interiority.

When we are Interiority powered, we take time to reflect and get with the larger picture of this endless transference of energies. We are not flummoxed.

For my treatment of polarities, I draw extensively from the book by Barry Johnson, *Polarity Management*.[135]

I use the typical polarity of the individual vs. the organization to show both the benefits and weaknesses of both sides. The explanation of the Polarity Map, Figure 22, is there are two poles, one of which represents the individual and the other the organization. In the illustration, the left half represents one pole that is the individual. The right half represents the other pole, which is the organization. Both poles, individual and organization, are also divided into levels, representing top and bottom respectively. The upper level of each pole represents the positive outcomes that result from focusing on that pole. The positive outcomes are also shown by the L+ sign and the R+ sign, for the left and right sides respectively. The lower level of each pole represents the negative outcomes that result from focusing on only that pole and neglecting the opposite pole. These are the disadvantages of that pole or its downside(s).

The negative outcomes are also shown by the L- sign and the R- sign, for the two sides respectively. Dynamic movement from one side to the other occurs when workers experience the downsides of the present pole—which they identify as the *problem*—and they are attracted to the upsides of the other pole—which they see as the *solution*. This dynamic movement is shown by the arrow moving diagonally from the L- side to the R+ side. In illustration 23, the movement continues as the downsides of focusing only on the organization begin to become apparent. This starts the movement through the four quadrants in the form of an infinity loop, as shown in the same illustration.

The whole movement from the bottom left to top right through the bottom right and top left is shown in the direction of the arrows. This illustrates the dynamic movement between polarities that occurs in all organizations and communities and about which it is necessary to be aware when it is happening in our own work-

FIGURE 26: **POLARITIES TRANSITION ON AN INFINITY LOOP**

place. The main reason for becoming aware of this dynamic movement is workers do not embrace just one side of an argument to the exclusion of the other. If we adopt the organization or group viewpoint only, then we are in danger of losing the benefits that come with individual activity and vice versa. The solution is to be flexible enough to examine both sides and take them into account when solving a problem that involves both. It can be said adopting only one side of the polarities is a fundamentalist position and probably represents an immature view. The ability to view both polarities and accept the dynamic energies flowing between them is both realistic and represents a more mature stance.

In the world of consultation on organization development and improving worker productivity, many useful models follow a four quadrant cycle or loop as in the polarity illustration. The fact there are four quadrants is not as important as the movement between them that signifies our involvement and growth. Our involvement in the cycles or loops of our growth is not perfect when we begin our work. But with increased awareness, we insert ourselves consciously into the flowing energies that characterize our journey toward maturity.

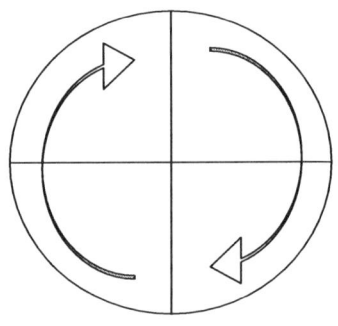

FIGURE 27: **TRANSITIONING CYCLES OF ENERGY**

We are restless oceans of energies.

These energies are constantly flowing between our minds and our emotions; between us and our environment; and especially between us and our co-workers. Along with these energies are tensions that are necessary and normal. Our normal reaction to these interactions: we *like the energies*, but we *dislike the tensions*, especially between opposites.

As we become aware of these energies, we first develop a level of *tolerance* for co-workers. In other words, we form a *long-term view* that prevents us from over-reacting to immediate events. The second application of this cyclical movement relates to the *energies flowing through all things* in the wider world beyond the workplace.

We are not alone in our efforts to achieve positive results in our lives—and organizations. The energies in the macro world around us are also engaged in moving all things forward toward successive stages of growth…and positive outcomes, even through negative experiences. Again, such growth occurs in never-ending cycles that move from one polarity to another.

The lesson here is to trust the process of forward movement, even though it is incremental and may seem at times to retrogress. Because of the challenges of under-

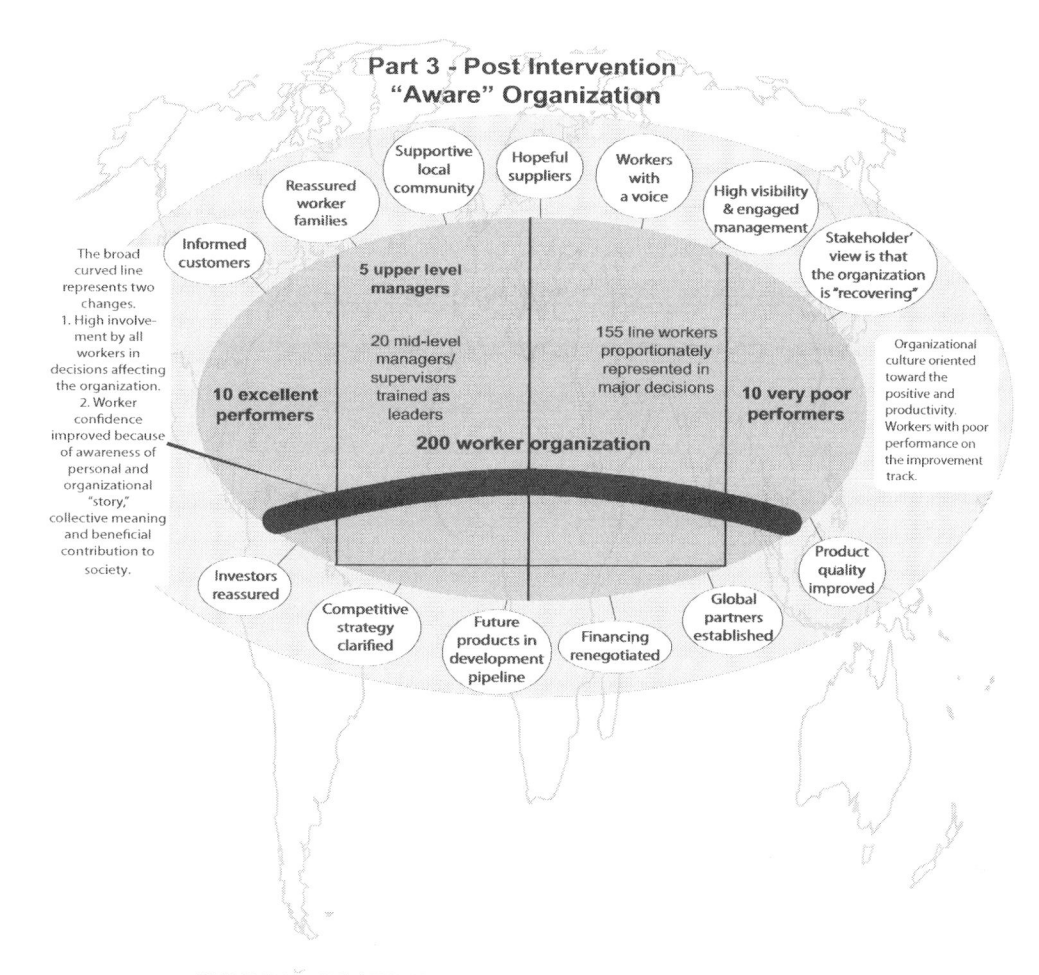

FIGURE 28: **POST INTERVENTION "AWARE" ORGANIZATION**

Part 3 - Post Intervention "Aware" Organization

The broad curved line represents two changes.
1. High involvement by all workers in decisions affecting the organization.
2. Worker confidence improved because of awareness of personal and organizational "story," collective meaning and beneficial contribution to society.

- Reassured worker families
- Supportive local community
- Hopeful suppliers
- Workers with a voice
- High visibility & engaged management
- Informed customers
- Investors reassured
- Competitive strategy clarified
- Future products in development pipeline
- Financing renegotiated
- Global partners established
- Product quality improved
- Stakeholder view is that the organization is "recovering"
- Organizational culture oriented toward the positive and productivity. Workers with poor performance on the improvement track.

200 worker organization:
- 5 upper level managers
- 20 mid-level managers/supervisors trained as leaders
- 155 line workers proportionately represented in major decisions
- 10 excellent performers
- 10 very poor performers

---

standing these models of how organizations work, many of us end up being defeated by the complexity of the process. The worst result is that we give up playing our parts; our contributions are consequently lost to the emerging states of our workplaces, our work and our communities.

When we began this chapter, we started with the assumption there is not a lot we can do about our situation at work because that is *just the way things are*. The fact is, we can do something about situations we all too often perceive as overwhelming. It is our involvement through Interiority that is often painful. The Greeks have a proverb that says "we suffer our way to wisdom." If we focus on the wisdom, the suffering makes sense.

Workers need to make sense of life in their own way. Considering the intervention that I conducted in this aware-but-weak-organization and its struggling-with-meaning workers, there is nothing quite equal to the worker/thinker who tackles the thoughts that come unbidden through the dynamic tensions of the polarities, and makes them part of his/her store of wisdom.

An examination of the post-intervention aware organization, (See Figure 28) reveals that the bell curve line has changed in two ways: 1) the former bell curve has become a consistent line curving like the upper part of a circle and 2) the width of the line has expanded substantially. Both of these changes indicate that workers' awareness regarding the issues and their sense of belonging has transformed into more positive approaches to work and healthier relationships in the workplace.

Prepared – sure! But really ready??

Chapter 7

Challenges

> "Skate to where the puck is going to be,
> Not where it has been."
> —Wayne Gretzky (celebrity athlete)

These days, we are constantly challenged to fundamentally *change ourselves*—and quickly. Unfortunately, the ability to face up to the challenges and adopt relevant practices is in short supply. The kind of change to which we are all invited is not so much a one-time event as a way of life. Connecting with the energies of Interiority is the only way any of us truly changes.

The sources of increased productivity (targeted by Interiority) are primarily the energies released within us when we face these challenges. These energies require that we know ourselves so well, and value our growth so much, that we become the change to which we are invited. If we recognize our patterns of activity and continually adapt our behaviors in an ever-deepening process, then "skate to where the puck is going to be" gradually becomes "skate to where the puck is."

If we practice changing according to the soulful voice that echoes from within, it becomes simply "skate."

The skate orientation to change is a key step in the inward progression of Interiority, which hopefully leads to maturity over the span of our lifetime. When we are skating, we are moving effortlessly in union with the energies of everything that constitutes *self*. We are bringing everything we are into the moment in which we are skating, and into the next moment, and so on. We are engaged, not detached; we are actively moving, not reactively stuck. When we are really "skating," improvements in productivity do not flow as much from innovative technology, updated machinery, emerging market opportunities, newly developed strategies or reconstituted teams; but from the comfortable relation to *self*.

The transition from *skate to where the puck is* to the intuitive *skate* signals we know and practice the basic skills required for doing our work. Similar to when we are skating effortlessly, we come to do our work tirelessly, productively and enjoy the results. An ongoing task for us, while we are working, is to define our personal, developmental goals and imagine the steps and processes whereby we will arrive there. When we commit to that goal and process, no amount of external buffeting can deter us. We will arrive. Of that we are sure, but the fears and risks in the intervening moments will hardly diminish. Of those difficulties, we are also sure. No one ever learned to skate by holding on to the side of the rink. The fiercest risk is to let go of the fear of failure. In a similar fashion, when we work according to the language of our souls, we have to let go of the wall of the *status quo* and commit ourselves to skating, freely.

We will explore four areas of constructive change that will help us to skate: Changing Ourselves, Personhood through Work, Relationality as Truth and Embracing Interiority.

Changing Ourselves

In this first challenge of constructive change, I ask what it means to change ourselves. The obvious answer is about changing our behaviors by upgrading an ineffective habit into one more successful. But since such behavioral change is brought about by our rational minds, it is perhaps superficial. The kind of change I envision allows our souls to guide transformation. This type of transformation is much deeper than the change within the control of our rational minds. The changes managed by our souls derive from several sources, namely:

- our sense of sacredness
- our need to serve
- our experience with pain
- our need to belong

We begin with the work that is considered sacred.

Sacredness

For workers, the choice to change something within themselves involves seeing that one's engagement with work is neither profane nor meaningless, but sacred. Perhaps that choice involves initially seeing that they are not merely collaborating co-workers but a *self-organizing organism* driven by inner energies to *solve major problems*. When we do what we are designed to do at work, namely solve problems, we are entering the sphere of the holy. Then, work which was formerly labeled profane, is revealed as sacred. The activity of honeybees is an example from nature. When invaders threaten the hive and the queen, the bees organize themselves to repel the invaders at the cost of their own lives. Such activity is a sacred endeavor because it reflects the elementary nature of the bees at work.

Similarly, when threatened by the oil spill in the Gulf of Mexico in 2010, people from everywhere organized to stop the gusher, protect and clean the environment and establish more specific regulations to ward off further disasters of a similar kind. Work gets no holier than that.

Conversely, consider the case of regulating the out-of-control financial services industry: we can predict that merely expanding regulations will prove ineffective. In this case, more regulations are profane. We easily recognize such profanity because the effort is false, inauthentic and wasteful. We enter the sphere of the holy when we make sustained efforts to change our inner selves to be truthful, authentic and prudent. Then we can act ethically on the industry because we vibrate in tune with Interiority-fueled integrity.

It will come as no surprise that there is a rising chorus of marketers "selling change" in these early decades of the 21st Century. Examining the language and models of such popular change efforts, we realize they serve but to dim our understanding and disconnect us from the *vox populi, (voice of the people)*. People are tired of hearing about change—because nothing substantial ever changes. The changes noised abroad are not based on Interiority, so they devolve into mockery and drivel. So too, it will be with me if I am pulled outside of myself in response to self-generated delusions of change. Effective change must often be Interiority powered—and *disruptive*.

Disruptive change means *nothing that went before pertains*. Disruptive change refers to the kind of change that completely *ends a previous period* and *begins the next*. Disruptive change means if I am to join in greater work than perfunctorily doing the tasks that consume the hours that usher my life along, I must rebel against a static view of life. Such change means I must not wait for external circumstances to usher me into a different way of working but I must become actively disruptive on my own behalf. If I am to change at all, the one requirement I give myself is to remain *rooted within, fed from within* and *guided from within*. For that to happen, we must consider our motivation for changing ourselves.

Called to Serve

One of the greatest motivations to engage in the work of changing ourselves is to be of service to something beyond our own interests. For those of us who respond to the challenge of finding greater meaning in our work, we can get there by being in service to the needs of our souls—and of all things. In short, the reason for changing our ideas and behaviors: we are worth it and so is the community we influence. An essential component of such service is the embrace of necessary pain as a path to the deeper self.

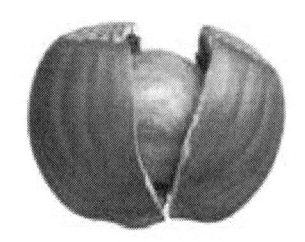

FIGURE 29: **BROKEN SHELL OFFERS FRUIT OF UNDERSTANDING**

There are two aspects for coming to terms with the reality of pain. The first concerns *individual pain* with which we must learn to cope. The second connects to the pain that is the *burden of all living beings*. The first kind of pain is treated in the following story:

My Story – Reconciling the Spirit

When I pushed back the little door in the wall of the confessional I heard a gasp. I knew this confession would be different. A voice from beyond the 12-inch square opening moaned. In the darkness, I leaned closer to the veiled mesh. It was a woman's voice. I tried to picture her, to no avail. The voice was trying to put shape on words. I knew she meant, "I need help."

I said, "I'll help. Just follow my lead. I will go slowly. If you want to speak, just begin and I will listen."

I began, slowly. "Lord, I am here. I have a story to tell. It is difficult for me to talk about it. I have no suitable words. The journey has been long. I have been lost and in exile. But I am here."

I waited in the silence. I asked for a word to guide me. She whispered, "Betrayal," as if the word included a crime, trial, condemnation and punishment all in one.

I continued. "I am so ashamed of what I have done. I never thought I would be so selfish. But I was. I can't go back. I can't undo my deed. What's done is done. I have injured those who trusted me. I have betrayed that trust. That trust meant more to me than anything. I have been wandering for a long time, alone and suffering and now I am here for this work that I have to do."

I again waited in the silence and then asked for a word to guide me. The voice said, "Remorse."

I continued slowly, "I am left in my solitary remorse. I hate what I have done. I regret my deception with all my heart. I thought I was strong but I was weak. I thought I was dependable but I was a broken reed. I thought I was courageous but I was a coward. What's worse is I have betrayed myself. I deceived myself. I made excuses for my behavior. I made up stories that would allow me to do what I knew was wrong. I thought I was so smart but in the end, I was so foolish. I am so ashamed; so disappointed in myself. How could I have been so foolish?"

I waited in the silence. Again, I asked for a word to guide me. A sobbing voice said, "My family."

I continued even more slowly, "I love my family. Yet I betrayed them and now I am full of sadness. I feel useless and worse than bad. How can anyone betray those who depend on you?"

I waited in the silence. Then I asked, "What do you want?"

The voice, in coming to terms with the seeming impossible, breathed, "Forgiveness."

I continued. "By everything that is holy, good and pure in this world, I want to be forgiven. I want to look into my soul and direct that forgiveness to the deepest, darkest corners so I am released. I want release at that level for I know if I am not healed there I will go back again, as I did many times before. I want to acknowledge the wrong deed, my wayward heart and let go of the sad burden I am carrying."

Again, I asked for a word. The dreaded word came on a breath itself distrusted, "Abuse."

I continued. "I have suffered harshly at the hands of another, when I was an innocent. I wanted to never think about it. I wanted to blot out the memories. I fled into the clutches of substitutes. Nothing helped. I turned against myself as punishment for being alive. I suffered the pains of self-hate, self-destruction and exacted on myself abuse worse than that of the abuser."

I waited in the silence. I asked, "How will you forgive yourself?"

The voice said, "All I have is the love of my family. That's where I might begin. I want to look my family in the eyes and feel their forgiveness. I want to make amends. I want to change."

I waited in the silence. I asked, "What is holding you back?"

Again, the whispered voice said, "Hopelessness."

I continued slowly, "My heart is heavy with my deceit. I am close to despair. I feel weighed down by darkness and coldness and my future is bleak. How can anyone—anyone be so lost? The problem is I want to hope again and I am wondering if that is alright. I want to hope in my basic goodness. I want hope to rise up in my heart and comfort me in the face of what I have done. I want to hope in the future. I want that future for myself and my family. I want hope to help me through the doubts and difficulties that will come in reconciling with my family."

I waited in the silence. Then I asked, "What are you going to do?" A clearer voice said, "Return."

I continued slowly, "I will return to my family. I am sure that they will receive me as they have always done. They are good and I believe in their goodness."

Then the voice said, "Yes, they are not the problem. They will take me back. They—the voice trembled, got caught, and in a tone that was husky with the saddest of feeling murmured—they have always loved me." The voice sighed deeply, "The only problem is me, my behavior, my habits and my out-of-kilter life."

"What ways do you have for making sure you do not do the same again?" I asked.

"I can tell them what I am going to do. I can ask them for their support in specific ways. I can remove all sources of temptation from around me," the voice said.

"What are you going to do for you?"

The voice hesitated then said, "I don't know."

"I am going to ask two questions. Is that alright?" I asked.

"Yes."

I continued, "Usually, after you do the problem behavior, what do you say inwardly to yourself?"

Again, silence. Then thoughtfully, "I call myself bad names; really bad names; I feel bad, I nurse bad feelings, and I treat myself badly and I don't let up till I am driven to the edge of despair."

"My second question is: If you do the behavior again, what can you say to yourself that would be more sympathetic and helpful?"

Again, silence. Then the voice said quietly, "I have never said sympathetic or helpful things to myself. I'm afraid, I don't know how."

I waited in the silence.

Then the voice said, "I could say, you are human but you are good."

"Good." I said and I waited.

"Maybe I could be more loving toward myself," the voice said.

I asked, "How?"

"I don't know if I could say, 'I love you' toward myself," the voice said.

I waited. "But that would be the best thing, wouldn't it?"

"Yes," she sobbed.

I waited. The sobs came in great gasps, moans, sniffles and the voice shook with grief. "Oh God, I never . . . I can't . . ."

I said, "I am going to pray now in your place as if I am you. You just lean on my prayers or pray along in whatever way you like."

I began: "Great God of the universe and of our hearts, I thank you for my life. I thank you for this day and for my family for each of them is a reflection of your love. I acknowledge your great power, love and forgiveness for me. I have wandered far from your love. But now wrap me in your love, heal me from my weaknesses, hold me close and every minute let me realize your support. Let me walk in the knowledge I am your beloved. Let me feel that love in the deepest levels of my heart and soul. Help me accept your forgiveness for it is my hope. Let me embrace my own life again in freedom and hopefulness. In times of weakness when I am faced with doing the bad things that cause my loved ones and me unbearable pain, help me to say to myself the loving words I never could; that I never said before. Help me not to go to the place of hating and despising myself. Let me not pursue myself into the dreadful places of darkest blame and pile hurt on hurt until I am raw with pain.

"Let my days be loving of myself. Let my mornings be filled with hope and my evenings filled with thanks. Let me serve my family as best I know how. Strengthen me now, fill me with your love and walk with me always." I concluded and waited in the silence.

"Thank you," said the voice.

"You take good care of yourself," I replied. "Amen."

She was gone. I slowly closed the little door and breathed a prayer of thanks for all brave people who confront their weaknesses and their pain and enter the great battles for life. For her, I was just a nameless priest murmuring prayers, but that hardly mattered. What mattered was her reconciled spirit that allowed her to grow again.

My Story – Reflections

Sometimes, we are happy we have been born for just one particular moment. None of us know why. We just recognize it as a moment of profound truth.

I knew it was for this person that my life's journey had brought me to that dark confessional. Most of the time in the confessional, I had only the dark for my companion. But this one time, I was not alone. This was my turn to be there.

I only hope when it is my turn to encounter my own failings I will find a willing ear. A willing and understanding ear is one of the greatest treasures of humanity.

My Story – Applications

In working together, making mistakes, feeling guilt and remorse, we do not need to get to the gory details of any life. Better not to know the details if not knowing will suffice. All we need to know is ourselves.

In our humanity, we are everyman. We are prone to weakness, to self-deception, self-aggrandizement and doing what is not in our best interests. When we fail to live up to our own expectations, we can get down on ourselves and perhaps become bitter about our weaknesses. But in doing so we are compounding the pain and further weakening our resolve. Still, in spite of repeated failures, it is possible to turn toward ourselves even though painful. Often, because of the pain, we can return to a home within. We all live with pain and so we need to treat ourselves with care and love, always. Rather than avoiding the pains that will inevitably come, we need to embrace them in ourselves and in everything. The pain is part of us.

Your Story

What then might be your story of some addiction, obsession or compulsive behavior that causes you grief or shame? Perhaps you may have tried repeatedly to change this pattern but without success. Is it possible that this pattern has been a means of escape from stress or internal pressures? Perhaps you can forgive yourself and develop a more comfortable relationship with yourself. To achieve relief, it may be necessary to practice a more understanding and compassionate approach toward yourself—and gradually free yourself from the unnecessary burden.

Pain and Compassion

In this section, I return to the second aspect of pain which connects to the suffering of all sentient beings. Because of the universality of pain, compassion is a necessary attitude regarding ourselves, work, co-workers, workplaces and organizations. We all suffer because, by our very lives, we serve, even unconsciously. All living things have lives marked with maturing stages, inevitably accompanied by pain. As we progress through life, hopefully we learn to cope with it. Initially, we play our parts by doing our work well.

We also play our parts on a different level by embracing the world as imperfect. This world, which generally flees from pain, can take a breath when it—and all its pain—is embraced by even one of us. When the world in its pain is held, it can be healed. An intimate connection exists between the pain affecting the world and the pain we experience in our work, and vice versa. When we enter into our own healing at work, we enter into the healing of the world.

On the other hand, when we resist or deny the presence of pain in our work lives, we can experience deep hurt. Pain becomes acute when we work only for transactions, such as sales. When we are operating in a world of our own making, we become increasingly loaded with the pain we deny. Pain that is embraced as part of the condition of life, especially at work, is an indication of a healthy attitude and work style. Ironically, pain accepted makes all things easier to bear.

The Need to Belong

We belong in the world – not above or apart from it. In a way, we have ownership of the world and the world has ownership of us. This way of belonging is different from the sense of us as individuals, acting on sensory data that is analyzed, judged and acted upon—independent of others. The relationship of belonging denotes a quality of affectivity entirely different from the anemic connections in the world of independent objects.

In a workplace full of objects and objectified workers, there exists only transactional relationships—no belonging to each other, no shared pain and no feeling. This type of relationship derives from the logic that has driven workers and institutions throughout the evolution of the western world at work. If there *is no belonging, neither is there feeling or respect for others*. Nor is there any reciprocal feeling. If there is no feeling for each other, there is no ownership of the pain that permeates one's life. If there is no sharing of the pains of life, then we are alone in the midst of everyone and everything that could provide shelter and succor.

But if we are in *relationships of belonging*, of *shared pain and joy*, then we *are alive with everything*. The notion of belonging to all things is at once a concept, an image, a practice and a way of being.

To live consciously in belonging to all things is to influence them deeply and be influenced by them. The idea is to belong so intently, we vibrate in tune with our workplace surroundings—even though we scarcely think so. When we belong, we are comforted by our chairs, our desks, the keyboards, the photos and frames that hold them and the palpable presence in the cubicles next to us. We feel at home in our work. Everything is ours, in the sense of belonging to it all. Everything can call on us.

We work through Interiority by remembering *all things serve us* and *we serve all things*.

My Story - "If You do it, it will be Done"

It was in mid-May. I stood in the hall of the clapboard house where I lived, in the snowy valley of Yonezawa. I had just tramped around the drying slush outside the door and thought to myself, "It's getting to be time for the shoes." As I opened the door to the shoe closet in the hall, I thought to myself, "we have seen the last of the snow and it's about time." Snow typified the city's streets and sidewalks, little mountains of it everywhere, so much of it that it became hard-packed into icy ridges, which beat back all attempts at dispersal.

With the first snowfall in November, everything changed, especially the shoes in the hallway that disappeared into the closet. Out came the knee-high rubber boots and in went the shoes that were not to be seen until the following May. As the Yonezawans used to say, "You put on Long Johns and rubber boots in November and keep them on until May." But now as I looked into the closet, a sorry row of misshapen, salt-lined leather clumps looked out at me as if to say, "You left us alone here in the cold since last November, what did you expect?"

As I sat on the hallway step and struggled to squeeze my feet into the snooty shoes, I realized how shrunken the soles had become from lack of use. Chastened by the challenge, I looked again at the row of nasty looking shoes on the closet shelf. I remembered how, as the previous autumn came to a close, they had served me well. I remembered the mossy-green sheen on the stone lanterns that lined the leaf-strewn pathway to the shrine of the local hero-statesman, Uesugi Kenshin (1530-1578). Appropriately old, the imposing lanterns called to mind his immortal deeds, his style and qualities of mind and heart. He was a man of Interiority in action. Fondly, I imagined his tombstone inscribed with the words:

> *If you do it, it will be done.*
>
> *If you do not do it, it will not be done.*
>
> *Nothing will be done.*
>
> *As I moved along the pathway toward the shrine, my inward eye momentarily caught the tatami (woven grass) mats in the teahouse and their slightly musty smell. They reminded me I had work to do and if I did not do it, it would not be done.*
>
> *All of that from the sight of turned-up shoes in the hall closet, as I came in from the slushy street in Yonezawa.*

My Story – Reflections

My story is not about misshapen shoes but of being grateful for all times. *All things serve*. They serve in good and bad times. They serve in *all seasons* and *conditions* and then they die. All things are born, grow, diminish and die, but not before they serve. While moving through the stages of life, they experience the pain of change that eventually leads to death. We tend to deny the pain and look only to the health of things and the beautiful displays of nature in the sunlight. But the source of life lies quietly in the darkened earth of the pain we mostly deny. In so doing, we think to protect ourselves. But if we deny the pain endured in the transience of things, we refuse their struggle and suffering. In not seeing and respecting their pain, we show disdain for any appearance of diminishment and become filled with fear, anger and resistance to the conditions of life around us.

So it is with the workplace. Change is a constant. Every man sets about his task oblivious of the tasks others do. What will save us from total meaninglessness unless it is the capacity to be shaped by the enduring struggles that punctuate our days? What will heal us if it is not the sight of every other living, enduring thing… and choosing to belong to the struggle that is part of living?

My Story – The Question – Why did you Leave?

> *I had been in the priesthood for 20 years. It was all I had ever wanted to do. But at age forty-five I found myself exhausted and burnt out. I decided to leave the priesthood. In my inner shadows were the fears of life outside the clerical state, of embarrassment among my peers, of having no network of resources, of having to learn everything about the business world from scratch. The biggest shadow,*

however, was in the act of letting go. I was not just leaving a job but a life that had sustained me for 27 years.

The next shadow came with the question most asked of me, "Why did you leave?" The question typically came with a mixture of disappointment, bemusement and chagrin. For most questioners, the vocational aspect of the priesthood presumes a lifetime of dedication to others. This comes with the assumption that once such a commitment is taken on, it is there for good. Oddly enough, many know the phrase, "Once a priest, a priest forever." For some, the question, "Why did you leave?" came toward me as a rebuke. In their eyes, entering the priesthood involved a sacred promise and those who break a promise to God would deserve to die roaring.

Die roaring, indeed.

The whole process of leaving the priesthood took years of soul-searching. I was letting go of a way of life that was in many ways deeply fulfilling. I knew I would miss being with people, especially in their times of great need; providing consolation during periods of grief; helping to make sense of the chaos in the midst of disaster. I left the priesthood for reasons that made sense to me. Ironically, those reasons varied depending on the questioner.

For the casual questioner, I responded with the routine burn-out answer: I was emotionally exhausted from picky and nonsensical church regulations and dogmas.

For friends, I told of becoming lonely in non-exclusive relationships and realizing that I was never destined to become a clerical priest in the first place. The distinction of "clerical" priesthood refers to the ceremonial, ritualistic, church-organization aspects of priestly work. None of those held much attraction for me. For me, the priesthood was a way of serving people, especially when they were encountering the imponderable mysteries at work in their lives. For me, serving people did not mean providing canned answers, but rather accompanying them in their struggles.

To myself, I admitted to being lost and searching for a complement, for a stable presence in my life. In retrospect, I wanted—and needed—companionship. On the practical level, the choice was to leave in time to have a chance of making a new life. I was also following the beat of a distant drummer—or that "something else"—that remembered and was at work within me.

On the other hand, I thought that if I remained in the priesthood, I could not accomplish what I thought was important. I was following a hunch that there was important work for me to do in the non-clerical world. I believe that I was

> *correct. Presently, I believe I am making a contribution I could not have made had I remained and not had the experience of working in the secular world.*
>
> *That "something else" like a friendly prompt, has led me here.*
>
> *Perhaps the most incisive question about my reason for leaving the priesthood came from an elderly relative, who asked, "Are you happy now that you have left the priesthood?" Her simple question put the emphasis on my inner state of doing the right thing. If I was doing the right thing, then happiness would resonate within me.*
>
> *In response, I told her that I was—very.*

My Story – Reflections

The priesthood—or the religious life for either men or women—is a state defined more by the individuals than by the externals; more defined by the quality of their *inner lives* than by the works they do. Furthermore, their inner lives are more defined by radical encounters with the *great mystery* of life than by any amount of prayer.

That being said, there is no difference between people on the basis of their accomplishments or status in society. What makes people different depends on how much they are able to *love themselves* and *others*. The encounter with love is cloaked more in mystery than in transparency.

My Story – Application

All strivings for notoriety, status or achievements do not substitute for an inner life. An inner life is the greatest gift one can receive. An inner life well lived is the greatest gift one can give to the world…and leave behind. The rest is a mystery. Ultimately, this is the only answer I can give to the question, "Why did you leave?" The rest is still to be lived. So I trusted the call of my soul and stepped out into a society outside the monastery without much ado or plans for survival. In at the deep end I went, and after a drenching shock, I found I could swim.

I remember walking down Central Avenue in Glendale, California one day. I knew with absolute clarity in one cleansing moment I was going to be okay if I only trusted the abiding spirit within me. It was as if a weight lifted from me and I breathed deeply, merely because the air was there and I was alive and ready to tackle the challenges before me.

Your Story

What then is your story of leaving a life to which you had dedicated yourself but at some time found that you could not continue? How did you manage to make that decision? How did you recover from being separated from your previous life? Did you have support in your decision to pick up and go on from people whose friendship you valued? Did you find that people upon whom you depended in your former life, no longer supported you? What did you learn from having to begin again to make another life? What was your key resource in finding your way forward?

Personhood through Work

One's prevailing self-image may be as a doer, a mover and shaker in getting things done, but we are called to the greater state of authentic personhood through our work. The challenge is in building that personhood while engaging in work. Being authentic refers to being a true reflection of what is going on inside and out, and not a construct of characteristics according to the needs and expectations of others. Authentic personhood includes having thorough *self-knowledge*, an inner *ethical compass* that seeks integrity in everything we are and do and the *ability to reflect and grow* through our experiences at work.

There are *three perspectives* we can take with regard to embracing authentic personhood. One is the fulfillment that comes from concentrating on *specific tasks and events* of each day. We can develop personhood by keeping our souls engaged as we attend to the details. Everything is already filled with soul, but only when we work with soul is the connection uncovered. Taking time for reflection on the tools with which we work and how they benefit us is a way to connect with the soul. Seen this way, the details may seem insignificant, but they become the avenues to our deeper selves when we imbue them with skill and mindfulness of the sacred encounter taking place.

The second perspective on authentic personhood comes from the totality of our lives as *journeys of growth*. The latter journey is the one we mostly ignore, possibly because it seems so large. We can visualize and wrap our arms around the achievements of a single day, but the achievements of a lifetime are daunting.

Not surprisingly, the potential of the second perspective affords the most meaning and satisfaction. From this greater perspective, we can use everything to grow—both as individuals and as community members. As we have seen in the first part of this chapter, we can grow through our suffering. Rather than silently enduring those sufferings, we can reflect on the source of pain as partly self-generated, integrate our insights into our outlooks on life and work, tolerate the tensions of life's contradictions, gain the wisdom that arises in our awareness and appreciate our lives as unique gifts.

A third perspective on authentic personhood includes the ability *to reconcile everything within ourselves*. This mainly includes the *contradictions*, *chaos* and *shadow* elements about which I have written in Chapter 3, Foundations. Reconciling contradictions means being able to tolerate the anomalies of life and not become defeated; instead to endure with patience and insight as the work of life occurs within us. Reconciling chaotic situations includes being able to remain centered in the face of the most inexplicable conditions.

Not being thrown into a tailspin in crises is an indicator of maturity. Mature personhood is available through the work we do. We will know we are approaching such maturity if in our personhood we begin to glimpse a reflection of integrity throughout.

It follows then, that at work, being a person of living truth, a truth seeker and a truth teller can be truly challenging. This depends on reconciling ourselves to justice as an inner condition of how we work. We must diligently seek out what is real and not just our preferred versions of reality. We have to make such truth-seeking part of our work; that is, to know our biases, our cultural prejudices and their influences on us—our values and belief systems.

In all humility, we must seek to know what we do not know, namely the *blind spots* and *weaknesses* easily apparent to observant others. By reflection, we become conscious of our *patterns of behavior* and our *fundamental needs*. We must be able to *dialogue within ourselves* when we become aware of neediness and pretension.

Above all, we *cannot lie to ourselves*. We have to be open to hearing the other side's views. We must solicit feedback from those who know us well and who will honestly tell us about our behavior and its impact on them and others. Such people are treasures. As Shakespeare said about friends, "The friends thou hast and their allegiance tried, grapple to thy soul with hoops of steel." [136]

Aligned with truth seeking, an associated challenge at work is to *always learn*. Listen to your senses, your intuition and your soul. Learn from your mistakes by taking the time to reflect on what your mistakes have to tell you— and us—that we have conveniently forgotten. Learn from others, especially those who have learned something real from vital experience. Always have a definite project that deals with the subjects on your learning edge.

Relationality as Truth

Throughout Western history, conceptual statements about life situations have been offered to us as descriptions of the *truth* about how things are. This can be a challenge because: *statements of truth are just one element in the truths emerging in our lives.* Letting go of one historical assumption to replace it with an expanded version means we may have to confront an array of legacy assumptions and learn to live according to an adapted reality.

This adaptation process is something I learned from my experience in Japan, where relationships are more definitive of truth than abstract statements. In Japan, the *quality of one's relationships is a more foundational guide for behavior than statements about truths*, revealed or otherwise. This aspect of *truth* is what I call *relationality*.

Just as we strive for authentic truth, learning and growth in our individual selves, so must we acknowledge relationality with other human beings as truth, especially co-workers. Relationality means we are never merely individuals but are *interconnected to everyone and everything*. However, relationality is not a given because each of us brings our personal histories to our relationships, especially at work. Nevertheless, we become persons primarily through our relationships and the verbal and unconscious dialogues we conduct with them. Just like the inner dialogue that we conduct with ourselves is effective for our growth, so the dialogue in which we engage with others at work is effective for enlarging awareness.

The key to effective dialogue with others is to value them for their own sakes and avoid trying to get them to behave according to our expectations. If we value our unique self as a gift, perhaps we can value the uniqueness of others as a gift also. It is the respect for the special qualities of others that helps us grow through the exchange.

There is integrity in our vital relationships when we can safely be ourselves when we are together, when we can share our thoughts and wishes openly and, while we are in search of some common good, we do not hide our reservations or withhold commitment. If we are unable to tolerate the differences between us and others, it may indicate controlling behaviors, manipulation and even outright conflict in ourselves.

If I find these behaviors in myself, this may present an opportunity for reflection on what is going on within me. I may have to come to terms with dysfunctional patterns of reactivity or attend to the shadow components in such patterns to achieve release and growth. If the relationship between me and another is severely wounded, it may be that there is little hope of reconciliation and the relationship realistically needs to end. However, when there is still some tolerance and respect for the other, there may yet be an opportunity for growth as conditions change.

We are essentially social beings and must live responsibly as organic parts of the living system that depends on our cooperation for its health and wholeness. We are already being compensated with the gift of our lives for doing our parts. When we work, we are, of course, earning a livelihood. At the same time, by our work we are a cooperating part of the living organism of the earth and we are moving the universe along its evolutionary path toward greater consciousness. Seen from this angle, allowing ourselves to be directed by a purpose beyond our own interests is of benefit to us *and* to the community.

The challenge of keeping the ecologies of the earth vital and in balance becomes the obligation of individuals who are supported by a vibrant Interiority at work. Just as virtue is its own reward, so also is work that has a personal and a higher purpose, its own reward. At work, such a purpose becomes a *calling* and a *credo* for us to live by. Remaining dedicated to such a purpose is difficult because of our human limitations. It follows that becoming believers in that purpose is essential so we can access the energies of our souls. However, belief tends toward dependence on externals such as rituals and ceremonies, so we must strive to remain on target. To do so, we should keep the practice of Interiority as simple as possible.

Embracing Interiority

There are many reasons why we should embrace Interiority at work. The most important is that workers must have a strong inner core to withstand work challenges and grow through them both personally and professionally. The need to manage one's self is the most radical requirement of our times.

In his book, *Drive*, Daniel Pink notes "The secret to high performance and satisfaction at work … is the deeply human need to direct our own lives … and to do better by ourselves and the world."[137] When we embrace Interiority, we are embracing the world and its needs at a deeper level than normal. We all need to embrace Interiority in ways that allow us to deepen ourselves to the level of unshakable commitment to integrity. Lest anyone think Interiority means people must shrink from the more corrupt manifestations of evil in the world and in the workplace, I am saying the opposite. My point here: there is a necessity to embrace Interiority because of the *increasingly pervasive culture of deception that currently surrounds business and social life*.

We are furious; as we pick up the pieces left over from the great recession of the past few years, we realize we all have been the victims of a societal culture of graft and deceit. I referred to this culture as an ethic of self-absorption when I wrote about the historical legacies of work in Chapter 1, Questions. Recalling Hamlet that, "something is rotten in the state of Denmark," we realize we live in the midst of a miasma of deception and betrayal in which all are enveloped and only the sincere are deceived.

Deception breeds more deception, and to extricate ourselves we need Interiority.

The great deception of the 2008 recession was the creation of financial instruments so complex that no one could understand them and, in the intentionally created confusion, to deceive people of their livelihoods. This deception revealed the complicity of so-called organs of process inspection that allowed the flawed financial instruments to pass as legitimate. The purpose of creating such complexity could only have been to defraud investors, especially the gullible and poorly informed. Sadly, this was only the opening salvo in an ongoing battle in which the integrity of all of our institutions is at stake.

The political response has been to regulate the financial industry, but the source of the problem is much deeper than mere regulations can patch up. As Neal Gabler puts it in his *LA Times* article, "Can't Stop the Greed," "Why does financial reform fail? It ignores human nature." He continues,

> If we've learned nothing else about investment banking over the last two years, we've learned that it operates like a virus. You can devise all sorts of economic antibiotics—from stricter regulation and more oversight to limiting certain institutional arrangements, as Glass-Steagall did—but sooner or later they all fail because financial instruments keep mutating to escape destruction. Investment bankers reconstitute highly risky, highly profitable schemes such as credit default swaps or unit contingent options or other exotic inventions. That's why reform never works. It will always be outsmarted.[138]

It seems clear if the hearts and minds of those who want to deceive are set only on profit, then they will find ways to subvert any regulation or process. The best kind of regulation is not a proliferation of rules and processes for financial institutions to follow, but *self-regulation chosen by workers everywhere* that will offer a counter-balance to the avaricious greed of those who have access and opportunity to abuse financial systems. The most effective regulation is for workers to *self-manage*, to be *informed* about the requirements of their decisions and to be *centered* in Interiority-based values.

The challenge for all workers is to absorb the necessary information, do their own thinking, and make decisions compatible with personal values and the needs of the community. A healthy society requires that workers keep informed, reflect intently on what is happening, challenge suspect activities and provide warnings and direction aimed at consensus among co-workers and citizens.

For that we need robust Interiority, which requires battles be fought continuously in inner forums so when we act, we will do so with integrity.

Growing Up with War

The war I knew was of the vicious, knock-down, drag out, no-let-up, no-holds-barred conflict—not of the military type, but the inner one. That war made me think that one side of me was good and was to be kept alive and cultivated, while the other side was bad and needed to be destroyed. The war inside was provoked by the often misapplied words of Jesus in Matthew 26:41: "The spirit is willing, the flesh is weak." If I heard these words once when growing up, I heard them a thousand times. I believed them so much that everything non-physical (or so-called spiritual) was lumped into the good side and everything related to the physical was lumped into the bad.

In other words, I was infected with the belief that we humans are divided into two parts, the spirit and the flesh, and these two are constantly at war with one another. I was caught in the struggle in between the two sides. And it was hell.

The view that affected me most was of a heaven not connected to this life but one that lay beyond my death. The impact of such a view was to dissociate my yearning for fulfillment from this life, this world—and work—and attach the most profound aspirations of my soul to whatever lay beyond. This was the war within. I grew up when this thinking was at its height in society so it was not just me that got caught in this war. While I try not to believe such dualism anymore, my reactions are still so infected with this kind of thinking that I have to catch myself.

My thinking today is based on the existence of only one world in which everything has a spiritual core. At the same time, this world is so filled with mysteries that understanding it is like trying to predict when and where the wind will blow. "The wind blows where it will. You hear its sound, but you don't know where it comes from or where it is going." John. 3:8. For me, the important words are, "You hear its sound." This refers to my awareness of everything the wind stands for in the mysteries of both my inner and outer worlds. The wind reflects the constant spirit which is the dependable source of the inspirations of my soul.

My Story – Belief in the Constant Spirit

I sat by the bay across from a jetty adorned with countless seagulls hunkered against the faded dock planks. Here and there the whipping winds ruffled feathers and lowered eyelids over black eyes squinting against the gale. Around

> *them, the winds roiled the waters in rivulets, one dark wavelet following the last; like the chaotic ripples of our universe, suggesting other possible worlds, brimming with potentiality.*
>
> *I was reminded that the constant spirit running in front of the whirling wind is ever-faithful in drawing our attention to the work to be done. This spirit we call soul remembers one's unique call and whispers to each of us, suddenly, constantly and unexpectedly. So that we will respond from that deeper, truer place within—that we call our home in the world—this spirit calls at our attention to become whole and make our contribution.*
>
> *Up from the squadron rose a flapping gull. The bird battled into the wind, almost level with the flowing fronds of the straining dockside palms. Upward it struggled, then sideways seeking headway, banking sharply, sliding and gliding, arcing widely, circling, and finally settling among the serried ranks of the flock. The gull landed in a triumph of a questing, creating, irrepressible spirit.*
>
> *Similar to this gull, nothing is separate from the questing spirit. Every moment of life is an act of creation. Happily, such thinking lies far from the mentality (and lifestyle) that the "spirit is willing but the flesh is weak." The spirit is en-fleshed and tirelessly at work. Heaven is here in the rippling possibilities of every task, every day, every relationship and every inspiration. This is the message I live for and strive to live within.*

My Story – Reflections

In the face of the rising gull that is each of us, the gale force of history, tradition, culture and entropy (a measure of the energy in a system or process that is unavailable to do work) blows against the feeble flapping of our chaotic minds, pushing us, wheeling sideways, downward, back into ranks lined up with eyes half-closed against the storm of creativity, stoked by the spirit within. Again and again, the gull rises to challenge everything it ever knew about gravity and the flimsiness of feather, wing and aerodynamic flow; but rise it must.

My Story – Applications

The message here: within each of us there is an exigency of spirit to rise, not bemoan the past, but challenge the status quo. I need to tackle the shadows of my life, to learn as if the act of learning itself was just so I could leave knowledge behind, and reach beyond the disappearing horizon once more. I sense the need to deepen within me an appreciation for Interiority, to engage in inner disciplines against intimidating odds, to integrate and train for a life made whole; and to do all this in the context of my work…and all of my life.

Surprisingly, one inspiration for engaging the shadow manifestations in our lives comes from the words of the former world heavyweight champion boxer, "Iron Mike" Tyson: "Whenever stuff goes well for me, I just wait on the bad stuff to come."[139] This is a man who in his words is un-compromised by shadows but waits expectantly for them. Like Job, he is a man acquainted with troubles and realizes the spirit of living arrives in all shapes and sizes, throwing punches more lethal than knockout blows to the jaw.

My turn came when it seemed that winter shadows were all that was left for me; with no spring in the air. The vignette above of the rising gull, is a reminder that we have to be true to the story that has been shaped in us by our souls, by the work we do, and the work of our lives. Among our most incisive tools: listening to our soul's intent to hear the truth of ourselves, then to grow up, to become the person we are called to be and thereby be fulfilled.

This can all happen most readily by building a culture of Interiority in the workplace.

Your Story

What, then is your story of learning from the *recovery of some natural phenomenon* that became an inspiration for getting on with your tasks? What was particularly *inspirational* about the nature of the recovery? What did you learn about *beginning again* in the face of life's storms, such as major mistakes and failures that caused you grief? Were you able to learn some *wisdom* that carried you forward?

Friends are strangers we have yet to meet

Chapter 8

A Culture of Interiority

That is true culture which helps us to work for the social betterment of all.
—Henry Ward Beecher

In regard to work and the workplace, there are many ways to define the word *culture*. Generally, culture means, "The way we do things around here." Every family, group, organization, society and nation has a culture. Culture can be created, developed, built on, assessed, changed, merged and integrated. The culture of any organization is influenced by its mission, purpose and output, but it usually emerges over time from the personalities and interactions of the workers.

From a consultant's point of view, organizational culture includes: structures, values and processes that characterize the life of an organization. Culture provides the glue that *binds the workers and the organization together*. Valuing and celebrating one's culture is extremely important for group affiliation. Traditionally, these varieties of cultures merge into one identifiable set of customary practices that derive from formative experiences of people at work and from external influences on the organization.

In addition to externally-derived cultural influences, let me add the element of *inner resources* that might enormously enliven individual workers and the enterprise as a whole. An organizational culture that is partially derived from Interiority should be distinguishable from traditional workplace cultures by the *depth* and *integrity* of its character. A culture of Interiority emerges from the inner energies of workers. Those inner energies are formed by the physical, mental, emotional and spiritual resources of individual workers as they grow through their personal stories. As the workers attend to their tasks, those energies that have been cultivated by the practices of Interiority gradually empower co-workers, the organization and stakeholders.

Not only is an Interiority-Powered worker identifiable by external behavior, but he/she is distinguishable by a *centered attitude*, a *cogent identity* and *inner resolve*.

A culture of Interiority in the workplace enables workers to begin each day as if it is a new opportunity to produce the products and provide the services at the heart of the enterprise. A culture of Interiority is one in which each worker is aware he/she is a unique and wonderful majority of one. A culture of Interiority is one in which each worker is working with others in a unique collaboration: one team engaged in meeting customers' needs, in a way that has never before been revealed.

A culture of Interiority is fueled by Interiority-Powered (IP) workers. Throughout this Chapter, I will focus on a culture of Interiority and on Interiority-Powered workers.

Realism in Embracing Interiority

Above the ornate white and gold entrance gate to the shrine of Nikko in Japan are small statues of three monkeys. One has its hands clasped over its eyes, another over its ears and the third one over its mouth. The inscription reads, "See no evil, hear no evil, speak no evil." The implication is those who enter the

FIGURE 30: **SEE NO EVIL, HEAR NO EVIL, SPEAK NO EVIL**

precincts should preserve their integrity by avoiding seeing evil, listening to it or speaking it. Few realize that only one admonition is positive—"speak no evil." The other two are challenges to do the opposite. It is our responsibility to see and hear all the evil and all the good that is part of the reality of our lives. If we live in a cocoon, avoiding seeing and hearing the evil that is happening around us, how can we prepare for the realities of life?

There is work to be done in the world that can only be done by us and there is only so much time in which to do it. In the spirit of seeing, hearing and knowing the evil of the world, Interiority enables us to take responsibility for the following:

- Seeing poverty and destitution with compassion to do something about it. Compassion requires that some action be taken, however small.
- Noticing abuse in any form with a view to relieving it. Just taking time to notice it changes the circumstances—and us.
- Working against manipulation by an organization of its workers, consumers and the public in general. Choosing not to consume the goods of such organizations is a move against its unacceptable practices.
- Naming the demons of greed, corruption and manipulation that affect our societies and then striving to break the chain of causation that births them. Choosing not to belong to the chain of causation, as much as possible, is moving against those energies.
- Joining the discussion in community to avoid the abuse of power and the manipulation of people's misfortune.

Interiority allows us to foster unique qualities in our self-expression, including:

- Voice: Firm, confident and persuasive. These vocal qualities enable the listeners to be influenced, in their own way, toward development of their inner selves.
- Philosophy: Experientially-based and fitting for the individual. Embracing a clear philosophy allows workers to work consistently and productively, regardless of contrary conditions and models.
- Lifestyle: In keeping with the individual's values. A lifestyle that is comfortable yet simple is supportive of one's work, convictions and behaviors.
- Self-expression: Natural, unforced and deferential. Self-expression that reflects an integration of the inner and outer person and is natural to the worker, is convincing to the listeners and commendable by co-workers.
- Accountability: Accountability that derives from within the worker is strong and enduring. When a worker holds himself/herself accountable, he/she becomes a credible and dependable resource in the workplace.

Interiority enables one to avoid negative tendencies that can corrupt human nature, namely:

- Perverse satisfaction at the misfortune of others. We can guard against this by helping victims recover from any kind of hardship.
- Triumphal displays of material wealth. Ostentatious display creates resentment, which can be avoided by judicious choices of simple ornamentation.
- Misuse of wealth for wasteful purposes. Use one's belongings generously so others may also benefit.
- Nurturing resentment only drains our energies. Intentionally let resentments go and don't revisit.

Becoming an IP Worker Requires Awareness of One's Power

According to Executive Coach Marshall Goldsmith, "Every decision in the world is made by the person who has the power to make that decision, not the 'right' person, or the 'smartest' person, or the 'most qualified' person…"[140] He did not explain whether such power comes from one's position in the organization, by attribution from others or from within the individual. I like to think that such power derives from within ourselves because we are already connected to everything and the only condition is awareness of that reality. We live and work in a condition of radical relatedness to everything, although most of us are hardly aware of that reality. Our existential challenge is to say yes to that human condition of being in relationship to everything and to the power that is already at work in us. The extent of our power at work derives from the reality that *we are actually influencing everything all the time* and we need only to become aware and use that power.

Furthermore, the greater our awareness and application of our inner resources to work and relationships, the greater the impact on our own and others' productivity.

We are already powerful people. Allowing power to flow through us enables others to make their contributions according to their unique power and calling.

Shoes Too Small

Productivity can be magnified if we approach our work as an encounter with what needs to be created in the human community. Again, we recall Carl Jung's saying, "We all walk in shoes too small." This reminds us that when we are Interiority powered, we have greater influence than we imagine. Why then should we walk according to any other dictates except those coming from our inner core? By his comment, Jung pointed the way to the relocation of meaning from the institutional structure to the individual worker—because of the radical power within the worker.

Workers then have the responsibility for raising their consciousness, recognizing that they have the energies of the universe within and that their lives are constitutive of the emerging whole. As workers, we are carriers of cosmic power, even if that awareness escapes us or we are tempted to flee in fear from its requirements. To be truly productive at work requires that we are alive to the energies of our inner worlds and the ways in which we can harness them.

This radical relatedness is what provides ultimate meaning at work and access to the only real power there is. In this sense, there is no more powerful resource on earth than an IP worker. The IP worker has the potential to change the nature of work and how work is done.

IP Worker Awareness

The world of work causes constant (though almost imperceptible) shifts in IP worker awareness. Among those that affect us directly are the following:

- A shift of the moral center from the structured yet amorphous institution, to the inner workings of each and every responsible person engaged in work.
- A shift in who benefits most, from the privileged few, to the responsible majority who are seeking the common good.
- A shift in priority, from making money only for the shareholders, to recovering the initial inspiration of the organization, which is providing goods and services needed by customers.
- A shift in authority and power, from its location in an organizational hierarchy, to networked communities of common concern.
- A shift from information (including personal) being held by the powerful few for marketing purposes, to non-personal information being held by anyone with sufficient interest and access to the Internet; for the purpose of bringing about necessary and beneficial changes in the systems in which we work—and live.
- A shift in worker emphasis, from merely making products and providing services to gain compensation, into collaborative groups that not only make a profit but also make a positive contribution through their work.
- A shift from dense legalese surrounding products and services and mendacious methods of marketing, to providing truth in simple, easy-to-process ways beneficial to consumers.

- A shift in consumers, from mindless and uninformed, to researchers who screen the suppliers and offer their loyalty only to socially responsible and ethical organizations.

Even though in our time there are many more areas where the ground is shifting, the shift we are most interested in is the one from the *institution as model and arbiter* to the core of the *individual worker as the center of values and decisions*.

Institution to Individual

One paradigm shift well under way is the shift from institution to individual. Under this shift, we can include both the internal and external characteristics of the institution and the individual. The transition of power (in its concepts and structures) from the paradigm of hierarchical authority to the paradigm of the Interiority-Powered worker has already happened. In fact, the paradigm of power vested in hierarchical authority has already been largely superseded, though this transition may not be at all obvious.

Historically, the prevailing paradigm has been dominant: the institution holds sway over the lives of individuals. However, the institutional structure is no longer at the center. We have been in the midst of this paradigm shift for over a century, but few acknowledge it and even fewer implement it in the pursuit of their work. An examination of some of the following characteristics of the IP worker will substantiate this transition.

Characteristics of an IP Worker

An Open System

IP workers maintain themselves as an open system, as distinct from a closed system. A closed system is static. Because it lacks the energy for change, it remains fixed and will eventually be outdated and no longer viable as a living system. An open system (in the form of an IP worker) demonstrates the awareness that we are not isolated parts in a mechanical universe but are interacting with the whole, all the time. Such awareness allows the IP worker to dialogue with his/her inner self regarding needs, areas of weakness and opportunities for development.

Among the weaknesses workers discover in themselves is resistance to changing their own dysfunctional behaviors. If a worker confronts personal resistance and works through it using inner dialogue, then he/she is beginning to challenge the resistance in the organizational systems. His/her inner dialogue enables freedom of choice. When such freedom of choice is present, the worker is no longer locked into habitual patterns of behavior.

In addition, an IP worker is constantly interacting with the environment and with others. Together, they are open to receiving the information vital for the emergence of new opportunities. This dynamic interaction also means that they avoid the "them and us" mentality that poisons even the most effective working relationships. IP workers keep their communications open regardless of circumstances. The IP worker constantly learns from interactions and applies new-found knowledge in creative problem-solving. As an open system, this IP worker is always creating alignment with the other open systems. In that way, the IP worker can ride the waves of potential change that constantly flood the workplace.

Life Viewed as a Whole

Shifting focus from the institution to the individual does not mean individuals experience themselves as isolated units. IP workers experience themselves as always being in relationship with everything else. This means that the worker knows the needs of the whole and acts for the benefit of the whole and not just for personal interests. IP workers understand that the whole is alive and the way to absorb the energies of life is to interact and be a participant. They understand that progress can come from negative workplace situations as well as positive. Even when the system begins to break down, they don't waste time digging the graves of whatever systems are nearing expiration; they don't wait until they implode from creeping irrelevance or are torn apart from internal feuding. IP workers move to generate new direction and goals from the remnants of the old. Nothing is wasted as long as it provides new direction and becomes a resource for creativity and innovation. IP workers see problems as challenges to come up with new ways of working and opportunities for changing the way the systems work.

From the Center Outward

Just as hierarchically-structured institutions were emblematic of previous centuries, so too are the practices of taking our action cues from external circumstances emblematic of today's mentality. When cues took the form of managerial orders, the usual orientation of the workers was to turn their inner world around so they could be in alignment with the external circumstances of commands from above.

With the advent of the *knowledge worker*, *flat* organizations and the need for *innovative responses*, that process of beginning from the outside has changed so workers now begin to act from an inside source of creative energy. IP workers begin with an awareness of what is going on in their inner worlds and then use those inner resources to decide on what to do in the external. They act from the center outward.

Awareness of an IP Worker Regarding Action and No-Action

The prevailing consciousness of an IP worker is that all power comes from the energies of the universe and one has to stay in alignment with those energies whether that means being active or in waiting. Sometimes, the IP worker is waiting for action to happen. When we realize it is time for events beyond our control to guide what happens, our contribution is perhaps to avoid taking action (or to adopt a no-action stance).

This course of waiting might be the polar opposite of what we are inclined to do, and it takes some discipline to manage the tension within ourselves. This polarity might be referred to as the tension between being a collaborator with energies beyond one's control, but it is the ultimate effectiveness of which we trust. IP workers are cognizant and respectful of the processes inherent in the natural development of things. They have an innate trust in the process and are assured, if the process is followed, the correct result will certainly happen.

Co-creators and Contributors

IP workers see work as unique opportunities to contribute and fulfill their unique callings. They see themselves, not so much as individual agents operating in isolation, but as co-creators with everyone and everything in producing the goods and services for which the organization is established. As in the words of Gandhi, they "become the change they wish to see in the world." They believe that if they live the changes they want to see that the system eventually changes in accordance with their beliefs.

IP workers also understand that creativity depends on interdependent action. They take seriously their responsibility to be and do what they wish others to be and do. To avoid duplication of effort, they scan the situation for possibly complementary contributions to the work of others and they do their parts without delay. They seek opportunities to empower others with knowledge and introduce opportunities.

They can do so because they see their own power as gifts received for empowering others. At the same time, they are not dissuaded by mistakes or failed outcomes. They understand that not all forms of power are positive. There are forms of power that derive from lack of power, from being weak or needy. Being without knowledge or resources can also open doors to creativity that could not have been imagined if one had the necessary knowledge or resources.

Competencies of the IP Worker

The IP worker profile consists of sets of competencies that characterize Interiority; providing an overview of the worker who has grown to become Interiority powered. That means they are operating on energies that flow from their inner cores. While the following outline is comprehensive, it is not complete for every worker or circumstance. Variations will depend on the individual and the organization.

Centering Competencies

Centering is the main practice for connecting to one's inner core, accessing resources, acting from that center regardless of the task.

- *Sitting:* Deals with correct posture while sitting; being centered in silence, stillness and in the moment.
- *Breathing:* Being aware of and following one's breath in order to have fuller realization of being alive; filled with life's energies and connected to everything.
- *Presence:* Being fully present to one's work, without distractions; engaged in the flow of doing the work effectively, creatively and productively.
- *Integrated and Whole:* Engaging in work with all of our resources operating together.
- *Practicing Centering Consistently*: Competent in and dedicated to the practice of centering in its various forms.

Self-Aware Competencies

Being self-aware includes knowing our strengths and limitations, and the unique styles of behavior through which we express ourselves.

- *Physical, Mental, Emotional, Spiritual, and Relational:* Workers take responsibility for the care and maintenance of all of these dimensions of their lives. No one of them is more important than another because they all work together to make the worker productive and fulfilled. This kind of holistic self-care must be done consistently to have the desired effects.
- *Self-Care and Growth through Work:* Self-care is the first competency in being self-aware. In practicing self-care, I am taking care of my human needs. In being aware of personal growth through my work, I am effectively including every activity of my life as holding potential for growth and maturity.

- *Story Awareness and Integration:* Becoming aware of my story includes reflecting on the key experiences of my life and how they are linked into one narrative. Integration means taking the learning I have gained through those reflections and making use of them in accomplishing my work.
- *Focus on Meaning, Purpose:* I am motivated to seek meaning in the work I do and to direct my activities toward achieving a purpose beyond my own concerns.
- *Inner-Anchored and Self-Motivated:* My inner self becomes the place from which I act and in which I find security. Being self-motivated means rather than acting from external stimulus, I act from a conviction that has its source in my inner self. Self-motivation leads to constant self-assessment and self-management.
- *Behavioral Style Aware:* I know the pattern of my behavior and even though that pattern differs from that of my co-workers, we generate more energies and results by working effectively together than we might separately.
- *Problem-Solving Style Aware:* Everyone has a problem-solving style and each style is correct for that person, even though it may be greatly different from that of co-workers.
- *Growth through Reactivity, Tension:* I become aware of my reactive complexes and tensions, and I engage with them so I am not blocked; in so doing, I establish connections to the energies that have been inaccessible to me up to this point.
- *Maintain Self as an Open System:* I consistently open myself to the possibilities that surround me while I am doing my work. This stance allows me to use creative options for its completion. Openness means that I solicit feedback from co-workers and supervisors regarding the impact of my behavior. In this way, I proactively engage with the most effective means to further my growth as a worker—and as a person.
- *Perceives Self as Co-creator:* I am aware that I am only one of innumerable sources of inspiration and energy for the completion of my work.

Right-Relationships Competencies

I can develop and maintain viable relationships, even though I experience great differences of approach as compared with that of my co-workers.

- *Care of Others:* I extend myself to know, understand and take care of my co-workers.
- *Forgiveness Initiatives:* I take the initiative to forgive; to ask for forgiveness and to make recompense for the harm I have caused to others.

- *Compassion for Weaknesses:* I am able to feel compassion for the weaknesses of my co-workers so I do not have unrealistic expectations of them.
- *Accommodates Differences:* I have the capacity of allowing for differences between myself and co-workers and of making use of those differences to effectively complete the work.

Communications Competencies

This competency includes skills and positive attitudes in all manner of communications between me and co-workers.

- *Information Sharing:* I share all the relevant information I have with my co-workers, especially to the extent it is necessary for them to complete their work.
- *Emotionally Expressive:* I am able to be descriptive of my emotions related to the work and the relationships between me and my co-workers.
- *Supportive:* I provide the content of my communications in ways that are positive and constructive of my co-workers.
- *Problem-Solving Orientation:* I am ready to work at solving any problems encountered by me and my work group.
- *Reveals Vulnerability Appropriately:* I am unafraid of having others see my weaknesses, mistakes or failings. I work at overcoming those limitations to the extent I can and progress through them so the best results are generated.

Organizational Competencies

This includes awareness and skills at working for the collective and the organization's stakeholders.

- *Belonging to the Organization:* Besides managing my own Interiority and productivity, I contribute to the spread of a culture—and practices of Interiority—throughout the organization and among the stakeholders. I do these things as an expression of belonging to the organization.
- *Systems-Thinking Oriented:* When I set about doing my work, I am thinking about the impact that the completion of my work has on all of the other stakeholders. I also think about the influence that their work has on the completion of my work and likewise how those influences spread throughout the system.
- *Learning Centered:* I reflect on how I did my work and how it was completed so I can learn about how to improve upon it and then implement those improvements into the system.

- *Shared Vision, Ownership of Work Processes:* I invest myself in sharing the vision I have of the organization and I use my energies for its achievement. At the same time, I consider myself an owner of the work I do and of the organization in which I do it. I also take ownership of the work processes and if they are not effective, I take initiatives to improve them.
- *Open, Flexible, Change Capable:* I maintain myself as open, curious and in a developmental mode so I can adapt to the requirements of the work, the organization and the stakeholders.
- *Interdependency Aware:* I am aware of the interdependency among all of the stakeholders and all who are connected in any way with my work. This awareness will influence me in my attitude toward my work and help its completion with the highest possible productivity.

Client-Centered Competencies

This set of competencies focuses not only on external clients but also those internal workers who are the immediate clients of my work.

- *Present to Clients, Understands their Needs:* I work hard at understanding the needs of all the clients. Major approaches to the completion of the work depend on accurate understanding of client needs and responding to them to the best of my ability.
- *Uses Empathy in Communication:* Particularly in services work, I use empathy in communicating with my clients so they know I have feelings in common with them regarding the difficulties we might be facing.
- *Coaches them to Problem-Solve:* Rather than always solving the problem for the client, I coach them on how to solve their own problems.
- *Feedback Capable:* I am able to provide both positive and constructive feedback and also to receive both types of feedback so my co-workers and I can maintain effective working relationships.

Good Work Competencies

I do high quality work—in which I am interested—and I feel good about doing it.

- *Involved, Engaged, Self-Directed:* I pursue my work with interest and consistent involvement. I engage with my work so all my attention—and resources—are available for its completion. Self-Directed means doing my work on my own initiative in order to work effectively.

- *Learning from Our Work:* I engage with the work in a way that it teaches me personal life-lessons and helps me improve my techniques.
- *Alignment with Tasks and Goals:* I align myself with the work so it gets done with everything I can provide from my resources and from all the other resources available. I so orient myself to my work goals that I achieve them expeditiously.
- *Appreciation of the Opportunity to Contribute:* I do my work with appreciation of the opportunity to be creative and to make a contribution to the organization, to my family and to the wider community.

Teamwork Competencies

- *Shared Ownership of Tasks:* The members of the team share the ownership of the required tasks. All members work on the tasks as if they had exclusive responsibility for its completion.
- *Cross-trained for Doing Each Other's Tasks:* Regarding our co-workers' tasks, we know enough about the contents and processes involved to be able to fill in for them in their absence.
- *Knows Each Other's Resources:* Team members take it upon themselves to become known to each other. This means that all the resources of all members are shared by the team.
- *Plays Collaborative Roles:* Members play different roles so they do not duplicate efforts or waste resources.
- *Achieves Results Together:* We collaborate in such a way that we achieve results more efficiently than if we were working in isolation.
- *Accountable to Each Other:* Team members hold each other accountable for doing the tasks to which they are assigned within the parameters given to the team.

Productivity Competencies

This means being capable of completing the work in an effective manner, with all of the needed competencies. The competencies include:

- *Clear Tasks, Goals, and Deadlines:* There is clarity concerning all of the key aspects of the work.
- *Organized in Work Processes:* The work is laid out according to the most effective steps necessary for its completion.

- *Creative and Effective in Resource Usage:* There are usually many resources that can be used for the completion of the work but it requires creativity to achieve effectiveness in using them.
- *Unblocked Flow of Energy:* I have done the inner work necessary to remove blocks to my energy in the achievement of my work.
- *Admits Mistakes and Shortcomings:* I own up to whatever mistakes I have made so others are not inconvenienced by them. I also own up to imperfections in my work that make it somehow incomplete. I make myself available to receive feedback that will assist me in overcoming those imperfections.
- *Accepts Human Imperfections*: I understand and take into consideration that there will be some imperfections in the work that is done, especially if many team members are involved.
- *Completes Assigned Work with High Quality:* There are ways of doing the work with barely acceptable results. In my work, I always do it to the best of my ability and with the highest quality results.
- *Assists Others in Completing Their Tasks:* When I complete my tasks ahead of schedule, I look to assist others in the completion of their tasks, or I do work that is no one's specific responsibility.

Social Benefits Competencies

I do my work with an eye to providing social benefits for the local community.

- *Community-Supportive:* I use the opportunity of doing my work to support the local community in whatever way possible.
- *Responsive to being "Called" to Contribute:* I do my work as much as possible in response to a sense of being called to do this particular work at this time.
- *Ensures Results by Autonomous Action:* I do my work without having to be supervised. I am able to make decisions about all of the key parts of my work and I can do so without having to get permission.
- *Aware of Stakeholder's Needs:* I make efforts to understand the needs of all of the stakeholders and, as much as possible, respond to them in the completion of my work.

A CULTURE OF INTERIORITY 255

IP (INTERIORITY POWERED) WORKER PROFILE

1. Centering Competencies
 a. Sitting – Correct Posture
 b. Breathing comfortably
 c. Presence – Complete attention
 d. Integrated and whole
 e. Practices consistently

2. Self-Aware Competencies
 a. Physical, mental, emotional, spiritual
 b. Self-care and growth through work
 c. Story awareness and integration
 d. Focus on meaning, purpose
 e. Inner anchored and self-motivated
 f. Behavioral style aware
 g. Problem-solving style aware
 h. Growth through reactivity, tension
 i. Maintains self as an open system
 j. Perceives self as co-creator

3. Right Relationships' Competencies
 a. Care of others
 b. Forgiveness initiatives
 c. Compassion for weaknesses

4. Communications Competencies
 a. Information sharing
 b. Emotionally expressive
 c. Supportive communications
 d. Problem-solving orientation

5. Organizational Competencies
 a. Belonging to the organization
 b. Systems-thinking oriented
 c. Learning centered
 d. Shared vision, ownership of work processes
 e. Open, flexible, change capable
 f. Interdependency aware

FIGURE 31: **IP WORKER PROFILES (2)**

IP (INTERIORITY POWERED) WORKER PROFILE

6. Client-Centered Competencies
  a. Present to clients, understands their needs
  b. Uses empathy in communications
  c. Coaches them to problem-solve
  d. Feedback capable

7. Good Work Competencies
  a. Involved, engaged, self-directed
  b. Learning from our work
  c. Alignment with tasks and goals
  d. Appreciation of opportunity to contribute

8. Teamwork Competencies
  a. Shared ownership of tasks
  b. Cross-trained for doing other's tasks
  c. Knows each other's resources
  d. Plays collaborative roles
  e. Achieves results together
  f. Accountable to each other

9. Productivity Competencies
  a. Clear tasks, goals and deadlines
  b. Organized in work processes
  c. Creative and effective in resource usage
  d. Unblocked flow of energy
  e. Admits mistakes and shortcomings
  f. Accepts human imperfections
  g. Completes assigned work with high quality
  h. Assists others in completing their tasks

10. Social Benefits Competencies
  a. Community-supportive
  b. Responsive to being "called" to contribute
  c. Ensures results by autonomous action
  d. Aware of stakeholder's needs

FIGURE 31: **IP WORKER PROFILES (2)**

Here I want to take a break from the seriousness of this topic with a story about the culture from which I came. The reason is culture is profoundly formative of who we are and what we become and we neglect it at our peril.

My Story – Spirituality of the Ordinary

I grew through the culture of Northern Ireland. If our town represented the structured world populated by churches, pubs and houses, then Uncle Hughie's house, in a lonely place on the side of a remote mountain, represented all that was wild, wonderful and warm in the Celtic heritage of the Irish culture. Even during the best of times, Irish weather and terrain requires a tough constitution to survive. But Uncle Hughie's mountainous environment was especially rugged, making human survival as difficult as it could possibly be.

His house was built on the wildest, boggiest land on the mountain and was almost impossible to cultivate. That was only one of the reasons there was no other house within miles. In fact, it was the last house out on the mountain. But it was not just the remoteness that made it seem as if we—the visitors from the town—had gone back hundreds of years in time. Mixed in with the wild bleakness of the mountain and the remoteness of the house were great examples of people loving life, loving love, loving learning and coming to terms with birth, sickness, dying and death.

It was on that mountainside that an unheralded epic of the human struggle with the earth played out. Somehow, new life was always emerging in a dance of wild and untrammeled fertility, mostly through cooperation of the humans and nature in a fierce mutual embrace. No matter the experiences of being battered down by the weather, illness and bad luck, they always seemed to rebound. Here, I felt there was less of a consciousness of the struggle of good and evil that troubled my life in the town, and more of an emphasis on human survival among the briars and the ferns and the whitewashed walls—and going to the toilet in the great outdoors in all types of weather.

We loved to go there because of the welcome by Uncle Hughie and his family. I loved it also because of the immediate and mysterious connection with the earth, the animals, the forest, the bogs and the fields that seemed alive with the ferocious beauty and begrudging fertility of nature on the barren mountainside.

Uncle Hughie's house was more like four whitewashed walls set in a long rectangle, divided up into six small rooms covered with a thatched roof; dug into the side of the hill to get as much shelter as possible from the elements. In spite of the fact there was no electricity, no running water and only an open, leather-bellows-blown hearth and turf-fire for warmth and cooking, the hospitality was warm and genuine.

Uncle Hughie's family had only the most rudimentary implements in the house but there was nothing rudimentary about their ability to talk, to laugh and to enjoy the beauties and the sorrows that came along with living life close to the earth. The living room/kitchen had a flagstone floor that was swept with a broom of heather sprigs and gorse, all tied with string called, "Hairy Ned." The newborn chicks were kept in a cardboard box next to the hearth so that they would not freeze. The turf for the hearth fire was dug from the bog during the summer and dried so that the fire was warm enough to heat the main room. A bedroom flanked the kitchen on one side and on the other a pantry held the provisions for cooking. The next room held the dairy where the milk was churned into butter. The rooms at both ends of the house held the horse and the pigs respectively and, for obvious reasons, they could only be reached through outside doors.

Warmth, welcome, wildness and wonder prevailed. During the daytime, we children were sent on many an egg hunt because the hens would lay their eggs in the hedgerows or in the nests in clumps of grass. In the evenings, we all crowded around the hearth on three-legged stools and listened to the funny stories and the tales of the mysterious natural coincidences that drew fascinating interpretations of the great "powers that be." Ghost stories were told as the darkness highlighted the blustering flame of the oil lamp on the wall. We did our best to keep quiet so they would not stop.

Besides being a rugged challenge for survival, it was an opportunity to touch the Celtic culture that celebrated life in one piece. In the Celtic world, the sacred could be immediately experienced. There was a natural quality to Uncle Hughie's spirituality in the sense that prayer came easily. There were prayers for every aspect of daily life, like herding the cows, feeding the chickens, cleaning the pigsty, churning the butter, cutting the hay, driving the horse and cart, working with the dog to round up the sheep or cattle. Prayers uttered through deep-sighed whisperings, prayers of want, need, gratitude for blessings, and the needs of the community all came around to "thy will be done" in warm recognition of the powers that be—for all things to happen, all things to happen in due time—all done in God's time, sacred time.

Compared to our urban, rule-bound lyrics and prose, Celtic traditions were like poetry and music. All of these elements came together when small glasses of poteen (moonshine) were filled and brought around. Invariably, Uncle Hughie, who

> was small of stature, pulled himself up to his full height in his good suit, waistcoat, hobnailed boots and with hand and glass held high greeted us all, in a loud voice, that rang out, "Healths Apiece," and we were drawn into that circle of hospitality and friendship. This was magic to me because Uncle Hughie, who had little else but his hearth, had everything in his ancestry, his family, his store of knowledge and wisdom; and most memorably, the sharing of his goodness that we from the town, with our busy concerns, could take pleasure in.
>
> To be sure, in that house it was survival amid tough times, but mixed with an air of aristocratic civility that created interdependent, genuine relationships in that mountainside community. Such civility came from poetry recitations, songs, stories, music, a shared hearth and work, shared beliefs about life and the rules learned from working with the earth.

My Story – Reflections

This aspect of the spirituality of the ordinary is missing in great part in our generation because we have not inherited accessing the spiritual dimension of our lives at any moment. We do not know the swish and rhythm of the scythe as it cuts sweetly through the swath of grass or corn—releasing the scented smells of the new-mown crops. We do not have the immediacy of lifting the still-warm eggs from under the hedge where the hen just laid them. We do not have our senses awakened by the rhythmic rustling of the bushes shaking the rain-drenched leaves, fluttering along the hedgerows, spattering us into shivering flight.

We are less centered in life, from not having that sense of the mysterious energies bringing life to all—and all happening within eternal time.

My Story – Applications

We fear the irresistible decisiveness of nature's ways. We fear the racing forest fires, the violent shaking of the earth's crusts, the surging waters flooding the plains, the swirling winds that flatten homes and lives—leaving nothing behind but dust.

Further, we need quiet times to let the sun's rays warm us from our cores. We need to stand on solitary hillsides and smell the perfumed breezes flowing round us. We need to realize that nature is making itself fertile and productive once more. We need the magic alchemy to make the energies that drive our mills, and we need the nourishing waters that bring nutrients to the roots of everything on which we live.

And in the middle of it all, we need to hum tunes and celebrate the culture that binds it all with hearty "Healths Apiece."

Your Story

What then is your story of spiritual inspiration in the ordinary events of your workday? Is it not in the doing of the routine that your spirit is nourished? Do the dishes in the break room need to be cleaned, filing cabinets kept orderly and wastebaskets emptied? In our attention to the routine details, do we not keep our lives in good order? How does your attention to the ordinary chores and circumstances of your work keep you balanced and in good shape?

Becoming an IP Organization

Throughout the course of history, it could be argued that while workers lived out their lives attending to immediate workplace tasks, the overall mentality that governed the human community has seen several major shifts. Perhaps these shifts could be identified as *three ages* in which a dominant idea held sway and according to which the majority ordered their lives. The main idea in the first age might have been *God*, followed by *Nation* in the second age and *Self* in the third age.

During the age in which the dominant idea of *God* prevailed, different communities organized themselves into religious institutions and led their daily lives according to uniquely defined beliefs. During the age in which the idea of *Nation* dominated, different communities were conscious of themselves as tribes/nations/states. Their citizens pursued goals based on the domestic ideas of zero-sum resources and the absolute rights of private property, law and sanction. During the age in which the dominant idea of *Self* prevailed, workers became aware of themselves as individuals possessed of a self that became the focal point of action. During this age, they conducted their lives as consumers of goods and services that had been marketed as necessary to maintain social status.

We are transitioning into the age of the *Universe* in which belonging to the whole has registered in the consciousness of all. Because of the influence of scientific discoveries and the effects of global warming, we are becoming aware of the nature of matter, energy, ecological interdependence and how everything influences everything else. We are approaching the age when the *collective* will become as important as the individual self.

Connecting the ages, the predominant ideas from the previous ages have not been lost but have been subsumed into the prevailing idea. In spite of the historical evolution of these dominant ideas, people have organized themselves in groups around work that produces goods and services; in general, because of the efficiencies of doing the work together.

In addition, we can say that the pace of change from one dominant idea to another has quickened, but it is still dependent on the impact of transformative events, such as the re-election of Barack Obama. Such events have a profoundly transformative influence on the human community, indicating that a threshold has been crossed and the consciousness of the community can never revert to the way it was before.

Accordingly, the traditional hierarchical form of organization has been slow to change but is giving way to new structures for worker collaboration. As an impetus for transformative change, it may be helpful to consider we are always in the process of becoming more effective and productive through our interactions with everything else. We belong to, and influence everything, and therefore are able to effect much more in collaboration with the whole than we could by ourselves. This is the foundation of the move away from our focus on externals and individual effort and toward Interiority.

Currently, in this dominance of *Self* age, organizations are changing, but not at the fundamental levels required for tapping into the powerful resources of all the shareholders. In order to show the public they are changing with the times, organizations sometimes adapt their processes and outputs, but seldom enough to provide vital and responsive solutions to their customers' needs. They even add corporate social responsibility (CSR) programs (perhaps) to convince observers that they are serving the wider community. When these changes are not accompanied by upgrades in Interiority, the results usually show up as cosmetic and the organization immediately reverts to the unproductive patterns of the past.

When fundamental change does come, it usually percolates through the organization from IP (*Interiority-Powered*) workers and incrementally spreads throughout the system. These IP workers model paradigm shifts that allow them to leave behind traditional models and propel themselves onward to new ways of thinking—and working.

Just as paradigm shifts have occurred in the case of IP workers, so are paradigm shifts occurring in Interiority-Powered (IP) organizations, albeit comparatively slowly. These shifts toward IP organizations will take much longer to become the norm than for individual IP workers because *organizations resist change*. They do so because they are weighed down by *vested interests* of management, are inhibited by the *outdated mental models*, struggle with *inertia of legacy systems* and are subject to the drag of *psychic entropy*.

Also, workers very often claim they want change to happen, yet still resist changing themselves because of an unwillingness to assume responsibility for their own lives—or for the whole. Nevertheless, while the greater resistance to change tends to occur at the management level, the advance of revolutionary technologies (such as technology-based networks) almost ensures the obsolescence of the hierarchical model and the adoption of the network structure.

Characteristics of the IP Organization

It is the Network

New models of organization and leadership have emerged to challenge the traditional hierarchical systems. These new models reflect the IP organizations that we anticipate will become the norm because of competitive necessity. These changes have appeared in knowledge management, information access and networks that have almost eliminated the distance between suppliers and clients. The most obvious change in organizations has been driven by emerging technologies, especially by *interconnected networks*. The technology of networked systems has virtually *eliminated time and distance* as major factors in how organizations work.

This change is apparent in the illustrations of the typical hierarchical organization and the newer networked, collaborative organization.[141] The networked organization also aligns with the advent of cloud computing. Cloud computing is a general concept that incorporates software as a service, to which access can be established from anywhere.[142] This is also where individuals can gain access to enormous computational power of a "cloud" of computers.

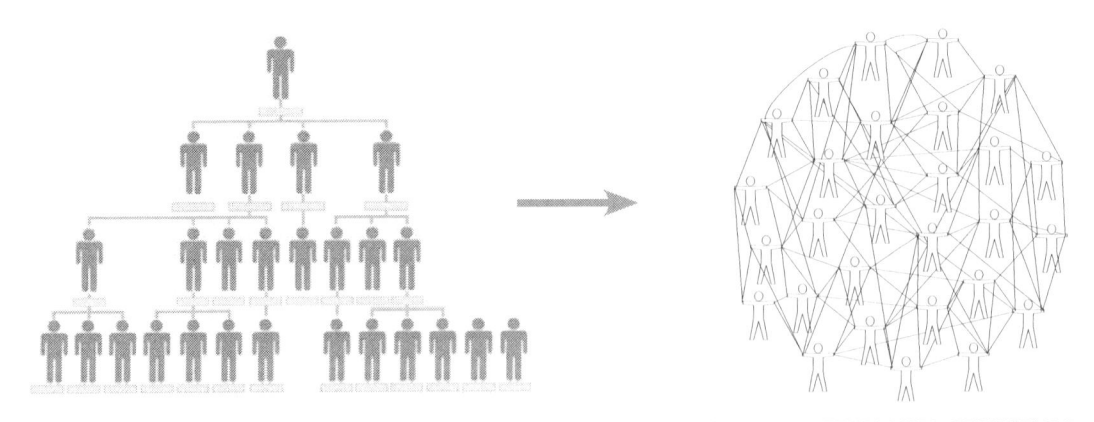

FIGURE 32: **HIERARCHY STRUCTURE**

FIGURE 33: **NETWORKED STRUCTURE**

The inefficiencies of communication, management and information-sharing in the hierarchically structured organization are enormous compared with the fast and effective methods of the collaborative type organization. The scale is also vastly different because the hierarchical organization is usually confined to a geographical location while the collaborative type can be extended globally with only minor lessening of efficiencies. One of the outstanding characteristics of the collaborative model is the ability to flexibly adapt to emerging client requirements. One look at the collaborative organization is sufficient to confirm that the networked model looks like an amoeba organically growing and adapting to even the most chaotic environments.

Open Systems

Just as IP workers maintain themselves as open systems, so do IP organizations maintain that openness to being available for serving the whole community. That means constantly discerning the needs of the whole through listening to the voices of the stakeholders. This is how an organization discovers its own voice. That voice is connected to the purpose and mission for which the organization exists.

The responsibility of the stakeholders is to constantly listen and discern the voices of the communities to which they belong and then to communicate those "voices" to the appropriate functionaries in the organization. If the stakeholders are maintaining attitudes of openness, the voice of the whole will communicate itself through every phenomenon which strikes a chord in their consciousness. This also means that the stakeholders will be attentive not only to the positive side of the organization's life but also to the shadow material inherent in its activities. (An investigation of the shadow sides of organizational life is just as important for discerning the voice of the whole community as is a look at the positive activities.)

Generally, we come into the circumstances of our work as a fait accompli (an established fact). Even though we may want to change the world, we first have to accept the realities of our work situations as we find them. That requires an initial love and acceptance of one's fate. The love of one's fate reminds us that it is in the life we have and are called to fulfill that we discover real power. For organizations, this *amor fati (love of one's fate)* does not mean passive resignation to the forces of life that might lock the leaders into one view of the world. Again, just as the individual worker is living in the tension between being an individual and belonging to the collective, so does the organization operate within that tension of the ideal and the real or imperfect. The organization must have an independent existence but not an absolute independence.

The organization is fundamentally a part of the collective and it must maintain itself as an open system by managing the tension between independence, belonging to the collective and responding appropriately to its needs.

Flexible Leaders and Workers Collaborate

There's a challenge to the collaborative organization: *leadership skills are required more than management skills*. The traditional role of management has been to define, assign and manage tasks—and expected outcomes. The emerging role of leadership supersedes management's conventional role and establishes the direction toward which the company should move. The leaders inform the workers about what needs to be done, why and when, while listening to what they have to say. Then each worker creates his own portfolio of tasks according to those company priorities and the workers' qualifications. Of course, this portfolio has to be integrated with the portfolios of co-workers and coordinated with the goals of the organization.

This structure is more informal and flexible than in a hierarchically-structured organization and incorporates three aspects: *project*, *people* and *profession*. Workers form themselves into teams according to needs (of the individuals, clients, company and society). Based on these emerging needs, the *organization constantly changes*. Workers collaborate with managers to initiate changes and then inform the leaders of the reorganized teamwork. In accordance with holding each other accountable, worker compensation is largely determined by peer review. Rules for working hours are reduced to a minimum.

The work environment is a place where personal growth and development is possible, and achievement and innovation are supported. Workers learn from experiences, share their knowledge and support the achievements of others.

Worker Innovation a Necessity

Fundamentally different from the hierarchically-structured organization, an IP organization is necessary for innovation to happen. In general, we have left the era of mass production and entered the *era of mass customization* of products and services. Customization requires *creativity* and *innovation*. Customers today want what fits their needs and they will search until they find that customized product. This means that organizations must be filled with workers who are multi-skilled and diverse in their approach to innovation. In other words, especially workers who deal with customers, must be familiar with trends in style and technology, so they can produce products and services responsive to the customer's requirements. They are an innovative part of the new paradigm that thinks beyond the mass-produced product or service.

In this focus on innovation, it is necessary to leave transaction processing as much as possible to computers. This requires a workplace that puts its focus on interactions with diverse workers and a shared context that challenges conventional thinking, links to customers and end-users, uses change-process tools and facilitates worker involvement.

Shared Values, Assumptions and Norms

The hierarchically-structured organization has been traditionally governed by rules, regulations and common processes. This type of rigid adherence to the rules was effective in eras dominated by manufacturing. However, in our time of mass customization, *rigid adherence to the rules is a recipe for stagnation*. Shared values, assumptions and norms—rather than rules—guide the IP organization and bind the workers in a psychological contract that allows them to pursue innovative products and services.

One of the shared values is the meaning that comes to the workers through products or services that fulfill the customers' needs. In the wider context, *meaning* emerges from the consciousness of collaboration with life, from cosmic energy expressing itself through the workers and the work they do. As a result, the workers recognize that something larger than themselves is intending itself through the experience. They are also energized by participation in that larger goal.

Another value that should permeate the IP organization is the emphasis on both the masculine and feminine approaches toward responding to stakeholder needs. An outcome of this approach: no function that cannot be fulfilled by either a male or a female. Androgynous (a combination of male and female psychological characteristics) approaches and behaviors are the norm for worker relationships.

In the IP organization, it is assumed that workers embrace responsibility and accountability. This assumption alone should cause leadership to avoid using resources to control worker behaviors. Other leadership assumptions for an IP organization are that workers will:

- take on *several tasks* at one time
- *connect with others* who have necessary expertise
- use the *openly available information* for doing their jobs
- make *more efficient work processes*
- become *creative* in advancing the organization's growth and development
- *Self-assess* their level of productivity, self-management and performance improvement and customarily discuss this with their supervisor
- solicit *feedback* from co-workers on how they are doing their work
- develop their *skills* so if it is necessary to move on they will have excellent prospects elsewhere

Norms are the unwritten but effective rules that grow up around the workers in an IP organization and extend to include the stakeholders. A norm in a technologically advanced organization might be the use of digital information for communication, search and storage rather than books, filing cabinets and paper documents. Legacy systems may remain but gradually fade to allow for the speedier and more accurate digital systems.

Recapping the Past for "Jumping" Forward

To develop an IP organization, it is necessary to stress in the emergence of new organizational forms that the past is not discarded or lost but subsumed under the new. As William Faulkner wrote, "The past is never dead. It's not even past." Evolution does not move in constant forward steps. Evolutionary development takes place in what might be called "jumps" forward, and all of the past is not lost but is recapitulated in the new forms that emerge from the old. This process is similar to the momentum of an athlete who takes 20 paces back in order to leap 30 paces ahead.

In applying these thoughts to organizations, all of the learning of the past is not forgotten but to be recapitulated in a new expression more in step with the needs of customers. The past organizational forms are contained in the new—but transformed—fashion. In the sense of recapitulation, we can look at our own efforts at deepening and implementing Interiority as a period of preparation, so together the human community can move forward in such a jump. Then workers will say of the new dispensation, "This is how it should be."

This does not mean that our specific efforts are in vain because what transforms reality is a person who is living out of Interiority in every moment. The dynamics of one's own contribution to Interiority is based on the notion of *threshold of consciousness*. When we engage with something new and embrace it through repeated actions, we are not just developing habitual patterns but we are crossing a psychic threshold; thus, the human community can never regress to the way it was previously.

There is a price to be paid for such movement because *systems resist change*. After transformative discoveries have long penetrated the minds and hearts of individuals everywhere, there are still change-resistant organizational structures and co-dependent worker behaviors that, like invisible prison bars, block healthy growth and productivity. Perhaps the last things to change are the habits, addictions and traditions that support dysfunctional and painful lives.

Such weaknesses notwithstanding, as long as the will to work from a place of Interiority is there, every worker and every organization has the capacity to grow, be innovative and influence the whole community for the better. During periods of history when much of the work could be done by manual labor, it may have been acceptable to withhold inner commitment. However, in our age of the knowledge worker and multiple intelligences, it is more necessary than ever for workers to initiate action from their inner cores. If they do so, they can bring all of their innate resources to bear on the innovative completion of their work, and correspondingly, personal and organizational fulfillment.

The IP Organizational Profile consists of sets of competencies that characterize Interiority. As you can see in the profile on pages 276-277, the center of the organization is represented by concentric circles that diminish to the smallest group of executives who make the key decisions. This is called the *core group* and is essentially stable over the long term. The wider fields around the core are called the *cloud* and include many suppliers or sales people who work on projects and when finished, move out of the cloud. While this is a comprehensive view of the characteristics of an IP organization, it is not complete. Variations will depend on each separate organization, its identity, stakeholders and management.

Competencies of the IP (Interiority-Powered) Organization

Empowerment Competencies

Management empowers workers with as much autonomy as they can handle in doing their work. They also challenge workers to engage in manageable risk that will continuously stretch them in cycles of maturation.

- *Invites the 'Whole Person' to Work:* Every human dimension is legitimate and acceptable in the workplace. This includes limitations, mistakes and the darkness of our un-integrated shadow energies. This invitation recognizes that workers have the right to grow through their work.

- *Puts the Human at the Center:* The individual person is seen as the center of the organization's life rather than the hierarchical power structure. Introducing the concept of worker centrality is a leadership challenge.

- *Encourages Career Self-Development in Workers:* Supports workers in selecting their own career paths and related development activities. A system of senior members mentoring less-experienced workers—by making available their own transformative experiences—is encouraged.

- *Supports Worker Settlement in a Local Community:* Provides support for workers in settling down in the local community. Communities need the stability that allows for maturity to happen.

- *Supports Teamwork over Individual Productivity:* Sees teamwork as enhancing productivity and satisfaction because of resource sharing and the potential for growth through relationships.

- *Nourishes Growth-Oriented Mindsets:* The work of growing up through the work (and work relationships) provides an ongoing opportunity for reflection and development.

- *Cross-Trains for Team Productivity:* Workers are trained in team members' tasks so they *can* do each other's work when necessary.

- *Self-Selection of Team Members by the Team:* Team members are supported to take part in the selection of the members they want on their own team—while keeping the achievement of the task and the required competencies in view.

- *Opts for Culturally Diverse Teams in Assigning Projects:* Sees advantages in the dynamism of culturally-diverse teamwork.

- *Team Members Hold Each Other Accountable:* Each member is held accountable in terms of productivity, quality and teamwork.

Work that Matters Competencies

Management emphasizes work that provides benefits for both the workers and the community regarding the content of the work and the way it is done.

- *Meaningful Work:* The work itself carries within it meaning for the worker, the customer and all the stakeholders.

- *Work for a Purpose:* The work is chosen because it is oriented toward a useful outcome for all concerned.

- *Purpose Provides Energy for Work:* The objective of the work is emphasized in such a way that doing the work becomes motivational for the workers.

- *Access to the Whole Self at Work:* The work itself provides development opportunities in every aspect of the worker's life.

- *Worker Submits Work Plans, Results Expected and Deadlines - to the Supervisor:* The workers generate the plans for doing the work, the results they expect to generate and the deadlines for completion. They provide all of these to the supervisor who works with them to ensure that they are appropriate to the needs of the organization.

Work for the "Greater Good" Competencies

In all of its practices, culture and results, the organization is dedicated to the greater good of the stakeholders—as well as the local and global communities.

- *Invests in a Purpose Larger than Profitability/Products/Services alone*: The organization primarily invests its resources to achieve benefits for the stakeholders over and above profitability, products or the services themselves.

- *Uses Sustainable Business Practices*: The work is done with a view to achieving sustainability in all of the resources used for the end product.

- *Ethical Integrity in all Decisions*: All decisions are made with a view to effective business practices and ethical integrity. Ethical integrity is built from the center of each worker's Interiority. Key decisions have both a business and an ethical dimension and neither can be dispensed with.

Management Competencies

Management does their work in alignment with the Interiority of the worker and the organization.

- *Monthly One-on-One Discussions Re. Results and Job Satisfaction*: Rather than the annual performance appraisal (PA), managers might discuss the worker's productivity, one-on-one on a monthly or more frequent periodic basis. Traditional PAs are measured by how many widgets a worker produced over a defined period. More comprehensive PAs also factor in worker behaviors on the job. The most effective PAs are based on the worker's self-assessment of their productivity and on a self-administered plan for improvement and self-management. This plan is reviewed with the worker's supervisor and becomes the basis for compensation and career advancement.

- *Relinquishes Control to Aid Self-Generated Innovations*: Managers delegate work to the workers so they are not so much controlling outcomes as facilitating results.

- *Involves Workers in Goal-Setting*: Managers collaborate with the workers on setting goals for productivity, results, deadlines and other key aspects of work.

- *Autopsies Mistakes Without Blame*: Managers review mistakes, consult with workers on the reasons why, integrate valuable lessons and plan for the avoidance of such mistakes in the future.

- *Leads with Questions:* Rather than telling workers what they must do and how to do it, they lead the workers through coaching questions along a path to where they are able to do the work with autonomy, quality and satisfaction.

- *Engages in Dialogues:* Rather than creating separations between management and worker levels, the manager engages the workers in dialogues so they are both involved in achieving the results that fulfill their function in the workplace.

Interiority Culture Competencies

Management engages the workers to the extent that they create their own plans and practices for improving their Interiority.

- *Nourishes a Culture of Interiority:* Workers are encouraged to engage in the practices of Interiority that lead them to higher productivity and greater personal satisfaction.
- *Shows Respect for Interiority:* The organizational culture is oriented toward respecting the development of Interiority and its practices in all of the stakeholders.
- *Workers Manage Own Self-Development Plans:* In addition to having a self-development plan for completing the work assigned to them, managers ensure that the workers have individual plans for the development of their Interiority.
- *Relationality Activated at the Core:* The organization places equal focus on individuality and relationality in the achievement of the mission.
- *Optional Activities for Self-Care:* Workers develop their own Interiority from a range of acceptable activities within the culture of the organization.
- *Allows 10% of Time for Personal Projects:* Workers have the option to use 10% of their work time to do projects related to their regular work, but which they have not been able to do. The point here is to leave the disposition of that time to each worker's will so that he/she can develop personal initiatives.

Worker Self-Management

The organization allows workers a high degree of autonomy in doing their work. In accordance with required criteria, this does not include the freedom not to work at all or to avoid doing it.

- *Autonomy in Performing Work, Use of Time, Teamwork and Technique:* To the greatest extent possible, workers are provided with autonomy in the performance of their work, how they use their time for doing the work, with whom they collaborate and the means whereby they complete it.

- *Workers Self-Organize to Do the Work:* Following the prescribed criteria, workers have autonomy to organize themselves to make all the decisions involved in the completion of the assigned work.

- *Works from any Location from which the Results can be Produced:* Workers can work from any location and not necessarily the workplace. This is true as long as the work meets prescribed standards and workplace relationships are maintained.

- *Matches Work to Skills, Knowledge and Capabilities:* Workers can choose to do work that most effectively matches their knowledge, interests and abilities.

Stakeholder-Centered Competencies

The organization puts its focus on providing for the needs of the stakeholders.

- *All are Connected to the Organizational Story:* All stakeholders are aware of the original story of the organization and are involved in carrying on its vision and mission even though one or both may change due to time and circumstances.

- *Connects Worker's Story and Organizational Story:* Workers are enabled to find expression of their unique stories in the context of the organization's story.

- *Maximizes Value for all Stakeholders:* The organization keeps its focus on providing value for all those who have a stake in the success of the enterprise.

- *Practices Reciprocity toward the Stakeholders:* The organization makes it a practice to reciprocate to an appropriate degree the investment of any stakeholder resources.

- *Embraces the SRM (Stakeholder Relationship Model):* The organization fosters relationships with all stakeholders so their needs are fulfilled as much as possible. This follows the example of COSTCO.

- *Network-Centered Structure:* The organization shifts as much as possible from the hierarchical structure to one that embraces the network of interdependent units. Hierarchy is dispensed with to allow leadership to emerge from within individual workers—and teams.

- *Skillful Use of the Digital Marketplace:* The organization adapts, changing from the traditional bricks and mortar retail business model to one that is online.

- *Operates through Cloud and Core Workers:* The organization evolves from the traditional, hierarchically-structured and managed model to one that has its workers located in a distributed, constantly changing cloud structure; with a small headquarters of core workers that retains its identity and mission over time. Nevertheless, even though separated in terms of function, all members of the organization are treated as equals in terms of their productivity—and their humanity.

- *Creates Value for the Whole (local) Community:* The organization practices reciprocity in providing for the needs of the local community.

Good-Work Competencies

The organization puts the focus on doing good work as a source of high productivity and satisfaction in the workers.

- *Results Only Work Environment (ROWE):* ROWE does not mean exclusive emphasis on objective results. Rather, it emphasizes the growth of whole persons working within holistically operating organizations. The ROWE acronym was first developed and implemented at Best Buy Corporation, producing high corporate productivity and positive personal satisfaction for the workers. Many other organizations are moving in this direction. In a ROWE workplace, workers have flexible schedules. They just have to get their work done. How they do it, where and when they do it, is up to each worker.

- *Supports Work as a "Calling":* The organization views workers as working because they have a "calling" to be engaged in doing the kind of work they are tasked to do.

- *Contributes to Personal Fulfillment:* The organization puts a high priority on workers' growth and development—both as professionals and individuals—so they are fulfilled by the work they do.

- *Celebrates Worker Achievements:* The organization recognizes the achievements of workers and the contributions they have made to the organization and its stakeholders.

- *Allows Workers Time for Personal Contributions to the Community:* The organization recognizes that workers are aware of the specific needs of the community and supports them in providing for those needs through the use of company time and resources.

Productivity Competencies

The organization emphasizes the priority of productivity over other considerations.

- *Promotes Work Mastery and Self-Mastery:* The organization promotes skills development in the workers so they are masters of their work. In addition, they promote self-development to the point where workers are capable of bringing their whole selves to work.

- *Knows all Available Resources, Energies:* Management ensures that workers are aware of all the resources throughout the organization, making them available so they can be fully utilized.

- *Stretches Workers through Increasingly Complex Tasks:* The organization increases its productivity by taking on and producing more complex products or services. This magnification of challenges stimulates the workers to increase their capabilities and improve outcomes.

- *Learns from Mistakes and Imperfections:* Management takes mistakes or imperfections in its products or services seriously; they see them as opportunities to learn new skills and technologies for future prevention of such defects.

- *Arranges Workplace for Maximum Worker Exchange as well as Isolation for those Working Alone:* Management arranges the workplace for maximum worker exchange, and for those who are working alone, provides a distraction-free environment.

- *Structures Work Processes for Maximum Innovation:* Management structures work processes so there are challenges to and rewards for innovations that improve key aspects of production or services.

Organizational Competencies

The organization emphasizes organizational effectiveness in the achievement of goals and in worker management.

- *Operates on a Long-Term Perspective:* The organization avoids operating on a short-term-profitability-only basis and works from a long-term view that supports all of the stakeholders who have more settled interests in organizational viability. This long-term perspective influences the fulfillment of society's aspirations for justice and equitable opportunities for all.

- *Information Transparency to all Stakeholders:* The organization makes information available as much as possible to all workers and then to all stakeholders.

- *Practices Servant-Style Leadership:* Leadership is exercised in such a way that leaders serve the needs of the workers and the stakeholders.

- *Emotionally-Intelligent Leadership:* Leaders are characterized by their ability to empathize with workers and stakeholders.

- *Practices Distributed Co-Creation of Products:* Management recognizes the participation of all workers in the creation of innovative products; thus, reward systems are brought into alignment with structured innovation.

- *Bases Culture on Integrity in all Processes:* The organization considers integrity in all of its decisions and acts from integrity in all of its activities.

- *Moves all from Compliance to Engagement:* The organization tries to move all of its worker/management relationships from compliance with rules to full personal engagement with work and the activities of the stakeholders.

- *Values-Centered Management:* Management practice is guided by and based on values rather than on expediency or any other practical goal.

Business Cycle Competencies

The organization recognizes that the business cycle must be considered when running operations.

- *Manages Business Cycles Effectively:* Management considers the cycles of business as an important part of maintaining some level of viability in running the organization.

- *Promotes Market Literacy:* Management makes available as much information as possible about market conditions so that those in charge of key operations are enabled to make sound decisions.

- *Practices Strong Forecasting:* Leaders are expected to forecast conditions in the market so all concerned can make preparations to adapt to emerging conditions.

- *Tracks Consumer Sentiment:* Leaders must constantly be aware of how consumers are reacting to market conditions and take measures to effectively cope with those conditions.

- *Makes Corporate Information Available:* Leaders proactively make corporate information available to the widest possible number of stakeholders for the purpose of strengthening affiliation and identity.

- *Includes Workers' Input in Decisions:* Leaders take seriously the input of workers on every operational aspect.
- *Selects well from the Talent Pool:* Since success depends on the people who work for the organization, selection from the available talent pool is one of the chief skills of management.
- *Opts for Social Networking and Viral Marketing over Traditional Marketing Methods:* Consumers are becoming non-responsive to traditional marketing pitches so organizations must move toward word-of-mouth methods—such as those used in viral marketing models.
- *Structure Facilitates the Flow of Forecasting Data:* Organizational processes must be structured so forecasting data can flow effectively to those who need it to make decisions.
- *Works for Organizational Longevity to Sustain Workers and Dependents:* For sustenance of workers and their families, a balance is maintained between necessary change, flexibility and the need for stable local communities.

IP ORGANIZATIONAL PROFILE

    1. Empowerment Competencies
      a. Invites the whole person to work
        b. Puts the human at the center of the organization
          c. Encourages self-managed career development
            d. Supports worker settlement in a local community
              e. Supprts teamwork over individual productivity
                f. Nourishes growth-oriented mindsets
                  g. Cross-trains for team productivity
                    h. Self-selection of team members by the team
                      i. Opts for culturally diverse teams in assigning projects
                        j. Team members hold each other accountable

    2. Work that Matters Competencies
      a. Meaningful work
        b. Work for a purpose
          c. Purpose provides energy for work
            d. Access to the whole self at work
              e. Worker submits plans and expected results

    3. Work for "Greater Good" Competency
      a. Invests in purpose larger than profitability
        b. Uses sustainable business practices
          c. Ethical integrity in all decisions

    4. Management Competencies
      a. Monthly one-on-one discussions with workers
        b. Delegates control for self-generated innovation
          c. Involves workers in goal-setting
            d. Autopsies mistakes w/out blame
              e. Leads with questions
            f. Engages in dialogues

    5. Interiority Culture Competencies
      a. Nourishes a culture of Interiority
        b. Shows respect for Interiority
          c. Workers manage self-development plan
            d. Relationality activated at the core
          e. Optional activities for self-care
        f. Allows 10% of time for personal projects

    6. Worker Self-Management
      a. Autonomy in performing work, use of time, teamwork
    b. Workers self-organize to do the work
  c. Works from any location from which the results can be produced
d. Matches work to skills, knowledge and capabilities

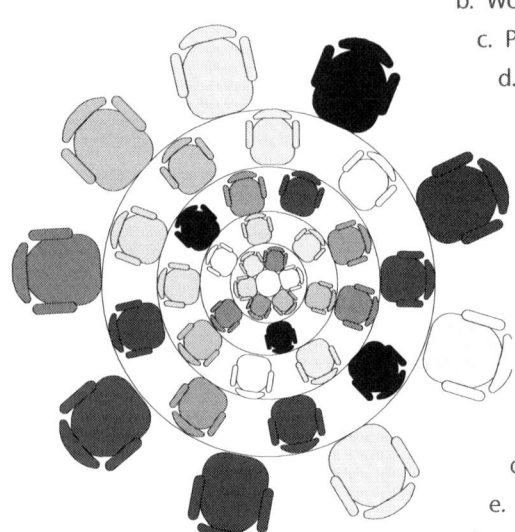

FIGURE 34: **CORE ORGANIZATIONAL STRUCTURE (2)**

A CULTURE OF INTERIORITY   277

IP ORGANIZATIONAL PROFILE

7. Stakeholder-Centered Competencies
a. All are connected to the organizational story
b. Connects worker's story and organizational story
c. Maximizes value for all stakeholders
d. Practices reciprocity toward the stakeholders
e. Embraces SRM, (Stakeholder Relationship Model)
f. Network-centered structure
g. Skillful use of the digital marketplace
h. Operates through cloud & core workers
i. Creates value for whole (local) community

8. Good-Work Competencies
a. Results Only Work Environment (ROWE)
b. Supports work as a "calling"
c. Contributes to personal fulfillment
d. Celebrates worker achievements
e. Allows time for contribution to community

9. Productivity Competencies
a. Promotes work and self mastery
b. Knows all available resources, energies
c. Stretches workers through increasingly complex tasks
d. Learns from mistakes and imperfections
e. Maximizes opportunities for worker exchange
f. Structures processes for maximum innovation

10. Organizational Competencies
a. Operates on a long-term perspective
b. Information transparency to all stakeholders
c. Practices "Servant" style leadership
d. Emotionally-intelligent leadership
e. Practices distributed co-creation of products
f. Bases culture on integrity in all processes
g. Moves all from compliance to engagement
h. Values-centered management

FIGURE 34: **CORE ORGANIZATIONAL STRUCTURE (2)**

11. Business Cycle Competencies
a. Manages business cycles for benefit of all stakeholders
b. Promotes market literacy
c. Practices strong forecasting
d. Tracks consumer sentiment
e. Makes corporate information available
f. Includes workers' input in decisions
g. Selects well from the talent pool
h. Opts for social networking as well as traditional marketing methods
i. Structure facilitates the flow of forecasting data
j. Works for organizatioanl longevity to sustain workers and dependants

The Integrated IP Worker and IP Organization

For the IP worker and the IP organization to have real validity, both must be sufficiently integrated so they can work for the fulfillment of the goals of all involved. An examination of an Interiority-Powered worker/organization will reveal that the *profile of the workers is much larger* than in any previous views of the organization and that they are Interiority Powered. The next most evident characteristic is that the organization has a culture of *integrity* and *productivity*. These two elements go together and are indispensable for the implementation of each other.

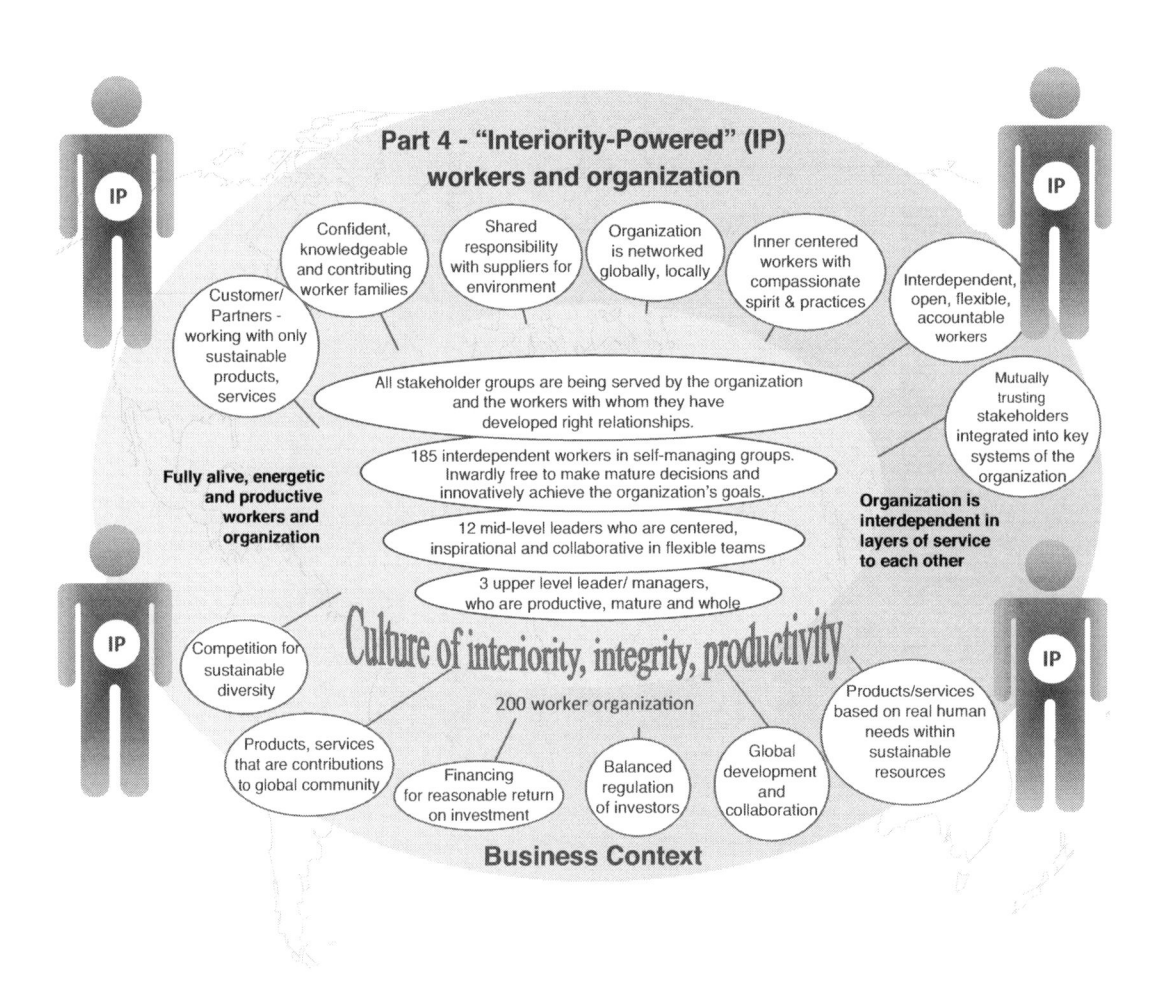

FIGURE 35: **IP WORKERS AND ORGANIZATION**

A CULTURE OF INTERIORITY

The next outstanding characteristic is that the organizational structure is *no longer hierarchical* from the top down. In the illustration on page 278, the inverted structure reveals that the stakeholders are central at the top of the organization. The next level down reveals the workers divided into self-managing groups innovatively managing the organization's goals. The next level down reveals the mid-level leaders who are collaborative in a team and each of whom is leading several worker teams. The final level is the core group of leaders / managers who are leading and guiding the IP organization. Their major challenge is to keep the workers adequately informed. This means helping the workers assimilate the enormous amounts of available information into relevant and digestible chunks. The leaders work hard to keep the organization and all of its activities transparent to the stakeholders.

The major characteristic of the organization's layers is interdependence: they are in service to and held accountable by each other. Beyond the organization's boundaries lies the business context, which require that the products/services really are a contribution to the whole community.

> ### My Story – Interiority Rings a Bell for Some and Not for Others
>
> *I had coached the CEO for several years. He had made great progress in the basics of management skills. He was an above-average leader, was very successful in the company business and was well liked by the workers and stakeholders. He liked what I was doing, as a coach. So, I thought hard about the awareness and skills that he might benefit from tackling next. I figured that he might be open to aspects of Interiority. I thought that he might want to develop deeper levels of self-awareness and how that might further improve his key business and organizational relationships. I looked for an easy way to broach the subject.*
>
> *I ran into a blank wall. He did not understand what I was talking about. Nothing I did or said elicited the slightest response or acknowledgment of the validity of the topic. It was as if he did not recognize the subject or its relevance to himself.*
>
> *Now, this was a smart guy who had all kinds of education and experience. Yet, I had to conclude he had no clue about his inner world or if he did, he did not want to go there. This does not mean that anything was wrong with him. Nothing was wrong. But subjects like reflection, shadow, maturity or Interiority did not compute in his world. Such subjects simply did not ring a bell as important.*
>
> *So I backed off and continued to coach him, as before, for skills development. Subsequently, it became highlighted for me as to why the inner world—and growth— is important for some people and not for others.*

> This question prompted me to think of the great leaders I knew who were successful and well liked, but who also had cultivated a deep inner life based on Interiority. I knew leaders who empowered both IP workers and organizations. They would not have considered themselves so talented, which is part of what made them effective models of IP leadership. They got things done often by not acting themselves but allowing and supporting others in their actions. I remember a leader who would consider decisions in their total context and not just from his own self-interest. He would locate himself in the chain of others who, by their work, would support everyone in the human community—including those who, because of lack of capacity were unable to work. He would say, "Everyone needs a chance to live."
>
> I recalled a leader who, in true self-respect, chose what was of lasting inner worth and not what was of temporary and material importance. He would invest his products and services with thoughtful touches that his customers found helpful and so kept coming back for more.
>
> I thought of the leader who would model customer service by knowing and serving the needs of her co-workers. She did so by giving credit to others and by embracing silence and deference even while diligently serving them.
>
> I recalled the leader who could get things done without recourse, without force or pressure of any kind; by the power of example, he empowered workers toward the highest productivity.
>
> So, what made them different from the CEO in this story? Perhaps they were able to reflect on their experiences and choose to learn and become wise. It may have been that nothing came easy to them and therefore life, in its hardships, pain and disappointments, taught them what was important—and that was everything they needed to know.
>
> I hesitate to say further except to point to the great mystery of how different we all are and how each has his/her call and contribution to make.

My Story - Reflections

As a coach, I was reminded about how dangerous it is to think I might know what the client needs in terms of his/her personal development. That kind of thinking would surely get me into deep trouble. As a person, I was reminded about the folly of judging another person in terms of who I am. The simple truth: I know nothing about the inner world of another. There is so much that I do not know even about myself that the greater part of me will remain a mystery as long as I live. As a member of the wider community, I was reminded that *there are energies at work in everything about which we have no inkling*. We know some things but so much more is cloaked in mystery. Nothing more need be said.

Your Story

Dear reader, what about the challenges you have encountered? Did you experience moving through the stages of learning about life and living to the point where you were able to let go and "skate"? Assuming you did, how have you continued to improve your skating ability (living through the disappointments, glories and diminishments of living)? In what ways have you become an IP worker? In what ways have you supported your company into becoming an IP organization? In what ways are the behaviors associated with an IP worker and an IP organization integrated into your company culture? When called to face the kinds of challenges outlined in this chapter, how does your sense of inner being influence your behavior? Are you appreciative of the challenges that guided you in the fulfillment of your unique contributions?

Communication = effort, practice and action

Chapter 9

Practices

"The kingdom of heaven is within you."
—Luke 17, 20

After all the talk and theories, the question is, "How does one implement Interiority?" In a word, *practice*. Without practice nothing happens, so this treatment of practices is perhaps the most important piece of all. Presented here is a *dialogical framework* for practices. A dialogical framework refers to the inner dialogue carried on between self and soul and upon which the effectiveness of the practice depends. The goal of practice is *integrated wholeness*; the goal of dialogue is *integrity* and *authenticity* in the process.

Ideally, the practices and dialogues go on all the time, with the key result being individuals becoming centered within themselves. They become centered in their physical beings and in their mental/emotional/psychological beings. They sit centered; they stand centered; they walk centered; they sleep centered; they work and live in a centered way; they draw their wisdom from the center of their beings.

The outcome: wisdom born of experience, externalized in one's behavior and implemented in one's life.

To develop routines of centered behavior, it is necessary to set aside time for specific practices. Only through repeated practice will centeredness become a habit—with emerging wholeness carrying over into all our activities at work. Supportive habits form from repeated behavioral changes that are powered from Interiority. We cannot think ourselves into Interiority. Interiority is not what you think it is, but ultimately what you practice. *Interiority comes from* a combination of *thought*, *reflection* and *practice*. Of these, the most difficult is practice because it requires time, discipline and letting go, all of which we are inclined not to do over the long haul.

Achieving the state of Interiority means that you let go of the anxieties that threaten inner balance and live out of an intrinsic self—your innermost reality.

When we live from within, we begin to wake up to the *true reality*, of *this moment*, in *these circumstances*. Through the practices of inner centeredness, we come to realize that *this is the only moment* so it brings us the *greatest potential for living*. Consequently, we gradually become committed to living life in this singular moment…and then in the next…and so on.

This moment is not a product of our minds, imaginations, fantasies, hopes or activities, but of being fully present to self, now. That's what makes this moment of living *real*. This quality of inner presence to all reality is relatively easy to attain for a second at a time. However, to continue to live fully aware, from moment to moment, in the always-changing circumstances of life requires practice; *continuous practice,* for as long as we live.

Our Reality

Some hold that it is impossible to know reality because it is only through our sensory impressions that we can come to know anything and those senses are often unreliable. Others hold that reality is whatever our brains tell us it is. For the purposes of this discussion, we take the position that the reality we perceive is ours and not an objective view of what is out there. Francis Crick, the neuroscientist who helped discover the structure of the DNA molecule in 1953, once said, "What you see is not really there; it is what your brain believes is there … Seeing is an active construction process. Your brain makes the best interpretation it can according to its previous experience and the limited and ambiguous information provided by your eye."[143]

This is a sobering thought and an affirmation of the importance of knowing ourselves—and our stories. In addition, the fact that our brains perceive only subjective stories should warn us to understand other people's stories before we make judgments based on what we think is objective reality.

The human tendency is to perceive reality as if it were always comfortable, compatible and without pain of any kind. In fact, we have a strong tendency to secure the creature comforts that will allow us to experience reality without having to endure grief, disappointments and sorrow. In line with the limitations built into the realities of life, one of the purposes of the practices of *Interiority* is to comprehend the nature of reality as inclusive of *pain, disappointment* and *sorrow* and to live deeply within that framework. One possible consequence is that we will not be thrown into debilitating cycles of frustration when difficulties and disappointments come around, instead we can acknowledge them with patience and forbearance.

Suffering and patience do not cancel each other out but can be in harmony at the center of the maturing self. If we can arrive at such a realization of reality through the practices of Interiority, then we can extend our acknowledgment of reality to others. In this, we practice empathy and compassion for the human condition. If we are able to accept this mixed nature of reality while we are at work, we can maintain equanimity in working through troublesome issues. We can then influence others in working through their troubling issues. In the same way, we can gradually influence how the organization expresses compassion for the issues that bother stakeholders using the organization's products and services. This kind of compassion can be the basis of excellent customer service and is likely to lead to healthy business expansion and help promote a model society where citizens opt for compassion over cupidity.

Five Approaches to Practicing Interiority

Here are five dimensions through which human growth might be approached. Each dimension is further divided by various practices.

- Dimension 1:   Personal Story
- Dimension 2:   The Body/Physical
- Dimension 3:   Psyche/Psychological
- Dimension 4:   Others/Relational
- Dimension 5:   Spirit/Spiritual

The choice of which dimension to pursue at a particular time depends on the needs of the individual. Just as we cannot take every road in life, in our quest for Interiority, we cannot follow every approach to human growth at the same time.

Dimension 1: Personal Story

Awareness of our evolving personal stories allows us to become ourselves through the experiences of work. When we are fully living and growing while at work, then more of our resources become available for completing work.

Step One – Experiences: The first practice is a four-step sequence of elements. The first element is to recall the formative experiences of one's life. This is done by searching through key or pivotal life events, becoming aware of the formative experiences of one's unfolding life story. Formative experiences are those that made such a strong impression on one's inner world that they remain a vivid memory. Formative experiences do not have to be comparatively large or dramatic, as even seemingly insignificant images or behaviors may have had a powerful influence on us. To be formative experiences, they would have remained somewhere in our consciousness and influenced our lives. As we recall those experiences, we may remember how we originally felt, even though the experience may have occurred a lifetime ago.

Steps in Cultivating Interiority

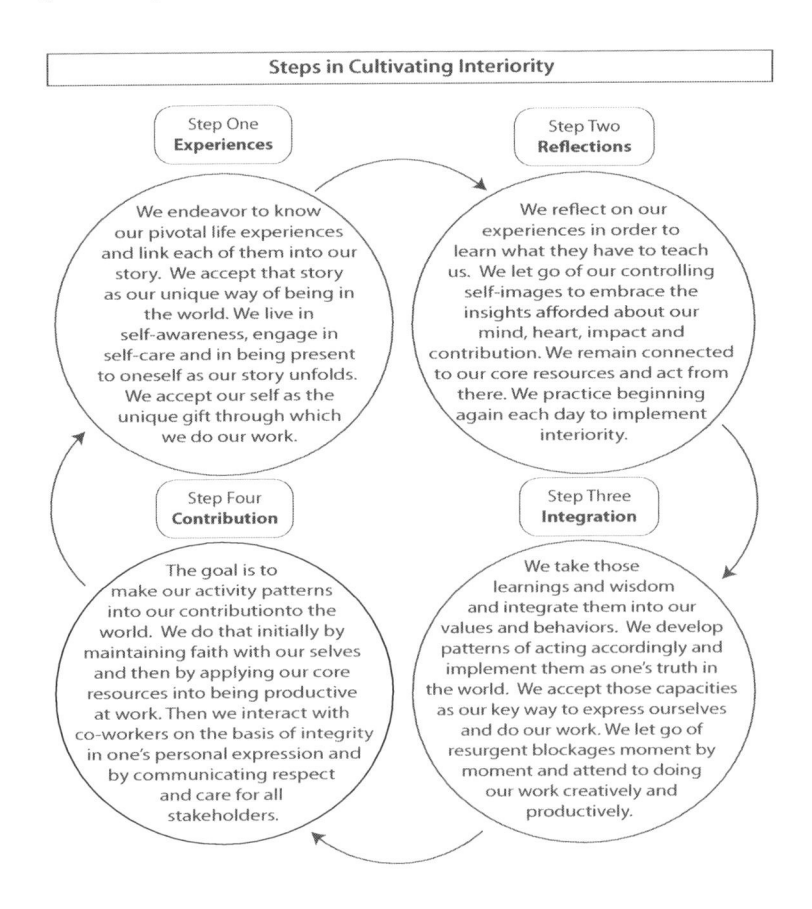

Step One – Experiences: We endeavor to know our pivotal life experiences and link each of them into our story. We accept that story as our unique way of being in the world. We live in self-awareness, engage in self-care and in being present to oneself as our story unfolds. We accept our self as the unique gift through which we do our work.

Step Two – Reflections: We reflect on our experiences in order to learn what they have to teach us. We let go of our controlling self-images to embrace the insights afforded about our mind, heart, impact and contribution. We remain connected to our core resources and act from there. We practice beginning again each day to implement interiority.

Step Three – Integration: We take those learnings and wisdom and integrate them into our values and behaviors. We develop patterns of acting accordingly and implement them as one's truth in the world. We accept those capacities as our key way to express ourselves and do our work. We let go of resurgent blockages moment by moment and attend to doing our work creatively and productively.

Step Four – Contribution: The goal is to make our activity patterns into our contribution to the world. We do that initially by maintaining faith with our selves and then by applying our core resources into being productive at work. Then we interact with co-workers on the basis of integrity in one's personal expression and by communicating respect and care for all stakeholders.

FIGURE 36: **STEPS IN CULTIVATING INTERIORITY**

In remembering those experiences, a word of caution: depending on the trauma level of the original experience, we may need professional help to work through it in healthy ways. When we pay attention to our inner lives, dark and repressed energies—including feelings which tend to overwhelm us—might also come to the surface.

In addition to formative experiences, we also need to know the links between each of the incidents that shape our unique stories. Each person's linked experiences hold a special value, meaning and purpose that are the basis of one's contribution at work—and in life.

The first condition for becoming aware of my formative experiences, and story, is *presence*. Presence is taking time to be alone, in silence, in stillness, accepting the person that I am and that I am becoming. As an example, consider the formative experiences that I shared in the My Story sections of the preceding chapters of the book. Without this quality of presence, it is difficult to even begin to practice Interiority.

Please take a moment to review the four-step sequence (page 286), in cultivating Interiority.

Step Two – Reflections: Meaning has both a personal and a universal aspect. Reflecting on the significance of our experiences and the linked episodes of our story affords a powerful context for our life and work. It requires that we let go of false images we might be holding on to, perhaps an inflated self-image or an exaggerated fear of certain realities in our life. Letting go of whatever is not true or real in ourself and choosing to embrace what is authentic usually requires profound acts of courage.

Courage is necessary when we have formed habits of seeing ourself in a false light due to compromises we made to live according to the expectations of others. In that case, we may have lived a life not of our own making and may have lost touch with our own reality. Becoming aware of the forces that may have dominated our story allows the opportunity to let them go in favor of our emergent story.

Recovery of our real self is often a painful and difficult undertaking and requires repeated practice to become familiar and comfortable again. The unadorned self, however, is worth the efforts necessary to let go of crutches we may have relied on to prop up a false ego. Eventually, this authentic reality provides the most effective resources for our work and the greatest personal satisfaction. The prize: we come home to ourself and rest comfortably within; trusting the person we are is the greatest gift we could receive and make available to the community of all things.

Reflection centers one's awareness on the core of the self, allowing growth, maturity and the emergence of the whole person we are all meant to be. *The practice of reflection is a journey toward becoming whole.*

Step Three – Integration: Here we integrate the lessons and wisdom that derive from reflections on our experiences and use them to establish a firm and resourceful identity. Our identities are composed of self-concepts, values, attitudes, behavior patterns, life choices and activities. Identity is affirmed when we engage in activities that are true reflections of our aspirations and contributions. Thus, identity becomes the source from which we approach our work, rather than emanating from external sources. There is no intrinsic conflict between fulfilling assignments from our supervisors and motivations confirmed by our own identities.

The point here: rather than simply being compliant with the directions of others, I actively engage with my work on the basis of an undivided, unblocked and resourceful self.

Step Four – Contribution: In making our contributions, we draw together the disparate parts of our experiences while becoming whole; expressing our thoughts, insights and contributions through our work. Our contributions are shaped consciously and unconsciously as we find ourselves true to our patterns, and yet emergent, as we discover new expressions in the challenges we encounter. Good work emerges from integrated workers who know who they are, who engage wholeheartedly with their tasks and make responsible contributions. Being integrated means that we show only a unified self to the world. When we make our contributions through Interiority at work, we are able to *positively influence* others, including team members, stakeholders and the wider community. Ultimately, it is for that contribution that we are at work and alive to all aspects of living.

Finally, there are two aspects to our integrated stories: *personal* and *universal*. Both must be considered together as we are never merely individuals; we are always interconnected with the whole, the living universe. We are always giving to and receiving from *everything*. In that sense, the obligation to practice Interiority is not only for the completion of one's personal story but for the completion of the universal story, the emergence of the story of everything. When we engage in the practices of Interiority, we are not only taking care of ourselves, but at the same time caring for all things. Most of the time, we are not conscious of our interdependence on everything, but as we practice we become profoundly aware of our connections with all things.

Dimension 2: The Body/Physical

> *"Though the world is torn and shaken*
> *Even if your heart is breakin'*
> *It's waiting for you to awaken*
> *And someday you will-*
> *Learn to be still*
> *Learn to be still"*
> —Don Henley and Stanley Lynch - The Eagles[144]

Modern man is living a fast-paced life as if being active is the ideal way to live. Restless and driven, we end up being so active we can barely enjoy moments of solitude. It takes effort to quiet the fidgeting, twitching and involuntary movements that characterize people at work. Bringing a halt to this frenetic activity and entering into inner solitude is something we have to learn by practice. We have to learn to be still, silent and solitary so the world turns around us. We need to develop a point of stillness, a still point, within.

It is only when we stop and listen that we can enter into an authentic encounter with self.

As we learned in Chapter One, the habitual western orientation in life and work is toward the rational/conceptual/behavioral. Because this orientation is so pervasive, we have to learn how to slow the action of thinking so we are aware of the totality of being alive in this moment.

Rather than the rational/conceptual, we need practices that feature the physiological approach to Interiority. The first practice that involves the body focuses on posture. The reason for treating posture is not so we can exhibit good manners or breeding in our physical stances. Rather, it is to express our attitude toward the inner worlds of our physical beings and to demonstrate respect for everything through positive relationships with all things physical.

Posture: Even though we are seldom aware of it, the body is the most immediate way we express ourselves. We are a composite of body, mind, emotion and spirit but we often live in only one or two of these elements. Becoming whole means we are being healed from rifts between the different dimensions within, and are living and working through all of them together.

Correct posture depends on the proper location of the center of gravity within our body. In the Japanese tradition, this is called *hara* or belly. Hara is the area just below the navel and one-third into the body. According to certain cultural traditions, some people tend to shift their centers of gravity upwards into the chest or even into the head and thus find themselves out of gravitational alignment. When we use our thinking faculty to control every specific action, the rhythm of our movements tend to become stilted and can even cause symptoms of vertigo.

In our treatment of posture, rather than using our heads to control movements, let us try to connect with hara and move from our centers of gravity. A simple practice for achieving right posture is described by Karlfried Graf Durckheim in his book entitled, *Hara, The Vital Center of Man*. He writes: "Right posture can be acquired only if one does three things: drop the shoulders, release the lower belly and put some degree of strength into it. For this it is sufficient to say, 'I am, I feel myself down here, a little below the navel.'"[145]

An added benefit of the hara posture is the reduction of the primacy of the ego and a shifting of awareness to a much deeper level that centers on the self within. This shift of one's center of gravity is not simple to achieve because most people are in the habit of thinking the head is the center of action. By locating our centers in hara, we can restore familiarity with our physical selves.

If you are centered and upright within, then you will become centered and upright in all of your external activities. If you continue to practice being centered within and without through the posture of your body, then every activity at work and in life becomes another opportunity to *deepen awareness* and the *expression of being whole*.

In short, the goal is to bring consciousness of your whole self to your work and—your life—beginning with the body.

When your activities proceed from your true center, you become a testimony to authentic personal presence. The way you inhabit your body is an indicator of the way you approach all of life—especially work. If you are aware of your physical needs and take care of them, you are attending to your body so you can maintain it in healthy ways. Unfortunately, many people abuse their bodies by using toxic substances, eating poorly, failing to rest and not exercising adequately.

The following are some archetypal physical postures that express attitudes toward the world—and other people:

- Standing or sitting upright and facing squarely toward the other shows we are *paying attention*.
- Bowing one's head forward or inclining the upper half of the body forward in the direction of the other demonstrates *respect*.
- We show respect when we begin and end an activity by bowing in reverence for all *beginnings and endings* (and in recognition that we are *one with everything*).

- Raising one's arms with hands turned upward and holding them outstretched in front of oneself demonstrates that we are *offering something* to the other.
- Walking straight forward with upright carriage shows a *positive attitude* and *optimistic behaviors*.

As you practice adopting a posture expressive of your true self, try to get a sense of your body and of its intimate connection to the earth and all things. A suggested practice: in the early morning stand with your face lifted to the rising sun and allow your body to be bathed in light and warmth as you breathe in fresh air.

At work, whether sitting, standing or walking, you should always be aware of the many immediate opportunities for centering. For example, in walking to the printer, if your only awareness is to collect copies, then the opportunity for practice is lost. However, if each step becomes a practice of presence to one's self, then you are growing through seemingly unimportant activities. *Every activity at work holds potential for growth toward wholeness.* Even activities that may seem boring and repetitive can be transformed by the inner experience of Interiority to become steps in one's journey to self.

Proper posture allows us to be centered within the body. When we are fully occupying our bodies in organized ways, then we are organized for work. When we adopt proper posture in our work situations, we are manifesting the energies of life at work within us. Our bodies are storehouses of energy that optimally should be available for our work. Adopting good posture allows our energies to flow smoothly in the direction of completing our tasks.

Fortunately, there are many methods for achieving relaxation using our mind—such as the following:

When you feel tension and stress, you can concentrate on any of the muscle groups in your face. Begin with the forehead, and after exerting some strength in those muscles by tightening them, proceed to relax them. This tension-and-release pattern can be followed by concentrating your mind on the muscles of the cheeks, lips, chin, neck, shoulders, etc., until you have achieved a state of relaxed posture and smooth energy flow around your head. A similar state of relaxation can be achieved by clenching your fists, forearms and arms and holding that position for five seconds before releasing them. Similarly, you can achieve relaxation by standing and gently shaking out hands and arms and swinging them in moderate semi-circles around the body.

A good reference for these kinds of exercises and many others is the book, *The Way of Energy* by Master Lam Kam Chuen.[146] The point of good posture is for our bodies to be fully alive in each moment and to symbolize the truth of ourselves at work. A further purpose of proper posture is to realize the unity of the body and the mind. *Living in each moment is to make one's self real.*

As a sidebar, many of us feel disconnected from our bodies because we think we have some physical aspect that is inadequate or inferior. Because of this disconnect, we are in need of reconciliation with our physical selves as the precious physical partners in everything we are.

To practice reconciliation, look at your hands and begin to address them inwardly. Appreciate the way they are shaped and how well they have served you in your work: expertly, strongly and expressively. Express remorse that you may have taken them for granted and perhaps used them roughly. You can reconcile yourself with your hands so you are appreciative of them in doing your work. You might consider reconciling other parts of your body, even those that might have caused you embarrassment in the past—such as the shape of your face, your nose, or some part of your skin that may be discolored.

The practice here is to spend some time with a particular part of your body, express appreciation for its service and thus begin a healing reconciliation; in the process, becoming upright and centered within.

Breathing (practice): The second body practice is breathing. Many of us have learned poor breathing habits through the fear of being out of control. This results in holding onto the breath and not letting it out in a natural sequence. The first action in the practice of breathing: notice how you are breathing and whether your breath is flowing freely. For this, you might pay attention to your abdomen, chest, throat and shoulders. Try to notice if there is any constriction or habit of controlling your breath by muscular tension. If there is, then allow the breath to come and go as if it is in alignment with everything else—giving and receiving—in its environment. In breathing this way, you allow your breath to come in and out in a natural way. By breathing in without constriction, you are simultaneously accepting the life you are living in this moment. By allowing your breath to go out, you are letting go of the previous moment and embracing life in the present.

Similar to the practice of hara to achieve correct posture, the purpose of paying attention to our breathing is to dissociate from the rational mind and concentrate only on breathing. This allows for the rise of *intuitive consciousness*, the *integration* of all of our capacities and the *unimpeded flow of energies* for work.

One popular breathing practice is found in the Chinese *Tan Tien*. Similar to hara, the *Tan Tien* indicates a location one-third of the way inside the body and about three centimeters below the navel. What follows is a description by Master Lam Kam Chuen:

Most people breathe by raising and opening the chest cavity. Our goal is different, however. We want to return to the powerful, deep breathing that we were born with... Natural breathing is centered on the Tan Tien inside the abdomen. Breathing from the Tan Tien refocuses your energy in the original center of the body.[147]

He continues:

Stand with your feet apart at shoulder-width, toes pointing forward. Fold your hands over your abdomen, putting your right thumb over your navel and resting your left hand on top of your right hand. Keep your mouth gently closed. Press in slightly as you breathe out. Quietly and slowly breathe out through your nose. As you exhale, draw your belly in so you feel you are squeezing the air out of your torso from the bottom up. Breathe out smoothly and soundlessly, until you feel you have emptied your lungs. When you are ready to breathe in, inhale through your nose and allow your belly to expand outward as if the incoming air is filling your abdomen. All this to happen naturally, don't force your belly out. Just let the air filter in smoothly and steadily without tension.[148]

The emphasis here is on the natural process of breathing from the deepest place in your physical self rather than the controlled holding and letting go of the breath.

Counting the Breath (practice): In the following breathing practice, I quote from the book by Kalichi entitled *Dance, Words and Soul*:

Pay attention to the breath going out from your nostrils and breath coming in. In this, we listen to the inner sound of breathing, not just the sounds of air coming in and going out through our nose.... Traditionally, 'counting the breath' is the first practice within Zen meditation training. The aim is to follow the breath while counting; nothing more. While breathing out, you say internally, 'one.' The beginning of the exhale begins the sound of the number. With the end of the exhalation, the inner sounding of the number ends. With inhalation, just allow the breath to come in. On the exhalation, count two and continue to the end of the exhalation. Continue this counting to the count of five. When you get there, just begin again at one. If you drift and lose count, start again at one. Let the breath dictate the pace. The sound of the counting follows the pacing of the breath. Notice the rhythm of sound and silence. Upon exhalation, hear the sound of your internal counting. With inhalation, you just let the breath come in. When you are able to focus on one number leading into the next without losing count, then try following the breath without counting. The practice of listening to the sound of breathing is the first of all mantras.[149]

We now move on to the practice of sitting.

Sitting (practice): We spend more time sitting than in any other posture, whether at work or elsewhere. The practice of sitting therefore requires our attention so we are always nurtured, healed and energized as we sit. The practice of sitting quietly and in stillness is a way of being fully alive and present to oneself from the center of awareness, letting go of distracting thoughts, emotions, images and mental preoccupations, allowing our energies to flow freely.

Our first consideration: the variety of postures of sitting. For the following postures, we take our cues from classical Zazen postures, as illustrated and explained by Kosho Uchiyama in his book *Opening the Hand of Thought*.[150]

Regardless of the sitting posture you use, the focus is always on being wide awake to the reality of the moment and the truth of ourselves. The objective of sitting in one of these postures is not to get comfortable, waste time or solve problems, but to become aware of the self in the moment. Through practice, this awareness of the core of self becomes an anchor that keeps us stable and allows us to work using energies flowing from deep within.

*The **Full Lotus Posture**. Two cushions are placed on the floor. One is a large flat cushion that is called a zabuton. On top of that and toward the back side is placed a smaller round, firm cushion, called the zafu to support the spine. Each foot is resting on the opposite thigh. The knees should be resting on the zabuton. In this way, the body is supported in three areas. Both knees are on the zabuton and the buttocks are on the zafu.*

FIGURE 37: **FULL LOTUS POSITION**

*The **Half Lotus Posture**. Two cushions are placed in the same way on the floor. In this illustration, the right foot is placed on the left thigh. The left foot is resting on the cushion. The knees are resting on the zabuton.*

FIGURE 38: **HALF LOTUS POSITION**

The **Burmese Posture**. This is similar to the two postures above but the knees and feet are resting on the zabuton.

FIGURE 39: **BURMESE POSTURE**

The **Kneeling Posture**. In this posture, the buttocks are resting on the zafu as shown.

FIGURE 40: **KNEELING POSTURE**

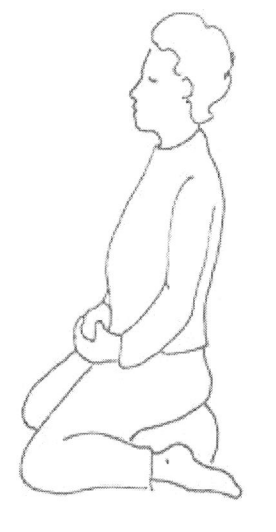

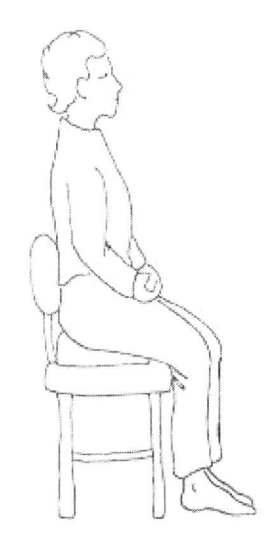

The **Chair Posture**. In this posture, the objective is to have the knees lower than the hips and the feet solidly on the floor.

FIGURE 41: **CHAIR POSTURE**

*The position of the **hands** while sitting in any of the positions is also key. This is called the Cosmic Mudra. The hands are resting in the fold of the torso and thighs. The right palm is facing upward while resting in the palm of the left hand and the thumbs are touching slightly. The hands thus form an oval that is reminiscent of the shape of the cosmos.*

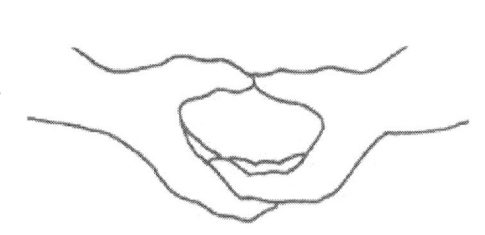

FIGURE 42: **COSMIC MUDRA**

Centering (practice): Now that we have considered posture, breathing, muscular relaxation and sitting, it is time to put them together into one coordinated Interiority practice I call centering. Centering is all about locating one's awareness within his/her core. Centering is a practical meditative activity that can be done whenever the need arises. (Many are familiar with this activity in the form of meditation.) Workers find centering useful because they can arrive at a place of simplicity, yet summon an energy-filled intensity in the complexity of the workplace. The centering practice is a way to be present to self, acting from a place within and having more of who we are available for our work.

To begin the practice of centering, we must again cultivate silence, stillness and solitude. The first step is to spend a couple of minutes each day in silence and stillness, then gradually extend the duration as we become more accustomed to the practice. Silence may initially be difficult, but if the time of silence is spent on listening within, a foundation will grow. The end result is that we can live and work continuously from an inner spiritual center of gravity. A centered self is an enormous benefit amid the constant demands and distractions of the workplace.

When I lose patience, gossip, idle, back-bite and slander, or become depressed, I must return to my center, remain anchored within and allow my energies to flow toward productive activities.

As I am sure you are well aware, an inordinate amount of inane chatter takes place in the world around us—and in our minds. Because we are unaccustomed to silence in both the exterior and interior worlds, we may need to mentally let go of the noise just to gain a modicum of quiet. The chatter of the world outside is insignificant in comparison to the amount of chatter that occurs within our minds. In this sense, real silence is the absence of noise within ourselves.

When we fail to arrive at times of silence and solitude, we miss the magic of what can be heard only when we are quiet, still and solitary. Stillness is the absence of physical activity; no bouncing around in our inner beings, instead concentrating on one point at the core. Stillness is a prerequisite for real engagement with our work and for the experience of inner work to take place. It is only in the silent and still engagement with one's work that high quality results can happen. Here, I am reminded of the Yeats poem about Michelangelo working on the creation scene in the Sistine Chapel.

There on that scaffolding reclines
Michael Angelo.
With no more sound than the mice make
His hand moves to and fro.
Like a long-legged fly upon the stream
His mind moves upon silence.

—Yeats[151]

For your reference, I am including a framework of a Centering Practice on the next page. Please use this framework, at least at the beginning of your practice of silence and stillness.

It takes concentrated energy to quiet the mind, center on a point of stillness within and remain in expectation and waiting. What might we be waiting for? One purpose of the silence and stillness is to allow for listening to the inspiration and messages coming from our inner worlds. The most profound listening occurs when we are attentive to the *resonance of our own existence* among all other living things.

Another purpose for the stillness is to allow the image of what is emerging in us to actually take shape. In a moment of silent thought, a sudden realization of what makes a product or service more effective may dawn on us. How often is it that the issues with which we wrestle at work can seem impossible to resolve with our ordinary, fragmented minds? It is not unusual however, for those same issues to become resolved when we allow the energies of our inner selves to work in the silence and stillness.

The issues also seem more open to resolution when we are in the presence of a good man (or woman).

> **A Centering Practice**
> **For Individuals and Groups**
> The practice below can be done by oneself or with a group of others. I recommend that you do both. You should have your own time and place to do the Centering Practice, by yourself.
> **Groups** You should also have a time and place to do the Centering Practice with a group of others.

Centering Practice

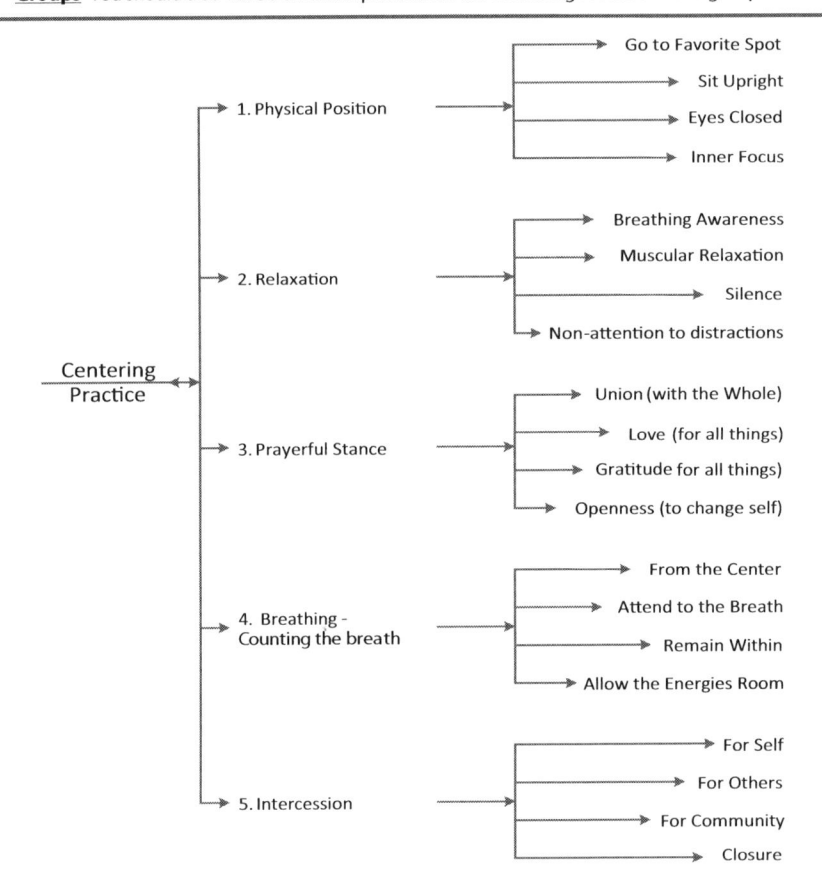

1. Physical Position
   - Go to Favorite Spot
   - Sit Upright
   - Eyes Closed
   - Inner Focus

2. Relaxation
   - Breathing Awareness
   - Muscular Relaxation
   - Silence
   - Non-attention to distractions

3. Prayerful Stance
   - Union (with the Whole)
   - Love (for all things)
   - Gratitude for all things)
   - Openness (to change self)

4. Breathing - Counting the breath
   - From the Center
   - Attend to the Breath
   - Remain Within
   - Allow the Energies Room

5. Intercession
   - For Self
   - For Others
   - For Community
   - Closure

FIGURE 43: **FIVE-STEP CENTERING PRACTICE**

My Story – A Good Man

They say a good man (woman) is hard to find, but when you do find one, you recognize him/her immediately. We've all met them before. I met one during a workshop I was conducting. I will call him George. His persuasive power came not from his looks, his clothing, his walk or his choice of seating in the room. It was his voice that first made me perk up my ears. It was well-modulated, steady, assured and had a ring to it that reverberated deeply within.

The scenario wherein George spoke emerged when we were well into the afternoon of the first day of the workshop. After the feedback session, the behavior of management was at issue. Of particular concern was the behavior of a manager named Catherine. Accusations of poor decision-making, budget mismanagement, collusion with her supporters in apportioning resources and manipulation of information were lobbed like missiles in her direction. Catherine sidestepped the barbs, reversed the arguments, rebutted the key points or merely shrugged them off. The representations made by various workers were going nowhere. Both sides seemed to be heading for worst-case thinking; conflicts that hardened positions, name-calling and aggravated moods and relationships. It appeared to me that the grievances and complaints of the disaffected workers were either too general or unfocused, and their recommendations too unclear to have any effect on Catherine. She appeared untouchable and intent on staying that way. Hers was a splendid isolation: impervious and impregnable.

During a particular impasse, when people leaned grumpily back in their chairs, George spoke. What he had to say became a turning point in the discussion. He faced Catherine squarely and spoke about his experience. His words were brief, to the point and irrefutable. They reflected his experience. He described his work and how Catherine's recent pronouncements had caused considerable difficulties for him. He gave specific times and dates, projects and snafus. He connected his difficult experiences with the directives Catherine had issued. He described the negative impact on workplace projects, clients, co-workers and other stakeholders. Then he asked if Catherine would specifically address his experiences and the negative outcomes to the organization. Catherine began by constructing her argument with a Miss Piggy-like Moi??? tone of mock horror. She claimed she was not to blame and argued her position from tradition, training, company regulations, expert opinions and conditions in the workplace.

George firmly pressed on. He noted that Catherine's response was inadequate, only presented a defense and added no benefit for resolving the issues. By providing parallel instances of poorly-considered worker needs, he made the case that she had neglected to do her homework before making her decisions. George pointed to specific instances when he had informed Catherine of the potentially dubious outcomes of her decisions. He cited Catherine's easily recognized dismissive behaviors in ignoring him. He also poked fun at his own easily recognized reactions. Then he outlined some simple ways the workers' difficulties might have been avoided. After this exchange, Catherine recognized how her oversight had caused the problems. However, Catherine's arguments now took a different tack.

She referred to meetings in which she took up George's suggestions with her management committee. Her committee of supervisors, who were seated in a protective circle around Catherine, looked decidedly uncomfortable at such a reference. Suddenly everyone knew the plain truth had not been told. Sensing the discomfort of her committee, Catherine quickly brought up the pressure of her boss' decision and tried to support her argument from that direction. She finally argued about the inability of workers to follow her precise directions. George said nothing. In the face of the glaring deficiencies in her positions, Catherine was now the decidedly uncomfortable one.

George then switched tactics and inquired how Catherine might redo her decisions based on the new information that had been presented. Catherine took the cue to review her decisions. George listened. She gradually came around to see the possibilities in the positions George had outlined. George acknowledged Catherine's strengths and how they had produced some excellent outcomes. Now, it seemed George was taking Catherine's side and supporting her strengths.

Finally, George summarized the ways in which the workers' needs could best be met and the preferred outcomes for all assured. He pointed out how management might easily make sure of those outcomes, with less expenditure of resources. George stopped as suddenly as he had begun. The group was quiet. They knew they had witnessed a potential confrontation that because of skillful positioning, accurate statements of facts and acknowledgment of the contributions of the management had become a situation in which both sides had been enabled to do their jobs more effectively.

There's always a consequence. The group and I knew George would suffer for taking on the issues and directly facing Catherine. George had done a good deed. But we all knew the adage, "No good deed goes unpunished." We also knew that those who do good deeds had better be prepared for punishment or else not try.

George's demeanor registered that he knew the score even as he stepped into the ring with Catherine. He would pay the price, suffer the consequences and go about his business.

That was the kind of man he was, a good man.

My Story – Reflections

Even though George had deftly led Catherine along through the dialogue, it was not the content that was the most impressive. It was George's attitude that drew the admiration of everyone present. There was no grandstanding, no better-than-thou innuendos, hidden personal agendas, condescension or intent to injure.

It was an Atticus Finch moment similar to when he walked decisively from the courtroom. The case had been tried, the prisoner's honor restored even though found guilty and later killed. Atticus had done his duty and urged others to do theirs. The workers knew a good man had done good work. The medium was the message. Dignity and respect had won the day. So much was evident from how the group leaned in toward George, as if to participate in his aura or relax in the non-judgmental range of his self-presentation. When he spoke his truth, it was taken as speaking truth to power. No one thought it was anything other than the truth.

My Story – Applications

There is no more lasting power than a man or woman who does their work in dignity and respect. How memorable the person who rises above confining circumstances to achieve a good that is difficult to attain. How credible when one is able to lose with equanimity. How impressive the person who knows the way and pursues it with restraint and composure. Rather than joining in the confrontation, George's assumption was that we could solve the issue. Easy, if you know how. Easy, but not simple. Easy only if you *get involved, use your resources* for the purposes of the group, *take no credit* for the work done and *exact no revenge*. Virtue is its own reward. Exact no "pound of flesh" from anyone, even the crassly guilty perpetrators. Deed done, no more need be said.

Your Story

What about you? Have you ever suffered because of doing the right thing? Has justice ever not been on your side? Have you ever had to endure the taunts, bitter comments, or irascible asides when your intentions were right and your deeds impeccable? You know you have. How did you continue to do your work in spite of such treatment? Were you tempted to even the score? Did you try to repay the insults by delivering the same or better, in kind? Or did you learn that petty tactics of revenge turn on you, in the end?

Perhaps you learned to pay the price of doing the right thing just because it is right.

Group Centering (practice): Work is done either individually or with the cooperation of others. Centering is able to be practiced either by oneself or with the cooperation of others. I belong to two meditation groups and practice centering on my own. I can testify to the power of the group-centering practice as a source of encouragement and support. That is why I recommend both individual and group centering practices.

Members begin the sitting practice by bowing toward the center of the circle. Then each member resumes sitting in the same manner as when alone. The basic requirement for participation is to trust in the good will of the members that the practice will be healthy and beneficial and that there is a certain commitment to the process. In the practice of centering by sitting together in a circle, participants acknowledge the power of the group. The group centering practice is based on the assumption that trust is developed through sitting together and means the individuals are able to be alone together. This practice is a reflection of the larger reality that all of us are ultimately separate human beings but at the same time interdependent. The practice is ended by bowing toward the center of the circle.

Trust in the group-centering process is built by the members who engage in it together. The understanding is that they are holding open a space within which each can learn, grow and receive support from the group. In centering together, creative energy is shared by the people who are being present to each other in the most elementary way. Because of the deeper levels of awareness that can be reached through centering, it is possible to establish more accepting and respectful attitudes toward those with whom we may be having difficulties.

FIGURE 44: **GROUP CENTERING**

Standing (practice): Besides the practices of posture, breathing, sitting and centering, it is important to practice standing in a centered way so, regardless of the tasks we are doing or the activities involved, we are being nourished and energized.

When standing, it is preferable not to be rigidly at attention. The posture should be upright and the knees unlocked and slightly bent. Your weight should rest easily on your two feet. The top of your head should feel somewhat as if it is suspended from above, as if held up by a golden cord. This helps with the alignment of the four centers of awareness, as represented by the four black dots in the illustration.[152] The most effective posture in standing is to have your attention centered, as explained previously, in the Tan Tien, just below our navel.

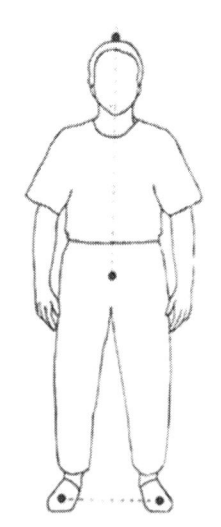

FIGURE 45: **STANDING IN CENTERED POSTURE**

Walking (practice): Besides the practices of sitting and standing, walking is a most beneficial physical practice. Just like standing, walking is best conducted while attention is centered within us, we are in balance and our energy is flowing with the fluid movement of our legs and bodies. All my life I have tended to be a fast walker, intent on getting to the goal, doing what was required and getting back. I was so intent on the goal I did not take note of the process or the environment and almost never of what was happening within me. However, recently, walking slowly has become part of the centering practice I perform.

The goal of slow walking such as this, usually in a fairly wide circle, is not to get somewhere but to become more present to oneself during the walking. There is an abundance of things to notice. One is the movement of the body in alignment with the breath, in proper posture and centered in self-awareness in the present moment.

FIGURE 46: **WALKING WHILE IN CENTERED POSTURE**

The walking practice is begun with hands folded left over right in front of the breast, putting the *left foot forward*, which begins the *exhalation* of the breath. Putting the *right foot forward* begins the *inhalation* and thus the pace is slow and aligned with other physical movements. The concentration is on the breath, the physical movements of the feet, ankles, legs, knees, thighs, torso, spine and head. The purpose of the practice of slow walking is to be aware of our true self and gradually this awareness is transferred to all of our activities at work.

Dimension 3: Psyche/Psychological

Therapy/Self-Care *(practice)*: Therapy includes activities related to the restoration of health to some malfunctioning aspect of our lives. Therapy related to the psyche/soul means "attending to" (from the Greek *therapeuein*, meaning attend) those needs of the soul which are made manifest in our daily lives, perhaps through discomfort or pain. In our time, hundreds of therapies have become available for every kind of illness or dysfunction. Under the heading of psychotherapy in Wikipedia, there are 163 listings and more are emerging all the time.

Our approach might be listed under self-help, but only because the initiative is adopted and guided by the individual. I wish to distinguish it from the burgeoning genre of self-help media that purport to provide immediate solutions to all kinds of human dysfunction. In contrast, our meaning for therapy is a *daily discipline* for the *maintenance of inner personal health* and the *free flow of energies for work*.

Some caveats regarding the use of the term *therapy* as a practice seem appropriate here. The first caveat: our treatment of therapy is necessarily *general*. Only in the widest possible sense is this practice something that can be done without the aid of a psychotherapist or other professional with specific training relating to the psyche.

The second caveat: *we do not have as much control of our inner workings as we might like to think*. The unconscious is like an iceberg, almost all of which is below the surface of our awareness and is in control of the majority of what we do and think we are about. The most effective therapeutic discipline one can choose is a tempering of the needs of the ego and an alignment with the dominant operations of the psyche or soul—giving one's best to fulfill the calling in that direction. When we align with the intent of our soul, we experience comfort, wholeness and energy for our work. When we ignore the needs of our soul in our individual or communitarian lives, we experience dislocation, discomfort and conflict with ourselves.

In short: self-help therapy means staying in touch with the *intuitions* arising within regarding the *core reality* of one's psyche/soul; being aware of its *emerging direction and needs*; and *directing efforts toward fulfillment* of the same.

Psyche is a Greek term for soul and refers to the essence of what makes us human. The function of the soul is to maintain alignment on what is meaningful. Consequently, when you align with the intent of your soul, you experience comfort within, wholeness, harmony and energy for your work. When you ignore or disrespect the needs of your soul, either as individuals or as communities, you experience discomfort, alienation and conflict within.

So, there you have it. When we—either as a society, families of origin, cultures or as individuals—*violate the needs of our souls, we experience emptiness* and symptoms associated with *lack of meaning*.

There are no completely common symptoms but only those unique to your own story. Some symptoms may relate to boredom or lack of energy toward those things that previously provided satisfaction. Conversely, if you are responding to the real needs of your soul, then your energies rise to the task at hand. Such engagement constitutes therapy in its widest interpretation.

Many readers may be surprised at the inclusion of therapy in the context of everyday work, Interiority and productivity. Keep in mind, healing, satisfaction, meaning and productivity go along with finding the agenda of your soul and engaging in its related tasks, while doing your work. On the other hand, whatever we deny in the instincts of our souls will tend to produce compulsions, addictions, projections or other discords.

What then are the practices of therapy related to the psyche/soul?

- *The first therapeutic practice is a constant choice to listen to the promptings of the soul and allow the emergence of the real self.* Anything and everything can be a bearer of messages from our soul into our awareness, even the daily newspaper or the fleeting glimpses of passing freeway traffic. When a newspaper column catches our eye and pulls us into its story, we are receiving a message of meaning from the soul. Not all such messages are of the same depth of importance so we must still work at deciphering the meaning and applying it to ourself, personally.

We can do no better than to take note of the recurring intuitions of our souls and choose to serve the becoming of self. It is easy to say "choose to serve," but in reality our choices become viable only after we begin efforts to let go of blockages from past conditioning between the inclinations of the ego and the aspirations of the soul.

The ego thinks it is in control and does not give way easily to any other source of inspiration, especially when that source is within us. Whether we are aware or not, the soul is in charge of the becoming of one's self and will lead us to make efforts in that direction. Because becoming our real self is difficult, we usually do not collaborate easily with the guidance of our souls. The choice to collaborate often means letting go of the dictates of institutional messages and opting for living our own life script. As we surrender the scripts coming from outside ourselves, we will generally be prompted to generate our own scripts. For this, we may have to let go of the behavior patterns that mainly characterized our personas up to this point and opt for something more authentic. If we continue to let go of the inhibitions to self-awareness, we will begin to intuit some measure of satisfaction and comfort within as well as greater flows of energy. *Choose to serve the soul.*

- *The second therapeutic practice is to realize that the self you are called to become is much greater than what you could have imagined under the control of your ego.* Recall the previous quote from Jung, "We all walk in shoes too small." Because our lives are necessarily in service to making a comfortable living for ourselves and our families, most of us diminish the roles we are called to play. The typical mistake here is to think we are called to *do* something "great" such as developing a breakthrough technology that brings extraordinary benefits to mankind. However, the more persistently echoing call is toward *being* the self it is within one's destiny to become.

When we respond to calls to authentic selfhood, energies are released to sustain us in that quest. The quality of our being derives from something larger than might have been imagined by our ego. For example, when we use our imagination to see the suffering of those who have hurt us and feel empathy for those hurts, we are rising above petty revenge. Revenge only mollifies bruised egos and keeps us arrested in negative and reactive cycles. When we practice letting go of our egotistical needs and enter into alignment with the needs of our souls, we are taking the road less traveled.

Again, the practice is to breathe deeply and take note of the inspirations that float into our awareness—perhaps about how we are greater than what we have been trained to be by early programming or choices. The more we engage in this practice, the more likely it is our authentic expression feels more familiar. Consequently, we are led to a magnified way of being in the world with expanded energies for the work of the whole. The challenge is to not deceive ourself that we are already living authentically. Even if we do deceive ourself, our soul will not forget or allow such dissimulation. It is not in the nature of our souls to let go of the core message of our lives. *Serve a greater call.*

FIGURE 47: **ONE STEP AT A TIME**

- *The third therapeutic practice is to continue on the daily journey toward self rather than getting caught in the expectation of the arrival at some goal and then cease your search for wholeness.* The temptation is to think of the arrival so we can rest from the effort of fully lived lives. Our daily life is not static and this too applies—in a deeper way—to our inner life, which is dynamically continuing on its journey toward wholeness. That journey is toward our whole self—what we might call our home, as it becomes more of a psychic residence. Come to think of it, our daily preoccupations are inclined to be caught up in avoiding risk, replaying grudges, revenging injuries real or imagined and remaining anchored in the small world of the wounded ego. In the process of letting go of those wasteful preoccupations, more energy becomes available for the journey. To live a life of contentment with the status quo is likely more comfortable, but less interesting or engaging than a life that invites us onward to wrestle continuously with the mysteries of our existence. *Focus on the journey more than the arrival.*

Be aware of some great goal for which we are alive and at work. However, pay attention to achieving each comparatively little task in this moment, then in the next and so on. Gradually, the whole work for which we are responsible emerges. In a similar fashion, the great work of our becoming whole and the person that we are called to be, is accomplished. In a similar fashion, the all-encompassing work of emerging consciousness in everything is accomplished. *Be aware of the great goal but attend to the little tasks required for its achievement.*

- *The fourth therapeutic practice is to treat authentic sufferings as opportunities to grow.* Authentic suffering, as opposed to neurotic suffering, occurs when our energies are most invested and, therefore, most open to meaning. Neurotic suffering appears meaningless to the sufferer. Life involves painful choices, risks and conflicting desires that must be endured and lived through if we are to experience authentic living. If we choose a road that appears more meaningful than that chosen by the crowd, we open ourselves to criticism, blame and rejection—and thus to suffering. We naturally seek what is comfortable and avoid what is painful. In that quest for comfort, so-called healers and leaders of various kinds would testify that a painless life is possible if we only follow their lead. Nonetheless, the condition of *living fully involves some form of suffering.*

In the face of inevitable pain, we are helped if we think the suffering will lead us to deeper levels of awareness. When we accept that legitimate suffering is part of living, our energies are freed-up to find meaning in the inevitable pain. The emphasis here is on the suffering that enhances one's life rather than diminishes it. The practice is to become so aware of everything in our lives that we gain satisfaction from the glories of the moment and, at the same time, tolerate the difficulties and attendant suffering. *See suffering as a constant opportunity.*

- *The fifth therapeutic practice is to be aware that, in daily life, we are never abandoned by our soul, but enabled by its energies, one way or another.* When we reflect with confidence on the loyalty of our soul to the becoming of self, we can adopt a more risk-taking approach to our life. Our soul never stops working for wholeness. Even though we are resistant to its initiatives, it keeps coming in our direction as if it were from the future of our potential fulfillment. Whether we adopt a more negative and destructive approach to life or a more positive and constructive one, we will always be called to account by the results produced in our awareness by our soul.

When we embark on becoming our authentic selves, we tend to complain that it is too difficult, requires too much discipline and usually runs counter-intuitive to the normal course of our thoughts and actions. Nevertheless, we are already being helped in this achievement by the unabated energy of our souls, of intuitions, dreams, life-stages and inspirational prompts that arise spontaneously. The practice then is to take advantage of those inspirations to redirect our thoughts and actions, collaborate with the energies released and integrate them into our lives at work.

The practice involves paying attention to the soul which does not rest but is helping us to move closer to authentic living. For example, consider our dreams. Dreams are always in service to our health and wholeness. It may not be so simple to understand them, but they somehow prefigure in symbols, locations, context and images—the direction our soul wants us to go. *Note we are already being helped.*

Shadow Work (practice): Shadow work carries great potential for the release of powerful energies for work. Two items bear repeating: First, shadow refers to *repressed or disowned energies* that *seek integration and expression*, especially in the second half of our lives. Second, *not all shadow energies are constructive* and some dark shadow energies can be the cause of evil behaviors and outcomes. One caveat: since there is an extraordinary amount of practices for the integration of shadow energies, the practice that works for some may not work for everyone.

The shadow work that has been effective for me combines dream-work and the four-step process called "Active Imagination" described below. Robert A. Johnson originally presented this method in his book *Inner Work*. In my own case, I bring the dreams uncovered in the shadow-work to sessions with my spiritual director. In that way, I have another qualified person to reflect with me on the content of the dreams, discuss what the message might be and help with how the lessons might be applied in my life. The headings of the four-step approach to Active Imagination are:

- *Invite the unconscious*: Pay attention to the images and the feelings that surface in a dream or sequence of dreams.
- *Dialogue and experience*: Initiate a conversation between the dream ego (*the person who appears as the central actor in the dream*) and the self. The purpose is to clarify the message the dream ego might want us to notice.
- *Add the ethical element of values*: Examine all messages so they might align with our value systems.
- *Make it concrete with some physical ritual*: Decide on some way to implement and ritualize the targeted change.[153]

In conclusion to the above, I add the following advice from a book called: Meeting the Shadow by Connie Zweig and Jeremiah Abrams.[154]

- "Even with great effort to own the shadow involving prolonged internal negotiations, the outcome is uncertain."
- "Mining the dark recesses of the human psyche is endless."
- "In this war between the opposites, there is only one battleground—the human heart.

And somehow, in a compassionate embrace of the dark side of reality, we become bearers of the light. We open up to the other—the strange, the weak, the sinful, the despised—and simply through including it, we transmute it. In so doing, we move ourselves toward wholeness."

As always, please exercise care. Make sure you are comfortable with the methodology before initiating the practice. If you are not comfortable with any practice, then make contact with a professionally qualified person who can guide you in selecting and working with your practice.

Emotions – *(theory and practice)*: There is a good reason why the topic of emotional intelligence has come to the fore in our times. Emotions are keys to self-knowledge and personal growth, and are essential for creativity at work and personal satisfaction. Emotions are at the core of soft skills, such as listening, empathy and managing interpersonal relationships. On the other hand, emotional ups and downs can be the source of severe mood swings that throw us out of balance in managing our lives at work. These vagaries notwithstanding, it is up to each of us to take charge of our unique emotional patterns and expression. Each of us have the responsibility to come to terms with these powerful forces that enliven our moments and our relationships, contribute to maturity or disintegration—and can make for creativity and energetic productivity at work.

For the effective use of emotions, the starting place is within. We begin by *knowing our emotions* and *taking responsibility* for them. Men, more than women, tend to have difficulty in accepting emotions as legitimate parts of their humanity and can find it challenging to express feelings. Some men have repressed their feelings for so long, they have become emotionally detached.

Certain cultures program children to stoically hide their emotions as if it is criminal to have them at all. Fortunately, emotions do not go away and are recognizable when they make their appearance in unguarded situations, such as during competitive games or in moments of shame or embarrassment. Even if we have strongly repressed emotions, it is still possible to regain the legitimacy of feelings and learn how to release those energies for wholeness at work. However, to get in touch with our emotions, we first have to work at feeling them. It is comparatively easy to feel the positive emotions such as happiness, pleasure and sensory gratification. Most can differentiate and name them with little difficulty.

We tend to deny or repress the so-called negative feelings such as fear, anger, sorrow, sadness, shame or impatience. Denial may be okay if those repressed emotions disappeared, but unfortunately all they do is go underground, only to appear again as backaches, headaches, stress, ill-humor, grouchiness, self-loathing and many other self-destructive feeling states, including depression. This is why it is essential to work at emotional integration.

Five Steps to Emotional Integration

1. Become aware of and feel the emotions
2. Examine and name the emotions
3. Accept and allow the emotions
4. Describe one's emotions
5. Learn from and integrate the emotions

- **Become Aware of and Feel the Emotions:** Becoming aware of feelings is not always simple, especially if they are repressed so much they have become lost to us. In that case, we may have difficulty in knowing what we are feeling, much less naming the feelings accurately. Usually, when we have repressed our emotions for a long time, the stress from pent-up and unrecognized feelings becomes overwhelming and compels us to search for and recover some authentic feelings—and expressions. Especially if we have endured spontaneous surges of aversion, jealousy and even hatred of co-workers, we may be stimulated by these difficulties as motivation to get started on journeys of recovery. The first condition for such recovery is to acknowledge that *our emotions are not caused by co-workers*. When we get angry, we are the ones who are feeling those feelings. The behavior of the other(s) may have given occasion for our emotions to surface, but we own those feelings—no matter how reluctant we are to recognize that fact. *Become aware of the emotions.*

We can start by taking note of our positive emotions, beginning with happiness. The first step is to feel it. Think of a loved one and note the feeling in your body as the warm and positive energy surges in a general sense of well-being. Allow the feeling to find its natural expression, by smiling or relaxing muscles and try not to overdo it. Hold on to the feeling as it changes shape and notice the subtle shadings of happiness as you imagine soon meeting your loved one.

To continue feeling emotions, do the same for the more difficult emotions, such as sadness. In imagining parting from your beloved or a friend, you may feel the tug of sadness. Especially at the death of a loved one, you may be overcome by sadness, loneliness and loss. Again, recall a loved one who has passed away some time ago and feel the feelings. Allow them to rise and stay within you. As time passes, notice how they change. Feelings of loneliness may deepen, grief may be overwhelming and find expression in tears and sighs. *Feel the emotions.*

- **Examine and Name the Emotions:** We can learn a lot about ourselves when we examine the *sources* of our feelings, the *patterns* in which they emerge and their *connection* to a complex, such as inferiority, superiority or victimhood. It may be helpful to periodically stop what we are doing and focus on what we are feeling. We might ask ourselves, What am I feeling? Are there associated feelings? Am I in the grip of a charge of complex emotions? Can I associate that complex of feelings with some self-image such as victimhood or inferiority? Examine the feelings, how they change, how intense they are and how some feeling groups give rise to separate feeling patterns.

We can follow the connection between feelings and trace them back to the feeling or thought we noticed originally. When we feel a negative emotion, we might ask ourselves: What experience, thinking pattern or action of mine led to that emotion? Only when we notice some distortions in thought or action that may have caused the emotion, are we in a position to correct the outcome. Until we directly face the problem—such as erroneous logic that is causing the painful emotions—they will likely keep recurring. When we know the source of our feelings and patterns, and if they are part of a familiar reactive pattern triggered by certain stimuli, we are on the road to deepening self-awareness and enhancing the ability to moderate those reactions.

As we examine our emotions, it may be beneficial to consider the potentially erroneous thinking that accounts for them. We should *avoid blaming others,* especially parents, for what we feel. Most people grow up with some emotional baggage, including unhealed sensitivities and wounds. If we persist in blaming our parents for our victimhood, we may continue to embrace resentment in various aspects of our lives, at work and in relationships, for example. The danger: we can become obsessed with maintaining a *rigid stance* or become *depressed* and *drained* of vital energies. It is preferable to take the energy we usually use to blame others and instead achieve a higher purpose with it. By examining our unique pattern of emotional expression we are in an advantageous position to deepen self-acceptance. *Examine the emotions.*

One effective way of examining our emotions is to put names on the emotions we feel. There are hundreds of ways of naming our emotions. Not all of them can accurately be applied to what we are feeling at a certain time. It may sound mechanical, but it can be helpful to find a list of ways for naming emotions, then picking a name that closely represents what we are feeling. If we can't find a name, we might choose a color, such as red for anger, blue for sadness; or a shape: bright, jagged, round. If we can't name the color or shape of the feeling, we might notice our reaction to certain music or art that might draw forth what we are feeling. *Name the emotions.*

- **Accept and Allow the Emotions:** We have to realize that emotions are part of our human apparatus, a necessary, difficult and yet wonderful part of our lives. Being able to feel a wide range and a depth of emotions is a way to taste the variety of experiences that life brings. Emotions help us cope. When we sense danger is near, spontaneous feelings of fear galvanize us into action to keep us safe. At enjoyable occasions, we share the emotions we feel through uplifting participation in celebrations.

Emotions are helpful and acknowledgment of our emotional nature is a most human thing to do. Granted, it is fairly easy to accept an optimistic and positive view of ourselves. A positive self-image can be tremendously helpful, but it must be realistic. We may actually portray a variety of negative emotions in our self-presentations but rationalize that our patterns are positive. We may build up a façade of positivity based on those delusions that easily crumble under pressure. It is then that the real self-expression appears, causing confusion to others and embarrassment to us.

It is helpful to honestly look beneath the surface to note the emotions we deny having and allow them their rightful place within our lives. *Accept the emotions.*

Allowing the emotions we are feeling is a way to know ourselves and grow; a way to tap into the energies we have not been able to release, a way for us to ventilate what has been repressed for too long, a way to communicate and a way to develop trusting relationships. Allowing our emotions adequate description and expression is a loving act toward ourselves and toward our loved ones. *Allow the emotions.*

- **Describe One's Emotions:** In the case of negative emotions, our tendencies are to project the causes on to the perceived offenders. We blame them for the discomfort we feel. We argue with them in the hope of justifying our negative projections. We nurse our injured feelings and sometimes we burn with resentment. When we harbor venomous feelings toward others, we tend not to forget the rancorous situations of perceived mistreatment, playing them repeatedly in our imaginations. When those emotional fires are kept stoked, there is a high possibility that we will express the associated emotions in inappropriate ways.

There are *many taboos* associated with extremes in emotional expression. There are situations where is it inappropriate to express our emotions, such as laughing loudly during a funeral or exploding in anger at the insignificant mistakes of a co-worker. So, how do we find legitimate expression for what we feel in the grip of high levels of exasperation? Here is an example of what to do.

When a person shows up late and does not apologize for the delay, how do you react? Do you lose control, shout in frustration and blame him/her for causing you to waste time? Or do you describe how you feel, the reason why, inquire about the cause of the delay and hear him/her out respectfully? Do you exact some kind of revenge, or do you negotiate how to handle such a delay the next time it happens?

Obviously, the most effective way of dealing with such feelings is to calmly and objectively describe how you feel while maintaining respect for the other person. Such emotional transparency allows unique emotional truth to become known by others and can form the basis of a solid relationship. Being known by someone is one of the greatest gifts in life. Knowing others through their emotional transparency is likewise a great gift. *Practice describing the emotion.*

- **Learn from and Integrate the Emotions:** Depending on what your response is in the above scenario, you might have learned quite a bit about yourself in that encounter, whether that learning was positive or negative. Regardless of your response, it is important to reflect on your learning and decide how you will integrate it into your behavior patterns so they are more balanced. *Learn from your emotions.*

Emotional integration is a coordination of the physical, rational, spiritual and social energies with productive results in the workplace. Coordinating these inner resources takes time to mature into wholeness at work. One caveat: not fully identifying with distress or anger. Even though we may feel taken over by some feeling, we are always more than a singular emotion. Remember, we can distance ourselves from, and rise above even the most absorbing feelings, and make purposeful behavioral decisions.

Our emotional lives are high among the greatest gifts we have for tasting the variety and spice of life. However, our emotions are not all we are. Our emotions need to be integrated: with our values, intellects, physical attributes and limitations; our social contexts, relationships, and souls. Emotions are ways to gain access to the subconscious. In that way, they are constant companions in getting to know more about ourselves and our soulful journeys. Our emotions are too precious to be used only for depression of self or to abuse others. They are to be used mostly to enliven us so we can taste the joys of living and creative satisfaction at work. In that way, they are made ever more precious. Our emotions are the energetic drivers of our imaginations that seek to create, produce and achieve the projects that come our way in the workplace. *Integrate the emotions.*

Now we move on to the integration of the rational with the intuitive aspects of our psyche.

Rational/Intuitive (practice):

"It is the polarity and the integration of these two modes of consciousness, the complementary workings of the intellect and the intuitive, which underlies our highest achievement."

—Robert Ornstein, The Psychology of Consciousness.[155]

Ornstein refers to how the left and right brain work most effectively together. The functions and energies of both sides of the brain are necessary for arrival at wholeness. It bears repeating that the right side of the brain controls the functions of the left hand, and the left side of the brain controls the functions of the right hand. It also bears repeating that both sides of the brain are physically connected, but most of us have developed habits of using the left-brain more than the right, especially if we are right-handed. Of interest here are the practices that lead to integration of the two hemispheres of our brain, the release of energies for such collaboration and an arrival at more profound levels of Interiority.

Left brain	Right brain
conscious thought	subconscious thought
logical analysis	emotional reaction
outer awareness	inner awareness
use of language	use of intuition
methods, rules	creativity
truth	flexibility
forceful	complex

FIGURE 48: **LEFT AND RIGHT-BRAIN COMPARISON**

For our purposes, the deeper integration of the left and right brain cannot be treated only in theoretical terms but must be experienced by some specifically creative work process. In this practice, for deeper integration of the two sides, I offer four stages that are aimed at the invention of an idea; but the reader must supply the details and bring the item to actual fulfillment. The stages in the achievement of integration are:

- **Generating an Idea:** In the first part of this exercise, focus on using your *right-brain* for the generation of some specific idea. Find a quiet space where there are few distractions and spend some time there in stillness and silence, without doing anything. When an image flashes by your inward eye, use a pad and pencil to make note of the *ideas* or *images* that stream forth. At this point, do not evaluate or arrange the notes into any order. Your subconscious mind is not inactive; even when you are awake, it releases random pieces of data that have significance.

In the second part of this exercise, focus on using your *left-brain*. *Review* the notes you made, *evaluate* them and put them in some kind of *order*. This is a simple example of using both sides of the brain. Now, as you arrange the results, concentrate only on the ones relevant to a dominant idea on which you have been working. In this stage, you are arriving at some kind of breakthrough by the creative use of the right and left sides of your brain working together.

- **Allowing Commitment to the Idea:** When you first have a breakthrough idea, it emerges as a vision, a possibility. As it begins to take hold of your energies, then you have a choice to commit to fulfilling the idea. My emphasis here is on allowing choice because the process is more intuitive and imaginative (right-brain), than analytical and linear.

As an exercise in allowing your commitment to become stronger, write words, draw images, make drafts or in some other way frame up the idea. By allowing the idea to take shape in this way, it will gradually occupy significant portions of your conscious and unconscious life. When faced with the choice of committing to fulfilling the idea, it is necessary to invest energy in choosing to make it real or you run the risk of losing the opportunity. At the same time, allow the persistence of the idea or image to surface and take note of the patterns by which it establishes itself in your awareness.

- **Incubation of the Idea:** The third stage involves incubation of the idea over an indeterminate length of time, and perhaps with fluctuating investment of energy. This is when you live with the idea, allowing it to germinate in your mind (and emotions) and physically engineer it into a product or service. This is a time of *collaboration with the idea* as it takes shape. Puzzling gaps may appear in the arrangement as you struggle with various representations emerging from your conscious and unconscious mind, and from the right and left-brain. This is a time for quiet intuition, still listening, cocooning, noticing connections, exploring options and developing relationships connected with the idea or product.

Take time to be quiet and direct your energy toward listening with no particular outcome in mind. Allow the ideas to rise to the surface of your consciousness without analysis or discrimination. Don't worry about whether it is good or bad, useful or frivolous. Try to follow the vagaries of your inner state, as sometimes doubts and indecision punctuate this period. Spend some time learning to tolerate the *ups and downs*—which may be characterized by sensations of darkness, emptiness and boredom. Assist yourself in not giving in or giving up on the pursuit of the idea or image; and discipline yourself to begin again in the struggle to maintain attention on the fermentation of the ideas.

- **Invention of the Idea or Product:** This is the stage in which the idea or product takes shape in reality. Here you have an outline or a mockup/model of the idea. This is a time for planning, which is more of a left-brain function, but even during this period take time to be with the product in terms of its artistic impact, of how it feels, how it appeals to your senses and what it provokes in your imagination. These are right-brain functions and in the iterative process of planning and generating imaginative scenarios in which the product might be used, it takes its final shape. This final stage is the result of the labors of the prior three stages.

The point of going through these four stages is to practice generating an idea, using the left and right-brains working together.

Take the time to write down the idea or put together the product and observe it from the point of view of the user, client or co-worker. Get feedback, comments or questions, and see them as opportunities to make the idea or product stronger, more efficient and clearer. Rewrite the idea or restructure the product in several recursive

> **My Story – Ghost in the Church**
>
> iterations to make it ready for presentation.
>
> *How many times did I hear the story of the ghost in the church at midnight? One ghost story that got better with the telling related how "A man was locked inside the church and woke at midnight to hear a voice calling from the direction of the altar."*
>
> *'Is there anyone here who can serve mass?' the voice calls.*
>
> *The man rubs his eyes and sure enough, it was the ghost of a priest all dressed up in his vestments. He spoke up and volunteered to serve mass for the ghost. At the end of the mass, the man asked the ghost if he was okay now that mass had been celebrated?*
>
> *The ghost answered, 'Aye, I have been coming here every night for 500 years and only now am I free from the obligation to say mass. I promised to say mass for the soul of a person who had died and sadly, I died before I could. Now I can go to my grave in peace.'*

> *While the man was trying to figure out how many nights 500 years entailed, the ghost disappeared. He didn't even leave his name or mention which parish he was from. The man had forgotten to ask him some of the big questions, but he'd had one too many and he couldn't think quickly enough. Anyway, the ghost was gone and the man lived to tell the story. But when he was let out of the church the next morning, his hair had turned as white as the driven snow—surely, a fitting end to the story just so the man could let the people know that the story was true.*
>
> *Those kinds of ghost stories were told and retold in my youth, always with the ending that went, "That's the God's honest truth." Told around the kitchen fire, the stories made sure we scampered up the stairs and flew into bed as fast as our legs could carry us. I liked those kinds of ghosts. They were innocent enough, but carried with them a twinge of excitement. They made up an important fabric of my life and the society around me.*

My Story – Reflections

Ghosts are generally thought of as spirits of the dead who, for some reason, have not found a resting place. Most are supposed to be benevolent, though I would not know for sure. People in many traditional societies were highly aware of the energies of the spirit world. All things were supposed to have a spiritual energy flowing in them. People communed with such energies in order to have a sense of belonging and to make friends with the more benevolent kind. In our secularized world, people have seemingly lost touch with the energies of everything. Since nothing substantial supports their lives, their awareness has shrunk to the objects immediately around them. Preoccupied with materials things, their connections no longer extend to the whole or any part of the natural environment anymore. What a loss!

My Story – Applications

However we might wish to address the energies of this universe, we need to make some personal connection with it. Whether that connection is in the form of a spiritual or physical energy, plant life or the universe, we need the consciousness of belonging to something during our lifetime. The most immediate way to do so is through our capacities for Interiority. For that to happen, nothing quite matches a solitary moment of deep awareness of being a living part of everything.

Your Story

What then is your story of connection to everything? Were there times when the natural world flooded into your awareness? When were you most aware that the energies pulsing through everything also enlivened you? Were you ever conscious of spiritual energies coursing through everything…which might influence your life in some way? Did the spirit of some ancestor—familial, tribal or social—energize the orientation of your life? Did the inspiration of some memory from people long past move you to act—or keep you from acting—at a particular time?

Dimension 4: Others/Relational

We now concentrate on the relational dimension with other co-workers and on developing effective working relationships based on Interiority. The importance of the orientation to others derives from the fact that *reality is relational*. This aspect of our lives at work is a *psychic* reality that binds us together and by which we are influenced and influence each other.

The relational dimension is the *basis of healing*. In the face of personal tragedy, such as major illness or natural catastrophes, we become ever more aware of the churning morass and the sometimes-brokenness of nature on our planet. In spite of the enormous scientific discoveries and development of technological wonders, we humans are often defenseless and defeated. Sometimes, we have the impression that mankind is in charge and will eventually gain control of rampaging forces of nature, but alas it is often us humans who are unwittingly the cause of natural disasters, such as global warming. In every way and in every circumstance, the answer is healing.

The first practice of healing is reflective of the energies released in the practice of sitting. In his book *Silent Music,* William Johnston refers to the Zen master as one who "sits for the whole universe."[156] In this understanding of the practices of Interiority, the healing that takes place through our work is beneficial for us. The healing is also effective for others with whom we work and through the quality of the energies we generate, exerts a beneficent influence on everything. Since the first humans walked the earth, the illnesses from which they sought healing, such as possession by evil spirits or diseases of the digestive tract, improved or did not, depending on their circumstances. For us, the illness from which we seek healing seems to include isolation, loneliness, loss of human values and a general sense of meaninglessness in our lives. This lack of meaning is magnified in our time when we have so many creature comforts and yet we feel empty.

The meaning that can come to us through Interiority at work: I am a healing presence for myself and others and ultimately for the universe.

- **Healing of Self (practice):** We should first distinguish between healing and curing. To cure someone is to relieve the symptoms of their suffering by the use of a medical remedy. The healing about which we are speaking does not happen by some similar application of an external remedy. Inner healing takes place within the individual and belongs in the practices of Interiority. Healing is not so much a one-time event but a process of becoming more fully the self by growing through engagement with complexes, shadow manifestations and symptoms, such as reactive patterns—which leads to the *release of unused energies* for work. This kind of inner healing engagement takes place over a life span.

- **Know Our Limitations:** *The first step for healing self is to know our limitations.* Remember the only real sin in life is *missing the mark* and is largely the consequence of omission. Acknowledgment of our limitations comes through accepting that we have, by various maneuvers, avoided responding to the call to full engagement with *self*. One indicator that healing has begun is when we address a question to ourselves regarding what matters most in our lives. By addressing such a question, we become open to the possibility that we can know. An example may be the limitation brought on by extreme reactivity toward authority figures such as supervisors and managers. *Know our limitations.*

- **Okay to Feel Guilt:** *The second step in healing is to feel sorrow and normal guilt for detrimental actions or omissions against authority figures.* As an example, we might reflect on the damage we may have caused to authority figures by impugning their motives or bad-mouthing them in front of co-workers. Normal guilt is differentiated from guilt that is neurotic or derived from the experiences of some other person whose guilt has somehow been transferred to us. Feeling sorrow for behaviors of omission or from damaging the reputation of an authority figure is apt and justified. *Okay to feel guilt.*

- **Open Ourselves to the Energies of Renewal:** *The third step is to open ourselves to the energies of revival and renewal that arise from the core of our being at the promptings of our soul.* This core energy for renewal is oriented toward resolving specific limitations but is also effective for *personal transformation*. Extending the above example further, we cooperate with inspirations rising from within to heal the damage we have done to the reputation of the authority figure. *Open ourself to the energies of renewal.*

- **Renew the Intention of Becoming Ourselves:** *The fourth step in practice is to renew our intention to engage in becoming ourselves.* As mentioned before, we engage in questions of meaning again as circumstances and levels of awareness have changed. In the above example, we plan the behaviors that will lead to restitution of the good name of the authority figure and renewal of our inner state. *Renew the intention of becoming ourselves.*

- **Engage in Practices of Reconciliation:** *The fifth step is to engage in the behaviors that are a necessary part of becoming ourselves—in this case, reconciliation.* Here, in the presence of the same co-workers, we acknowledge the damage we have caused to the authority figure and act to restore his/her reputation. When this is taking place, healing is also occurring in the inner forum. Again, nothing happens without practice. The credibility of these steps toward self-healing depends on the continuation of efforts toward changing the damaging reactive habits in regard to authority figures and the inculcation of restorative behaviors.

Along with the healing of self, we might consider *healing the ancestors* whose oppressive influence might have been partly causative of our reactive behavior patterns. *Engage in practices of reconciliation.*

As a side note, through Interiority, we can collaborate in healing ourselves from the *shadow disturbances* we have inherited from our ancestors, who (perhaps) unintentionally passed on their unresolved conflicts to us. By the hard work of daily practice and dialogue with the inner complex of energies, we can continue the healing, lose the divided selves and become more whole. In this way, we can become conscious of the influences of our families-of-origin, our cultures and our tribes and choose to live out of self-generated inner convictions; thus, becoming healed in the process.

Similarly, it is not at all impossible to imagine that we can even heal our parents and ancestors from the negative agendas passed on to them—with the burdensome expectations that they would live their lives according to some heritage from their parents and ancestors. Perhaps we can achieve this healing by simple dialogues within ourselves, wherein we mentally and emotionally embrace our ancestors and walk forward with them in a healed manner…as we live our lives.

Who is to say that we do not have healing power and that we cannot extend this power to our ancestors as a gift? After all, the activity of our souls or the energies of the spirit in all things is not determined by time and place. Likewise, we can project healing on our descendants and those younger generations who are influenced by us, as we heal our own contaminated agendas. We do this so we do not pass on to them incomplete agendas, burdens for them to carry or resolve. The possibility then increases that we do not hand down to the proverbial *seventh generation* the conflicts we have inherited from our ancestors, tribes and cultures. That is, if we do the hard work of dialogue within and implement the practices for achieving Interiority.

- **The Healing of Others: (practice):** Who is this *other*? On the surface level, the other is any individual we meet, but especially the co-workers with whom we interact. However, below the surface, there are many others we need to be aware of. There is the other represented by our *families of origin* upon whom we have depended for nurturance; until we struck out on our solitary journeys, and who stuck by us, if we were lucky. There is the other represented by the *womb*, which took care of us for nine months before release into the world. There is the *magical other* (powerful individuals and heroes) upon whom we project our needs and expectations; this is the other we can depend on to relieve us of our fears and sufferings so we do not have to take responsibility for ourselves.

Then there are the relationships with those others that have exerted significantly *positive influences* on our lives. These are the others who, because of their love or hatred for us, became so important we have grown into the people we are because of them. There are also the others with whom we come in *daily contact,* including co-workers, loved ones, passersby and those whose very presence is a cause of our constant state of anxiety. These others can be a heavy burden for us to carry, particularly if we are not aware of their influence or have capitulated to our inner needs for their presence, even though the relationship is toxic to one or both.

It is important to remember that before we can interact equitably with another person, we need to be aware of his/her image that is contaminated with negativity and which we may have internalized. It follows that before we can heal any part of the relationship to the *external other*, we have to heal the relationship with the *internalized other*. If we realize that we are estranged from the internalized other and do nothing to heal that negative condition, then those perceptions and feelings will be projected onto the external other.

The path to healing is again *dialogical*. The inner dialogue with our estranged self is the place to begin. Then the dialogue moves to the estranged inner other, then to the external other. The following are the steps in the healing of relationships with the other.

1. **Recognize What We Dislike about Ourselves:** The first stage of the conversation begins with recognizing what we do not like within ourselves. All we need to do is to name one thing we dislike within us. For example, we do not like our avoidance of normal guilt feelings for things we do wrong. We can heal that dislike by directing expressions of self-acceptance within, based on the knowledge that everyone makes mistakes and normal guilt feelings are

part of growth and enlargement. *Recognize what we dislike about ourselves.*

2. **Note the Rejected Internalized Other:** The second stage in the dialogue addresses the image of the "other" we have within us, whom we reject. For example, we reject the image of the "other" because it seems to project violence toward us. We can heal that rejection of the image of the "other" as prone to violence by acknowledging that the image is only made up by our stereotypical judgment of people who resembled an individual in our past. We can heal the image if we pay attention to its source in our own negative experiences and recognize our fears of the same pattern happening again. *Note the rejected internalized other.*

3. **Know the Behaviors of the Other that Occasion Our Reactions:** The third stage in the dialogue addresses the behaviors of the *real* other to whom we react in a negative way. For example, we perceive the disposition, expressions and gestures of the other person as an authority figure we experienced as oppressive when we were younger. We need to briefly take note of the behaviors of the other that trigger our reactions. Then we need to take ownership of the connections between the internalized oppressor's behaviors and the other's behaviors—as belonging within us. We can only heal the images and the connections if we pay attention to the real qualities of both and deem them worthy of our efforts at healing the broken parts. The consideration of worthiness here is a critical component in the healing process. *Know the behaviors of the other that occasion our reactions.*

4. **Consider the Worthiness of All Involved:** If we perceive the "other" as merely another object unworthy of our attention, then we can do anything to the "other" without compunction. However, if we perceive that person as worthy of our attention, everything changes in our attitude and behavior. We allow the "other" to be a "person"—if for no other reason than self-respect. If we respect ourselves, we will accord to others the respect that is due them. Whatever is true of us is true of others. Therefore, by extension, we should allow them their ambiguities and ambivalences and let go of believing they will act according to our expectations or for our benefit. *Consider the worthiness of all involved.*

5. **Allow the Soul's Intent to Guide Our Healing.** The final stage of healing is to allow the intent of our soul to guide our behaviors. We may not necessarily feel reconciled or satisfied with any aspect of our relationships, but the practice of healing behaviors leads to the subsidence of hurt and the acceptance of

others and ourselves. When we understand that our soul and body are not two but one, we recognize our inextricable connection with all things. Thus, what we do to ourselves is ultimately done to others and vice versa.

Jung said: "Ultimately, every individual life is at the same time the eternal life of the species."[157] Nowhere is this unity more necessary in the workplaces of our time than in the relationships among co-workers, and, of course, within us. The process of refocusing on our soul's intentions is what promotes healing. *Allow the soul's intent to heal.*

Conflict Management *(practice)*: Conflict is ubiquitous in our places of work. When conflict happens, the usual reaction of workers is to locate the cause of tension in the actions of others or in institutional systems and its representatives. An Interiority approach is to initially examine the possible sources of such conflict as *originating within*, as we experience ourselves out of harmony with the environment. The question is: what kind of practice will enable us to grow through workplace conflicts? Undeniably, when conflict happens, we feel a surge of energy that often finds expression in emotional outbursts and negative behaviors toward others. It is this energy surge that is of interest to us.

Pointing to the surging energies of all things, Heraclitus said "All is fire." Similarly, Einstein and Heisenberg supported this expression in quantum dynamics. We moderns have come to identify energy as an elemental force driving the birth and death cycles of all things. We have to recognize that we work in fields of energy that dominate our behaviors. Nevertheless, we are still responsible for the management of those energies in our workplaces and in relationships with co-workers. What then can we do to manage those dynamic energy surges within us? The first step is to be aware of emotionally-charged, energy complexes at work within us.

There are many types of complexes to choose from. Some that are prevalent in our culture: the *inferiority* complex, the *Oedipus* complex, the *God* complex and the *authority* complex. Actually, people can have a complex about almost anything. A psychological complex is defined in Wikipedia as "a group of mental factors that are unconsciously associated by an individual with a particular subject or connected by a recognizable theme and influence the individual's attitude and behavior."[158] Core complexes are those energy clusters under which we were controlled as children and generally have to do with parental images. Even though we have physically grown up, the same energy clusters can control our lives unless we discover which complex owns us, which values we have internalized and then move to dissipate their negative influences.

Generally, we live in two worlds: 1) the *conscious* world of *immediate action* and 2) the *unconscious* world wherein we are influenced by *energy-charged complexes* which essentially govern our lives. Only when we feel deep discord between these two worlds do we opt either for the traditional mode of self-repression or set out to discover our own authentic voice. The following steps in the practice are necessary to manage any complex and the conflicts that emerge from it:

1. **Notice the Energy Cluster—the Complex:** Become aware of the surge of energy that defines a complex by which we are "controlled." For example, we may be subject to the energies that surround the image of the life that our mothers wished for us and which still exerts a powerful influence on how we live. She may have wanted us to become a doctor and so we became a doctor in spite of our misgivings and resistance to the image of ourselves in medical garb. Over time, perhaps we became aware that our true calling and talents lay in fixing automobiles.

    When the complex serves the agenda of our soul, our energies are positively charged and we feel elation and fulfillment. In the example, this would be when we are fixing an automobile. When the complex serves the energies of another, we experience surges of negative energy. For instance, when we are practicing medicine. To clarify the complex, when we feel satisfied, we can ask ourselves, "What energizes me?" In the midst of an angry outburst, we might ask, "Where is this energy coming from?" The answers will indicate the deeper reason for the happiness, the anger or the ennui. *Notice the energy cluster—the complex.*

2. **Notice Our Projections onto Others of What We Dislike in Ourselves:** Our next step is to notice how we project negative energy clusters onto those who appear to us as the cause of our uncomfortable feelings, when in fact, they may originate from within us. Others sense our projections and resent being made into the carriers of our unrecognized or disowned negative emotions. Reversing the action, they project their disowned negative emotions onto us, as if we were the source of their tensions. In doing so, a cycle of projections begins to characterize the relationship and drains both sides of the energies necessary for work. *Notice our projections onto others of what we dislike in ourselves.*

3. **Tolerate the Tensions Arising from the Complex:** Decide to tolerate the tensions from that energy cluster and choose some manifestation altogether different, but fulfilling. In the case of the example, say we choose to open an automobile maintenance service we have long imagined would make us happy. In this way, we are stepping away from the one-sided entrapment of the complex into tolerance of the tensions between the two points of focus in our lives (the mother complex and the embrace of our soul's agenda). In embracing the two

points of focus and tolerating the tensions between them, we experience a release of energies that become available for the work we have to do. *Tolerate the tensions arising from the complex.*

4. **Learn to Live with the Ambiguities and Tensions:** These two or more lifestyles may have little to do with each other, but they can be reconciled within us. This style of living—and working—is more realistic and mature. Living with ambiguities and tensions is not simple, but over time, the practice will lead us to wisdom and discernment. Accordingly, in our example, we might develop a way to manage our professional medical responsibilities and pursue our calling by making a significant contribution to the automobile maintenance industry. *Learn to live with the ambiguities and tensions.*

5. **Serve the Values of the Soul:** From the beginning of this book, I have highlighted the light and the dark, the good and the evil and other apparent contradictions that are the yin and the yang of the reality in which we live. Our life has integrity when we adhere to the values consonant with the agenda of our soul. The practice: serve the values inherent in our soul's agenda wherever they appear. Therefore, we must know which values are operative in our life and harmonize them with our highest aspirations. *Our life gradually takes on the agenda of our soul,* so no matter what we are engaged in on a practical level, we experience ourselves in balance, integrated and whole. *Serve the values of the soul.*

Forgiveness (practice): I grew up in a large family. Invariably, we siblings squabbled with each other by the hour and by the day. However, even after the most heated battles, our parents would demand that we make friends before going to bed. And so, forgiveness and its behaviors, however reluctant, took root and stuck. Similarly, in workplace conflict, we eventually come to the act of forgiving ourselves and each other to ameliorate hurt feelings and restore relationships. As one can expect in practicing Interiority, the practice of forgiveness *happens more within us* than in the final expression toward the other party.

We may not realize it but some of the damage we endure derives from a refusal to forgive. This kind of repression leads to depression and anxiety, self-estrangement, irritability and bitterness toward ourselves and others; and it often ends in *self-punishment.*

On the other hand, if we can practice forgiveness and self-acceptance on a regular basis, we can become peaceful within and arrive at maturity and stature. Forgiveness of self is a never-ending challenge, but it becomes easier if we let go of self-criticisms during our centering practices. The following are some recommended steps toward forgiveness:

1. **Understand the Fault** Understand the actions of self and of the other that precipitated the conflict that led to the injury and hurt. *Understand the fault*.

2. **Be Aware of the Feelings:** Become aware of feelings of anger, grievance, or desire for revenge generated within us and note how they are connected to similar and unresolved emotional conflicts felt in the past. *Be aware of the feelings*.

3. **Center Within:** Practice breathing deeply, taking walks, putting time and space between ourselves and the perceived incident that caused the hurt. When our emotions allow, we practice centering. This will allow us to go deeper into where the healing is taking place, by being in silence, stillness and solitude. Commit to do what we have to do to restore inner calm and balance. Forgiveness is for ourself more than for the other. *Center Within*.

4. **Show Forgiveness in Some Practical Way:** Find a way to express forgiveness to the other, whether by writing or speaking to them, but always by forgiving them inwardly as the basis of outward reconciliation. *Show forgiveness in some practical way*.

5. **Allow the Possibility of Enlargement:** Open to the possibility that through the practice of forgiveness, we may develop a stronger and healthier relationship with that person, both within ourselves and in the workplace. One possible outcome: the perception for each of us, which is that the unpleasant conflict is one of those *paradoxical gifts* we come across unexpectedly in life. If we reflect on how we have grown through our significant relationships, it is often those relationships characterized by conflict that turn out to be the most growth-producing of all. *Allow the possibility of enlargement*.

6. **Humbly Accept Limits:** Try to see the bigger picture of the unintended, unavoidable consequences of our actions. By the very fact of living, we are already committing some kind of injury to others. Through practicing acceptance of the imperfect nature of all things, we can grow through our tolerances of the tensions and dilemmas. *Humbly accept limits*.

7. **Visualization of Forgiveness and Reflective Healing:** If our preferred way to achieve inner reconciliation is to use non-verbal methods, we might try using visualization of forgiveness. The visualization is done through exercising the imagination. The process includes "seeing" ourself forgiving the person with whom we had a difficult experience and now achieving inner reconciliation. The method is as follows:

Sit in a comfortable position with our eyes closed and take a few deep breaths.

Relax and concentrate on our breath moving in and out and allow our heart to expand with each breath. Using our imagination, bring up an image of the person we have decided to forgive. Imagine we have been connected all these years by a negative energy. Choose to let go of the negative vibrations of that energy by silently forgiving the person and wishing them well. Turn the energies into positive support for going forward. Continue to imagine behaving in ways that are positive reflections of forgiveness and healing.

Conversely, if *we need* forgiveness from that person, then use the same exercise and ask for the forgiveness we need. Understand: we are being healed just by asking for it. These exercises can be done repeatedly or until we have the sense they are no longer necessary. *Visualization of forgiveness and reflective healing.*

Dimension 5: Spirit/Spiritual

Things spiritual refer to the regions of our inner selves (or souls) and to the constant spirit that pervades all things; just as energy is the building matter of the universe. Rather than looking upward for spiritual sustenance, we look inward to the regions of Interiority and its practices while we are doing our tasks. The spiritual task is to find the path that is uniquely ours in this world; and in following it faithfully we come to fulfillment, step-by-step. To do this, we must leave the path designed by others for us to follow, especially if it obstructs our growth. While following our uncovered paths, we have the guidance of our souls to move us toward wholeness. Following the path can become a religious experience.

Religion/Ritual (practice): One meaning of the word religion is derived from the Latin term, *ligare*, which means to be bound again (to the world and to one's emerging self). Our use of the word suggests some form of *transcendence* in the encounter with transformative life experiences—especially in the performance of work.

When transcendence happens, we are made new; we live out of that newness until another opportunity for potential transcendence presents itself. True religious experiences lead us to transformation, especially the spiritual kind. However, as nature always changes and we are invited to change with it, the religious challenge is to hold ourselves open to the next transformative opportunity. If we avoid the new opportunities in favor of earlier transformations, we run the risk of choosing comfort and the security of a form of religious institution, and perhaps a form of repetitive ritual.

This leads us to consider the two general types of *ritualized practices* that are 1) merely repetitions of *lifeless formats* or 2) practices that lead us consistently into *in-depth encounters* with mystery, ambiguities, paradoxes and dilemmas, and present us with choices to change and grow. The practices presented in this chapter often take the latter form of living rituals. Living rituals are opportunities for the liberation of energies that drive the enlargement of our minds, our work and, of course, our lives.

The way to ensure that the religious practices we adopt and the rituals we perform are life-giving and authentic sources of spiritual energies:

1. **Test Our Religious Responses and Rituals:** The first stage of religious response is to find out whether the religious practices and rituals we performed when we were young have changed and new ones have been put in place that match our needs. If those rituals are much the same as before, we might ask ourselves whether we are repeating them because of *tradition* or because they are fertile sources of *inspiration* for our present work and life needs. If the latter, then we have been investing energies in the evolution of those forms so they remain transformative. In the same way, we might ask ourself whether our present religious practices are aligned with our spiritual needs, and whether they are enabling us to grow spiritually. *Test our religious responses and rituals.*

2. **Heed the Promptings of Our Soul:** The second stage is about what our soul is requiring of us at this time so that we remain vital and involved on our journey toward maturity. This is certain: our soul is requiring something to do with *health* and *wholeness*. How our soul demands that development is unpredictable, but if we are alert to what is happening in every part of our life, we will be able to discern our soul's promptings—especially in workplace interactions. Indeed, for the alert mind everything is speaking to us. *Heed the promptings of our soul.*

3. **Question, Listen and Dialogue Within:** The third stage deals with how we heed the requirements of the soul as distinct from the agendas acquired from other sources. Recall the important practices already addressed: question, listen and dialogue with one's soul. As we respond to those inspirations, there is no doubt that we will be enlarged and will be more intently in service to the needs of the world. *Question, listen and dialogue within.*

4. **Press Forward toward the Fulfillment of Our Person:** The fourth stage of responsiveness to the soul's requirements is to become more acutely aware of our ultimate destination and the service we will perform that leads to fulfillment. The ultimate destination is not merely the drawing of our last breath but the quality of personhood we have lived, even momentarily and however imperfectly. In that moment of insight into our call and response is our affirmation of what ultimate value represents for us. *Press forward toward the fulfillment of our person.*

5. **Collaborate with Energies Released:** The fifth stage is a collaboration in the release of repressed energies within to make them available for the work that is ours to do. We are saying "yes, yes" to our soul when we race along, energies surging, engaging in the hard work of the inner dialogue, in any of its forms. These energies are the source of increased creativity and productivity. *Collaborate with energies released.*

Wisdom *(practice)*: "The Serenity Prayer," by Reinhold Niebuhr, ends with the words, "the wisdom to know the difference."[159] How precious is the particular virtue of wisdom whereby we can discern about the journey of our lives, work that is of the soul and let pass what is not. Wisdom applied to decisions is essentially different from ordinary decision-making. Making ordinary decisions includes:

1. Selecting the correct issue on which to work
2. Clarifying the optional solutions available
3. Calculating the consequences of each option
4. Making trade-offs on a range of achievable results
5. Linking the consequences of one's decision over time
6. Measuring one's tolerance of the risks involved
7. Selecting a course of action

The components of wisdom decisions involve:

Choosing to do the right thing based on its *moral implications*

Balancing the *ethically compelling* values with the astute *business-related* option

Allowing the *intuitions* of all parts of one's being to play roles in the decision

Considering the emerging needs of the *greater whole*

Selecting the *altruistic* and *compassionate* alternative over other possibilities

Including the intuition of the *heart,* the immediate *emotional response* and the calculation of the *mind*

Being *patient* by allowing the implications of the decision for persons and communities to rise to the surface from within

Steadily reflecting on the *lessons* of one's experience and possible applications to the present issue

Considering the optimum course in view of the emerging human context and being fully *at peace* with the decision made

In comparison to ordinary decision-making, a wisdom decision is more fully human. When we practice wise decision-making, we become *fully vested* in our choices and can work *without fear*.

In view of the span of our lives, why is wisdom decision-making so important? Above all, we want to grow wise. Everything speaks to us about wisdom. As Emerson said, "Every moment instructs, and every object: for wisdom is infused into every form. It has been poured into us as blood; it convulsed us as pain; it slid into us as pleasure; it enveloped us in dull, melancholy days, or in days of cheerful labor; we did not guess its essence, until after a long time."[160]

Learning Wisdom *(practice)*: In the springtime of life, most adolescents spend time deciding what they will be "when they grow up." At such an early age, most are thinking about good jobs as opposed to worthwhile work—work that will truly fulfill them, work that leads to wise lives, work that leaves no room for regrets over talent wasted. In the New Testament, the word sin comes from a Greek word that means "missing the mark" or "missing the target." One interpretation: the only real sin is a life that collusively misses the mark for which it was brought into existence. Many people come to sense halfway through the journey that they are indeed off the mark and strive to make corrections, either in career choice or how they approach work altogether.

Although many people have strong intuitions about why they were born, most fail to follow their intuitions, even to clarify the possible lives from which they might choose. Few have let go of all else to find the treasure hidden in the field. Only the very few find and commit to a purpose from which flows passion and enthusiasm. Once they have found all-consuming work, the implications resonate in everything they do. These few are in the grip of a passion so evident that their enthusiasm influences everyone with whom they come in contact. For these enthusiastic people, wisdom means they know—and are consumed by—the *difference between the mundane and the transformational*.

Being wise then means that we have the ability to discern what is of the *soul* and what is of the *ego* or some *lesser god*. The following are some steps toward learning the wisdom that surpasses everything:

1. **Know the Work for which We Are Here:** Step one is to spend the time to know the unique work for which we are here. Go beyond mere information or opinions and seek to practice the wisdom that reverberates with the aspirations of our soul. Such wisdom includes:
   - insight into self including our reactive patterns
   - courage to select the values that are priorities over all others

- foresight to imagine how our life and work will unfold
- realistic estimation of the variety of resources at our disposal
- balance between competing passions that might unduly sway our preference
- honest fear of hasty choices that might bring overwhelming complexities—far more than one can handle

Wisdom is no simple gift. For most people, it is hard won from infelicitous experiences. The practice of making wise decisions takes its cues from the practice of cultivated Interiority and the enduring growth of the self. *Know the work for which we are here.*

2. **Let Go:** Step two is to let go of the diversions and distractions that might intervene so we miss the mark. These distractions might include old agendas belonging to someone else's story, which we have claimed as our own because we found them comfortable. When the marketers try to persuade us to purchase entirely unnecessary items, our wisdom-based intuitions are quick to let go of both the object and the desire for it. *Let go.*

3. **Sustain Enthusiasm for Our Work:** Step three is to allow ourselves to be taken up emotionally until we are enthused and made passionate by the work that is ours to do. On the one hand, our emotional reactions can trap us into negative spirals of self-defeating behaviors, but on the other hand emotional reactions are supremely accurate barometers signaling that we are on the right track in what—and how—we are doing our work. The wise person learns to read the inner emotional barometer to sustain enthusiasm and to regulate negative reactivity patterns, which would drain needed energy. While embracing the emotional side of enthusiasm, it is also necessary to constantly discern the nature of our passions so we are not deceived by passing fancies or deluded by lesser expectations. *Sustain enthusiasm for our work.*

4. **Do the Work, Employ Wisdom:** Step four is to do the work, fulfill the purpose and pursue the dream, so in the doing we are ourselves fulfilled and wisdom becomes our steady companion. By dint of repetition, we learn what it takes to balance the competing sides of ourselves, especially the left and right hemispheres of our brains; the rational and the emotive. In the process, we become skillful at discerning which option is best for us; in other words, which choice makes us a little bit wiser. *Do the work, employ wisdom.*

Loving Behavior at Work (practice): Love is a familiar word that has a down-to-earth ring to it and yet the labors of love ripple so widely that the universe vibrates with its power. As we have described love earlier, it is the energy, *the strange attractor*, which holds everything in place; while the constant spirit goes about its evolutionary journey toward consciousness. As such, the giving and receiving of love is our most creative activity.

The vocabulary of love has been little used in the workplace because work has been perceived as a burden put upon workers by management. Nevertheless, conscious or not, the need to give and receive love is unquestionably present in every action of every worker. We are more familiar with the vocabulary of love as romance, eroticism, sentiment and as enticements to love one's car, pet or homeland. Yet all these pale when we are inspired to act selflessly on behalf of a co-worker in need. By extending ourselves to serve the other, we are doing the fundamental work of our lives. When no return is needed or expected, we are building something sacred, without even a conscious thought. Moreover, the more we behave in loving ways in the face of rejection, cynicism and injury, the more value-impelled the deed—and the truest form of love.

When we act from a source of love within for the only purpose of doing what we know is right, we are building the self, the community and the earth. It bears repeating: the act of love is reflective of the nature of things, for all things are eventually oriented toward the positive and the benign. As the Chinese say, *jen* (goodness) is what makes us human.

How then do we come to know ourselves as loved? We do so by following these loving practices:

1. **Know Ourselves As Loved:** We come to know we are loved initially by realizing that we have been given the gift of life. This kind of realization is one of those mysterious experiences when we come to know we are alive, along with all the other living things in our period of history. Sometimes this happens because of a confrontation with death that shocks us into recognizing that we are sustained and loved by the gift of life.

We learn further about being loved from our families of origin, from the reflections of friends and our loved ones. In our response to the needs of others, we come closer to knowing the meaning of love. Fortunate are those who have heard the phrase "I love you" addressed to them, and in the risk of their responses have entered more deeply into the meaning of life than they ever thought possible.

It is through the union of love that we can overcome the sense of separateness. This is when we really embrace our work so it becomes our way of life—and love. The initial practice: love self because love is the great healer and serves as the basis for co-workers. If we have love and compassion for ourselves, others will pick up on that, will want to be around us and will love themselves more. *Know ourselves as loved.*

2. **Vulnerability—a Condition of being Loved:** A condition of being loved is to be vulnerable in some way to the love of others; meaning, open up to allowing love into our self-awareness.

   Moderns barely tolerate this kind of vulnerability. They cannot endure the limitation of feeling vulnerable to the love of another. This is a major reason why being "loved for oneself alone," to paraphrase Marilyn Monroe's heartfelt cry, is much more difficult than loving others. Vulnerability is the *price of admission to one's humanity*. Without being vulnerable to love, the only form of humanity accessible to us is on the outside. The inner gift of being loved by another remains a foreign country, an unknown trackless waste where one wanders, lost and wondering why. *Vulnerability– a condition of being loved.*

3. **Cultivate the Ability to Be, and to Act for Another:** By evolutionary growth, humans are conditioned to feel compassion for others. But, when it comes to practical applications, love is a learned behavior. We do not automatically know how to love properly. Naturally, we will come to have some sentimental attachment to those who have nurtured and reared us, and for the family members we grew up with. However, sentiment alone does not qualify us as knowing how to love others or to know ourselves as loved. Love requires that we take the time to know the needs of others, and then give of our resources in response. Sometimes, what another needs is not material but some inner resource we have, such as a listening ear, an understanding mind, a sympathetic heart, or a positive attitude. In these examples, the action of love is to simply *be* for the other. *Cultivate being and acting for the other.*

4. **Know the Other and Be Known:** "Knowing" another person is one of the greatest gifts we can give them. I'm not referring to intellectual knowledge here, but knowing someone in the mysterious depths where they scarcely know themselves. This means that we spend time with them, are open to their influence and work together on some common interest or project. In doing a task together, gradually the other person appears; and we also become a known quantity to them.

The reciprocal side of knowing another is to allow ourself to become known. This dynamic requires that we *be* ourselves as much as possible, and be strong enough to tell the other about any difficulties in self-disclosure.

When others come to *know* us, we feel both a great sense of gratitude and some fear they will not respect the information we have disclosed to them. After all, our inner selves are our most sacred and intimate parts and there is no greater devastation than when they are trampled. It is insufficient to only know, and be known by others. Showing concern for their welfare is the next requirement. *Know the other and be known.*

5. **Show Concern:** Love requires that we show concern for others; that we look out for them and provide for their needs to the best of our abilities. Concern also requires that we take time to *understand what others need*. Without concern for others' needs, the quality of our love is shallow. When we share what we have, even though it is not necessarily material goods, then we are showing love. *Show concern.*

6. **Show Respect:** One of the greatest needs of modern man is to be respected. We can give material things in the name of love, but if there is no respect, the love shown is hardly deserving of the name. The meaning of respect is derived from the Latin word, *respicere*, which means we *take another look*. When we respect another, we are looking deeper than surface appearances and valuing the inner qualities of the person. *Show respect.*

7. **Practice Love through Our Work Behaviors:** Love consists of behaviors that are done on behalf of the other. Loving behaviors subtly expressed are all the more effective because only the recipient notices. For example, *acknowledging* the meritorious results achieved by a co-worker. A word of genuine appreciation is treasured by the co-worker long after the incident itself is forgotten. Another loving act: *honest feedback* delivered with sensitivity in response to a request for comment. A third loving practice: lending a *helping hand* when a co-worker is in need. Just *inviting a co-worker* to do what he/she can do best for the achievement of the work is usually appreciated. Also, *letting others take the credit* will usually earn their gratitude. If the credit does not come back to you, let it go.

Practicing these few behaviors will generally be sufficient for you to fulfill love in the workplace. *Practice love through our work behaviors.*

8. **Pursue Love as It is Communicative of Itself:** We need to think of ourselves as being constituted of love, by love and for love. We need to purposely *search for love within* and cultivate generosity of heart so loving behaviors become our normal expression. Be ready when opportunities come along to express love in the workplace. When love is expressed in behaviors, it is diffused outward to others and influences them, in turn, to love co-workers. Genuinely loving behaviors are recognizable and co-workers will imitate such behaviors themselves, in their own contexts. *Pursue love as it is communicative of itself.*

9. **Know Love as the Fulfillment of the Whole Person:** Aware or not, when we behave in loving ways, we are fulfilled in every aspect of our being and so are those with whom we come in contact. St. Augustine says, "Love and do what you will." It is as if loving behavior is the pinnacle of what a human being can achieve. It is not necessary to achieve any visible results because the results have already reverberated within us, and in everything.

Our lives depend on the quality of our loving behaviors. When we become loving from our core, we are influencing our family, friends, co-workers, company, stakeholders and community. Nothing is outside our reach and we become a healing presence. *Know love as the fulfillment of the whole person.*

The Holy and Mystery *(practice)*: Certain phenomena in human experience transcend comprehension and are considered sacred, regardless of creed or culture. Examples are the sacred nature of birth, a stirring response to newfound love and the urge to search for what fulfills the longings of the human heart. In the Shinto religion, *kami* or gods, such as the rising sun, are recognized as divine because of their ability to inspire awe in people.

We are transported by great natural wonders, profoundly moving works of art, mesmerizing forces of nature and the cycle of our lives rolling along their winding paths. During these experiences, we find ourselves in the presence of *awe-inducing energies* and the *power of the moment*. The only guide is our own spirit and to gain access to it, we have the following practices:

1. **Follow Spirit as Our Guide:** Because the nature of the search involves mysteries so impenetrable, it is normal to look for guides to show the way. Some people depend on "revealed" truth, some look to gurus, while others follow the teachings of established religions, and many abstain from the search altogether.

Our quest leads to the *workplace*, where work itself teaches us; our co-workers evoke learning through efforts to collaborate; and we are led within to the place where *we become the only work that matters*. That work is spirit-led, evoking agenda items with which to dialogue, learn and grow in a self-realization process. The size and scope of the agenda items are not nearly as important as the engagement process through which we evolve. Spirit is the grower—tilling the ground, planting the seeds and assisting in reaping the only worthwhile harvest: wisdom. *Follow spirit as our guide.*

2. **See the Holy as Our Destination:** Instead of the word *destination*, perhaps union is a more appropriate term for describing the condition toward which we are being led by spirit. Union does not depend on our reasoning power,

instead on an inner faculty that can only be described by what it is not, a way of unknowing. The union that I'm referring to allows us to experience *non-separation from everything* while *retaining* the unique *consciousness of self*. Union with the ground of one's being is the life condition—and work—of any person who is pursuing wholeness as a human being. When we enter into this union experience, we are already part of the *unspeakable, unknowable mystery* we might call holy. As is evident, when we attempt to deal with the mysteries, words and meanings fail to adequately explain anything. In this pursuit of Interiority, everything manifests the holy and in our union with things, we are made whole. *See the holy as our destination.*

3. **Engage Mystery as Our Way to Enlargement:** While we are alive, and especially while we are at work, we do not remain static and unchanging. Because we are *engaging* and *dialoging* within as a practice of Interiority, we are moving and *invited to grow continuously larger* than we could have imagined. On one level, we grow in knowledge and skill because of our engagement with assigned tasks. But when the task is to engage with mystery itself, our only recourse is to be still and *in the stillness allow ourselves to open to enlargement*. Action in this case would be counterproductive. Mystery does not reveal itself to any human faculty, which is why it is called mystery.

Humans are not without recourse, however. We can still develop a relationship to mystery. Such a relationship can be ineffably intimate and ineffably transcendent. As the Eagles sing, "Learn to be still" and perhaps the butterfly will land on our shoulder. In that moment, the ineffable relationship will deepen and grow larger. Stillness allows us to come together within and to be receptive to the larger task that is ours to fulfill. That is why the directive to "just sit" is so rich in the potential for our enlargement. *Engage mystery as our way to enlargement.*

4. **Know the Holy at Work in Our Work.** At this point, we come full circle to our work, the tasks we do, the contribution we make under the guidance of spirit. Nevertheless, even if the holy and mysterious are not accessible through ordinary efforts at setting goals, implementing plans and generating results, we are invited to go deeper into the fertile state of Interiority by the practices enumerated. It is within the deep awareness of our unfolding *stories*, *dialogues* between self and soul, the *search for union* along the byways of our journeys that we gain access to the energies of *creativity*, *productivity* and *enlargement*.

All of these are available to us while we are doing our work. When we reach this state of Interiority at work, we are making our contribution. *Know the holy at work in our work.*

My Story – Engagement with My Work

By now you will have read about various episodes in my story and considered key episodes in your own story. On the surface, I have moved through most of the stages as described by Shakespeare when he wrote:

"All the world's a stage,
And all the men and women merely players:
They have their exits and their entrances;
And one man in his time plays many parts"

I have played many parts, in many places—but surprisingly none as important as the one in which I am presently engaged. Of course, each of the previous parts had validity during the times I was engaged in them. And, depending on the integrity of this final stage, the real value of all the previous parts will become evident or not.

On the outside, I am putting together this book and the workshops through which workers aspiring to Interiority will engage with their lives and work. On the inside, I am fearful that I will not be as good an example of Interiority as I would like to be. Ultimately, such modeling is the proof of the pudding that the whole work of Interiority is a viable work-style. So, I am left with the question about whether I seriously engaged with my own life on the basis of Interiority? That is the question, response, proof and validity.

Also, on the inside, I have the desire to be and to do the necessary work, in my own way. If I am following the inspirations of the spirit within, I will be able to work comfortably with confidence that the same spirit is at work in everything.

In the present context, I feel buoyed up by the sense that others are heading in the same direction as myself. I see that direction and the efforts of those in alignment with Interiority as signs of hope.

My Story – Reflections

I am grateful for the life that I have experienced and still enjoy. My usual *self-criticism* is that I begin many different ventures in the area of human development and do not see them through to operating businesses—which is exactly the same as my usual *self-acknowledgment*: I begin many different ventures in the area of human development and do not see them through to operating businesses. In that way, I will eventually leave to others the task of carrying this work further.

Your Story

What then about you, reader? Do you have practices for developing Interiority at work? Have you put together for yourself a number of dimensions to develop inner sensibilities so your energies are released for greater productivity? How well have you incorporated silence, stillness and solitude as a practice for creative energies to rise up in your awareness? What about the psyche and psychological practices whereby unconscious energies can flow into your work life? Perhaps you might write notes on what struck you while reading this chapter.

Building the self is done bit by bit

Chapter 10

Programs

Three Workshops for Implementing Interiority

In this final Chapter, I describe three two-day workshops for making Interiority a functioning practicality and available to a group of workers and their organization as an intact program. The themes of the three workshops are: **Person**, **Work** and **Interiority**, respectively. In this discussion of the six days of the Interiority-related workshops, I begin with the premise that everything in the interconnected workshops begins and ends with the worker, work and the workplace. Workshop participants are expected to do pre-work before the first workshop and during the one-month (at least) period between each of the next two workshops. This pre-work ensures *customized treatment* and very *specific facilitation* of the process for the participants as a group. Participants also agree to ground rules, which include openness to *participation* in exercises, *feedback* on observed behaviors and *group sharing*.

Initially, I engage with clarification of *expectations*. The reason is that participants bring their perceptions, from their previous experience of workshops, about what will happen and pre-set notions about how they will participate. I inform them that the Interiority workshops are not like any in which they have previously participated. When

I have finished describing the objectives, processes, skills and requirements of all three workshops, I revisit the topic of expectations and verify each participant's *willingness to participate*. If they are willing, we proceed with the program. If not, we make appropriate adjustments, which might include the exit of some participants and then we proceed. Enrollment in these workshops is on a *voluntary* basis because of the personal and challenging nature of the content and interactions.

The **First Workshop** starts out with the *experiences of work*. Although the theme is Person, I approach the development of the person through his/her specific experiences at work. For this, I enable the participants to clarify their self-identity and practices of self-management in the work context. We proceed from there through the topics of story, meaning, context, calling, foundations, the great work (*as described in this book*) and self-care. From this line-up of topics, you can understand that this workshop does not deal directly with creativity or productivity but such topics are developed through the processes and practices of the participants' interactions. The dimensions of creativity and productivity are part of the experience of the three workshops. The participants are expected to exercise creative energies in the engagement with their own tasks and increase their productivity over the projected three-four month duration of the Interiority project.

The **Second Workshop** deals directly with the theme of Work. Initially, I enable the participants to clarify their work-style, work-style challenges and the fit between individuals and their chosen profession in terms of their inner aspirations. We proceed from there through the topics of historical development of work, how we are shaped by the work we do, good work habits, poor work habits, cultivation of the IP (*Interiority Powered*) worker and IP organization, visioning and contribution. Again as in the first workshop, the participants deal with improving their creativity and productivity through the exercises, processes and practices of the participant's interactions.

The **Third Workshop** deals directly with the theme of Interiority. Initially, I enable the participants to clarify their level of Interiority in terms of the existential challenges we all face in life and work. We proceed from there through the topics of the energies available at work, how they might be blocked, how to break the ingrained patterns that act as barriers to the release of those energies, how we move through cycles of growth and maturity to become whole, how we heal ourselves and others at work, clarification of the resources necessary for implementation of wholeness, and how each participant plans to make his/her contribution to the organization and the communities of belonging. Again as in workshops one and two, the participants deal with improving their creativity and productivity through the exercises, processes and practices of the participants' interactions.

In all three workshops, I review the basics of listening, clarity of expression, emotional expression, feedback, dialoguing, observation skills, accountability and coaching. This review is not one of the main purposes of the workshops but it is often necessary to remind the participants of these communication skills. Another set of competencies that I emphasize is the ability to develop *relationships with the other participants*. The dynamics among the participants greatly help motivate each one to keep on track, while promoting learning and skills development.

To differentiate the Interiority approach from the usual methods of conflict resolution, I offer the following example of how I used a conflict scenario to define the Interiority factors that become grist for the interactions of the three workshops.

My Story – Reconciling the Workers with their Inner Resources

The workers who were gathered for the workshop sat rigidly along the rows of tables. Their unsmiling and resistant demeanor was challenging to the point of defiance. I was the consultant, mediator, coordinator, educator, facilitator and any other -ator you care to mention. I was there to help them work on the conflicts that surged among them and hopefully dissipate the negativity that drained co-worker relationships. Constant squabbling had been reducing worker output, the organization's productivity and the shareholder's profit. The workers and their managers were at an impasse regarding what to do about the issues that divided them.

In brief, this interminable situation of conflict was the purported reason for the workshop. Management wanted these conflicts resolved so that everyone could get back to doing their work productively. The main emphasis was to have the participants define and take ownership of the issues that caused the conflict.

Once they had taken their seats, it was up to me to assist them in dealing with their issues and putting an action plan together for the targeted improvements. Just as in previous conflict-management workshops in my experience, this workgroup wore its history of conflict in hunched-up shoulders, rigid jaw-lines and nervous fidgeting. The divisions in the group were even apparent in the sociogram (a structural representation of the social links of individuals) of where they sat in the room. Like birds of a feather, they sat huddled with their buddies and those with whom they generally saw eye-to-eye. It was a classic scene of Us vs. Them.

The room fairly crackled with pent-up tension. Occasionally the tension was given voice but then words came spluttering forth in distorted speech that flew incoherently and served only to harden those for whom they were intended, me included. Words with barbed edges, hopscotched from table to table and in the cold

> *silence rose like transparent stone walls between us and them. Small groups often divide themselves according to workplace affiliations that serve only to highlight the anomaly: everyone on one side thinking of themselves as the good guys, the others deserved only to be known as the bad.*
>
> *Good intentions notwithstanding, in such a climate of tension, it is entirely possible for a facilitator to become a target of the unresolved emotional entanglements in the group. My approach was that none of these would be effective. To me, the best option for the purposes of development was to give recognition to legitimate emotional expression and guide the energies wherever they would go.*
>
> *As always, the "us" at the other tables could scarcely be spoken of without contempt, while secretly wishing they might be banished and thereby solve all problems forever. Bearing such grudges, each side nurtured its own hurts and angers.*
>
> *This then, was the appearance of repressed, untreated emotions that had for too long found no normal, healthy outlet in workplace interactions. The bottom-line: one group of participants wanted to have the other group, the "bad guys" fixed. They wanted their behaviors changed and with that all of the systems in which they participated.*

The Way of Interiority

In view of the turmoil affecting the above group, as well as the assumptions about workshops on conflict resolution/management strategies, it is usually my considerable task to *refocus a group's energies inward*. Rather than the usual definition of the source of the conflict being in the external, observable behaviors of the co-worker, I enable the participants to become aware of the sources of the conflict deriving from within themselves. These sources in turn derive from one's experiences, which result in patterns of reactivity and feeling clusters among the many other possible causes. The challenge is for the participants to redirect their awareness inward to face the causes of the conflict as they are originating from within themselves.

The way forward does not lie in programmatic solutions based on adapting external behaviors and systems alone. The way lies in allowing blocked energies to be released and for the individual—and group—to become Interiority Powered. This way requires disciplines of stillness, quiet, silence and openness to listen inwardly. If they are able to refocus their energies from the externals to what lies within and I am able to do the same, we engage with the real work of Interiority together. In so doing, we engage with the only effective method for increasing creativity and productivity: the *energies* which emanate from within by way of Interiority.

Just as in any similar challenge to workers who have been accustomed to traditional paradigms for solving problems at work, the major process in conducting the workshops is in enabling the participants to *transition from external/behavioral solutions* to those that emerge from the energies of Interiority.

Additional Principles to Consider

In designing and conducting workshops to help workers tap into the rich reservoir of Interiority, several other dynamics and principles should be taken into consideration. Specifically, special attention should be given to the possibility of *deep personal issues* arising during the workshop sessions. Somewhat related is the idea of *managing difficult tensions*, aptly named as a "devils brew," *(see below)*. And finally, an approach to workshops on Interiority cannot be over-prescriptive. There is as much *art* and *spirit* as there is science involved in the design, as well as facilitation.

Personal Issues - Unworkable in the Context of such a Group

One question that might arise here concerns the possibility of some worker(s) divulging personal or emotional information that might be overwhelming to manage in the workshop. My approach is to make sure participants are aware of such a possibility and to take care of the individuals within the limitations of the group agenda. When such care is insufficient for their needs, I provide them with referrals to professional resources for further assistance. It must be remembered that my approach in these workshops is to develop the whole person and not necessarily to treat any specific personal issues.

A Devil's Brew

A devil's brew is but one interpretation of periodic workplace-tension blasts. Despised and outlawed, the devil, as the supposed cause of acrimonious conflict, comes in for an unfair share of the blame in the workplace. All too often, in conflicts we ascribe the causes to nefarious spirits who are useful only as scapegoats that allow us to escape responsibility. In a bygone entertainment era, the comedian Flip Wilson, using his falsetto, drew laughs by claiming, "The devil made me do it." Such scapegoats mostly assist people in *evading responsibility for personal wrongdoing* and avoiding the kind of conflict that can generate beneficial results for the workers. Most workers are taught only to solve workplace problems with a mechanical/engineering mind. Such a mind is not only devoid of personal responsibility but possibly collusive in allowing participants to avoid accountability. Thereby hangs a tale of the non-usage of energies of potentially inestimable value.

The oyster's irritation produces the pearl. Conflicts that are well-managed can defuse emotional tension and provide opportunities for listening, empathizing and problem-solving based on the way of Interiority. The irritant in the oysters are a necessary part of how things grow and become whole. The same is true of workers in conflict in the workplace. Quite simply, *conflicts are a necessary part* of workers and teams growing up to mature identities and *wholesome problem-solving*, if they are provided with opportunities for doing so.

While recognizing the pain involved, I have sympathy for the devil that justly disturbs the space inside oneself and in the relationships between people at work. I have sympathy for workers who are often caught and held in victimhood that is not unlike a hell on earth. If workers can emerge informed from that place of dysfunction, they will have grown to understanding those in similar circumstances and hopefully become a healing presence for them.

Science, Art and Spirit

Conducting the interactions and dynamic interchanges among workshop participants requires a combination of science, art and a spiritual quest for all involved. Specific details regarding these dimensions are beyond the scope of these pages. However, in alluding to them, I wish to emphasize the *diverse currents* of science, art and spirituality that intermingle in workers engaging with the depth of their realities; thus becoming open to the transformations that ensue.

Regarding the conduct of workshops that include all three dimensions at once, appropriately enough it is through reliance on my intuition and experience of what is suitable that perhaps elicits my most effective response. Here again, it is spirit at work in the group and in me which remembers. Spirit is at work when we are gathered to improve our work, as well as our relationships, calling us to become aware again of the richness we carry within ourselves. Despite repeated efforts that had limited effect, spirit calls us to try again, to learn from our failures, to mature and accept the world as it is and not as we would like it to be—and to be faithful to our call to work effectively together.

Spirit is abiding life's consciousness, which requires that our organizations *renew themselves*; to redirect themselves to their *original purpose* in new ways and to *make* the *contributions* for which they began their journey. The unique fusion of *science*, *art* and *spirituality* (all part of Interiority) enables substantial increases in productivity and profound satisfaction in the workers and stakeholders.

Conclusion

"Only compassion can save – the wordless knowledge of my own responsibility for whatever is being done to the least of God's children. This is the knowledge of the spirit."

—Peter Drucker

Introducing Interiority into Organizational Life

The following is a brief treatment of a Nine-Step Process for introducing Interiority into an organization. I will indicate the area through which Interiority is introduced and explain the function of each area in moving the whole process forward; so that over time Interiority becomes embedded in the culture.

1. **Worker Awareness and Initiatives:** This step derives its uniqueness from the proposition that the initiative for Interiority at work comes through the sensitivity of the workers; responding to the changing conditions of society—and the organization, necessitating a profound strengthening of their inner resources at work. This kind of sensitivity in the workers is the most dependable barometer of emerging trends and necessary responsiveness; and it is an assurance of vitality and accuracy in the use of the organization's resources.

   Every worthy CEO is especially attuned to what is happening in the vital center of the organization—which is the workforce. The CEOs are also aware that they themselves are the models which the workers imitate to establish their behavior patterns and attitudes. Additionally, they enable the voice of the workforce to be heard. They do this by clarifying what they hear regarding the need for Interiority, so a consensus is formed throughout the organization and action is taken accordingly.

   Practically speaking, the initiative derives from worker awareness that traditional methods of development at work are ineffective. Interiority-based methods offer the most comprehensive and effectively viable alternatives.

2. **The CEO and Adhoc Committee** *(a subcommittee organized for the specific purpose of introducing the Interiority Program):* In introducing the Interiority Program, the CEO demonstrates awareness of the areas critical to the success of the organization. He/she makes the connection between *Interiority, worker and stakeholder satisfaction* and *improvements in productivity*. It is the task of the CEO to initially practice Interiority and then persuade the Adhoc Committee of the urgency of implementing the program throughout the organization. When the CEO and Adhoc Committee have taken seriously their own

need for Interiority at work and implemented the practices to some degree, they are in a suitable position to implement the programs throughout the system. It is up to the CEO to communicate in general terms about the Interiority Program to all the workers.

3. **The Interiority Committee:** The Adhoc Committee works with Human Resources and an external consultant to assemble a *design and a program development committee,* (The Interiority Committee), *i*ncluding representatives from a cross-section of the workforce. The Interiority Committee decides on a course of action for implementing the Interiority Program.

4. **Human Resources:** The Interiority Committee, along with representatives from HR, designs and develops an Interiority Program, based on the original materials made available for the task, adapting them in ways appropriate for the organization. The adapted program may include a combination of vocabulary, values, documents, workshops, practices and policies that are part of the regular development materials of the organization and its culture.

5. **Pilot Programs:** The adapted Interiority Program is conducted in *pilot tests* on several groups that are representative of the organization as a whole. According to the lessons learned through these pilot tests, the program is further *adapted to fit* the specific needs of the workers, the organization and the stakeholders. Representatives of HR, along with some individuals chosen from the workforce by the workers, are also trained to become co-facilitators of the workshops and subsequent implementation processes.

6. **Adaptations to the Interiority Program:** The impact of the Interiority Program on each of the pilot groups is *assessed* and suitable *improvements* are introduced and the testing is repeated again with other similar groups.

7. **Inauguration of the Interiority Program:** The CEO explains and announces the *inauguration* of the Interiority Program. The *schedule* for the implementation of the program is established.

8. **Rollout of the Program:** The program is rolled out in small intact groups throughout the organization. The objective is to ensure that the concepts are *understood*, the practices are *implemented* and a culture of Interiority is *nurtured*.

9. **Suitable Adaptations are Incorporated:** The impact of the program is *monitored* and as circumstances and conditions warrant change, suitable adaptations and improvements are incorporated. Since an Interiority Program is aligned with the values and principles that guide an organization, it needs continuous support by a Champion who is appointed by the CEO.

CONCLUSION 349

Nine-Step Interiority Implementation Model

1. Management, workers and stakeholders become aware of the social and business challenges and needs for Interiority.

2. The CEO becomes aware of trends in the market that constitute threats and opportunities for the organization. Takes responsibility for his/her own interiority and then persuades an Adhoc Interiority Committee about the urgency of doing the same.

3. The Interiority Committee decides on a course of action and recruits members from a cross-section of the organization. This Committee enlists the help of an external consultant to enable the implementation.

4. This Committee, with input from representative stakeholders, designs and develops an Interiority program that is adapted to the needs of the organization.

5. The consultant and HR Trainer conduct pilot Interiority Programs with a cross-section of workers, including stakeholder representatives.

6. The impact and results of the pilot programs are reviewed and appropriate adaptations are made to both the content and process.

7. A schedule is planned for the rollout of the program throughout the organization. The CEO communicates to the organization about the Interiority Program.

8. The Interiority Program is implemented with the emphasis on embedding the culture and practices throughout the organization and as much as possible with the stakeholders.

9. The Interiority Program is implemented continuously throughout with adaptations as conditions warrant.

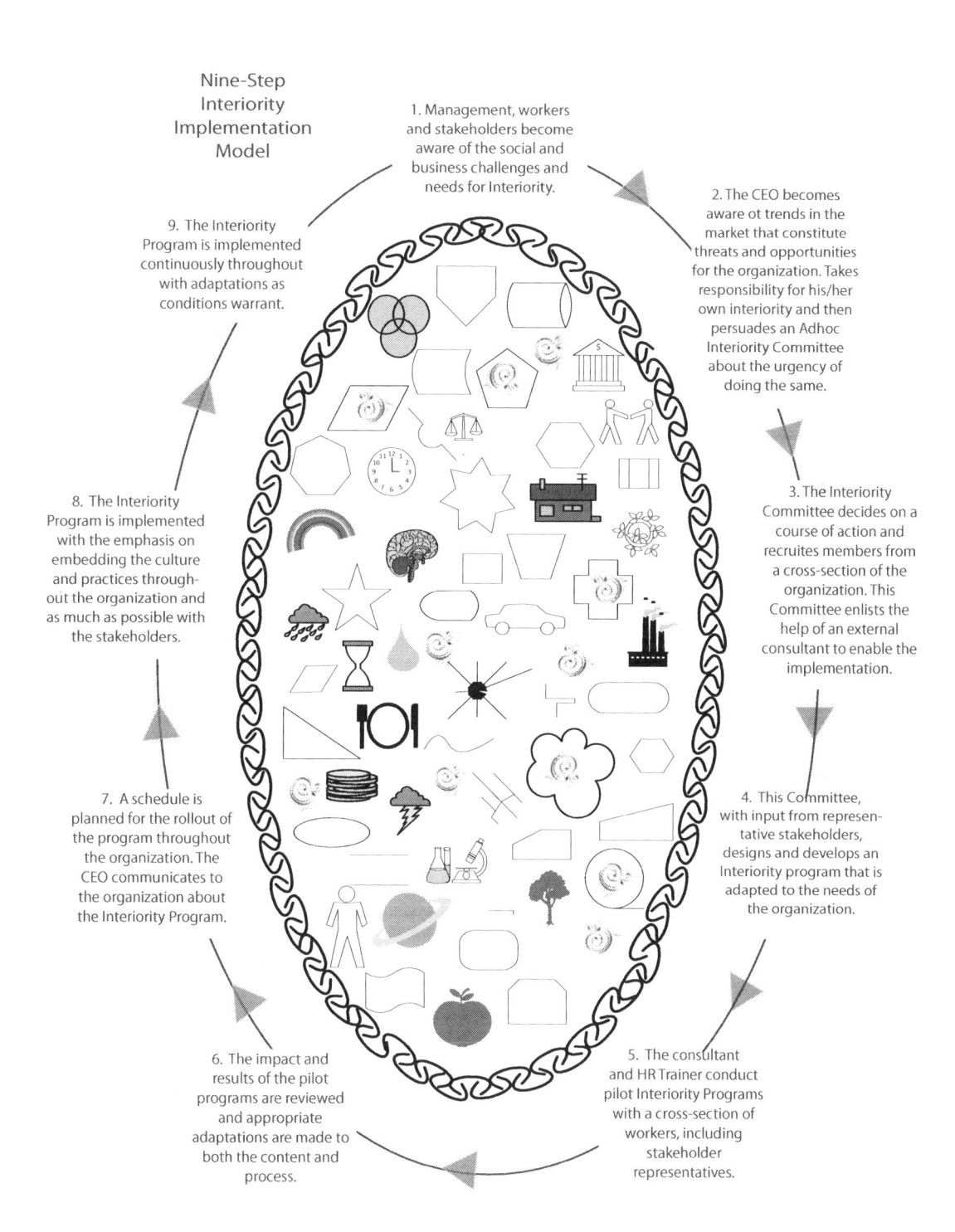

FIGURE 49: **NINE-STEP INTERIORITY IMPLEMENTATION MODEL**

In Figure 45, I present the foregoing nine steps in a visual model. In the outside oval, I present the steps themselves. In the inner oval, I present a visual representation of a variety of items that might influence the interactions of any group. Those dynamic energies must be taken into account in guiding the nine-step process.

Taking Heart

I often frighten myself. I do so when I get that shock of fear and despondency as I realize how little I know compared to what I would want to know and what I want to see happen in society. In moments like this, I recall the words, "Become the change you want to see in the world." I renew my energy and commitment to do that, but still I get frightened when I become aware of the continuous atrocities—even close to where I live. I frighten myself all over again when I recall how little I have done during my lifetime to alleviate the woes of the human community. I even become afraid at the impact of my carbon footprint on the environment.

For a moment, I take comfort at the great work of many good people and groups who are unapologetically working at improving the lot of their fellow man—to just get frightened all over again when I think of the structures of oppression that abuse and disinherit workers and citizens the world over. This becomes even more complex when I think of how difficult it is to change systems such as this, that exert the same oppressive influences that have taken place for centuries. Again, I take heart from the groundswell of resistance to this cruelty that helps people realize that their rights have been violated and their freedoms have been abused.

I take heart when I think of the movements to transfer power to the people and away from manipulative centers of control that take advantage of the ignorance of those they are supposed to serve but who serve only themselves. I take heart in the efforts of those who think of and work for the interests of the collective. I realize the only way to make viable the structures and activity of the human community is through constant efforts to raise the consciousness of that same community. In this way, I make my case for Interiority as the basis of such a movement. The human community needs such a consciousness. It is too often underserved by the religious communities and those entrusted with providing inspiration to the minds and hearts of all.

The workplaces are the temples, the work itself the sustenance, the relationships with co-workers—the support, and the context of growth and the hearts of the workers—the bases of hope for an earth and human community renewed.

CONCLUSION

Until we develop Interiority in ourselves at work, we are tempted to be distracted by the glitz of the market. Unless we develop our inner capacities for meaning at work, we are too easily diverted by the promises of the newest techno marvel. If we wait for circumstances—or others—to show us the way, we miss the potential wealth at the core of our beings. Until we invest in the core community of ourselves, we may not claim the world of our work as our sacred home.

These are possibilities for you and me to consider. These are the possibilities of Interiority at work.

Finis 6.17.13

About the Author

Hugh Leonard is Principal of Leonard Coaching, Training and Consulting of Los Angeles, California, USA. He has worked as an Executive Coach, Trainer and OD Consultant for a variety of clients, both locally in the U.S. and internationally for over 20 years. Regarding consulting for the theory and practice of Interiority, a good place to begin is his workshop called Life Integration Quest and Discovery, (LIQD) which he has conducted for small groups since 2004. Prior to beginning his professional life, he spent the most of 20 years as a Catholic priest and missionary in Japan and at the same time served 27 years as a member of a Catholic religious order. He has Masters Degrees in Asian Studies, Human Resource Development and Applied Theology and is a certified Executive Coach and Spiritual Director.

For this book, his website is www.interioritypowered.com. He welcomes your comments and questions on his blog. His other websites are www.nowwebecomeourselves.com and www.lifeintegrationquest.com. His e-mail is: hugh@hughleonard.com.

Endnotes

1. Drucker, Peter F. "The Rise of the Knowledge Society." *The Wilson Quarterly* 17.2 (1993): 52-+. Print.
2. Samuels, Alana. "*Productivity Is Up, Workers Worn down.*" *The Los Angeles Times* 20 Dec. 2009: 1. Print.
3. Coy, Peter, Michelle Conlin, and Moira Herbst. "*The Disposable Worker.*" *Business Week* 7 Jan. 2010. Print.
4. Soros, George. *A Chat with George Soros*. Newsweek, January 30, 2012. 56.
5. Gallup Management Journal. Gallup Study: Engaged Employees Inspire Company Innovation. 12 Oct. 2006.
6. Social Determinants of Health. The Solid Facts, Second Edition. Edited by Richard Wilkinson and Michael Marmot 18.
7. Stevens, Anthony. On Jung. London: Routledge, 1990, 250. Print.
8. Eiseley, Loren C. The Night Country: *Reflections of a Bone-hunting Man*. London: Garnstone, 1974. 137. Print.
9. Donne, John. "Meditation XVII." *The Literature Network: Online Classic Literature, Poems, and Quotes. Essays & Summaries*. The Literature Network. Web. 05 July 2011. <http://www.online-literature.com/donne/409/>.
10. Whitman, Walt. *Leaves of Grass*. New York: Modern Library, 1993. Print.
11. Hacker, Jacob S., and Paul Pierson. Winner-take-all Politics: *How Washington Made the Rich Richer-and Turned Its Back on the Middle Class*. New York: Simon & Schuster, 2010. Print.
12. Forster, E. M. Howards End. New York: Knopf, 1991. Print.
13. "Genesis 1 (Blue Letter Bible: KJV - King James Version)." Blue Letter Bible. 1996 – 2011. Web. 05 July 2011. <http://www.blueletterbible.org/Bible.cfm?b=Gen>.
14. Wessel, David. *The Factory Floor Has a Ceiling on Job Creation*. The Wall Street Journal, January 12, 2012. A6.
15. Miller, Laura. "SALON Features: David Foster Wallace." *Salon.com - Salon.com*. Salon, 1996. Web. 05 July 2011. <http://www.salon.com/09/features/wallace1.html>.
16. "The Internet Classics Archive | Theaetetus by Plato." *The Internet Classics Archive: 441 Searchable Works of Classical Literature*. The Internet Classics Archive. Web. 05 July 2011. <http://classics.mit.edu/Plato/theatu.html>.
17. Martin, Thomas R., Neel Smith, and Jennifer F. Stuart. "*Democracy in the Politics of Aristotle.*" *The Stoa Consortium*. Demos, 26 July 2006. Web. 05 July 2011. <http://www.stoa.org/projects/demos/article_aristotle_democracy?page=13>.
18. Applebaum, Herbert A. The Concept of Work: *Ancient, Medieval, and Modern*. Albany: State University of New York, 1992. 71. Print.
19. "Genesis 1 (Blue Letter Bible: KJV - King James Version)." Blue Letter Bible. 1996 – 2011. Web. 05 July 2011. <http://www.blueletterbible.org/Bible.cfm?b=Gen>.
20. Ibid. 3:23
21. Ibid. 3:19
22. "Paul's Epistle - 2 Thessalonians 3 - (KJV - King James Version)." Blue Letter Bible. 1996-2011. Web. 5 Jul 2011. < http://www.blueletterbible.org/Bible.cfm?b=2Th&c=3&t=KJV >
23. "Paul's Epistle - Colossians 3 - (KJV - King James Version)." Blue Letter Bible. 1996-2011. 5 Jul 2011. < http://www.blueletterbible.org/Bible.cfm?b=Col&c=3&t=KJV >
24. Applebaum, ibid, 193.
25. Applebaum, ibid, 189.

26. Applebaum, ibid, 321.
27. Applebaum, ibid, 188.
28. Applebaum, ibid, 287
29. Applebaum, ibid, 322.
30. Tilgher, Adriano. Work, *What It Has Meant to Men through the Ages*. London: G.G. Harrap, 1931. 47. Print.
31. Calvin, Jean. On the Christian Faith: *Selections from the Inst., Commentaries, and Tracts*. New York: Liberal Arts, 1957. Print.
32. "Protestant Work Ethic." *Wikipedia, the Free Encyclopedia*. Web. 05 July 2011. <http://en.wikipedia.org/wiki/Protestant_work_ethic>.
33. Ruether, Rosemary Radford. Gaia & God: *an Ecofeminist Theology of Earth Healing*. [San Francisco]: HarperSanFrancisco, 1992. 194. Print.
34. "Thomas Hobbes." *Oregon State University*. Web. 05 July 2011. <http://oregonstate.edu/instruct/phl302/philosophers/hobbes.html>.
35. Spittler, Gerd. Founders of the Anthropology of Work: *German Social Scientists of the 19th and Early 20th Centuries and the First Ethnographers*. Münster: LIT, 2008. Print.
36. Locke, John, and Peter Laslett. Two Treatises of Government. Cambridge [England: Cambridge UP, 1988. 314. Print.
37. Kramer, Matthew H. John Locke and the Origins of Private Property: *Philosophical Explorations of Individualism, Community, and Equality*. Cambridge, U.K.: Cambridge UP, 1997. Print.
38. Applebaum, ibid, 361.
39. Applebaum, ibid, 366.
40. Malone, Michael S. The Future Arrived Yesterday: *the Rise of the Protean Corporation and What It Means for You*. New York: Crown Business, 2009. 46 – 47. Print.
41. Kuczynski, Jürgen. France 1700 to the Present Day. London: Muller, 1946. 48. Print.
42. Tilgher, Adriano, Work: *What it has Meant to Men through the Ages*. Harcourt, Brace and Co., New York, 1930. 79.
43. Applebaum, ibid, 389.
44. Applebaum, ibid. 583.
45. Applebaum, ibid. 584.
46. Applebaum, ibid. 584.
47. Applebaum, ibid. 584.
48. Applebaum, ibid. 341.
49. Kolbert, Elizabeth. "*Why Work? A Hundred Years of The Protestant Ethic*." *The New Yorker* 29 Nov. 2004. Web.
50. Campbell, James M. "Hannah Arendt: *Prophet for Our Time*." *Religion-online.org*. Web. 5 July 2011. <http://www.religion-online.org/showchapter.asp?title=2074&C=1912>.
51. John, Paul. "Section 10." *Encyclical Laborem Exercens*. Homebush, N.S.W.: St. Paul Publications, 1981. Print.
52. John, Paul. Ibid. "Section 25.
53. Hopper, Kenneth, and W. J. Hopper. The Puritan Gift: *Reclaiming the American Dream amidst Global Financial Chaos*. London: I.B. Tauris, 2009. Print.
54. Ehrenreich, Barbara. Bright-sided: *How the Relentless Promotion of Positive Thinking Has Undermined America*. New York: Metropolitan, 2009. Print.
55. Ehrenreich, Ibid. 185.
56. Robert, Reich B. "*American Optimism and Consumer Confidence*." *The American Prospect* 18 Sept. 2001. Print.
57. Hill, Napoleon. Think and Grow Rich. New York, NY: Ballantine, 1996. Print.

58. Pilzer, Paul Zane. God Wants You to Be Rich: *the Theology of Economics*. New York: Simon & Schuster, 1995. Print.
59. Montgomery, David. Workers' Control in America: *Studies in the history of work, technology, and labor struggles*. Cambridge University Press, 1979, London, New York, Melbourne.
60. Abrams, John. Companies We Keep, *Employee Ownership and the Business of Community and Place*. Chelsea Green Publishing Company, VT, 2008.
61. Goleman, Daniel. Vital Lies, *Simple Truths: the Psychology of Self-deception*. New York: Simon and Schuster, 1985. Print.
62. Gardner, Howard. Five Minds for the Future. Boston, MA: Harvard Business School, 2006. 129. Print.
63. "Nearly 5 Percent Of U.S. Population Suffers From Persistent Depression Or Anxiety." *Science Daily: News & Articles in Science, Health, Environment & Technology*. Science Daily, 3 Dec. 2008. Web. 06 July 2011.
64. Yeats, W. B. Sailing to Byzantium, *Immortal Poems of the English Language*, Washington Square Press, New York, NY, P. 490. Print.
65. Auden, W.H. The Age of Anxiety, a Baroque Eclogue. New York, Random House, 1947. Print.
66. Capra, Fritjof. The Turning Point: *Science, Society, and the Rising Culture*. New York: Simon and Schuster, 1982. Print.
67. Jung, C. G. The Structure and Dynamics of the Psyche. [Princeton, N.J.]: Princeton UP, 1969. Print.
68. Hollis, James. On This Journey We Call Our Life: *Living the Questions*. Toronto, Ont.: Inner City, 2003. 91. Print.
69. Swimme, Brian. The Hidden Heart of the Cosmos: *Humanity and the New Story*. Maryknoll, NY: Orbis, 2004. 110. Print.
70. Swimme, Brian, and Thomas Berry. The Universe Story: *from the Primordial Flaring Forth to the Ecozoic Era—a Celebration of the Unfolding of the Cosmos*. [San Francisco, Calif.]: HarperSan Francisco, 1992. 226. Print.
71. Swimme and Berry, Ibid. 66.
72. Joyce, James. A Portrait of the Artist as a Young Man. New York: Viking, 1964. Print.
73. Swimme and Berry, Ibid, 74.
74. Gell-Mann, Murray. The Quark and the Jaguar: *Adventures in the Simple and the Complex*. New York: W.H. Freeman, 1994. Print.
75. Benyus, Janine M. Biomimicry: *Innovation Inspired by Nature*. New York: Morrow, 1997. Print.
76. Wheatley, Margaret J. Leadership and the New Science: *Discovering Order in a Chaotic World*. San Francisco: Berrett-Koehler, 1999. Print.
77. Surowiecki, James. The Wisdom of Crowds. New York: Anchor, 2005. 3. Print.
78. *Dartmouth College*. Web. 06 July 2011.
79. Malone, Michael S. The Future Arrived Yesterday: *the Rise of the Protean Corporation and What It Means for You*. New York: Crown Business, 2009. Print.
80. Hayes, Tom. Jump Point: *How Network Culture Is Revolutionizing Business*. New York: McGraw-Hill, 2008. Print.
81. Malone, Ibid. 28.
82. Malone, Ibid. 34.
83. Malone, Ibid. 33.
84. Malone, Ibid. xiii.
85. Malone, Ibid. 10.
86. Hayes, Ibid. 70.
87. Hayes, Ibid. 70.
88. Hayes, Ibid. 141.

89. Hayes, Ibid. 163.
90. Hayes, Ibid. 172.
91. Hayes, Ibid. 177.
92. Lewin, Roger, and Birute Regine. The Soul at Work: Listen, Respond, Let Go : Embracing Complexity Science for Business Success. New York: Simon & Schuster, 2000. 38. Print.
93. Jonas, Hans, and Lawrence Vogel. Mortality and Morality: a Search for the Good after Auschwitz. Evanston, IL: Northwestern UP, 1996. Print.
94. Groves, Chris. Teleology Without Telos: Deleuze and Jonas on the Living Future. 2006. TS. Mittel-Europa Foundation, Bolzano, Italy. Causality and Motivation Workshop. Web. 11 July 2011.
95. Berry, Thomas. The Great Work: Our Way into the Future. New York: Bell Tower, 1999. 169. Print.
96. Berry, Ibid. 170.
97. Johnston, William. Silent Music: the Science of Meditation. New York: Harper & Row, 1974. 55. Print.
98. Johnston, Ibid. 56.
99. Johnston, Ibid. 64.
100. Saint-Exupéry, Antoine De, and Katherine Woods. The Little Prince. San Diego: Harcourt Brace Jovanovich, 1982. Print.
101. Wheatley, Margaret J. Leadership and the New Science: Discovering Order in a Chaotic World. San Francisco: Berret-Koehler, 2006. 129. Print.
102. Hendricks, Gay, and Kate Ludeman. The Corporate Mystic: A Guidebook for Visionaries with Their Feet on the Ground. New York: Bantam Books, 1996. xix. Print.
103. Hsieh, Tony. Delivering Happiness: A Path to Profits, Passion, and Purpose. New York: Business Plus, 2010. Print.
104. Berry, Thomas. The Great Work: Our Way into the Future. New York: Bell Tower, 1999. 162. Print.
105. Chandler, Steve, and Duane Black. The Hands-Off Manager: How to Mentor People and Allow Them to Be Successful. Franklin Lakes, NJ: Career Press, 2007. Internet resources.
106. Quinlan, Joseph P. The Last Economic Superpower: The Retreat of Globalization, the End of American Dominance, and What We Can Do About It. Maidenhead: McGraw-Hill Professional, 2010. Print.
107. Abrams, Ibid. Foreword, pg. 105.
108. Ibid. 282
109. Ibid. 282.
110. Buechner, Frederick. Wishful Thinking: A Seeker's Abc. San Francisco, Calif.: HarperSanFrancisco, 1993. 119. Print.
111. Appleby, Joyce O. The Relentless Revolution: A History of Capitalism. New York, NY: W.W. Norton & Co, 2010. 80. Print.
112. Ibid.
113. Ibid. 86.
114. Ibid.
115. Dürckheim, Karlfried. The Way of Transformation: Daily Life As Spiritual Practice. Sandpoint, ID: Morning Light Press, 2007. 85. Print.
116. Swimme, Brian, and Thomas Berry. The Universe Story: From the Primordial Flaring Forth to the Ecozoic Era-a Celebration of the Unfolding of the Cosmos. San Francisco, Calif.: HarperSan Francisco, 1992. 70. Print.
117. Jung, C G, Herbert Read, Michael Fordham, Gerhard Adler, Lisa Ress, Barbara Forryan, Janet M. Glover, and William McGuire. The Collected Works of C. G. Jung. London: Routledge & Kegan Paul, 1989. Print.
118. Johnson, Robert A. Owning Your Own Shadow. HarperSanFrancisco, 1993. 18. Print.

119. Ibid. 26.
120. Smallwood, Jonathan, Daniel Fishman, and Jonathan Schooler. "*Counting the Cost of an Absent Mind: Mind Wandering as an Under-recognized Influence on Educational Performance.*" Psychonomic Bulletin & Review 14.2 (2007): 230. Print.
121. Jung, Carl G, and Richard F. C. Hull. *The Collected Works: Volume 16*. London: Routledge & Kegan Paul, 1954. Print.
122. Burns, Robert. "*To a Mouse.*" *The World Burns Club*. World Ferderation. Web. 12 July 2011. <http://www.worldburnsclub.com/poems/translations/554.htm>.
123. Keats, John. "*When I Have Fears That I May Cease to Be.* John Keats. The Oxford Book of English Verse.*" Bartleby.com: Great Books Online — Quotes, Poems, Novels, Classics and Hundreds More. Web. 12 July 2011. <http://www.bartleby.com/101/635.html>.
124. Williams, Oscar. *Immortal Poems of the English Language: British and American Poetry from Chaucer's Time to the Present Day*. New York: Washington Square, 1965. 489. Print.
125. Sharpnack, Rayona. Trade Up!: *Five Steps for Redesigning Your Leadership and Life from the Inside Out*. San Francisco: Jossey-Bass, 2007. Print.
126. Bohm, David. Wholeness and the Implicate Order. London: Routledge & Kegan Paul, 1981. Print.
127. O'Neill, Thomas P. A Thomas Merton Reader. New York, NY: Image, 1989. 506. Print.
128. Campbell, Joseph. The Hero with a Thousand Faces. New York: Pantheon Books, 1949. Print.
129. Thompson, Helen. Journey Toward Wholeness: *A Jungian Model of Adult Spiritual Growth*. New York: Paulist Press, 1982. 23. Print.
130. Frost, Robert. The Road Not Taken, *and Other Poems*. New York: Dover Publications, 1993. Print.
131. Liukkonen, Petri. "Christina Rosetti." *Www.kirjasto.sci.fi*. 2008. Web. 12 July 2011. <http://www.kirjasto.sci.fi/rossetti.htm>.
132. "Employee Engagement Survey: The Gallup Q12." *Survey Research & Enterprise Feedback Management | Voice of Vovici Blog*. Web. 12 July 2011. <http://blog.vovici.com/blog/bid/18535/Employee-Engagement-Survey-The-Gallup-Q12>.
133. Jackson, Maggie. Distracted: *The Erosion of Attention and the Coming Dark Age*. Amherst, N.Y: Prometheus Books, 2008. 26. Print.
134. Fromm, Erich. Escape from Freedom. New York: Farrar & Rinehart, Inc, 1941. 36-37. Print.
135. Johnson, Barry. Polarity Management: *Identifying and Managing Unsolvable Problems*. Amherst, Mass: HRD Press, 1992. Print.
136. Shakespeare, William, Tucker Brooke, and Jack R. Crawford. *The Tragedy of Hamlet, Prince of Denmark*. New Haven: Yale University Press, 1947. Print.
137. Pink, Daniel H. Drive: *The Surprising Truth About What Motivates Us*. New York, NY: Riverhead Books, 2009. Print.
138. Gabler, Neal. "*Disincentivizing Greed.*" *Los Angeles Times*. 22 Aug. 2010. Web. 12 July 2011. <http://articles.latimes.com/2010/aug/22/opinion/la-oe-gabler-greed-20100822>.
139. Samuels, Allison. "*Tyson Is the Hero of New Film. But Not to Himself* - Newsweek." *Newsweek - National News, World News, Business, Health, Technology, Entertainment, and More - Newsweek*. Web. 12 July 2011. <http://www.newsweek.com/2009/04/10/a-fighter-disarmed.html>.
140. Goldsmith, Marshall, and Mark Reiter. Mojo: *How to Get It, How to Keep It, How to Get It Back If You Lose It*. New York: Hyperion, 2009. 165. Print.
141. Kolind, Lars. The Second Cycle: *Winning the War against Bureaucracy*. Upper Saddle River, N.J: Wharton School Pub, 2006. 67. Print.
142. "Cloud Computing." *Wikipedia, the Free Encyclopedia*. Web. 12 July 2011. <http://en.wikipedia.org/wiki/Cloud_computing>.
143. Crick, Francis. The Astonishing Hypothesis: *The Scientific Search for the Soul*. New York: Scribner, 1994. 31. Print.
144. Henley, Don and Stanley Lynch, from the lyrics of, *Learn to be Still*, from the album, *Hell Freezes Over*.

145. Dürckheim, Karlfried. Hara: *The Vital Centre of Man*. Rochester, Vermont: Allen, 1962. 121. Print.
146. Lam, Kam C. The Way of Energy: *Mastering the Chinese Art of Internal Strength with Chi Kung Exercise*. New York: Simon & Schuster, 1991. Print.
147. Ibid. 42.
148. Ibid. 42-43.
149. Kalichi. Dance, Words and Soul. Ireland: Kalichi, 2001. 17. Print
150. Uchiyama, Kōshō, Thomas Wright, Jishō C. Warner, and Shohaku Okumura. Opening the Hand of Thought: *Foundations of Zen Buddhist Practice*. Boston: Wisdom Publications, 2004. 42 – 45. Print.
151. Yeats, William Butler. "*Long-Legged Fly*." *Welcome to Web Books Publishing*. Web. 12 July 2011. <http://www.web-books.com/Classics/Poetry/Anthology/Yeats/Long-Legged.htm>.
152. Lam, Kam C. The Way of Energy: *Mastering the Chinese Art of Internal Strength with Chi Kung Exercise*. New York: Simon & Schuster, 1991. 30 -31. Print.
153. Johnson, Robert A. Inner Work, *Using Dreams & Active Imagination for Personal Growth*. HarperSanFrancisco, A Division of HarperCollins Publishers, New York, 1986, P. 161. Print,
154. Zweig, Connie and Abrams, Jeremiah. Meeting the Shadow, The Hidden Power of the Dark Side of Human Nature. New York: Jeremy P. Tarcher / Penguin, 1991
155. Ornstein, Robert E. The Psychology of Consciousness. New York: Harcourt Brace Jovanovich, 1977. Print.
156. Johnston, William. Ibid. 90.
157. Stevens, Anthony, On Jung, *An Updated Edition with a reply to Jung's Critics*. Princeton University Press, New Jersey, 1999, P. 40. Print.
158. "Complex (psychology)." *Wikipedia, the Free Encyclopedia*. Web. 12 July 2011. <http://en.wikipedia.org/wiki/Complex_(psychology)>.
159. Neibuhr, Reinhold. "*Serenity Prayer* (full Text)." *Winternet™ - a BPSI.NET Company*. Web. 12 July 2011. <http://www.winternet.com/~terrym/serenity.html>.
160. Fromm, Erich. The Art of Loving. New York: Harper, 1956. 23. Print.

Glossary

360° (Degree Assessment): A 360° assessment means an instrument, (inventory, questionnaire) that is used by coaches or trainers to assess the capabilities or issues that people face in the execution of their job. Part of the assessment process is to ask, at least, nine individuals to complete the instrument on the individual in question. The people who complete the instrument are chosen from a range of individuals who occupy positions such as a supervisor, co-workers or subordinates. The questions included in the assessment instrument usually deal with the individual's skills in such areas as leadership, communications, problem-solving, job knowledge, etc.

Affirmation: The word affirmation comes from the Latin affirmare, which means to make firm, to strengthen, to make strong. Affirmation comes in many forms and those that are of interest to us are: Affirming the self – This type of affirmation implies a deep appreciation for life and a continuing sense of gratitude for the experiences life brings. Affirming the other – This type means the acceptance of the goodness of the other as he/she is. Affirmation reflects the goodness of the other to him/her. Victor Hugo says in *Les Miserables*: "Man lives by affirmation even more than he does by bread."

Archetype: "The idea of archetypes is an ancient one. It is related to Plato's concept of ideal forms: patterns already existing in the divine mind that determine in swhat form the material world will come into being. But we owe to Jung the concept of the psychological archetype: the characteristic patterns that pre-exist in the collective psyche of the human race, that repeat themselves eternally in the psyches of individual human beings and determine the basic ways that we perceive and function as psychological beings." Robert Johnson, *Inner Work*. P. 27.

Authenticity: The word authenticity refers to something that is genuine, not fake or false. In legal terms, the word refers to something that is legitimate. For our purposes, authenticity refers to that quality of a person's self-presentation that establishes them as genuine, truthful, frank and forthcoming in his/her expression.

Awareness: Awareness means having an abiding knowledge of something from having observed it, been told about it, experienced it, or sensed it through one's intuition. Here we focus on intentionally expanding our awareness of the influence that we have on the evolving consciousness of the universe and living our lives in accordance with that goal.

Barrier: A barrier (stumbling-block, wall) is something that obstructs or separates, often by emphasizing differences. Here, we are speaking of barriers to inner change in people. Often, we are not aware of the barrier that is preventing change from happening. That barrier may consist of anxieties, fears, projections, etc.

Becoming: The term "becoming" refers to the state of something coming into existence. Since everything is made of energy and is in constant movement; everything is in a state of becoming something it was not.

Being: The term "being" refers to the state of something existing in the present. A human being refers to an individual person. Being can also refer to somebody's essential nature or character.

Belief: A belief means acceptance by the mind that something is true or real, often underpinned by an emotional or spiritual sense of certainty. Beliefs also can refer to a statement, principle, or doctrine that a person or group accepts as true.

Call: A call is an invitation from life to serve, to activate your will toward a cause worthy of you and the community to which you belong. A call is sometimes heard as an inner voice that urges one to pursue something that is of lasting value.

Capitalism: Capitalism, which is also called free market economy, or a free enterprise economic system has been dominant in the Western world since the breakup of feudalism. In the capitalistic system, most of the means of production are privately owned and production is guided and income distributed largely through the operation of markets.

Center: When we use the word, Center, we do not use it solely in its physical meaning of the fixed point at the core. In our context, we use the word, Center, as the "center of our individual life, our driving force, reason and purpose." Karlfried Graf Durckheim, *The Way of Transformation*, p. 84.

Centering: Centering means to go to the center of things and that is the center of ourselves. If we can rest in the center of our consciousness, then we are in a position to accept ourselves and all things as they are. By centering in ourselves momentarily, we become able to live out the fullness of who we are.

Centering Practice: Centering practice means the discipline of going to the center of ourselves for at least five minutes and up to 30 minutes or more each day. This discipline involves the practice of becoming silent and still and locating one's awareness at the core of oneself. In this practice, we are leaving all other activities and engaging only with the core of our self. Because of the nature of our senses, minds and emotions, it is most difficult to just quietly be within our self. Nevertheless, the effort to be still and silent is what is important. This practice can be done by assuming any of the traditional physical positions associated with sitting or walking meditation and can be accomplished by oneself or with a group of people.

Centered Person: A person who is centered, refers to an individual who is acting from a place within themselves. That place is usually not the location of conceptual thinking, rather it means the source of a combination of beliefs, values, thoughts, intuitions and reflected-upon experiences that allows the individual to make decisions based on his/her own inner frame of reference.

Chaos: On one level, chaos denotes a state of disorder. However, the chaos that we are interested in refers to chaos as "a fermenting ground for creative order." O'Murchu, *Evolutionary Faith, p. 108*. This means that in the process of integrating our life, we might well embrace the cycle of life-death-rebirth, (a seemingly chaotic state), that signals the emergence of new and more complex life forms of which we are one example. If we can live in a comfortable relationship with the often chaotic circumstances of life, we will arrive at a wisdom that will promote our positive engagement with the world in whatever state we find it.

Character: What does it mean to have character? It means having values upon which one makes decisions. It means having a moral compass that sets clear parameters for what one will and will not do.

Coaching: Coaching refers to the practice of engaging with a person, who facilitates learning and implementing behavioral changes, which result in more developed abilities for that person or organization to function. A coach is someone trained to guide others toward increased competence and commitment in the performance of their work.

Collective (Unconscious): The ordinary meaning of the term refers to that which belongs to a group. The "collective," may also refer to such usage as: collective farm. In our context, we refer to the Jungian concept of the collective unconscious, which points to the existence of, "a vast psychic groundwork that is shared by all humanity." *(Gerald G. May, Care of Mind, Care of Spirit, 1992, p. 52).*

Complexity: According to Peter Senge, (the Harvard-based expert in management and organizational systems), there are two types of complexity, (1) detail complexity, (2) dynamic complexity. He maintains that the real leverage in most management situations lies in understanding dynamic complexity, not detail complexity. Dynamic complexity refers to situations where cause and effect are subtle, and where the effects over time of interventions are not obvious. Further, he says that, "for most people, 'systems thinking,' means "fighting complexity with complexity." Complexity in our usage of the term is not about things becoming more complicated. Complexity is about life itself becoming more enriched through the interactions of everything on everything else in varied and diverse ways.

Community – the Human Community: The human community refers to all of those interconnected communities of our time. The implication is that we belong to the human community because our actions have an impact on all other parts of the community. All people are communitarian by their very nature. It is especially true that we are connected to others when we live on a deep level in our inner lives. What we do in that inner core of our self is done to others and vice versa. What others do in that inner core reverberates into our lives and influences the quality of our lives.

Conflict: Conflict, in general, means a disagreement or clash between ideas, principles or people. Inner conflict can mean a psychological state resulting from the often unconscious opposition between simultaneous but incompatible desires, needs, drives, or impulses.

Conflict Resolution: Conflict resolution, in general, means the process of resolving something such as a problem or dispute. In our context, conflict resolution means to work with an individual or a group (system) to resolve the issues that created or gave rise to the conflict in the first place.

Contribution: Contribution in our sense of the term means that we find the purpose for which we are alive and proceed to live and work in accordance with that end. In this way, we make the contribution for which we are in the world, at this time, as the person we are.

Consciousness: On one level, consciousness means the state of being awake and aware of what is going on around oneself. In the context of this book, we are using consciousness in its more developmental aspect so that we understand our own constantly expanding awareness and ability to use our intuitive imagination for enhanced productivity at work. On another level it means awareness of or sensitivity to a particular issue. In the context of Interiority, consciousness assumes an extended meaning in that we posit the reality of a universe that is expanding in its consciousness of itself. If the quality of our awareness is comparatively profound, then our influence on the evolving consciousness of the universe is comparatively profound.

Codependency: Involves a pattern of thinking, feeling and behaving that looks to others or an organization for a sense of identity and self-worth.

Creativity: The ability to use one's inspiration, knowledge, skills and imagination to develop new and original ideas, products and services. Creativity is not only an action that is done by the individual acting alone. Creativity arises also out of the need of the moment for some solution. Creativity arises from within when one has lost one's ego investment in the outcome. It happens then that without such ego-based barriers, the creative energies flow in unforeseen or unimagined ways. Creativity arises from within one's core connection to the source of one's life. In that way, the individual becomes but a tool, as it were, for the music of the cosmos to sound or become the service that the human community needed to hear. Creative people refer to this sounding up from the depths of themselves as their muse.

Culture: Every society, family and group develops a culture out of the ways that they have for surviving, managing their tasks and making progress. Every culture, therefore, is a repository of all of the creative ways that people have devised in the tasks of living. Every culture then is necessary so that all cultures can avail of the richness of all the unique cultures of the human community.

Death: Death, for a living being, means to cease to exist in our physical form. Death comes to all living things. However, the meaning of death is much deeper than that which is referred to in one's physical demise. The real meaning of death means to accept, in a radical way, the limitations of one's existence and to embrace the moments in which we are present with deeply held awareness.

Deflection: Like all other forms of resistance, deflection is a way people have of protecting themselves. For example, deflection is a way that people have of changing the subject because they do not want to deal with the topic. Deflection is usually unconscious and not a strategic choice.

Denial: When I am in denial, I reject that a specific experience, insights, behavior or situation exists. People put their heads in the sand and refuse to see that things are different from what is objectively real.

Development: Development refers to the process of becoming larger, stronger, or more impressive, successful, mature, or advanced, or of causing somebody or something to change in these ways.

Discernment: Discernment means the process of uncovering the deeper meaning of one's experiences. Discernment in the context of Spiritual Direction usually refers to the uncovering of the inspirations that seem to be coming from the Spirit within. Discernment is oriented to understanding the source of the inspirations and whether they come from a spiritual source that is benign or toxic in terms of the impact on the individual concerned.

Discovery: Discovery means the process or act of finding out something that is of great importance about oneself, unexpectedly, which fundamentally changes the way one looks at life subsequent to that experience.

Dialogue: Dialogue is a way of finding common meaning through words, which lead to the deeper encounter of the people involved. Dialogue slows the conversation down so that the underlying assumptions, world views and values of each other can be heard. Dialogue is that address and response between persons in which there is a flow of meaning between them in spite of all the obstacles that normally would block the relationship.

Emergent: Refers to the coming into existence of something new from a confluence of elements that self-organize to form a complex whole. In our context, the word refers to the coming into being of our self from the experiences of our past, our call and our potential to make a contribution to the emergence of everything else.

Empowerment: Empowerment, in its simplest form, means to give somebody power or authority. Empowerment also means to enable someone else to have a greater sense of confidence or self-esteem. Empowerment in an organization means building a culture in which people take responsibility for themselves, the organization and the stakeholders and generate results accordingly.

Encounter: According to the dictionary meaning, the term encounter means to be faced with something difficult to deal with. In our context, the term means a meeting that is much more benign in its qualities and has a more profound impact on us, usually for the better. In an encounter with another, we are usually transformed in some positive way. Here, we use this term, encounter, according to the latter meaning.

Environment: Environment means the immediate surroundings of somebody or something, including events, circumstances, scenery, conditions, people and objects. In our context, we focus on the influence that we absorb, mostly unconsciously, from the people in our immediate surroundings.

Energy: The primal substance from which everything comes into being and which drives our activities, our being and becoming. Theologian Peter Hodgson, (1940) defines energy as "a primal, alluring, relational force."

Evil: Evil is referred to as the thoughts or acts that are profoundly immoral or wrong. Evil can be done to a greater or lesser degree. However, the evil is greater depending on whether it was done full knowledge, deliberately and caused great harm, pain or upset. It is possible to participate in evil by being active or by being passive while evil is being done with our knowledge.

Evolution: In scientific literature, this word tends to be used in a Darwinian sense, indicating the gradual emergence of species over time,s largely determined by natural selection or the "survival of the fittest," to use the more colloquial term. In popular writing,s evolution usually refers to the unfolding of cosmic and planetary creation over billions of years.

Experiences: Our experiences are the events that happen to us and within us as we live every moment of every day. The significance of our experiences can only be understood by ourselves when we reflect back on what happened to us and within us. We can understand the full impact of our experiences on ourselves when we reflect on the patterns of our lives that seem to appear with some regularity.

Guilt: An awareness of having done wrong or committed a crime, accompanied by feelings of shame and regret. Guilt may also mean the responsibility, as determined by a court or other legal authority, for committing an offense that carries a legal penalty. In our context, guilt is the burden on our conscience that we carry because we are part of some systems that have a seriously negative impact on the members of the human community. Recognition and acceptance of guilt for the wrong that we have done or participated in is the first step toward the reconciliation necessary for comfort in our inner life and in the community in which we participate.

Healing: To define healing, it is necessary to make a distinction between healing and curing. Curing refers to restoring efficient functioning to a body suffering from illness. Curing arises from the disease model of medicine. Healing, in the larger context, means making the connection within ourselves that will increase our love for ourselves and others. The power to heal is one of the powers that we have within us, as humans. We can heal ourselves by our reflective choices when we opt for wholeness rather than a restrictive view of our life. Healing has to do with meaning that comes through a certain insight into suffering. Healing does not mean that the suffering will end but that we may finish one painful episode and be better able to withstand another.

Heart: The term heart, in general, refers to the physical organ that pumps the blood throughout any living organism. In our context, the heart means the center of the emotional life of a person. The heart is a symbol of empathy, nurturing, caring, giving, love, among other human characteristics. To be a person with a "big heart," one is assumed to have a generous nature and to be generous in one's behavior. However, anything can be assumed to have "heart" if there is a perception that there is some warm human feeling about it.

Humanism: Humanism is a broad category of philosophies that affirm the dignity and worth of all people, based on the ability to determine right and wrong by appeal to universal human qualities — particularly our capacity for rational thought. Humanism entails a commitment to the search for truth and morality through human means in support of human interests. In some forms of humanism, there is a focus on the capacity for self-determination. In this way, humanism rejects the validity of justifications that appeal to a transcendent being. Not all forms of humanism focus on a rejection of the supernatural.

Identity: Identity means the set of characteristics that somebody recognizes as belonging uniquely to himself or herself and constituting his or her individual personality for life. In our context, for the growth, maturation and wholeness of the individual to take place, they have to become aware, in some way of their own unique, personal identity.

Institution: One meaning of the term institution is a large organization that is influential in the community, e.g. a college, hospital or bank. Another meaning of the term institution is an established law, custom or practice. The word institution can also be used to mean a person who has been well known and established in a place for a long time. In our context, institution means all of the systems that are part of how we live, work and manage our lives.

Integration: Integration means the process of bringing together disparate experiences, learnings and wisdom into one consciously-acting self-presentation. The word integration is derived from the Latin word integer, meaning **whole**. Being whole is what we seek when we yearn for and work at achieving a unity of all the elements and forces within ourselves. When we work at the integration of our self, we turn our attention to what brings everything that we have been, are now and will be into one unified presence of which we are conscious.

Interiority: In our use of the term, Interiority is the capacity of people at work to be aware of and be able to use the resources of their inner world for their own satisfaction, development, creativity and productivity at work. A second dimension of the term Interiority is the characteristic of all matter (energy), which exhibits a purposeful orientation toward increased consciousness and complexity.

Intervention: Intervention means to enter into an ongoing system of relationships, to come between or among persons, groups or stakeholders, for the purpose of helping them achieve the goals for which they are together. In our context, the kind of intervention that we speak of means to conduct a series of structured activities that have as their aim, the resolution of the issue in the systems that support the individuals or groups concerned.

Journey: In this book, we refer to the inner journey that is made up of the many journeys we make toward becoming mature in the course of our lifetime. These journeys bring about shifts in perception and awareness of where we are in our growth toward ourselves. Some of these journeys are chosen but most are forced upon us by the changes that we experience as we move through the seasons of our life.

Judgment: Judgment is about more than decision-making. It is not only coming up with the right solution to the right problem; it is also about producing results in a way that achieves balance between competing needs.

Legacy: The term legacy is associated with something that is handed down or remains from a previous generation or time. In our context, we focus on what an individual might want to contribute, as their "legacy" to future generations. Our context also keeps its focus more on the inner qualities of the person than on any external contribution that they might make.

Life: Life in our context refers to the 'examined life,' of Socrates or the life reflected upon, for the purpose of our maturation as a person. To taste life means that we encounter the core of our self, for the development of which we are born and live out our days in search of fulfillment.

Love : Eric Fromm describes love in this way: "Love is an active power in man; a power which breaks through the walls which separates man from his fellow man, unites him with others; love makes him overcome the sense of isolation and separateness, yet it permits him to be himself, to retain his integrity."

Maturity: Maturity means the state of being fully grown, ripe or developed, especially mentally, emotionally and spiritually.

Meaning: In our context, meaning is not something abstract but is something that is a byproduct of a life that is fully experienced, that is, well lived. Meaning is derived through an enlarged consciousness about what matters to the development of oneself and a commitment to living according to those things that really matter. Meaning is the awareness which we gain when we realize that our lives have significance, worth, integrity and is a contribution to the emerging community of all things. We are meaning-seeking beings and we can make our own meaning by doing the work of becoming whole as the person we are called to be. More often than not, our moments of potentially deepest meaning, come to our awareness through the chaotic circumstances in which we find ourselves as well as through various experiences of pain and suffering.

Mystery: The ordinary meaning of mystery means an event or situation that is difficult to understand or explain. However, the mystery that we speak of is something beyond our understanding but toward which we have a relationship. Mystery means the astonishing gift of life in all its wonders and contradictions and in which we are privileged to be a part. Living in relationship to mystery means to have a well-developed sense of the central mystery of our self.

Myth: A myth is a story set in a time and place outside history, describing in fictional form the fundamental truths of nature and human life. Such a story about heroes or supernatural beings is often attempting to explain the origins of natural phenomena or aspects of human behavior.

Ownership: Ownership is the personal and emotional investment that we make in our work. Ownership means much more than the literal notion of owning some part of the organization or product. If we take responsibility for all the good that results from the product or service that we provide, then we are taking ownership of the much wider context than the fulfillment of our immediate needs.

Paradox: A paradox is a statement, proposition or situation that seems to be absurd or contradictory, but in fact is or may be true. In our context, the paradoxes of life are part of the challenge of living. Those who embrace the paradoxical nature of life are probably able to derive real wisdom and creativity from such acceptance of the way things are.

Performance: A worker's performance is the degree to which they accomplish work requirements. Organizational performance is the degree that is reflected in the organization's success in achieving its goals. Human performance is a function of both the behavior and accomplishment of a person or group of people. Performance includes the actions of a person or people and the result of the action or actions. However, the performance that we refer to here is mainly about our ability to live a human life at work. That means to have a self, to take a position with regard to the mystery of which we are all a part, to be able to relate to others, to have a purpose in life and to seek to derive meaning in all of life's experiences.

Philosophy: In general, the term philosophy means the branch of knowledge or academic study devoted to the systematic examination of basic concepts such as truth, existence, reality, causality and freedom. In our context, philosophy is less theoretical and more apt to be used in ordinary life circumstances. However, sour usage is different from the term pragmatism. Pragmatism means a philosophical view that a theory or concept should be evaluated in terms of how it works and its consequences as the standard for action and thought.

Prayer: The general definition of prayer is a spoken or unspoken address to God, a deity or a saint. It may express praise, thanksgiving, confession or a request for something such as help, or somebody's well-being. In our context, the fundamental prayer is a person's orientation to living his/her life so that he/she achieves the purpose for which he/she is alive at this time and place and with the unique personhood with which he/she is gifted.

Principle: One definition of a principle is an important underlying law or assumption required in a system of thought. Another is a standard for moral or ethical decision-making. We use the word principle to indicate the standards whereby we conduct our coaching and Interiority-at-Work interventions or workshops.

Productivity: Productivity refers to the rate at which a company produces goods or services, in relation to the amount of materials and number of employees needed.

Purpose: Purpose, as used here, refers to the reason for which one is alive. Purpose is found within us and is discovered through reflection on our accumulated experiences. Having a clear purpose means that we have a motivational resource that provides a sense of direction and the energies to achieve our goals in life.

Quest: A quest means a difficult search for something of great value. Usually, a quest is not about material things but about such qualities of personhood as wisdom, integrity and involvement in causes that have a deep meaning and value for the world and the human community.

Question: A question usually involves a request for information or a response with some kind of answer. In our context, the questions are usually those that do not have definitive answers but require reflection that tends to deepen our awareness of what is important in life and living.

Reflection: One meaning of the term is the image of somebody or something that appears in a mirror or other reflecting surface. Another meaning of the term reflection is that which involves careful thought, especially through the process of reconsidering previous actions, events or decisions. It is in this kind of reflection that we can discover some valuable insight that enables us to live with greater clarity about what is important and appreciation for that with which we have been gifted.

Religion: The derivation of the word religion is the Latin language word, *religare*. This means to bind back or to bind to. In general, the term religion means anything relating to belief in religion, the teaching of religion or the practice of a religion.

Relationality: I use this term to denote the characteristic of everything being interconnected. This quality of always being in relationship with everything else is the foundation of authentic truth, learning and growth in our individual selves. Relationality refers to all things, especially our co-workers, representing truth in their whole being more than in what they say. Relationality reminds us to do (enact) the truth rather than merely to describe what truth might be.

Relationship: We are born into a community and we grow to become our own person through the significant relationships that we experience throughout the journeys of our lives. Because we are creatures that are born from the earth, we are basically relational in our essential being. We are never completely independent or totally an individual.

Resistance: Resistance is a force that slows or stops movement. Seen in a different light, resistance is energy. Resistance can also provide protection in case of danger. If we consider the properties of physics, we can understand that resistance is a natural part of any change. People feel resistance because of internal or external obstacles. Internal obstacles include anxieties, fears, outdated negative messages and ingrained habits. External obstacles include accidents, diseases and catastrophes.

Responsibility: We are responsible for the contribution of our lives, both on the micro scale of our immediate interpersonal relationships, and on the macro scale of our relationship with the universe to which we belong and our place in it.

SRM (Stakeholder Relationship Model): SRM refers to the way of thinking and acting of organizations and executives that put the emphasis on the needs of all of the stakeholders rather than just the profit-needs of the shareholders. In an expanded view of SRM, the concept includes many humanistic and spirit-based activities that empower the stakeholders to improve their lives and gain satisfaction from interacting with organizations that practice SRM.

Sacred: The meaning of sacred is that which is worthy of or regarded with veneration, worship and respect, usually within a religious context. Another meaning of the word sacred may be that which is dedicated to or in honor of somebody or event. In our context, the word sacred (holy) means that which is the source of everything in the universe. Because of being the source of everything, it is appropriate to designate that essence as sacred. Included in the source of everything are those things for which there are no rational explanations, such as the mysteries of life, death, fate, etc. Our awareness of the sacred evolves over the span of our lifetime. People usually progress from an undifferentiated intuition of the numinous quality of things to a mature sense of belonging to and contributing to "something greater than themselves," or that which is holy or sacred.

Self: Self most often refers to one's own person. Self is also often applied to the areas of our inner life that are called ego, soul and spirit. For our purposes, self indicates the ego, the soul and the spirit, taken together.

Self-Disclosure: In general, self-disclosure means the ability for us to reveal information that was previously kept secret. Self-disclosure refers to a skill in communication, a requirement in dialogue and in a sense is a measure of people's confidence in themselves and the validity of the content that they disclose.

Self-Management: Self-management means making written plans and committing oneself to action; monitoring progress toward measurable goals and setting new goals as they are necessary; forming the habit of working toward specific goals; holding oneself accountable for results.

Self-Identity: Self-identity means the name or essential character that identifies somebody or something. For an individual, self-identity means the set of characteristics that somebody recognizes as belonging uniquely to himself or herself and constituting his or her individual personality for life.

Shadow: Carl Jung, the great psychologist, teacher and researcher into human behavior, developed the concept of, "the Shadow." In his words, "the shadow is a moral problem that challenges the whole ego-personality, for no one can become conscious of the shadow without considerable moral effort. To become conscious of it involves recognizing the dark aspects of the personality as present and real." *"The Shadow," Aion, CW 9ii, par. 14.* The contents of our shadow side includes the energies that may have been repressed in some earlier part of our life. Surfacing and integrating such shadow energies into our conscious life is called shadow work. The shadow is a real part of every human being. To recognize its influence and assimilate its energies allows us to take charge of our life and its growth.

Sin: Sin is an act, thought or way of behaving that goes against the law or teachings of a religion, especially when the person who commits it is aware of this. Sin can be group or systemic depending on the responsibility of the person in authority at the time of the act.

Soul: Soul means the "essence of one's existence." "Soul represents the whole, living being of an individual person." May, Gerald D., *Care of Mind, Care of Spirit, p. 7.* Soul refers to the deepest and truest nature of a person, people or a nation, or what gives someone a distinctive character.

Spirit: Spirit is a vital, dynamic force of being; that which is afforded by the energies of life and brings the soul into living reality. Spirit implies energy and power.

1. Spirituality: Some popular definitions of spirituality are: "A quest for meaning in a sea of confusion and a world of emptiness.

2. A connection to the sacred, the belief in some higher power and the sacredness that goes along with that.

3. Bringing a sense of God into everyday life by looking beyond an individual reality.

Everything is interconnected with everything else. Everything is affected by everything else."

Excerpted from a presentation by Steve Phillips *of Phillips Associates, Malibu, CA on, Spirituality in the Workplace.*

Spirit is most often used to designate strength and heart in a person. Spirit is also used to designate the areas of our inner life that are also called soul and life-force. In religious contexts, the word is used for what is commonly called ghost, or that non-material part of us that lives for eternity. For our purposes, we will use the word spirit to denote the inner core of the person.

Stakeholder: A stakeholder means a person or group with a direct interest, involvement or investment in something, e.g., the employees, stockholders and customers of a business concern. In the organizational context to which I referred, stakeholders means all those people who influence or are influenced by an organization's actions or representatives. The ultimate stakeholder is society, in general.

Story: Story, in our context, means our personal story that we relate about who we are, what we are about and our life purpose. Our story is unique to ourselves and yet it is constitutive of how the consciousness of the human community evolves. Even though we are not aware of our impact on how the world evolves, there is no doubt that how we live out our story has an influence on everything.

Suffering: Suffering, in our context, is that enduring pain that is experienced in the deeper encounter with ourselves on our life journey. Suffering is not equated with physical or psychological pain. Suffering is part and parcel of the human condition. Many people try to escape all suffering as if it were not part of being human. In their efforts to escape the painful part of the human condition, they resort to what is usually referred to as, "bread and circuses." The part of the human condition that is labeled suffering" is about facing the real challenges of growing up, maturing, paying the price for what we really value, of relating to the mystery of our lives and to the great mystery in which we participate.

Transcendence: Transcendence refers to the inner activity of evolving awareness to go beyond the sum of our parts and become personally enriched, greatly more productive through collaborative working relationships and generating worthwhile results for the stakeholders. When we transcend something we move beyond our former state. In the context of this book, this means to move beyond the boundaries of our ordinary consciousness at work and enter into a more profound awareness of our inner resources and the possibilities of our maturing self and our influence on the organization to which we belong and the wider global economic system.

Unconscious: According to the dictionary, when one is unconscious one is unable to see, hear or otherwise sense what is happening. This state is usually temporary and often happens as a result of an accident or injury. In our context, this term refers to the part of the mind containing memories, thoughts, feelings and ideas that the person is not generally aware of, but that manifest themselves in dreams, fantasies and dissociated acts. The assumption that there is an unconscious realm depends on another assumption called repression. Many of our thoughts, feelings, imaginations and waking dreams are repressed because they are unacceptable to us for a variety of reasons.

Universe: Universe refers to the total physical entity from which all things originate and the energies that maintain all life forms including consciousness. We consider the universe itself to be evolving through several stages that were initially described by Teilhard DeChardin as *geogenesis* (geological unfolding), *biogenesis* (various life forms), *psychogenesis* (the mental development of humankind). In our context, we use the term universe to point to the evolving consciousness of everything. The typical usage of the word, universe indicates all the physical bodies that exist everywhere. Here, we accept that the physical bodies are filled with potential for greater consciousness. We, in the human community, because of our reflective awareness and abilities to make decisions that are generally centered on loving behaviors on behalf of everything, have a greater influence on the outcomes of that consciousness than we usually agree upon. The greater reality is that our influence in moving the "Universe" toward greater consciousness happens by our reflective choices and activities during the whole span of our lives and not just in single choices or actions.

Values: "Values define an individual's basic standards about what is good and bad, worthwhile and worthless, desirable and undesirable, true and false, moral and immoral." David Whetton, *Developing Management Skills, p. 52.* "A value is that which is explicitly or implicitly desirable to an individual or a group and which influences the selection from available modes, means and ends of action." Nancy J. Adler. *Organizational Behavior. P. 16.* Our values guide our choices and behavior. Values determine personal standards and moral judgment.

Whole: The whole means something that is complete, including all parts or aspects, with nothing left out. In another sense, being whole means healed or restored to health physically or psychologically. In our context, the "whole" means the whole universe being present in each of the parts. At the same time, the "whole" is constantly expanding in every way. What is important for us is that the "whole" is expanding in its consciousness of itself and we are all a part of that expansion. The whole is the larger system, the universe, the emerging process or life itself at work in all things.

"Whole Person" Approach: The "whole person" approach means that through Interiority, we approach all persons in the capacities and potential of their lives. This includes every dimension, such as good and evil; light and dark; inner and outer worlds; maturity and immaturity; past, present and future, etc. These are all included because nothing that is human is unworthy of treatment in the activities of becoming ourselves.

Wholeness: Wholeness is the state of inner unity whereby all of the physical, emotional, psychological, intellectual and spiritual dimensions are working together in unison. The feeling of being whole is akin to the feeling of belonging, the feeling of being where we are meant to be and doing what we are supposed to be doing in life. Wholeness refers to the state of being integrated within through the process of facing our limits, letting go of our fears, accepting that we are part of a greater whole and that life brings about this state gradually and not without our help.

Wisdom: The dictionary meaning of the term wisdom is "the ability to make sensible decisions and judgments based on personal knowledge and experience." In our context, wisdom means the accumulated knowledge of life, particularly of one's own, that has been gained through the experience of living an authentic life. We do not gain wisdom to hoard it for ourselves but to show through our self the way to live a life that is meaningful.

Work: Work is traditionally defined as the sum of the tasks that we do in our place of work. In the context of Interiority, we describe that body of work over our lifetime in the following ways:

1. The context wherein we are completing tasks and providing services and, at the same time, involved in our own coming to consciousness.

2. Where we develop various forms of self-expression that often appear as career changes.

3. Where we collaborate with our co-workers to contribute products and services and shape the future.

4. The occasion whereby our life takes shape, grows and changes because of the in-depth relationship that we have with the actual work itself.

5. The major life task through which we make our contribution in life.

6. The great enterprise in which we participate with the rest of the human community to transition our consciousness from one historical period to the next. When we are at work, we are the means whereby the universe is experiencing itself, hearing itself speak, moving, walking, talking, living and dying. Work is the occasion whereby we collaborate to sustain the earth by:

    a. Being aware that all workers united in pursuit of such a goal are the greatest force for the restoration of the living systems of our ailing planet.

    b. Being aware that economic viability depends on the ecological viability of the planet. This includes exercising an influence on the global economic systems.

c. Preserving the beauty of our environment, thus, preserving our own creativity.

d. Understanding that assuming responsibility for our work is intimately connected with assuming responsibility for the planet. This type of responsibility is closely related to being mindful or the state of mindfulness.

e. Producing products that transform the imbalances of consumerism into balanced and socially sustainable enterprise systems.

f. Protecting and maintaining the available natural resources by balanced usage.

g. Advocating for sustainable (green) policies and practices.

h. Standing up for justice for all stakeholders.

Bibliography

Abrams, John. *Companies We Keep, Employee Ownership and the Business of Community and Place.* White River Junction, VT. : Chelsea Green Publishing Company, 2008.

Adson, Patricia. *Depth Coaching.* Florida: CAPT, 2004.

Albrecht, Karl. *Social Intelligence, The New Science of Success.* San Francisco, CA: Jossey-Bass, 2006.

Applebaum, Herbert. *The Concept of Work, Ancient, Medieval, and Modern.* New York: State University of New York Press, Albany, 1992.

Appleby, Joyce. *The Relentless Revolution, A History of Capitalism.* New York: W.W. Norton & Company, Inc., 2010.

Benyus, Janine M. *Biomimicry: Innovation Inspired by Nature.* New York: Morrow, 1997.

Swimme, Brian and Berry, Thomas. *The Universe Story: From the Primordial Flaring Forth to the Ecozoic Era, sA Celebration of the Unfolding of the Cosmos.* New York: HarperCollins Publishers, 1992.

Berry, Thomas. *The Great Work, Our Way into the Future.* New York: Three Rivers Press, 1999.

Boshear, Walton. *Understanding People, Models and Concepts.* La Jolla, California: University Associates, Inc., 1977.

Buechner, Frederick. *Wishful Thinking: A Seeker's ABC.* San Francisco: HarperSanFrancisco p. 119, 1993.

Buford, Bob. *Finishing Well, What People who Really Live Do Differently.* Dallas: Integrity Publishers, 2004.

Buscaglia, Leo F. *Personhood.* The Art of Being Fully Human, Thorofare, New Jersey: Charles B. Slack, 1978.

Campbell, Joseph. *The Hero with a Thousand Faces.* Princeton University Press, 1949.

Capra, Fritjof. *The Turning Point: Science, Society, and the Rising Culture.* New York: Simon & Schuster, 1982.

Chandler, Steve and Black, Duane. *The Hands-Off Manager: How to Mentor People and Allow Them to be Successful.* New Jersey: Career Press, 2007.

Chuen, Lam Kam. *The Way of Energy, Mastering the Chinese Art of Internal Strength with Chi Kung Exercises.* London: Gaia Books Limited, 1999.

Csikszentmihalyi, Mihaly. *Finding Flow, The Psychology of Engagement with Everyday Life.* New York: Perseus Books, 1997.

—. *Good Business, Leadership, Flow and the Making of Meaning.* New York: Penguin Putnam, 2003.

Davies, Paul. *The Cosmic Blueprint, New Discoveries in Nature's Creative ability to Order the Universe.* Radnor, Pennsylvania: Templeton Foundation Press, 1988.

Durckheim, Karlfried Graf. *The Way of Transformation, Daily Life as Spiritual Practice.* Sandpoint, ID: Morning Light Press, 2007.

—. *Hara, The Vital Center of Man.* Rochester, VT.s Allen, 1962.

Dyckman, Katherine Marie, Carroll, L. Patrick. *Inviting the Mystic Supporting the Prophet. An Introduction to Spiritual Direction.* New York: Paulist Press, 1981.

Egan, Gerard. *The Skilled Helper.* Pacific Grove, California: Brooks/Cole, 2002.

Ehrenreich, Barbara. *Bright-Sided: How the Relentless Promotion of Positive Thinking Has Underminded America.* New York: Metropolitan Books, Henry Holt and Company, LLC, 2009.

Eiseley, Loren. *The Night Country.* New York: Charles Scribner's Sons, 1971.

Frankl, Victor E. *Man's Search for Meaning.* New York: Washington Square Press, 1985.

Fromm, Erich. *The Art of Loving.* New York: Harper & Row, Inc. 1956.

—. *Escape from Freedom.* New York: Farrar & Rinehart, Inc. 1941.

Gardner, Howard. *Five Minds for the Future.* Boston, Massachusetts: Harvard Business School Publishing, 2006.

Bell, Gordon and Jim Gemmell. *Total Recall, How the E-Memory Revolution Will Change Everything.* New York: Penguin Group (U.S.A.), 2009.

Goldsmith, Marshall and Reiter, Mark. *Mojo, How to Get It, How to Keep It, How to Get It Back If You Lose It.* New York: Hyperion, 2009.

Goleman, Daniel. *Vital Lies, Simple Truths, The Psychology of Self-Deception.* New York: Simon & Schuster, Inc., 1985.

—. *Working with Emotional Intelligence.* New York City, NY: Bantam Books, 1998.

Hacker, Jacob S., and Pierson, Paul. "*Winner-Take-All* Politics," *How Washington Made the Rich Richer And Turned Its Back on the Middle Class.* New York: Simon & Schuster, 2010.

Handy, Charles. *The Age of Paradox*. Boston, Massachusetts: Harvard Business School Press, 1994.

—. *The Hungry Spirit, Beyond Capitalism: A Quest for Purpose in the Modern World*. New York: Random House, 1998.

Havel, Vaclav. *The Art of the Impossible, Politics as Morality in Practice*. New York: Alfred A. Knopf, Inc., 1997.

Hayes, Tom. *Jump Point, How Network Culture is Revolutionizing Business*. New York: McGraw-Hill, 2008.

Hill, Napoleon. *Think and Grow Rich*. New York: Simon & Schuster, 1995.

Hillman, James. *Myth of Analysis, Three Essays in Archetyal Psychology*. Evanston: Northwestern University Press, 1972.

—. *The Soul's Code, In Search of Character and Calling*. New York: Warner Books, Inc., 1996.

Hollis, James. *On This Journey We Call Our Life, Living the Questions*. Toronto, Canada: Inner City Books, 2003.

—. *What Matters Most, Living a More Considered Life*. New York: Gotham Books, 2009.

Hopper, Kenneth and Hopper, William. *The Puritan Gift, Reclaiming the American Dream Amidst Global Financial Chaos*. New York: I. B. Tauris, 2009.

Howe, Reuel L. *The Miracle of Dialogue*. New York: The Seabury Press, 1963.

Hudson, Frederic M. *The Adult Years, Mastering the Art of Self-Renewal*. San Francisco: Jossey-Bass, 1999.

Hughes, Louis. *Body-Mind Meditation, A Gateway to Spirituality*. Dublin: The Mercier Press, 1990.

Johnson, Barry. *Polarity Management, Identifying and Managing Unsolvable Problems*. Amherst, MA: HRD Press, Inc., 1992.

Johnson, Robert A. *Inner Work, Using Dreams & Active Imagination for Personal Growth*. New York: HarperSanFrancisco, 1986.

—. *Owning Your Own Shadow, Understanding the Dark Side of the Psyche*. San Francisco, CA: HarperSanFrancisco, 1991.

Johnston, William. *Silent Music, The Science of Meditation*. New York: Harper and Row Publishers, 1979.

Jung, Carl G. *Youth and Age, Psychological Reflections*. n.d.

Kolbert, Elizabeth. "Why Work, A Hundred Years of the Protestant XE "Protestant" Ethic." *The New Yorker*, November 9, 2004.

Kolind, Lars. *The Second Cycle, Winning the War Against Bureaucracy*. Upper Saddle River: New Jersey, 2006.

Kuczynski, Jurgen. *France 1700 to the Present Day*. London: Muller, 1946.

Kurzweil, Ray. *The Singularity is Near*. New York: Penguin Group, 2005.

Lennick, Doug and Kiel, Fred. *Moral Intelligence, Enhancing Business Performance & Leadership Success*. Upper Saddle River, New Jersey: Wharton School Publishing, 2008.

Lewin, Roger, and Regine, Birute. *The Soul at Work, Listen...Respond...Let Go: Using Complexity Science for Business Success*. New York: Simon & Schuster, 2000.

Malone, Michael S. *The Future Arrived Yesterday, The Rise of the Protean Corporationand What it Means for You*. New York: Crown Business, 2009.

May, M.D. Gerald G. *Care of Mind/Care of Spirit*. New York: HarperCollins, 1982.

McDonnell, Thomas P. *A Thomas Merton Reader*. New York: Doubleday, 1989.

Merton, Thomas. *No Man is an Island*. New York: Harcourt Brace and Company, 1983.

—. *The Way of Chuang-Tsu*. New York: New Directions, 1969.

Moore, Thomas. *Care of the Soul, A Guide to Cultivating Depth and Sacredness in Everyday Life*. New York: HarperCollins, 1992.

Nachmanovitch, Stephen. *Free Play, Improvisation in Life and Art*. New York: Jeremy P. Tarcher / Putnam, 1990.

O'Donohue, John. *Anam Cara, A Book of Celtic Wisdom*. New York: Cliff Street Books, 1998.

O'Murchu, Diarmuid. *Evolutionary Faith, Rediscovering God in Our Great Story*. New York: Orbis Books, 2004.

—. *Quantum Theology, Spiritual Implications of the New Physics*. New York: The Crossroad Publishing Company, 1997.

Ornstein, Robert E. *The Psychology of Consciousnes*. New York: Harcourt Brace Janovich, 1977.

Palmer, Parker J. *Let Your Life Speak, Listening for the Voice of Vocation*. San Francisco: Jossey-Bass, 2000.

Pilzer, Paul Zane. *God Wants You to Be Rich, The theology of Economics*. New York: Simon & Schuster, 1995.

Pink, Daniel H. *Drive, The Surprising Truth About What Motivates Us.* New York: Riverhead Books, 2009.

Powell, John S.J. *Fully Human, Fully Alive, A New Life through New Vision.* Niles: Argus Communications, Inc., 1976.

Quinlan, Joseph P. *The Last Economic Superpower, The Retreat of Globalization, the End of American Dominance, and What We can Do About It.* New York: McGraw-Hill, 2010.

Ramo, Joshua Cooper. *The Age of the Unthinkable.* New York: Little Brown and Company, 2009.

Reich, Robert. "American Optimism and Consumer Confidence." *The American Prospect*, September 18, 2001.

Reuther, Rosemary Radford. *Gaia & God, An Ecofeminist Theology of Earth Healing.* New York: Harper Collins Publishers, 1992.

Riskas, Thomas. *Working Beneath the Surface, Attending to the soul's "hidden agenda" for wholeness, fulfillment, and deep spiritual healing.* Provo, UT: Executive Excellence Publishing, 1997.

Samuels, Allison. "Tyson is the Hero of New Film. But Not to Himself." *Newsweek*, July 12, 2011.

Sandburg, Carl. *Chicago Poems, (1916).* New York: Henry Holt and Company, 1916.

Senge, Peter M. *The Fifth Discipline, The Art and Practice of the Learning Organization.* New York: Doubleday, 1990.

Sharpnack, Rayona. *Trade-Up, Five Steps for Redesigning Your Leadership and Life from the Inside Out.* San Francisco, CA: Jossey-Bass, 2007.

Sheehy, Gail. *New Passages, Mapping Your Life Across Time.* New York: Random House, 1995.

Stevens, Anthony. *On Jung, An Update edition with a Reply to Jung's Critics.* Princeton: Princeton University Press, 1999.

Study, Gallup. "Engaged Employees Inspire Company Innovation." *Gallup Management Journal*, 2006: October 12.

Sullivan, Patricia. "Philosopher coined term 'deep ecology.'" *Los Angeles Times*. Los Angeles: Times Mirror, January 26, 2009.

Surowiecki, James. *The Wisdom of Crowds.* New York: Anchor Books, 2004.

Tagore, Rabindranath. *Fireflies.* n.d.

Tapscott, Don. *Grown Up Digital, How the Net Generation is Changing Your World.* New York: McGraw Hill, 2009.

Thompson, Helen, B.V.M. *Journey Toward Wholeness.* Ramsey, NJ: Paulist Press, 1982.

Uchiyama, Kosho. *Opening the Hand of Thought.* Somerville, MA: Wisdom Publications, 2004.

Wessel, David. "The Factory Floor Has a Ceiling on Job Creation." *The Wall Street Journal*, 2012, January 12: A6.

Westberg, Granger E. *Good Grief.* Minneapolis: Fortress Press, 1997.

Wheatley, Margaret J. *Leadership and the New Science, Discovering Order in a Chaotic World.* San Francisco: Berrett-Koeler Publishers, 1999.

Wilson, Eric G. *Against Happiness.* New York: Sarah Crichton Books, 2008.

Zweig, Connie and Abrams, Jeremiah. *Meeting the Shadow, The Hidden Power of the Dark Side of Human Nature.* New York: Jeremy P. Tarcher / Penguin, 1991.

Index

A

Abrams, Jeremiah 308
Abrams, John 105
accountability
  called to 201
  economic systems 92
  fallacy of 101
  for common good 102
  for resources 102
  implementing 103
  Internet 106
  lack of 206
  measures 194
  norms of 104
  self 105
Active Imagination 308
actualize 2
Adam 37
Adam and Eve 36, 37
Age
  of Interiority 13
Ages
  Dark, Middle 4, 39, 65
agnosticism 174
alignment 122
alive
  in the moment 291
  this whole thing is 11
  with everything 228
ambiguities 325
angst 87
anti-worker
  biases 34

Applebaum, Herbert 43
Appleby, Joyce 118
appreciation
  expanded 2
  for complexity 146
  for Interiority 239
  lack of 160
  life's mysteries 110
  of the sacred 99
  of your body 292
  word of 334
Appreciation
  psychic link 123
Aquinas, Thomas 76
Arendt, Hannah 45
Aristotle 35
assumptions 265
  legacy 234
  of leadership 265
  of the book 18
  unrealistic 172
attention 121, 290
  centered 302
  to breathing 292
  to little tasks 307
  to routine tasks 264
  to the soul 308
attractor (strange) 97, 293
Auden, W. H. 63
audience (primary) 15
authenticity 87
  acting truthfully 67
  in leaders 105

  in the process 283
Authenticity
  transparency 87
awareness
  belonging to whole 66
  center of 294
  expanded 96
  IP Worker 244
  levels of 302
  Occupy 51
  of being loved 333
  of biases 172
  of force fields 207
  of limitations 129
  of one's power 244
  of work 121
  prayer 116
  self 31
  transferral 303
Awareness
  of one's story 250

B

Bacon, Francis 41
becoming 1
  the self 71
behaviors
  incivility 204
being
  focus on 69
belong
  fail to 202
  in the world 22
  need to 220
  the need to 227
  to ourselves 97
  to the struggle 229
Bentham, Jeremy 44
Benyus, Janine M. 81
Berry, Thomas 98
Biblical quotes 107
Biomimicry 81
Black, Duane 99
bodies
  abuse their 290
bodies (our)
  storehouses 291
Body/Physical 285
Bohm, David 146
boids
  simulation 88
boredom 174
boss 3
  human touch 165
  male figure 37
  parent substitutes 202
brain
  believes is there 284
  left and right 67
  two hemispheres 314
breathing
  natural 293
  practice 292
  sound of 293
Breathing
  Centering 249
Buechner, Frederich 112
bullies 208
Burns, Robert 142
Bushido 50
business cycle
  competencies 274

C

Café (World) 52
calling 149
  and contribution 280
  discernment 151
  to serve 149
Calling
  work as a calling 272
Calvin, John 40
Campbell, Joseph 146
capacity for meaning 351
Capra, Fritjof 77
caring
  for all things 288
cartwheels 89
Catherine 299
Catholic Church 40, 139
center
  within yourself 326
centered
  attitude 242
  ego 144
  group 50
centeredness
  inner 284
centered (other) 2
centering
  in a group 301
  practice 296
Centering
  competencies 249
center outward 247
centers
  of truth 29
challenges
  and rewards 273

  and work-style 340
  to change self 219
Chandler, Steve 99
change
  agent 67
  disruptive 64, 221
chaos
  and order 49
  and tensions 144
  energies of 129
  intervention 155
Chaos
  happens 142
Chief Seattle 115
Christ, Jesus
  carpenter 36
Chuen
  Master Kam Lam 291
circumstances
  external 53
  internal 55
citizens
  disillusioned 18
civilization
  progresses inwardly 27
cloud
  computing 262
Cloud
  and core workers 271
cloud (probability) 86
co-dependency 202
  manifestations 204
collaborative
  organization 262
come within 112
committed (life) 12

communications
  competencies 251
  technologies 79
community
  and self 50
  building 21
  fulfillment 2
  human 19
  needs 173
  of living things 97
  renewed 350
  stakeholders 207
Companies We Keep 52
compassion
  and pain 227
compassionate 329
competencies
  client-centered 252
  good work 249
  productivity 253
complex
  adaptive system 45
  authority 323
  energy cluster 323
  God 323
  Oedipus 323
  tolerate tensions 324
complexes
  core 323
complexity 1
  and simplicity 88
  harmonious 93
concern
  show 334
confessional 222
conflict
  management 323

conflicts
  frequency 185
Confucian (Chinese) 50
conscience
  a matter of 199
  hardened their 175
  troubled 109
  uncreated 79
consciousness
  arriving at 97
  human 8
  meaning of 8
  of the universe 77
  seeking 1
  threshold 266
  transformative 99
Constantine
  Emperor 38
contemplation 3
contribution
  and fulfillment 92
  each has a 280
  to the whole 35
  unique 281
Contribution
  Step Four 288
contributions
  making our 288
contributors 248
control
  distributed 89
coordination
  horizontal 87
cosmogenesis
  self-organizing 78
Cosmology 94
cosmos

emergent entity 94
material 46
unfolding 65
creation
invisible acts of 8
creative
evolution 95
creativity
and emotions 123
and workshops 340
energies of 336
creativity erupting 79
cultivate
a voice 205
being for another 333
Interiority 93
our inner lives 113
silence, stillness 296
spirit of inquiry 64
trust 145
customer service 5
customization
product 264

D

dark
lost the 30
metaphorical 31
darkness
cursing the 77
healing in the 14
powers of 31
ruled 30
shadow un-integrated 267
dark side
embrace of 309
DeChardin, Teilhard 46

decisions
ordinary 329
wisdom 329
democratic systems
compromised 18
denial
escapist behavior 178
of complexities 48
of own issues 186
Denial
repression 310
depersonalization
of workers 5
de Saint Exupery
Antoine 96
Descartes 41
development
evolutionary 82
interior senses 96
of habits 9
organization 21
personal 149
self 44
devil's
not so bad 28
devil's brew 344
devils (noonday) 56
diagnosing 166
dialogical
approaches 51
framework 179, 283, 321
dialogue
inner 135
within 328
digitization 4
dimensions
ego and soul 144

ethical 175
infinite 32
interrelatedness 114
of experience 3
of Interiority 1
rational/empirical 42
Disney, Walt 17
distraction 178
  free from 122
  from escapes 78
  from lostness 34
  let go of 331
  work without 249
DNA strands 11
dominant
  culture 87
  hierarchy 36
  idea 260
Donne, John 12
dream
  consider your 308
  content of 308
  into opportunity 17
  sequence 308
  work 308
Drucker, Peter 2, 76
  only compassion 347
duality 96
  of things 142
Durckheim
  Karlfried Graf 290
Dylan, Bob 129
dynamic
  an inner 92
  attraction 213
  energies 144
  flow 214

flow of energies 214
interchanges 344
tensions 144
dynamics
  of polarities 213
dysfunctional
  areas 156

E

Eakes, Sharon
  Executive Coach 17
Earth's ecologies 80
Earth's Resources 92
ego (control) 305
Ehrenreich, Barbara 47
Einstein 17, 45, 76, 323
Eiseley, Loren 8
embattled 160
emergence
  of complex forms 363
  of greater order 83
  of meaning 93
  of shadow material 130
  of unique stories 3
Emerson 330
emotions
  accept the 312
  allow the 310
  describe one's 310
  feel the 310
  integrate 313
  knowing our 309
  name the 310
  theory and practice 309
empowerment
  as diminishment 196
  competencies 267

encounter
  intuitive 95
  manage the 212
  mysterious 16
  own failings 226
  resist the 131
  sacred 231
  transformative 327
  with self 289
encounters
  in-depth 327
energies
  dynamic 350
  repressed 329
  shadow 176, 287, 344, 375
energies released 329
energy
  sexual 96
  well-springs 3
engage
  in daily practice 137
  in reconciliation 320
  in self-integration 111
  mystery itself 336
  with each other 64
engaged
  attend to details 232
  disengaged 174
  employees 5
  in doing the work 124
Engaged
  in good work 5
enlargement
  mystery as way to 336
  open to 336
  possibility of 326
Enlargement 326

Enlightenment
  Age of 4
  philosophers 41
  secular view 43
Enron 205
enthusiasm 331
  for themselves 166
  sustain 331
entrepreneur
  within 17
escapism
  third response 178
Ethic
  Protestant 44
ethical compass 205
ethics
  God question 27
  in business 205
  lack of 205
  truthful lifestyle 201
everything
  is personal 10
evil
  all degrees of 14
  and dark shadow 308
  bad behaviors 31
  good and 3
  knowing the 243
  manifestations of 235
  sides of same coin 14
  soul as master 11
evil (see no) 242
evolutionary
  development 266
  march 4
  patterns 43
  process not random 95

existential
  challenge 244
  energies 128
  uncertainty 34
Existential
  energies 128
expansion
  of knowledge 26
  of the universe 77
experience
  integration 147
  lessons 329
  mystical 95
  pivotal 110
  reactive complexes 171
  reflect on 117
Experiences
  Step One 286
exploitation
  behaviors 178
Expression 123

F

Fair Day 58
Familiar
  energies 128
families 332
  of origin 304
farming 5
fate 263
Faulkner, William 266
fault
  finding 162
  recognition of 105
  understand the 325
fear
  factor 2
  inducing 180
  of failure 220
  of losing job 202
  of the system 182
  stressed by 190
  toxic 179
Fear
  used as a goad 180
fears
  are faced 179
  embrace of 180
fecundity 1
feedback
  reactions to 183
  solicit 265
feminine 265
fertile realities 3
fertility rituals 5
Finch, Atticus 301
Flow
  is mark of work 123
flummoxed
  by tensions 214
follow-through
  lack of 195
force-fields 207
forgiveness
  ask for 194
  practice of 325
  show 326
  visualization 326
Forgiveness
  of self 325
Forster, E.M. 20
foundation 1
  by way of trust 145
  inner 15

life integration 111
  makers of meaning 117
Fromm, Erich 206
Fukushima 108
fulfillment 370
  at work 18
  call 151
  diminish 64
  holistic 71
  materialistic 56
  of obligation 50
  of work 55, 138
  worker 21
  yearning for 237
Future Arrived 85

G

Gabler, Neal 236
Galileo 94
Gallup Survey 5
Gandhi 248
Gardner, Howard 55
Generation (Bubble) 87
generativity 11
George (story) 298
ghosts 317
gift
  of being loved 333
  of consciousness 8
  of maturing self 72
  of our lives 235
  of wisdom 329
  paradoxical 326
  the greatest 231
goal
  developmental 220
  of accumulating wealth 179

  of dialogue 283
  of life 12
  practical 274
  setting 165
God 35
  and sacred time 258
  appeared static 76
  as male 35
  is good 28
  is love 96
  laws of 189
  practice of co-opting 47
  prevailing image of 36
gods
  harvest 5
  the mills of the 170
  voices of the 116
Goldsmith, Marshall 244
Goleman, Daniel 54
goodness
  makes us human 332
  not one-sided 135
good work
  competencies 272
  elements of 120
  habits 340
  is hard won 12
Good work
  emerges from the work itself 64
greater good
  competencies 268
Gretzky, Wayne 219
grow
  and mature 124
grow and mature
  need troubles to 164
  opportunities to 104

growth
  and self-care 249
  barriers to 111
  cycles of 213
  five dimensions of 285
  happens through work 119
  personal 111
Growth 124
guilt 319
gull (rising) 238

H

Hacker, Jacob S. 18
  Winner Take All 18
Hara
  vital center of man 290
harvesting
  the crops 5
Hayes, Tom
  Jump Point 85
healing
  at work 227
  behaviors 320
  of others 321
  of our descendents 320
  of self 322
  our ancestors 320
  reflective 327
  the first practice of 318
  the occasion of 137
  working for 92
Heart 116, 164
heart (take) 350
Heisenberg 323
Hendricks/Ludeman
  Corporate Mystic 97
Henley, Don 289

Heraclitus 323
hierarchical
  chain-of-command 36
  control 144
  model 262
  organization 262
  organizations 81
  power structure 267
  structure 52
Hill, Napoleon 47
historical
  legacies 33
Hobbes, Thomas 42
Hollis, James 77
holy
  as destination 336
  everything manifests the 336
  is communitarian 140
  know the 336
  the science of 94
  the sphere of the 221
holy at the
  center of the self 95
Housman, A.E. 189
Hsieh, Tony 97
humanity
  admission to one's 333
  as equals in 272
  drain them of 119
  embracing 135
  maintain our 113
Human Resources 348

I

idea
  generation 314
  incubation 315

invention 316
  of God 260
  of Nation 260
  of worker 5
  of worker as philosopher 44
ideas 3
identification
  with work 122
identity
  personal 87
  retains over time 272
  soul strengthens 117
ills (systemic)
  in society 17
imagination
  allows us to 116
  messages to my 29
  our capacity for 116
impact
  of intervention 188
  of the program 348
  on the universe 79
Impact 123
implementation
  of the program 348
inclusivity
  of every worker 87
indifference
  choosing 173
individual
  freedom of 205
  journeys 54
  sustenance 2
individuation
  Carl Jung 76
inner
  condition of work 233

  discipline 64
  life well-lived 231
  resources 242
  world 3
inner dialogue
  self-talk 111
inner-directed
  compass 205
innovation
  of complex patterns 67
  source of 97
  worker 264
inquiry
  the core of Interiority 26
inquiry (spirit of) 64
Inspiration
  can happen any time 121
inspiration (at work) 10
institution
  as model 246
  disillusioned by 18
  to individual 246
  traditional 100
institutions
  as patriarchical 36
integrate
  resources 4
  the emotions 313
  the lost parts 130
integration
  cycles of 147
  life 111
  of shadow energies 164
  of two hemispheres 314
  the process of 111
Integration
  Step Three 288

integrity
  acting with 112
  compromised their own 199
  ethical, is built 269
  personal 86
intention of
  becoming oneself 320
interdependence
  of everything 115
interdependencies 3
Interest 121
Interiority
  a gift 17
  a right 17
  capacity for 1
  Committee 348
  embracing 235
  energies 3
  external case for 18
  flowering of 4
  implement 283
  internal case for 19
  introducing 347
  The Way of 343
  tools 167
  what is? 1
  Workshop Three 339
Interiority-culture
  competencies 270
Interiority Culture 213
Interiority-Powered
  organizations 261
internalized
  other 322
intervention (post) 217
Intuition
  is knowing 17

the capacity to sense 116
intuitions 3
involvement
  with work 120
inwardness
  tendency toward 94
IP
  Organization 260
  Worker 261
IP (Interiority Powered)
  worker profile 249
IP Organization Profile 267
IP workers
  as open systems 263

J

Jackson, Maggie 201
Japanese
  work culture 50
job insecurity 4
Johnson, Barry 214
Johnson, Robert A. 308
Johnston, William 95
Jonas, Hans 94
Journal
  Gallup Management 5
journey
  toward wholeness 306
Joyce, James 79
Jump Point 85
jumps (forward) 266
Jung, Carl 76
  shadow 130
  suffering 141
  thoughts 8

K

Kalichi
  Dance, Words 293
Kant, Immanuel 43
Keats, John 142
Keller, Helen 60
Kenshin, Uesugi 228
Kingdom
  of God 36
known
  as soul work 11
  by someone 313
Known (be) 333
Know yourself
  as loved 332
Koan, Zen 74
Krugman, Paul 175

L

labor union
  movement 48
Lao Tzu 125
lasting value
  focus on 104
leadership
  distributed 87
  skills 264
Leadership
  and the New Science 82
learning
  continuous 113
  edge of 233
  from experience 50
  style of 71
Learning
  from our work 253
  how to work 90

let go
  and simplify 331
  obstructive legacy systems 53
  of illusions 172
  of what is past 34
liberation
  of energies 17
Liberation
  frees the worker 17
Lichtenstein, Nelson 2
limitations
  know your 319
  of historical context 77
limits (accepts) 326
Lincoln, Abraham 104
living systems
  arrive at order 83
  restoration of 376
Locke, John 42
lostness
  dearth of meaning 34
love
  as fulfillment 96
  of compassion 96
loving
  behaviors 334
Luther, Martin 39
Lynch, Stanley 289

M

Machado, Antonio 25
male
  androgynous 265
  dominance 93
Malone, Michael S.
  Future Arrived 85
management

competencies 269
man (a good) 297
mantra 96
Marx, Karl 44
masculine 265
material
  shadow 129
material (things) 3
matter 94
maturity
  does not depend on 104
  journey toward 215
  professional 1
  tasks of 130
me
  what I dislike about 321
meaning
  seekers of 118
  the question of 92
  through work 65
measurement
  units of 2
Medieval Europe 39
Merton, Thomas 146
messenger
  was shot 184
Mexico (Gulf of) 221
Middle Ages 39
Milton, John 85
missing piece 204
missionary
  as a 21
  in Japan 8
monastic
  communities 37
monkeys 242

Montgomery, David 49
moral
  implications 329
mundane 330
mystery
  affinity for 41
  engage with the 116
  of our existence 14
mystery/wholeness 33
myths (contextual) 93

N

national debt 18
nature
  collaboration with 5
  of the holy 140
  our primary teacher 82
  paradoxical 141
  two-sided 141
Nayar, Vineet 103
Networked
  science 52
networks
  interconnected 262
Newton, Isaac 76
Niebuhr, Reinhold 73, 329
Nikko (shrine) 242
Norms 265
Novitiate 150

O

Occupy Movement 51, 106
Odyssey 54
Old Testament 35
open system
  IP worker 246

opposites
  tension of 67
optimism 47
organism
  self-organizing 221
organization
  troubled 155
organizational
  competencies 251
  resources 2
Ornstein, Robert 314
Others/Relational 285
ourselves (change) 220
Output/Input 2
overview
  of chapters 22

P

pain (individual) 222
paradigm shift 20
paradox
  of suffering 141
  tolerance of 96
paradoxical 3
parent's (unlived life) 134
Parmenides 27
Participation 124
passions 331
passivity
  patterns of 173
past (the)
  recapping 266
patterns
  behavioral 169
  unhealthy 93
people
  we are called to be 12
People Skills 199
Person
  Workshop One 340
personal
  issues 343
  relationship 140
  relationships 4
  resources 2
  story 286
personhood
  through work 232
Philosophy
  contemporary 7
Pierson, Paul
  Winner Take All 18
Pink, Daniel 235
plain crazy 177
Plato 35
Polarity
  management 214
  Map 214
politicians
  used by lobbyists 18
Pope John Paul II 45
posture (practices) 289
postures
  Zazen 294
potentiality 3
practice
  makes perfect 9
prayer 93
Prayer
  Serenity 329
pressures
  external 2

rising from within 66
withstand the 161
priest
  for twenty years 21
priesthood 229
processes
  efficient 265
  reasoning 1
productivity
  competencies 273
profane 221
Program
  Interiority 339
  Pilot 348
  roll-out 348
projections
  justify our 312
  notice our 324
Protean Corporation 85
Protestant 39, 44, 356
Proteus 86
Psyche/Psychological 285
Psyche (soul) 303
psychological
  growth 10
Puritan
  legacy 46
purpose 92
  fulfill the 331

Q

question
  everything 26
Questiones 25
questions
  coaching 269
  empowering 52
  ethical 55
  ignores 174
  pragmatic 32
  workers ask 25
questions (big) 27
Quinlan, Joseph P. 102

R

rational/intuitive 314
Reactions
  to other's behaviors 322
reactive complex 171
reactive patterns 319, 330
Reagan, Ronald 49
realism 242
reality
  nature of 51
  passively accept as 35
  shaping our 27
  subjective 98
reality (our) 287
Receptivity 122
reconciliation
  practices 320
reflection 3
Reflections
  Step Two 287
reflective
  awareness 375
  of who we are 117
  practices 61
Reformation
  Protestant 40
Reich, Robert 47
relationality 51, 67, 270

as truth 22, 234
  ethic of 51
relationship
  ritualize the 137
relationships
  cultivating 2
  everything is about 20
  of belonging 227
  with everything 98
  with parents 135
  work 94
Religion/Ritual
  Practice 327
religious
  rituals 328
Renewal
  Energies of 319
renewal of energies 319
Resignation 174
respicere
  respect 334
Responsible
  Engagement 172
Responsiveness 122
Reynolds, Craig 88
ritual 308
road
  less traveled 151
Rosetti, Christina 155

S

sacred
  character 5
  part of life 5
  reinterpretations 92, 94
  story 1
  work as 221
saints
  I grew up with 75
Satisfaction 124
science
  art and spirit 344
sciences
  revolutions in 93
security
  lifelong 4
self
  becoming of 12
  expression 117
  management 200
  reflection 117
self-aware
  competencies 249
self-care
  practice 303
self-expression 112
Seminary 132
serve a greater call 306
service to 222
shadow 263, 320
  bright 135
  dark 131
  dimension 135
  manifestations 239
  material 129, 139
  my 136
  repressed material 130
shadow-work 308
Sharpnack, Rayona 145
Shinto 335
shoes too small 244
shotgun 69

silence 14
  become used to 113
  listening within 296
  time to be in 287
Silent Music 95
simplicity 88
sin 330
sinful 309
sitting-practice 302
Smith, Adam
  Wealth of Nations 43
social benefits
  competencies 254
Socrates 33
something else 30
Soros, George 4
soul
  a benign energy 116
  daimon 11
  language of the 116
  of the world 13
  promptings 328
  serve the values 325
soulful
  experiences 10
souls
  needs of our 222
South Mountain
  Company 105
Spirit
  follow as guide 335
Spirit/Spiritual 285
Spiritual 327
spirituality
  at work 60
stakeholder
  competencies 268
St. Ambrose 38
Standing
  or sitting 290
  practice 302
St. Augustine 38
St. Benedict 39
stories
  are not accidental 3
  our own 3
  personal 7
  unique 3
St. Paul 37
Structures
  self-organizing 82
subjectivity 98
Submersion 178
suffering
  as opportunity 307
sufferings
  authentic 307
  self-generated 232
Superior-religious 164
Superpower 102
surface
  beneath the 200
Surowiecki, James 84
sustainability
  based work 92
Swimme, Brian
  Hidden Heart 77
symbols
  emergent 1
Systems
  repressive 92
systems-wide accountability 104

T

Tan Tien 292
Taylor, Frederick 2
teamwork
  competencies 267
technologies 4
teleology 67
terminology
  contemporary 66
The Eagles 289
the emerging whole
  servants of 114
the gift
  we are 115
the great mystery
  align one's life with 115
The Man 63
Thomas, Dylan 57
Thought
  Opening the Hand 294
three ages
  dominant ideas 261
Tilgher, Adriano 43
traditional (non) 2
transcendence 327
transformational 330
transformations
  irreversible 78
trends 4
trust
  is everything 87
Tyson, Mike 239

U

Uchiyama, Kosho 294
uncertainty
  tolerance for 113
unconscious
  invite the 308
Unfamiliar
  energies 128
union
  with the sacred 96
universe
  emerging 11
  expanding 77
  our sacred story 95
  why choose the 80

V

values
  ethical 329
  shared 265
viable relationships
  competencies 250
Vulnerability
  a condition of being loved 333

W

walking
  practice 303
Wallace, David Foster 34
war (within) 237
Weber, Max 44
we serve all things 228
Wheatley, Margaret J.
  Leadership-New Science 82
whistle-blowers 185
Whitman, Walt
  a great poem 16
wholeness
  achieving 7

growth toward 291
hidden 146
holiness 95
integrated 283
quest 11
Winner
  Take-All Politics 18
wisdom
  employ 331
  learning 330
  practice 329
  the beginning of 119
wisdom-decision 330
work
  a contribution 119
  a spiritual practice 119
  centrality 6
  for which you are here 330
Work
  meaningful 268
  Workshop Two 340
worker
  a good 64
  awareness 245
  disposable 4
  Interiority-Powered 242
  self-management 269
workers
  co-workers 2
  self-perception 21

Work Ethic 44
workforce
  guided from within 17
Workforce
  development depends on 199
workplace
  energy to the 10
  vocabulary of love 332
Workshop One 340
Workshop Three 340
Workshop Two 340
work-that-matters
  competencies 268
world
  inner 11
  outer 11
  work 12
worthiness
  of all 322

Y
Yeats
  Things fall apart 142
yin/yang 141
Yonezawa 229
Yunus, Muhammad 173

Z
Zweig, Connie 308

www.interioritypowered.com

Made in the USA
Charleston, SC
23 January 2013